Study Guide

Advanced Placement Edition*

American Government

ELEVENTH EDITION

James Q. Wilson and John J. DiIulio, Jr.

P. S. Ruckman, Jr.

Rock Valley College

Houghton Mifflin Company BOSTON NEW YORK

Publisher: *Suzanne Jeans*
Sponsoring Editor: *Traci Mueller*
Senior Marketing Manager: *Edwin Hill*
Development Editor: *Lisa Kalner Williams*
Project Editor: *Paola Moll*
New Title Project Manager: *Susan Peltier*
Editorial Assistant: *Nina Tamburello*
Marketing Assistant: *Edwin Hill*

Printed in the U.S.A.

ISBN 13: 978-0-618-95684-5

ISBN 10: 0-618-95684-0

23456789-VHO-11 10 09 08

Contents

To the Student

This *Study Guide* is a self-study accompaniment to *American Government,* Eleventh Edition, by James Q. Wilson and John J. Dilulio, Jr. It serves two purposes. First, it supplements, but does not replace the text. By using the *Study Guide* and the text together, you will reap maximum benefits from the course and enhance your general knowledge of the structure and operation of U.S. government. Second, this *Study Guide* will assist you in practicing and preparing for your exams and will improve your test-taking skills. These two purposes are inseparable. Good studying habits—hard work, practice, and review—are critical to learning and understanding any subject matter, and a thorough understanding is the best preparation for exams

This introduction begins with an overview of what you should expect to learn from a college-level course on U.S. American government. Following is detailed advice on how to get the most from this *Study Guide* as well as suggestions for obtaining additional supplementary information from the Internet.

THE STUDY OF U.S. GOVERNMENT

In colleges and universities, U.S. government is usually taught as part of an academic discipline known as *political science*. Political science differs from typical high school courses in two important respects. High school government courses customarily emphasize history. Furthermore, high school courses generally seek to promote citizenship by encouraging you to vote.

While this approach and goal is important, college-level political science develops a broader, more theoretical perspective on government. Political science is often about contemporary government rather than history. It compares the U.S. political system with other systems and does not necessarily assume that our system or Constitution is superior to others. It focuses mainly on how government really works. It provides, for instance, answers to and explanations for the following questions: Why do senior citizens have more political influence than college students? Why do members of Congress spend more time talking with constituents and lobbyists, attending committee meetings/hearings, and participating in fact-finding missions than they do debating legislation. How and why have presidential candidates and the media contributed to more candidate-centered campaigns that focus less on issues and party labels? Do the federal courts merely apply to law or do they make policy and are sensitive to public opinion? Why do interest groups sometimes seem to reflect the views of the top leadership of their organization rather than the views of the rank and file membership on policy issues?

Political science occasionally frustrates students seeking one correct or perfect solution to real-world problems. Political science theories often provide conflicting or even equally valid perspectives on issues. A case in point deals with the issue of *symbolic speech*: according to one constitutional theory, flag and draft card burning and painting exhibits that some people find offensive and indecent are forms of free "expression" protected by the First Amendment. Yet, according to another constitutional theory, only "speech" and "press" are protected by the First Amendment, while the First Amendment does not extend to flag and draft card burning and painting exhibits. Another case involves search and seizures: according to onc constitutional perspective, evidence obtained by police without a search warrant based on probable cause is a violation of the Fourth Amendment protection against illegal searches and seizures, and hence, inadmissible in court ("exclusionary rule"). Nonetheless, according to another constitutional perspective, evidence seized by police with the aid of a search warrant they believe to be valid is still admissible in court ("good-faith exception") if it later turns out that the warrant was defective (e.g., the judge used the wrong form).

Political science sometimes forces students to grapple with uncertainties. Students wrestle with debatable assumptions about human nature and with competing explanations for why humans behave as they do. For instance, they discover inherent contradictions between cherished ideals such as liberty and democracy. Moreover, they investigate basic value conflicts between interest groups, each with a good argument to support the assertion that its cause is just.

This is not meant to suggest that political science is an abstract or subjective field of study. To the contrary, political science requires precise conceptualizations and rigorous, objective analysis. It at times even involves the utilization of mathematical logic and quantitative data. Some have dismissed the importance of what political scientists do as nothing more than "precision guesswork." Yet, there is some truth to this claim because political science does attempt to explain government logically, and like any other science that tries to understand human beings, it is hardly exact. The complexities of humans create many challenges in political science. They also make it a fascinating subject, and one well worth your time and effort to study.

HOW TO USE THIS STUDY GUIDE

You should use this *Study Guide* do exactly what the title says—to guide you through the text material. This guide will highlight what is important in each chapter (the study objectives located under the rubric "Chapter Focus"). In addition, the guide will assist you in reviewing each chapter to make sure that you have covered and understood the pertinent facts, principles, and processes presented (Study Outline, Key Terms Match, Did You Think That…?, and Data Check). This guide also includes a Practice for Exams section that consists of true/false, multiple choice, and essay questions. You should not treat these questions merely as a practice exam. Use each set of questions as a way of furthering your understanding of what Professors Wilson and Dilulio have written and your instructor has presented in class. As you answer each question, review the text material, as well as your own notes (from both the text and your class). Understanding the subject will help you to do well on exams. Preparing for exams will, in turn, help you to understand the subject.

Chapter Focus

Before beginning each chapter of *American Government*, read through the study objectives in the Chapter Focus section. You can utilize these objectives to organize your thoughts and understand the textbook material. Keep the framework of each objective in mind as you read through the chapter, using each component of each objective as a heading for summarizing, in your own words, the important facts, concepts, ideas, and explanations presented. By the time you have completed each chapter, you should be able to write out a clear and accurate statement fulfilling each objective. You should always remember to think about how current U.S. government and politics conform, or do not conform, to the expectations of the Framers of the U.S. Constitution.

Study Outline

The Chapter Outline presents a section-by-section overview of the chapter. You should check the outline both before and after reading each text chapter. It should serve to reinforce in your mind the major chapter topics and clarify the relationships among them. But, you should not use the outline as a replacement for reading the text. You need to understand the material on its own terms. This can be done only by reading each chapter and not by simply relying on the chapter outline.

Key Terms Match

This section reviews the terms considered central to an understanding of the chapter's material. Test yourself on each of these terms, court cases, and political figures. If a term, make sure that you can give more than just a simple definition. When pertinent, give an example, cite an appropriate court case, and place the term in a broader theoretical context (answer the question: "so what?"). If a court case, be able to discuss the specifics of the case, the reasons why the decision was made, and its political significance or implications (again, "so what?"). If a political figure, discuss who that person is and how he/she has contributed to U.S. government and politics.

Data Check

The *Data Check* exercises emphasize points made in the various graphs, maps, and tables appearing in the text chapter. Too often, students neglect these helpful aids to comprehension. Completing this section will help you get the most out of the text's valuable visual resources.

True/False Questions

Mark the response you think is correct (true or false). Make sure that you understand, for each statement that you think is false, why it is false (space is provided after each true/false item to explain your choice). You can also use the space to indicate why you think a statement is true. Check your responses with the ones provided in the Answer Key.

Multiple-Choice Questions

A multiple-choice question will generally not have just one obvious answer. Each choice listed may have some term or idea that is related to the question, but *only one will correctly complete the statement introduced or answer the question asked.* Only one choice is correct.

Use the multiple-choice items to help you to review and understand the textbook material. Make sure that you understand why your choice correctly completes each statement or answers each question and why the other choices do not. Refer to the text to review the appropriate material addressed in each multiple-choice item. Check your answers with the ones provided in the Answer Key.

Essay Questions

Each chapter is accompanied by a series of essay questions. Most of these questions refer to specific details or an analysis provided in a particular section of a chapter. Others require you to tie together information from throughout a chapter, or, on occasion, ask you to connect themes and information from different chapters.

It is not unusual for college students (particularly, first-year students) to have great difficulty in answering essay questions. You may encounter questions that can be answered correctly in different ways from different perspectives. The best answers, however, are usually the most complete. Others may not be correct at all, either because they contain factual errors or, more commonly, because they do not address the question asked. To assist you with crafting successful answers to essay questions, the following simple guidelines are provided:

1. Read each question carefully. Focus. Reread. Figure out what the question really asks and answer accordingly. Do not simply read the question superficially and then start to write the first thing that comes to mind. Never write an answer based on "what you think the professor wants." If you approach the question in this manner, there is a high probability that you don't understand the question.

2. Organize. Outline each essay before you start to write. Use the outline to divide your essay into paragraphs, with each paragraph addressing a different part of the question. Begin each paragraph with a topic sentence or thesis statement, and use subsequent sentences in the paragraph to present supporting factual evidence, examples, finer points of logic, and conclusions. Organization saves time. Moreover, it improves both the strength of your reasoning and recollection of information.
3. Attack questions directly, and stay focused. Do not waste time restating questions. Use the first sentence of each essay either to introduce your major arguments(s) or to explain a term that reasonably requires explanation at the beginning of the essay. Then, develop your logic more fully, and discuss specific facts and examples. You should remember that summary is simply not enough. You should evaluate material and organize ideas into coherent, cogent arguments. If relevant, acknowledge opposing points of view without diluting strength of argument. Try not to repeat yourself. Stick to what the question asks. Do not get sidetracked onto peripheral arguments and constantly review your essay for contradictions.
4. Make sure to devote enough space and time to each part of the question. In short, be sure that your essay is balanced, while covering all aspects of the question.
5. Define key concepts clearly and accurately. Essay questions usually demand logical application of concepts to relevant facts, and good essays almost inevitably result from clear and accurate concept definitions. Conversely, vague, inaccurate, or even erroneous concept definitions almost always lead to confused and incomplete essays.
6. Always be as specific as possible. Try to find words that express exactly what you mean.
7. Explain fully. Never assume that certain points are obvious or that the grader of your essay can read your mind. If you want the grader to know what you mean, then say it! Develop *cause-and-effect* relationships as explicitly as possible. Support conclusions with well-reasoned arguments and evidence. If you claim that something is true, explain why you believe it to be true. Also, try to explain why possible alternatives to the correct answer can be logically refuted. Use examples to illustrate and clarify key points.

Answer Key

Answers to all chapter exercises (except for essay questions) appear at the end of each chapter of the *Study Guide.*

Classic Statements

In addition to these chapter components, the *Study Guide* includes five "*Classic Statements*" derived from the literature of American government and corresponding to one or more chapters of the text. These selections shaped political thought at the time they appeared and remain influential today. As you read each essay, consider (1) what the author is saying, (2) in what ways the author's central themes are relevant to American government and politics today, and (3) how the reading is related to the textbook coverage. Questions following each reading will help you focus on these three issues.

Following the last *Study Guide* chapter you will find two practice exams. The first covers Chapters 1 to 14. The second one covers Chapters 15 to 22 and includes some review questions from the first part of the text. Avail yourself of this opportunity to see how well you have integrated a large amount of material. And at the same time get some practice for your class exams.

In conclusion, it should be remembered that a study guide is useful only if it supplements your diligent study of the text itself. As mentioned earlier, it cannot replace the text, nor can it guarantee success on examinations. Used with the text, however, this *Study Guide* should noticeably boost your course performance and, hopefully, heighten your appreciation of American government.

PART I: The American System

CHAPTER 1

The Study of American Government

REVIEWING THE CHAPTER

CHAPTER FOCUS

The purpose of this chapter is to give you a preview of the major questions to be asked throughout the textbook, as well as to introduce some key terms in the basic vocabulary of American politics. After reading and reviewing the material in this chapter, you should be able to do each of the following:

1. List the two basic questions to be asked about American (or any other) government, and show that they are distinct questions.
2. Explain what is meant by *power* in general human terms and by *political power* in particular, relating the latter to authority, legitimacy, and democracy in the context of American government.
3. Distinguish among the two concepts of democracy mentioned in the chapter, explaining in which of these senses the textbook refers to American government as *democratic.*
4. Differentiate between majoritarian politics and elitist politics, explaining the four major theories of the latter.
5. Explain how political change makes political scientists cautious in stating how politics works or what values dominate it.

STUDY OUTLINE

I. Introduction
  A. Government failures
    1. The 9/11 attacks and the passage of homeland security measures
    2. Government response to Hurricanes Katrina and Rita
  B. Government successes
    1. Reducing poverty among the elderly
    2. Building the interstate highway system
    3. Improving public health
    4. Rebuilding war-torn Europe
II. Who governs? To what ends?
  A. Division as a source of "politics"
  B. Who governs?
    1. What is done to us and for us may depend on who governs
    2. Identifying who governs can be difficult
    3. Competing views cannot all be correct
  C. To what ends?
    1. Government affects our lives in many ways
    2. This can be seen in larger, longer perspectives
  D. Who governs does not necessarily determine to what ends

III. What is political power?
  A. Definition: the ability of one person to get another person to act in accordance with the first person's intentions
    1. Can be exercised in an obvious or subtle manner
    2. Can be found in all human relationships
      a) Text limits focus to power as exercised by public officials and government
      b) Recognition that, increasingly, matter once considered "private" are considered "public"
  B. Authority: the right to use power
    1. Normally easier to exercise power with a claim of right
    2. "Formal authority" when vested in a governmental office
  C. Legitimacy: what makes a law or constitution a source of right
    1. Historical struggles over what constitutes legitimate authority
    2. 2004 election and gay marriage
    3. Our sense of legitimacy is tied to the desire for democratic government
  D. What is democracy?
    1. Aristotelian "rule of the many" (direct or participatory democracy)
      a) Fourth-century B.C. Greek city-state or *polis*
      b) New England town meeting
      c) Abandoned as size of towns increased and issues became more complex
    2. Acquisition of power by leaders via competitive elections (representative democracy)
      a) Sometimes disapprovingly referred to as *elitist theory*
      b) Justifications of representative democracy
        (1) Direct democracy can be impractical
        (2) The people are affected by passions and demagogues
  E. Is representative democracy best?
    1. Text uses the term democracy to refer to representative democracy
      a) The Constitution does not contain the word democracy but the phrase "republican form of government"
      b) Representative democracy requires genuine competition for leadership
        (1) Individuals and parties must be able to run for office
        (2) Communication must be free
        (3) Voters must perceive meaningful choices
        (4) And other important questions—with multiple answers—remain regarding the number of offices, how many officials (elected and appointed), the financing of campaigns, etc.
    2. Virtues of direct democracy can be reclaimed through
      a) Community control
      b) Citizen participation
    3. Framers did not think the "will of the people" was synonymous with the "common interest" or the "public good"
      a) They strongly favored representative over direct democracy
        (1) Government should mediate, not mirror, popular views
        (2) Assumed citizens would have limited time, information and interest
        (3) Feared demagogues could easily manipulate fears and prejudices of the masses
        (4) Preferred a slow moving government
        (5) Believed representative democracy minimized chance that power would be abused by a popular majority or self-serving officeholders
      b) But were the Framers right?
        (1) Are their assumptions about direct democracy applicable today?

(2) Has representative democracy really protected minority rights and prevented politicians from using public offices for private gain?

c) Do people have more time, information, energy, interest, expertise, and ability to gather together for collective decisionmaking than they did when the Constitution was adopted?

(1) Today, there is unprecedented access to information about everything
(a) Five times as much mail as the mid-1990s
(b) Ten times as much e-mail as the mid-1990s

(2) Impact?
(a) Most people (and especially young people) still do not consume much political news
(b) Most Americans are not very active in political affairs
(c) Few citizens feel close to government or have great confidence in its leaders

IV. How is political power distributed?
A. Scholars differ in their interpretations of history
B. Variation in representative democracy
1. Majoritarian politics
a) Leaders constrained to follow wishes of the people very closely
b) Applies when issues are simple, clear and feasible
2. Non-majoritarian (or elite) politics
a) Sometimes the opinion of the people is not known, or even consulted
b) The shaping of policy detail probably reflects opinions of those who are more informed and motivated to participate
(1) The number of those who are informed and motivated is probably small
(2) They are probably not representative of the population as a whole
c) Elites: an identifiable group of persons who possess a disproportionate amount of political power
C. Four theories of elite influence
1. Marxism: government merely a reflection of underlying economic forces
2. C. Wright Mills: power elite composed of corporate leaders, generals, and politicians
3. Max Weber: bureaucracies based on expertise, specialized competence
4. Pluralist view: power is widely dispersed and no single elite has a monopoly on it; polices are the outcome of bargaining, compromise and shifting alliances

V. Is democracy driven by self interest?
A. Elite theories and cynicism
1. All four theories suggest politics is a self-seeking enterprise
2. Some important qualifications
a) Policies may not be wholly self serving
b) Democracy may be driven by other motives and desires
(1) 9/11 and self-interest
(2) Attitudes, allies and the temper of the times are as important
c) Some act against long odds and without the certainty of benefit

VI. What explains political change?
A. Great shifts in character of government reflect change in elite or mass beliefs about what government is supposed to do
1. Growth in federal power and subsequent attempts to cut back
2. Variations in levels of interest in international affairs
B. Politics about views of the public interest, not just who gets what

VII. The nature of politics
A. The answer to "Who governs?" is often partial or contingent

B. Preferences vary, and so does politics
C. Politics cannot be equated with laws on the books
D. Sweeping claims are to be avoided
E. Judgments about institutions and interests should be tempered by how they behave on different issues
F. The policy process can be an excellent barometer of change in who governs

KEY TERMS MATCH

Match the following terms and descriptions:

1. The ability of one person to cause another person to act in accordance with the first person's intentions
2. Power when used to determine who will hold government office and how government will behave
3. The right to exercise political power
4. The widely-shared perception that something or someone should be obeyed
5. Conferring political power on those selected by the voters in competitive elections
6. Term for the Greek city-state
7. An identifiable group of people with a disproportionate share of political power
8. A relatively small political unit within which classical democracy was practiced
9. A political system in which the choices of the political leaders are closely constrained by the preferences of the people
10. A philosopher who defined *democracy* as the "rule of the many"
11. A theory that government is merely a reflection of underlying economic forces
12. A sociologist who presented the idea of a mostly nongovernmental power elite
13. Individual who worried the new government he helped to create would be too democratic
14. A sociologist who emphasized the phenomenon of bureaucracy in explaining political developments

a. Aristotle
b. authority
c. bureaucracy
d. bureaucratic theory
e. citizen participation
f. city-state
g. community control
h. democracy
i. direct or participatory democracy
j. elite (political)
k. elitist theory
l. Hamilton
m. legitimacy
n. majoritarian politics
o. Marxist theory
p. Mills
q. New England town meeting
r. pluralist theory
s. *polis*
t. political power
u. power
v. representative democracy
w. Schumpeter
x. Weber

15. A political system in which local citizens are empowered to govern themselves directly

16. A political system in which those affected by a governmental program must be permitted to participate in the program's formulation

17. A North American approximation of direct or participatory democracy

18. A theory that no one interest group consistently holds political power

19. Structures of authority organized around expertise and specialization

20. An economist who defined *democracy* as the competitive struggle by political leaders for the people's vote

21. A theory that appointed civil servants make the key governing decisions

22. A term used to describe three different political systems in which the people are said to rule, directly or indirectly

23. A political system in which all or most citizens participate directly by either holding office or making policy

24. A theory that a few top leaders make the key decisions without reference to popular desires

PRACTICING FOR EXAMS

TRUE/FALSE QUESTIONS

Read each statement carefully. Mark true statements *T*. If any part of the statement is false, mark it *F*, and write in the space provided a concise explanation of why the statement is false.

1. T F It took the national government many years to implement just a fraction of the bipartisan homeland security policies and programs.

____

2. T F Politics exists in part because people differ about who should govern and the ends toward which they work.

____

3. T F Federal income taxes were higher in 1935 than they are today.

____

4. T F Most people holding political power in the United States today are middle-class, middle-aged, white Protestant males.

5. T F Constitutional amendments giving rights to African Americans and women passed by large majorities.

6. T F It is easy to discern political power at work.

7. T F The text suggests that, increasingly, matters that were once considered "public" become "private," and beyond the scope of governmental action.

8. T F In the 1950s the federal government would have displayed little or no interest in a university refusing applicants.

9. T F Much of American political history has been a struggle over what constitutes legitimate authority.

10. T F Alexander Hamilton worried that the new government would not be democratic enough.

11. T F Aristotle thought of democracy as the "rule of the many."

12. T F Everyone in the ancient Greek city-state was eligible to participate in government.

13. T F The New England town meeting approximates the Aristotelian ideal.

14. T F Some writers of the Constitution opposed democracy on the grounds that the people would be unable to make wise decisions.

15. T F Democracy as used in this book refers to the rule of the many.

16. T F The Framers of the Constitution did not think that the "will of the people" was synonymous with the "public good."

17. T F The Framers suspected even highly educated persons could be manipulated by demagogic leaders who played on their fears and prejudices.

18. T F The Framers hoped to create a representative democracy that would act swiftly and accommodate sweeping changes in policy.

____

19. T F People today have unprecedented access to information and consume more political news than ever.

____

20. T F Majoritarian politics probably influence relatively few issues in this country.

____

21. T F Marxist theory sees society as divided into two classes: capitalists and workers.

____

22. T F C. Wright Mills included corporate, governmental, and labor officials in his power elite.

____

23. T F Today, some would add major communications media chiefs to Mills' power elite.

____

24. T F Weber assigned a significant amount of power to appointed officials in the bureaucracies of modern governments.

____

25. T F Weber felt that bureaucrats merely implemented public policies that are made by elected officials.

____

26. T F Pluralists deny the existence of elites.

____

27. T F The bureaucratic view does the most to reassure one that America has been, and continues to be, a democracy in more than name only.

____

28. T F A policy can be good or bad independent of the motives of the person who decided it.

____

29. T F The self-interest of individuals is often an incomplete guide to their actions.

____

30. T F In the 1920s it was widely assumed that the federal government would play a small role in citizens' lives.

____

31. T F Who wields power—that is, who made a difference in the outcome and for what reason—is harder to discover than who did what.

____

32. T F Political change is not always accompanied by changes in public laws.

MULTIPLE CHOICE QUESTIONS

Circle the letter of the response that best answers the question or completes the statement.

1. Which statement best describes the performance of the government in the aftermath of the 9/11 terrorist attacks on the United States?
   a. Bipartisan homeland security policies and programs were adopted immediately.
   b. A fraction of the bipartisan homeland security policies and programs were implemented after many years of debate.
   c. Recommendations with respect to homeland security were summarily rejected.
   d. Almost all of the bipartisan homeland security policies and programs were implemented within a year.
   e. Homeland security programs and policies were considered too controversial for congressional action.
2. Today, on average, Americans pay _____ percent of their income to federal payroll taxes.
   a. 1
   b. 4
   c. 21
   d. 75
   e. 83
3. Most national political officeholders are middle-class, middle-aged, white Protestant males. Knowing this, we
   a. still cannot explain many important policies.
   b. have identified the power elite.
   c. can answer the question, "To what ends?"
   d. can predict little of importance to politics.
   e. can predict most of the policies that come out of Washington.
4. What do the authors define as "the ability of one person to get another person to act in accordance with the first person's intentions"?
   a. authority
   b. power
   c. influence
   d. legitimacy
   e. legislation
5. Which of the following statements concerning power is *correct*?
   a. Its exercise can sometimes be obvious.
   b. It can be exercised in subtle ways.
   c. It involves a person getting another person to act in accordance with the first person's wishes.
   d. It is found in all human relationships.
   e. All of the above.

6. Which of the following statements about authority is *correct*?
   a. It is defined as the right to use power.
   b. It resides in government, not in the private sector.
   c. It typically results from the naked use of force.
   d. It is the opposite of legitimacy.
   e. All of the above.
7. A survey of 450 history and political science professors resulted in ___________ being listed as the most significant achievement of government since 1950.
   a. devolution
   b. female suffrage
   c. social security
   d. the reduction of the federal deficit
   e. the rebuilding of Europe
8. Americans seem to agree that the exercise of political power at any level is legitimate only if, in some sense, it is
   a. systematic.
   b. democratic.
   c. bipartisan.
   d. partisan.
   e. traditional.
9. In Aristotle's view, democracy would consist of
   a. the effective representation of the interests of the whole population.
   b. political representation by all individuals in a society, regardless of race, age, or gender.
   c. participation by all or most citizens in either holding office or making policy.
   d. an elite group of policy makers elected by the will of the people.
   e. a nocturnal council that made decisions without regard to public opinion.
10. Aristotle's notion of democracy is also referred to as
   a. New York Democracy.
   b. direct democracy.
   c. commoner democracy.
   d. participatory democracy.
   e. b and d.
11. In the ancient Greek city-state, the right to vote was *not* extended to
   a. those who did not own property.
   b. women.
   c. minors.
   d. slaves.
   e. All of the above.
12. Which of the following is a basic tenet of representative democracy?
   a. Individuals should acquire power through competition for the people's vote.
   b. It is unreasonable to expect people to choose among competing leadership groups.
   c. Government officials should represent the true interests of their clients.
   d. The middle class gains representation at the expense of the poor and minorities.
   e. Public elections should be held on every issue directly affecting the lives of voters.

13. Sometimes, representative democracy is disapprovingly referred to as the _____ theory of Democracy.
   a. institutional
   b. elitist
   c. popular
   d. Aristotelian
   e. Jeffersonian
14. If you fear that people often decide big issues on the basis of fleeting passions and in response to demagogues, you are likely to agree with
   a. recall elections.
   b. the New England town meeting.
   c. the referendum.
   d. participatory democracy.
   e. many of the Framers of the Constitution.
15. The text suggests representative democracy is justified by all of the following concerns *except* that
   a. the people have limited information and expertise.
   b. direct democracy is impractical.
   c. the people may decide large issues on the basis of fleeting passions.
   d. the people cannot choose among competing leadership groups.
   e. the people may respond to popular demagogues.
16. In sharp contrast to the United States, very few offices in some European democracies are
   a. elective.
   b. appointive.
   c. full-time.
   d. constitutional.
   e. structured.
17. The text suggests the Founders thought the government should ____ popular views.
   a. reflect
   b. enlarge
   c. minimize
   d. mediate
   e. be guided by
18. The Founders granted that representative democracy would
   a. prevent factions from having any influence on government.
   b. prevent sweeping changes in policy.
   c. result in highly controversial elections.
   d. often proceed slowly.
   e. B and D.
19. The Founders might agree that ______ ought to hinge on popular vote.
   a. the right to a fair trial
   b. freedom of speech
   c. freedom of press
   d. freedom of religion
   e. none of the above

20. Issues can be handled in a majoritarian fashion if
    a. they are important enough to command the attention of most citizens.
    b. they are sufficiently clear to elicit an informed opinion from citizens.
    c. they are sufficiently feasible to address so that what citizens want can in fact be done.
    d. all of the above.
    e. none of the above.
21. In the Marxist view government is a reflection of underlying ________ forces.
    a. economic
    b. political
    c. ideological
    d. social
    e. teleological
22. Marx concluded "modern" societies generally feature a clash of power between
    a. farmers and industrialists.
    b. capitalists and workers.
    c. slaveowners and the landed aristocracy.
    d. monarchists and anarchists.
    e. intellectuals and spiritualists.
23. C. Wright Mills, an American sociologist, suggests politics and government are dominated by
    a. the tyranny of the majority.
    b. pork-barrel legislation.
    c. a nocturnal council.
    d. neo-Marxist policy.
    e. the power elite.
24. Which of the following statements is *not* consistent with Mills' position?
    a. Corporate leaders are the primary, dominant nongovernmental influence in policy making.
    b. Top military officials play an important role in the formulation of governmental policy.
    c. The most important policies are made by a loose coalition of three groups.
    d. A handful of key political leaders play an important role in the formulation of governmental policy.
    e. Nongovernmental elites play an important role in the formulation of governmental policy.
25. Max Weber felt that the dominant social and political reality of modern times was that
    a. "the Establishment" was dominated by Wall Street lawyers.
    b. all institutions have fallen under the control of large bureaucracies.
    c. capitalism is essential to modern-day forms of government.
    d. conflict increased between the government and the press.
    e. a dialectical process made communism inevitable.
26. Weber's theory suggests it would be wise for scholars who want to study power to focus on
    a. the President.
    b. mid-term elections.
    c. appointed officials and career government workers.
    d. members of Congress.
    e. critical national elections.

27. The view that money, expertise, prestige, and so forth are widely scattered throughout our society in the hands of a variety of groups is known as the
    a. pluralist view of American society.
    b. economic theory of democracy.
    c. elitist view of American society.
    d. dispersed power theory of American politics.
    e. monetary displacement theory of American politics.
28. A pluralist might agree with all of the following statements *except*
    a. political resources are not equally divided.
    b. mass opinion and the interests of citizens are irrelevant to policymaking.
    c. political resources are divided among different kinds of elites.
    d. elites are not a united front.
    e. policies are the outcome of complex patterns of haggling, compromises and shifting alliances.
29. The text suggests __________ theory "does the most to reassure one that America has been, and continues to be, a democracy in more than name."
    a. Marxist
    b. bureaucratic
    c. pluralist
    d. power elite
    e. Weberian
30. Ronald Reagan's policy initiatives on social and economic problems sought to
    a. return citizens' assumptions to what they had been during World War II.
    b. make the government more efficient and capable of addressing social problems.
    c. broaden government's social net for the truly needy.
    d. move the United States into the front rank of nations involved in forward social planning.
    e. return citizens' assumptions to what they had been before the 1930s.
31. American foreign policy, according to the text, tends to alternate between
    a. cold wars and hot wars.
    b. idealism and realism.
    c. bipolarism and multilateralism.
    d. interventions and isolationism.
    e. realism and existentialism.
32. The fact that people have been willing to die over competing views of the public interest suggests that
    a. such views are more than mere window dressing.
    b. politics concerns who gets what, when, where, and how.
    c. delusions are central to the political process.
    d. human nature is fundamentally inconsistent.
    e. political issues are rarely understood.
33. The kinds of answers that political scientists usually give to the fundamental political questions tend to be
    a. highly abstract and speculative.
    b. clear, concrete, and consistent.
    c. partial, contingent, and controversial.
    d. qualified to the point of unintelligibility.
    e. empirical and void of theory.

34. According to the text, before making judgments about institutions and interests, we must first observe them
    a. from a disinterested vantage point.
    b. as manifestations of underlying economic relationships.
    c. firsthand.
    d. on a variety of different issues.
    e. through the lenses of bureaucrats.
35. The logical place to begin the study of how power is distributed in U.S. politics is
    a. the Constitutional Convention and events leading up to it.
    b. your local town hall or courthouse.
    c. the day-to-day lives of Americans.
    d. the pages of this morning's newspaper.
    e. the Civil War.

ESSAY QUESTIONS

Practice writing extended answers to the following questions. These test your ability to integrate and express the ideas that you have been studying in this chapter.

1. Explain the difference between power, authority and legitimacy. Explain how Americans think of the last concept in particular.
2. Explain two senses of the word "democracy" and note historical examples of each.
3. What are some of the requirements for representative democracy and what are some ways that representative democracies in Europe are different from America?
4. Explain the sense in which the Founding Fathers expected the "will of the people" and "majority opinion" would figure into the new government.
5. What are three conditions of majoritarian politics?
6. Identify and explain four schools of thought about the distribution of power in society. Along the way, note which view suggests the widest distribution of power, which view is popular with political scientists and which view has the most positive ramifications for America.

ANSWERS TO KEY TERMS MATCH QUESTIONS

1. u
2. t
3. b
4. m
5. v
6. s
7. j
8. f
9. n
10. a
11. o
12. p
13. l
14. x
15. g
16. e
17. q
18. r
19. c
20. w
21. d
22. h
23. i
24. k

ANSWERS TO TRUE/FALSE QUESTIONS

1. T
2. T
3. F In 1935, about 96 percent of all Americans paid no federal income tax whatsoever. Today almost all families pay about 21 percent of their incomes.
4. T
5. T
6. F Sometimes is exercised in subtle ways that may not even be evident to those who are exercising it.

7. F Increasingly matters once thought to be "private" are becoming "public."
8. T
9. T
10. F Hamilton worried just the opposite, that it would be too democratic.
11. T
12. F Slaves, women, minors and those without property were excluded from participation.
13. T
14. T
15. F The text uses Joseph Schumpter's definition of representative democracy, not direct democracy.
16. T
17. T
18. F They did not. In their view, a government that could act swiftly and in radical ways could also do a great deal of harm.
19. F They do have higher levels of access to news and information, but they are not giving political news and information more attention than in the past. Most, especially young people, do not consume political news.
20. T
21. T
22. F Mills "power elite" consisted of corporate leaders, key military officials and key politicians.
23. T
24. T
25. F Weber saw power in the fact that bureaucrats also have discretion, which can cause their implementation of policies to vary widely.
26. F Pluralists do not believe everyone has power or that everyone has the same amount. They recognize that there are political elites (those with a disproportionate amount of political power and influence).
27. F The pluralist view is the more reassuring on this count.
28. T
29. T
30. T
31. T
32. T

ANSWERS TO MULTIPLE CHOICE QUESTIONS

1. b
2. c

3. a
4. b
5. e
6. a
7. e
8. b
9. c
10. e
11. e
12. a
13. b
14. e
15. d
16. a
17. d
18. e
19. e
20. d
21. a
22. b
23. e
24. a
25. b
26. c
27. a
28. b
29. c
30. e
31. d
32. a
33. c
34. d
35. a

CHAPTER 2

The Constitution

REVIEWING THE CHAPTER

CHAPTER FOCUS

The purpose of this chapter is to introduce you to the historical context within which the U.S. Constitution was written and in particular to the colonists' quest for liberties they felt had been denied them under British rule. After reading and reviewing the material in this chapter, you should be able to do each of the following:

1. Compare the American and French Revolutions of the same era with respect to the ideals that motivated them.
2. Explain the notion of higher law by which the colonists felt they were entitled to certain natural rights. List these rights.
3. Discuss the Declaration of Independence as a lawyer's brief prepared for court argument of a case.
4. Compare what the colonists believed was a legitimate basis for government with what monarchies—such as that in Great Britain at the time—believed was a legitimate basis for government.
5. List and discuss the shortcomings of government under the Articles of Confederation.
6. Discuss the backgrounds of the writers of the Constitution, and explain why these men tended to be rather mistrustful of the notion of democracy.
7. Compare and contrast the Virginia and New Jersey plans, and show how they led to the Great Compromise.
8. Explain why the separation of powers and federalism became key parts of the Constitution. Hint: the Framers' intention was not to make the system more democratic, nor was it to make it more efficient.
9. Show how James Madison's notions of human nature played an important role in the framing of the Constitution.
10. Explain why the Constitution did not include a bill of rights. Then explain why one was added.
11. Explain why the Founders failed to address the question of slavery in a definitive way.
12. Discuss whether "women were left out of the Constitution."
13. Summarize Charles Beard's analysis of the economic motivations of the Framers and the counter-analyses of those who disagree with Beard.
14. List and explain the two major types of constitutional reform advocated today, along with specific reform measures.

STUDY OUTLINE

I. Introduction
II. The problem of liberty
  A. The colonial mind
    1. Belief that because British politicians were corrupt, the English constitution was inadequate
    2. Belief in higher law of natural rights
      a) Life
      b) Liberty
      c) Property (Jefferson notwithstanding)
    3. A war of ideology, not economics
    4. Specific complaints against George III for violating inalienable rights
  B. The "real" revolution
    1. The "real" revolution was the radical change in belief about what made authority legitimate and liberties secure
    2. Government by consent, not by prerogative
    3. Direct grant of power: written constitution
    4. Human liberty before government
    5. Legislature superior to executive branch
  C. Weaknesses of the Confederation
    1. Could not levy taxes or regulate commerce
    2. Sovereignty, independence retained by states
    3. One vote in Congress for each state
    4. Nine of thirteen votes in Congress required for any measure
    5. Delegates picked, paid for by legislatures
    6. Little money coined by Congress
    7. Army small; dependent on state militias
    8. Territorial disputes between states
    9. No national judicial system
    10. All thirteen states' consent necessary for any amendments
III. The Constitutional Convention
  A. The lessons of experience
    1. State constitutions
      a) Pennsylvania: too strong, too democratic
      b) Massachusetts: too weak, less democratic
    2. Shays's Rebellion led to the fear the states were about to collapse
  B. The Framers
    1. Who came: men of practical affairs
    2. Who did not come
    3. Intent to write an entirely new constitution
    4. Lockean influence
    5. Doubts that popular consent could guarantee liberty
    6. Results: "a delicate problem"; need strong government for order but one that would not threaten liberty
      a) Democracy of that day not the solution
      b) Aristocracy not a solution either
      c) Government with constitutional limits no guarantee against tyranny
IV. The challenge
  A. The Virginia Plan
    1. Design for a true national government

2. Two houses in legislature
3. Executive chosen by legislature
4. Council of revision with veto power
5. Two key features of the plan
    a) National legislature with supreme powers
    b) One house elected directly by the people

B. The New Jersey Plan
1. Sought to amend rather than replace the Articles
2. Proposed one vote per state
3. Protected small states' interests

C. The compromise
1. House of Representatives based on population
2. Senate of two members per state
3. Reconciled interests of big and small states
4. Committee of detail

V. The Constitution and democracy

A. Founders did not intend to create pure democracy
1. Physical impossibility in a vast country
2. Mistrust of popular passions
3. Intent instead to create a republic with a system of representation

B. Popular rule only one element of the new government
1. State legislators to elect senators
2. Electors to choose president
3. Two kinds of majorities: voters and states
4. Judicial review another limitation
5. Amendment process

C. Key principles
1. Separation of powers
2. Federalism
3. Resulting powers
    a) Enumerated powers: those exclusively given or delegated to federal government
    b) Reserved powers: those given exclusively to the states
    c) Concurrent powers: those shared by both the national and state governments

D. Government and human nature
1. Aristotelian view: government should improve human nature by cultivating virtue
2. Madisonian view: cultivation of virtue would require a government too strong, too dangerous; self-interest should be freely pursued
3. Federalism enables one level of government to act as a check on the other

E. The Constitution and liberty

F. Whether constitutional government was to respect personal liberties is a difficult question; ratification by conventions in at least nine states a democratic feature but a technically illegal one

G. The Antifederalist view
1. Liberty could be secure only in small republics
    a) In big republics, national government would be distant from people
    b) Strong national government would use its powers to annihilate state functions
2. There should be many more restrictions on government
3. Madison's response: personal liberty safest in large ("extended") republics
    a) Coalitions likely more moderate there
    b) Government should be somewhat distant to be insulated from passions.

4. Reasons for the absence of a bill of rights
    a) Several guarantees in the Constitution
        (1) *Habeas corpus*
        (2) No bill of attainder
        (3) No ex post facto law
        (4) Trial by jury
        (5) Privileges and immunities
        (6) No religious tests
        (7) Obligation of contracts
    b) Most states had bills of rights
    c) Intent to limit federal government to specific powers

H. Need for a bill of rights
1. Ratification impossible without one
2. Promise by key leaders to obtain one
3. Bitter ratification narrowly successful

VI. The Constitution and slavery
A. Slavery virtually unmentioned
B. Apparent hypocrisy of Declaration signers
C. Necessity of compromise: otherwise no ratification
1. Sixty percent of slaves counted for representation
2. No slavery legislation possible before 1808
3. Escaped slaves to be returned to masters
D. Legacy: Civil War, continuing problems

VII. The motives of the Framers
A. Acted out of a mixture of motives; economic interests played modest role
B. Economic interests of Framers varied widely
1. Beard: those who owned governmental debt supported Constitution
2. However, no clear division along class lines found
3. Recent research: state considerations outweighed personal considerations; exception: slaveholders
C. Economic interests and ratification
1. Played larger role in state ratifying conventions
2. In favor: merchants, urbanites, owners of western land, holders of government IOUs, non-slave owners
3. Opposed: farmers, people who held no IOUs, slaveowners
4. But remarkably democratic process because most could vote for delegates
5. Federalists versus Antifederalists on ideas of liberty
D. The Constitution and equality
1. Critics: government today is too weak
    a) Bows to special interests
    b) Fosters economic inequality
    c) Liberty and equality are therefore in conflict
2. Framers more concerned with political inequality; weak government reduces political privilege

VIII. Constitutional reform—modern views
A. Reducing the separation of powers to enhance national leadership
1. Urgent problems remain unresolved
2. President should be more powerful, accountable, to produce better policies.
3. Government agencies exposed to undue interference

4. Proposals
   a) Choose cabinet members from Congress
   b) Allow president to dissolve Congress
   c) Empower Congress to require special presidential election
   d) Require presidential/congressional terms
   e) Establish single six-year term for president
   f) Lengthen terms in House to four years
5. Contrary arguments: results uncertain, worse

B. Making the system less democratic
1. Government does too much, not too little
2. Attention to individual wants over general preferences
3. Proposals
   a) Limit amount of taxes collectible
   b) Require a balanced budget
   c) Grant president a true line-item veto
      (1) A power held by most state governors
      (2) 1996 Act signed by President Clinton
      (3) Law declared unconstitutional by the Supreme Court
      (4) 2006 proposal by President Bush
   d) Narrow authority of federal courts
4. Contrary arguments: unworkable or open to evasion

C. Who is right?
1. Decide nothing now
2. Crucial questions
   a) How well has it worked in history?
   b) How well has it worked in comparison with other constitutions?

KEY TERMS MATCH

Set 1

Match the following terms and descriptions:

1. A set of principles, either written or unwritten, that makes up the fundamental law of the state
2. Rights of all human beings that are ordained by God, discoverable in nature and history, and essential to human progress
3. Individual who refused to attend the Constitutional Convention because he "smelled a rat"
4. A document written in 1776 declaring the colonists' intention to throw off British rule
5. The government charter of the states from 1776 until the Constitution of 1787

a. Articles of Confederation
b. Bill of Rights
c. Charles A. Beard
d. coalition
e. concurrent powers
f. Constitution
g. Constitutional Convention
h. Declaration of Independence
i. enumerated powers
j. faction
k. federalism
l. *Federalist* papers

6. An alliance of factions
7. Based on nature or God.
8. A meeting of delegates in Philadelphia in 1787 charged with drawing up amendments to the Articles of Confederation
9. Powers that are given exclusively to the states
10. A governing document considered to be highly democratic yet with a tendency toward tyranny as the result of concentrating all powers in one set of hands
11. A state constitution with clear separation of powers but considered to have produced too weak a government
12. An armed attempt by Revolutionary War veterans to avoid losing their property by preventing the courts in western Massachusetts from meeting
13. Those powers that are shared by both the national and state governments
14. A British philosopher whose ideas on civil government greatly influenced the Founders
15. A series of political tracts that explained many of the ideas of the Founders
16. A constitutional proposal that the smaller states' representatives feared would give permanent supremacy to the larger states
17. A constitutional proposal that would have given each state one vote in a new congress
18. Author of the Declaration of Independence
19. A constitutional proposal that made membership in one house of Congress proportional to each state's population and membership in the other equal for all states
20. A group with a distinct political interest

m. Great Compromise
n. Patrick Henry
o. Thomas Jefferson
p. John Locke
q. James Madison
r. Massachusetts Constitution
s. natural rights
t. New Jersey Plan
u. Pennsylvania Constitution
v. reserved powers
w. separation of powers
x. Shays's Rebellion
y. unalienable
z. Virginia Plan

21. A constitutional principle separating the personnel of the legislative, executive, and judicial branches of government
22. A constitutional principle reserving separate powers to the national and state levels of government
23. A principal architect of the Constitution who felt that a government powerful enough to encourage virtue in its citizens was too powerful
24. First ten amendments to the Constitution
25. Those powers that are given to the national government exclusively
26. A historian who argued that the Founders were largely motivated by the economic advantage of their class in writing the Constitution

Set 2

Match the following terms and descriptions:

1. A meeting of delegates in 1778 to revise the Articles of Confederation
2. The power of the legislative, executive, and judicial branches of government to block some acts by the other two branches
3. A form of democracy in which leaders and representatives are selected by means of popular competitive elections
4. An alliance between different interest groups or parties to achieve some political goal
5. Rights thought to be based on nature and providence rather than on the preferences of people
6. Change in, or addition to, a constitution
7. A group of people sharing a common interest who seek to influence public policy for their collective benefit

a. Amendment (constitutional)
b. Antifederalists
c. bill of attainder
d. Bill of Rights
e. checks and balances
f. coalition
g. confederation
h. Constitutional Convention
i. ex post facto law
j. faction
k. *Federalist* papers
l. Federalists
m. judicial review
n. line-item veto
o. Madisonian view of human nature

8. The power of the courts to declare acts of the legislature and of the executive unconstitutional and therefore null and void

9. The first ten amendments to the U.S. Constitution

10. A series of eighty-five essays published in New York newspapers to convince New Yorkers to adopt the newly proposed Constitution

11. Supporters of a stronger central government who advocated ratification of the Constitution and then founded a political party

12. The power of an executive to veto some provisions in an appropriations bill while approving others

13. Those who opposed giving as much power to the national government as the Constitution did, favoring instead stronger states' rights

14. A law that would declare a person guilty of a crime without a trial

15. A law that would declare an act criminal after the act was committed

16. A philosophy holding that accommodating individual self-interest provided a more practical solution to the problem of government than aiming to cultivate virtue

17. An agreement among sovereign states that delegates certain powers to a national government

18. A court order requiring police officials to produce an individual held in custody and show sufficient cause for that person's detention

p. republic

q. inalienable rights

r. writ of *habeas corpus*

DATA CHECK

North America in 1787 (Page 20)

1. How clear was it, in 1787, that the destiny of most of North America was to become English speaking and dominated by the United States?

___

___

Ratification of the Federal Constitution by State Conventions, 1787–1790 (Page 31)

2. How many states were strongly in favor of the Constitution and ratified it early?

___

3. Generalize about the geographic location of the states which were strongly in favor of the Constitution and ratified it early.

___

___

4. Generalize about the geographic location of the states which initially opposed the Constitution or ratified it initially after a "close struggle."

___

___

PRACTICING FOR EXAMS

TRUE/FALSE QUESTIONS

Read each statement carefully. Mark true statements *T*. If any part of the statement is false, mark it *F*, and write in the space provided a concise explanation of why the statement is false.

1. T F The delegates to the Philadelphia convention were not popularly elected.

___

2. T F The American and French Revolutions of the late 1700s were both fought for the ideals of liberty, fraternity, and equality.

___

3. T F The British Constitution was not a single written document.

___

4. T F Commonly listed among the natural rights to which colonists felt entitled were life, liberty, and the pursuit of happiness.

___

5. T F The Declaration of Independence contained more paragraphs naming specific complaints against the king than paragraphs announcing the goals of the Revolution.

___

6. T F Revolutionary colonists rejected the notion that the king of England had a natural prerogative to be their legitimate ruler.

___

7. T F Revolutionary colonists largely held that the legislative branch of government should have a greater share of governmental power than the executive.

___

8. T F The eleven years that elapsed between the Declaration of Independence and the signing of the Constitution were years of turmoil, uncertainty and fear.

___

9. T F Under the Articles of Confederation the national government levied relatively modest taxes on the people.

___

10. T F The Articles required nine votes for the passage of any measure.

___

11. T F John Hancock was elected president in 1785 but never showed up to take the job.

___

12. T F There was no national judicial system under the Articles of Confederation.

___

13. T F George Washington and Alexander Hamilton were strong supporters of the Articles of Confederation.

___

14. T F The Constitutional Convention lasted about one month.

___

15. T F The Pennsylvania state constitution was the most radically democratic.

___

16. T F Shays's Rebellion may have encouraged some delegates to meet in Philadelphia who may not have otherwise.

___

17. T F Rhode Island refused to send a delegate to Philadelphia.

___

18. T F Most of the Framers of the Constitution were experienced in government and were in their fifties or sixties.

___

19. T F Thomas Jefferson and John Adams did not attend the Philadelphia Convention.

____

20. T F The Constitution of the United States is the world's oldest written national constitution still in operation.

____

21. T F The Virginia Plan appeared to favor the larger states, whereas the New Jersey Plan was more acceptable to the smaller ones.

____

22. T F When the first decisive vote of the Convention was taken, the New Jersey Plan was favored over the Virginia Plan.

____

23. T F The Great Compromise is sometimes called the Connecticut Compromise.

____

24. T F James Madison enthusiastically supported the Great Compromise.

____

25. T F The Great Compromise, which essentially saved the Convention from collapsing, was directly opposed by, or not supported by, the votes of eight of the thirteen states.

____

26. T F The author of the Virginia Plan refused to sign the Constitution.

____

27. T F At the time of the Convention, most European systems spread authority between state and national governments.

____

28. T F The power to declare war would be a proper example of an "enumerated" power.

____

29. T F The power to issue licenses and to regulate commerce within a state would be proper examples of powers that are "reserved."

____

30. T F The Founders assumed most people would seek their own advantage and that some would exploit others in the pursuit of self-interest.

____

31. T F James Madison, like Aristotle, thought that government had an obligation to cultivate virtue among those who were governed.

____

32. T F The Framers considered the dispersion of power at both the state and federal levels to be a kind of "double security" to the rights of the people.

____

33. T F To be in effect, the Constitution had to be approved by ratifying conventions in all thirteen states.

---

34. T F The Constitution was initially rejected by ratifying conventions in two states.

---

35. T F The text suggests that many of the major fears and dour predictions of the Antifederalists turned out to be correct.

---

36. T F *Federalist* No. 51 argues that coalitions in large republics tend to be less moderate.

---

37. T F The possible addition of a bill of rights was never considered at the Constitutional Convention.

---

38. T F At the time of the Convention, most state constitutions contained bills of rights.

---

39. T F The Constitution did not contain a bill of rights originally, in part because the Founders did not believe that the national government would be able to infringe on those rights already protected in such bills.

---

40. T F The evidence suggests the personal economic circumstances of the Framers influenced their decisionmaking more than the interests of the states they were supposed to represent.

MULTIPLE CHOICE QUESTIONS

Circle the letter of the response that best answers the question or completes the statement.

1. The goal of the American Revolution was
   a. equality.
   b. stability.
   c. fairness.
   d. liberty.
   e. fraternity.
2. The colonists believed that most politicians tended to be
   a. aristocratic.
   b. idealistic.
   c. benevolent.
   d. corrupt.
   e. incompetent.

3. The colonists fought to protect liberties that they believed were
   a. discoverable in nature and history.
   b. based on a "higher law."
   c. essential to human progress.
   d. ordained by God.
   e. all of the above.
4. When he wrote the Declaration of Independence, Thomas Jefferson replaced _______ with "the pursuit of happiness."
   a. life
   b. property
   c. justice
   d. liberty
   e. equality
5. At the time of the American Revolution, most citizens were
   a. self-employed.
   b. indentured servants.
   c. highly literate.
   d. propertyless.
   e. concerned with economic rather than political issues.
6. The essential complaints itemized in the Declaration of Independence are remarkable because
   a. each had been primary features in other revolutions.
   b. they were never actually mentioned to the King.
   c. most of the colonists were unable to understand them.
   d. none spoke of social or economic conditions in the colonies.
   e. Jefferson got most of the material from Washington and Adams.
7. An "unalienable" right is
   a. supported by a majority of any society.
   b. created by legislators.
   c. based in a written constitution.
   d. without restriction.
   e. based on nature and Providence.
8. The colonists new vision of government insisted that
   a. the executive branch be superior to the legislative branch.
   b. the judicial branch be superior to the legislative branch.
   c. the branches of government be unified.
   d. each branch of government be equal.
   e. the legislative branch be superior to the executive branch.
9. One notable feature of colonial governments by 1776 was the presence of
   a. weak governors.
   b. authority in community groups and local organizations.
   c. bicameral legislatures.
   d. elected judges who could be removed from office by people.
   e. written constitutions with detailed bills of rights.

10. The Articles of Confederation attempted to create
    a. a league of friendship among the states.
    b. a centralized government.
    c. a strong state commitment to the national government.
    d. weak state governments.
    e. none of the above.
11. Under the Articles, Congress had the power to
    a. make peace.
    b. coin money.
    c. appoint key army officers.
    d. run the post office.
    e. all of the above.
12. All of the following were true of the government under the Articles *except*
    a. each state had one vote in Congress.
    b. the national government could not regulate commerce.
    c. the national government could not levy taxes.
    d. there was no national judicial branch.
    e. amendments required the support of nine of thirteen states.
13. The critical meeting that was scheduled by those who met at George Washington's house and later held at Annapolis, Maryland, focused on the topic of
    a. the quartering of soldiers.
    b. naval defense.
    c. trade regulation.
    d. qualifications for citizenship.
    e. the official recognition of several new colonies.
14. The original purpose of the Constitutional Convention was to
    a. draw up a bill of rights.
    b. discuss regulations on intrastate commerce.
    c. levy taxes.
    d. build an army.
    e. revise the Articles of Confederation.
15. What influential Founder concluded history — to that point in time — provided no truly desirable model of government?
    a. John Adams
    b. Alexander Hamilton
    c. George Washington
    d. James Madison
    e. Patrick Henry
16. French political pundits and Thomas Paine praised the state constitution of Pennsylvania because it was radically
    a. centralized.
    b. democratic.
    c. legalistic.
    d. monarchical.
    e. elitist.

17. Shays's Rebellion stirred the fears of some that state governments were
    a. becoming too powerful.
    b. about to collapse.
    c. controlled by British interests.
    d. opposed to liberty.
    e. seeking independence.
18. Thomas Jefferson responded to the news of the Rebellion by noting
    a. it was the logical result of the American Revolution.
    b. no such problems were likely to occur again.
    c. a little rebellion now and then is a good thing.
    d. confederations are always plagued by such disturbances.
    e. dissenters should be arrested and jailed as soon as possible.
19. The Philadelphia Convention attracted about ____ delegates from the states.
    a. 12
    b. 30
    c. 39
    d. 55
    e. 74
20. About ___ of the delegates at the Convention participated regularly.
    a. 12
    b. 30
    c. 39
    d. 55
    e. 74
21. The majority of the delegates to the Constitutional Convention were
    a. veterans of the Continental Army.
    b. lawyers.
    c. governors.
    d. doctors.
    e. intellectuals.
22. The text suggests some names made famous by the Revolution were conspicuously absent from the Convention, including
    a. Thomas Jefferson.
    b. John Adams.
    c. Patrick Henry.
    d. Samuel Adams.
    e. all of the above.
23. The various speeches given by the delegates at the Convention are known to us from
    a. an official report provided to Congress.
    b. newspaper reports and a series of leaks throughout the summer.
    c. detailed notes kept by Madison.
    d. a variety of speeches made by Alexander Hamilton.
    e. the personal diaries of Benjamin Franklin.

24. The delegates to the Constitutional Convention shared a commitment to
    a. democracy.
    b. equality.
    c. fraternity.
    d. liberty.
    e. competition.
25. When John Locke theorized about the "state of nature," he was speculating about a period of time when
    a. there was no private ownership of property.
    b. governments had legislative powers, but no executive.
    c. power was equally divided and there was no "instinct" for self-preservation.
    d. the people freely consented to detailed restrictions of their natural rights.
    e. there were societies, but no governments.
26. The philosophy of John Locke strongly supported the idea that
    a. government ought to be limited.
    b. property rights should be subordinated to human rights.
    c. the state of nature was without flaw.
    d. reason is an inadequate guide in establishing a political order.
    e. equality of goods and income is necessary to political order.
27. The Pennsylvania experience led the Framers to be concerned about the tyranny of
    a. lawyers.
    b. the executive.
    c. the judiciary.
    d. the legislature.
    e. the majority.
28. To many conservatives in the late eighteenth century, democracy meant
    a. political equality.
    b. mob rule.
    c. stability.
    d. liberty and justice.
    e. quality representation through competitive elections.
29. In the *Federalist* papers, Madison quipped that government would not be "necessary" if
    a. men were angels.
    b. laws were memorized.
    c. aristocrats labored in the field with commoners.
    d. Americans were not so stubborn.
    e. the King had no army.
30. The presiding officer at the Constitutional Convention was
    a. James Madison.
    b. Benjamin Franklin.
    c. Patrick Henry.
    d. George Washington.
    e. Thomas Jefferson.

31. Supporters of a strong national government favored the
    a. Virginia Plan.
    b. New Jersey Plan.
    c. Georgia Plan.
    d. Rhode Island Plan.
    e. Pennsylvania Plan.
32. All of the following were features of the Virginia Plan *except*
    a. the government was divided into three major branches.
    b. the national legislature was divided into two houses.
    c. each state had one vote in the national legislature.
    d. the executive was chosen by the national legislature.
    e. one house of the legislature was elected directly by the people.
33. The high degree of contentiousness at the Convention was evident in the fact that Benjamin Franklin suggested beginning each meeting with
    a. prayer.
    b. hand shaking.
    c. the sharing of positive experiences.
    d. informal chat.
    e. a formal pledge to be civil.
34. The Great Compromise
    a. required Supreme Court justices to be confirmed by the Senate.
    b. based House representation on population and Senate population on equality.
    c. solved the conflict between those who wanted a powerful House and those who did not.
    d. provided that the president be selected by the electoral college.
    e. dealt with, without mentioning by name, "slavery."
35. The Constitution called for Senators to be
    a. elected by the people.
    b. selected by members of the House.
    c. selected by the previous administration.
    d. chosen by the electoral college.
    e. selected by the state legislatures.
36. The Great Compromise was supported by the votes of delegates from ______ states.
    a. 13
    b. 12
    c. 10
    d. 5
    e. 2
37. Before a committee created the electoral college, convention delegates suggested the president be
    a. chosen by Congress.
    b. chosen by the state legislatures.
    c. selected by members of the Supreme Court.
    d. elected directly by the people.
    e. A and D.

38. With regard to the power of judicial review, the text suggests
    a. few scholars have ever doubted the widespread support for this power at the Convention.
    b. it is not clear whether the Framers intended the Supreme Court to have such a power.
    c. only state courts can exercise the power in relation to federal laws.
    d. the Constitution explicitly grants this power to the federal courts alone.
    e. the Constitution explicitly granted this power to local courts alone.
39. All of the following statements regarding the amendment process are correct *except*
    a. amendments can only be proposed by the Senate.
    b. Congress can call a National Convention at the request of two-thirds of the states.
    c. amendments must be ratified by three-fourths of the states.
    d. states may ratify amendments through their legislatures or special ratifying conventions.
    e. almost all amendments to date have been proposed by Congress and ratified by state legislatures.
40. The American version of representative democracy was based on two major principles:
    a. self-interest and institutionalism.
    b. separation of powers and federalism.
    c. commerce and competition.
    d. liberty and equality.
    e. unification and centralism.
41. The power to print money would be an example of a(n) "_______ power."
    a. enumerated
    b. reserved
    c. concurrent
    d. dispositive
    e. partitioned
42. Powers that are exclusively given the states are referred to as "_______ powers."
    a. enumerated
    b. reserved
    c. concurrent
    d. dispositive
    e. partitioned
43. The power to collect taxes would be an example of a(n) "_______ power."
    a. enumerated
    b. reserved
    c. concurrent
    d. dispositive
    e. partitioned
44. The Antifederalists are best described as
    a. nationalists.
    b. radicals.
    c. neo-institutionalists.
    d. Framers.
    e. states' righters.

45. The *Federalist* papers were written
  a. at the suggestion of Benjamin Franklin.
  b. to explain democracy to European governments.
  c. to help win ratification of the Constitution in New York.
  d. principally by Madison and Jefferson.
  e. principally by John Jay.
46. Which of the following liberties was included in the Constitution before the Bill of Rights was added?
  a. *Habeas corpus.*
  b. Freedom of speech.
  c. Right to petition the government for redress of grievances.
  d. Right to bear arms.
  e. Protection from double jeopardy.
47. In the Constitution, slavery was
  a. not specifically mentioned.
  b. recognized as a necessary institution.
  c. outlawed after twenty years.
  d. denounced as inhuman.
  e. expressly permitted in the South.
48. Sophisticated statistical analysis of the voting behavior of the Framers of the Constitution suggests
  a. they generally pursued the interests of wealthy land owners and businessmen.
  b. they generally acted in a manner to protect the interests of the poor.
  c. they consciously ignored the interests of the commercial classes.
  d. they generally represented the interests of their respective states.
  e. they consciously ignored the interests of the slaveowners.
49. Those who favor reforming the Constitution by lessening the separation of powers between the branches often draw their inspiration from the model of
  a. Germany.
  b. the Articles of Confederation.
  c. Great Britain.
  d. France.
  e. the United Nations.
50. Women are specifically mentioned in the original Constitution
  a. in the "privileges and immunities" clause [Art. IV].
  b. under qualifications for office [Art. I].
  c. in language regarding treason [Art. III].
  d. in Article I, Section 8, Clause 3.
  e. nowhere.
51. No women voted in state elections in the United States until
  a. 1838, in Kentucky school board elections.
  b. 1869, in territorial elections in Wyoming.
  c. the ratification of the Fifteenth Amendment in 1875.
  d. The Great Panic of 1872.
  e. the ratification of the Twentieth Amendment in 1920.

ESSAY QUESTIONS

Practice writing extended answers to the following questions. These test your ability to integrate and express the ideas that you have been studying in this chapter.

1. Describe the state of things during the eleven years between the Declaration of Independence and the Constitution.
2. Identify some of the government's major structural features and power arrangements under the Articles and note some aspects of the government which might reasonably have been "weaknesses."
3. Describe what happened in Shays's Rebellion and discuss its impact.
4. Summarize the basic views of John Locke in regard to the state of nature, government and liberty.
5. Compare and contrast the Virginia and New Jersey Plans.
6. What are some aspects of our government which suggest popular rule was to be only one element of the new government?
7. Identify and explain the three categories of governmental powers in this country.
8. Identify eight examples of checks and balances in our system of government. In doing so, identify both the branch of government that has the check and which branch of government which is checked.
9. Describe Madison's view of the relationship between human nature and government. Also identify two aspects of the new government which he considered most relevant to the topic.
10. Explain Madison's view of the relationship between liberty and the size of a republic.
11. What are three reasons why the Constitution signed in Philadelphia did not contain a bill of rights?
12. Summarize Charles Beard's view of the Constitutional Convention and what subsequent research on the topic has concluded.
13. What are four to five suggestions that might be made in order to reduce the separation of powers in our system of government.

ANSWERS TO KEY TERMS MATCH QUESTIONS

Set 1

1. f
2. s
3. n
4. h
5. a
6. d
7. y
8. g
9. v
10. u
11. r
12. x
13. e
14. p
15. l
16. z
17. t
18. o
19. m
20. j
21. w
22. k
23. q
24. b
25. i
26. c

Set 2

1. h
2. e
3. p
4. f

5. q
6. a
7. j
8. m
9. d
10. k
11. l
12. n
13. b
14. c
15. i
16. o
17. g
18. r

ANSWERS TO DATA CHECK QUESTIONS

1. Not at all clear.
2. Four.
3. All four are in the Northeast. They are somewhat small in size and a significant portion of their boundaries are coastal lines.
4. These states are distributed throughout the map, North to South and East to West and there are many more of them. They are a diverse group.

ANSWERS TO TRUE/FALSE QUESTIONS

1. T
2. F The primary goal of the American Revolution was liberty.
3. T
4. F The list would have included life, liberty and property.
5. T
6. T
7. T
8. T
9. F The national government had no power to tax under the Articles.
10. T
11. T
12. T

13. F Washington and Hamilton were both advocates of a strong national government, the kind which simply did not exist under the Articles.

14. F It lasted about four months.

15. T

16. T

17. T

18. F The Framers had amazing levels of political experience but were relatively young.

19. T

20. T

21. T

22. F The first vote favored the Virginia Plan.

23. T

24. F Madison opposed the Compromise.

25. T

26. T

27. F At the times, most European systems were unitary.

28. T

29. T

30. T

31. F Madison felt that the only way that a government could accomplish that goal would be for it to be too strong and, as a result, a threat to individual liberty.

32. T

33. F The Constitution called for ratification by only nine states.

34. T

35. T

36. F The argument was quite the opposite, that large coalitions tend to be moderate.

37. F A bill of rights was suggested at the Convention, but the idea was voted down.

38. T

39. T

40. F The evidence suggests that the Founders voted, more often than not, in terms of the economic interests of the states that they represented.

ANSWERS TO MULTIPLE CHOICE QUESTIONS

1. d

2. d

3. e

4. b
5. a
6. d
7. e
8. e
9. e
10. a
11. e
12. e
13. c
14. e
15. d
16. b
17. b
18. c
19. d
20. b
21. b
22. e
23. c
24. d
25. e
26. a
27. e
28. b
29. a
30. d
31. a
32. c
33. a
34. b
35. e
36. d
37. e
38. b

39. a
40. b
41. a
42. b
43. c
44. e
45. c
46. a
47. a
48. d
49. c
50. e
51. b

CHAPTER 3

Federalism

REVIEWING THE CHAPTER

CHAPTER FOCUS

The central purpose of the chapter is to introduce you to some of the complexities of government in the United States caused by the adoption of a federal system, that is, one in which both the national and state governments have powers independent of one another. You should also note how the nature and the effects of U.S. federalism have changed throughout U.S. history and continue to change to this day. After reading and reviewing the material in this chapter, you should be able to do each of the following:

1. Explain the difference between federal and centralized systems of government, and give examples of each.
2. Show how competing political interests at the Constitutional Convention led to the adoption of a federal system, but one that was not clearly defined.
3. Outline the ways in which the courts interpreted national and state powers and why the doctrine of dual federalism is still alive.
4. State why federal grants-in-aid to the states have been politically popular, and cite what have proved to be the pitfalls of such grants.
5. Distinguish between categorical grants and block grants or general revenue sharing.
6. Explain why, despite repeated attempts to reverse the trend, categorical grants have continued to grow more rapidly than block grants.
7. Distinguish between mandates and conditions of aid with respect to federal grant programs to states and localities.
8. Define *devolution* and its roots.
9. Discuss whether or to what extent federal grants to the states have succeeded in creating uniform national policies comparable to those of centralized governments.

STUDY OUTLINE

I. Introduction
    A. The story of Sussette Kelo
        1. Property condemned by city officials
        2. Desire to redevelop area with pricey townhouses, malls and a large hotel
        3. Supreme Court upheld the city's decisionmaking
            a) Property can be seized for public use
            b) Property can be seized for economic development in distressed communities
    B. What could anyone do about it?

II. Why "federalism" matters

A. Reaction to the *Kelo* decision and other examples of tension and variation in policy-making

1. Grass roots lobbying campaigns
2. Thirty-four states tightened laws to make seizures more difficult
3. Half of the states have a minimum wage standard that is higher than the federal standard
4. Sometimes, but not always, the national government leads in making, administering and funding expensive public policies

B. Federalism

1. Definition: system in which the national government shares power with local governments
2. States have a specially protected existence and authority (not merely junior partners)
3. The implementation and funding of federal decisions depends upon state and local government
4. The impact of federalism is widespread (roads, crime, civil liberties, civil rights, etc.)
5. The degree and manner in which federalism has mattered has changed over time

a) Recent highly visible attempts to scale back the national government

(1) Devolution - giving more power to the states

(2) Block grants – $ to states to spend more freely under broad guidelines

b) Long-standing tension between national and state governments

(1) Slavery

(2) Regulation of business and social welfare programs

(3) States rights

(4) Mandates

III. Governmental structure and assessment

A. Structure and examples

1. Definition: political system with local governmental units, in addition to national ones, that can make final decisions
2. Examples of federal governments: Canada, India, and Germany
3. Examples of unitary governments: France, Great Britain, and Italy
4. Special protection of subnational governments in federal system is the result of

a) Constitution of country

b) Habits, preferences, and dispositions of citizens

c) Distribution of political power in society

5. National government largely does not govern individuals directly but gets states to do so in keeping with national policy

B. Good or bad?

1. Confusion about responsibility for particular functions can have dire consequences

a) Hurricanes Katrina and Rita led to fighting between federal, state and local officials

b) First-responders and disaster relief workers were nongovernmental, volunteers

c) Some government agencies made delivery of aid harder

2. Negative views: block progress and protect powerful local interests

a) Laski: states "poisonous and parasitic"

b) Riker: perpetuation of racism

3. Positive view: Elazar: strength, flexibility, and liberty
4. Federalism makes good and bad effects possible

a) Different political groups with different political purposes come to power in different places

b) *Federalist* No. 10: small political units dominated by single political faction

C. Increased political activity
1. Most obvious effect of federalism: facilitates mobilization of political activity
2. Federalism lowers the cost of political organization at the local level

IV. The Founding
A. A bold, new plan to protect personal liberty
1. Founders believed that neither national nor state government would have authority over the other because power derives from the people, who shift their support
2. New plan had no historical precedent
3. Tenth Amendment was added as an afterthought, to define the power of states

B. Elastic language in Article I: necessary and proper
1. Precise definitions of powers politically impossible because of competing interests, such as commerce
2. Hence vague language—"necessary and proper"
3. Hamilton's view: national supremacy because Constitution supreme law
4. Jefferson's view: states' rights with people ultimate sovereign

V. The debate on the meaning of federalism
A. The Supreme Court speaks
1. Hamiltonian position espoused by Marshall
2. *McCulloch* v. *Maryland* settled two questions
a) Could Congress charter a national bank? (yes, because "necessary and proper")
b) Could states tax such a bank? (no, because national powers supreme)
3. Later battles
a) Federal government cannot tax state bank
b) Nullification doctrine led to Civil War: states void federal laws they deem in conflict with Constitution

B. Dual federalism
1. Both national and state governments supreme in their own spheres
2. Hence interstate versus intrastate commerce
a) Early product-based distinction difficult
b) "Original package" also unsatisfactory

C. State sovereignty
1. Mistake today to think dual federalism is entirely dead
a) Supreme Court has limited the use of the commerce clause
b) New life has been given to the Eleventh Amendment
c) Although not all recent Supreme Court decisions support greater state sovereignty
2. Constitutional basis of state and local government
a) New debates have resurrected notion of state police powers
b) State constitutions tend to be more detailed and expansive
c) Many state constitutions open the door to direct democracy
(1) initiative - to elect
(2) referendum- to vote down laws
(3) recall - remove someone from office
d) Existence of the states guaranteed while local government exist at pleasure of states

VI. Federal–state relations
A. Grants-in-aid
1. Grants show how political realities modify legal authority
2. Began before the Constitution with "land grant colleges," various cash grants to states
3. Dramatically increased in scope in the twentieth century

4. Were attractive for various reasons
    a) Huge budget surpluses in 1880s
    b) Federal income tax was created
    c) Federal management of money and the power to print more at will
    d) "Free" money for state officials
5. Required broad congressional coalitions
    a) Example: federal funds for increased public safety post-September 11
    b) Example: Homeland Security grants and fair share formulas

B. Meeting national needs: 1960s shift in grants-in-aid
1. From what states demanded to what federal officials found important as national needs
2. Impact of the rise of "federal activism"
    a) Increase in federal grants to state and local government
    b) Shift in the purposes for such money

C. The intergovernmental lobby
1. Hundreds of state, local officials lobby in Washington
2. Federal agencies have staff members that provide information, technical assistance, and financial support to state and local organizations
3. Purpose: to get more federal money with fewer strings

D. Categorical grants versus revenue sharing
1. Categorical grants for specific purposes often require local matching funds
2. Block grants devoted to general purposes with few restrictions
3. Revenue sharing requires no matching funds and provides freedom in how to spend
    a) Distributed by statistical formula
    b) Ended in 1986
4. Neither block grants nor revenue sharing achieved the goal of giving states more freedom in spending.
    a) Neither grew as fast as the states had hoped—categorical grants, on the other hand, continued to grow
    b) The federal government increasingly attached "strings" to what was supposedly unrestricted
5. Why block grants grow more slowly?
    a) Desire for federal control and distrust of state government
    b) No single interest group has a vital stake in multipurpose block grants, revenue sharing
    c) Categorical grants are matters of life or death for various agencies

E. Rivalry among the states
1. Increased competition a result of increased dependency
2. Snowbelt (Frostbelt) versus Sunbelt states
    a) Difficulty telling *where* funds spent
    b) Difficulty connecting funds to growth rates
    c) Focus on formulas and their impact
3. Census takes on monumental importance

VII. Federal aid and federal control

A. Introduction
1. Fear of "Washington control" and jeopardy of Tenth Amendment
2. Failed attempts at reversal in trends (block grants and revenue sharing)
3. Traditional and newer forms of federal controls on state governmental actions
    a) Conditions of aid tell a state government what it must do to obtain grant money
    b) Mandates tell state governments what to do, in some instances even when they do not receive grant money

B. Mandates
  1. Most concern civil rights and environmental protection
  2. Administrative and financial problems often result
  3. Federal-state disputes, fueling the friction
    a) Some mandates are not adequately funded
    b) Explaining the variation in funding
      (1) Number is high in environmental policy, low in education policy and moderate in health policy
      (2) Lower rates of spending are associated with more mandates
      (3) Waivers more easily obtained in some policy areas than others
  4. Additional costs imposed on the states through
    a) Federal tax and regulatory schemes
    b) Federal laws exposing states to financial liability
  5. Federal courts have fueled the growth of mandates
    a) Interpretations of the Tenth Amendment have eased flow of mandates
    b) Court orders and prisons, school desegregation, busing, hiring practices, police brutality
C. Conditions of aid
  1. Received by states voluntarily, at least in theory
    a) Financial dependence blurs the theory
    b) Civil rights generally the focus of most important conditions in the 1960s, a proliferation has continued since the 1970s
      (1) Conditions range from specific to general
      (2) The states and federal government disagree about the costs and benefits of rules
  2. Different demands result in complex bargaining among government officials
    a) Bargains originally favored local officials
    b) Emergence of Washington's needs over local needs

VIII. A devolution revolution?
A. Efforts of the Reagan administration
  1. Consolidation of categorical grants into block grants
  2. Less money sent to the states, but with fewer strings
  3. States started spending more of their own money as well
B. Republican efforts in the 1990s
  1. Attempt to cut government spending, roll back federal regulations and shift important functions back to the states
  2. Reform of AFDC
  3. Devolution
    a) An old idea led from a new direction, Congress
    b) Spending was considered a form of constituency service
C. Was the era of big national government over?
  1. Annual federal spending per household up
  2. Federal revenues and debts are at an all time high
  3. Spending by state and local government spending has increased as well
  4. Large, costly federal programs remained and were not turned into block grant programs (Medicaid)
  5. There have been more, not fewer government rules and regulations
D. Impact of devolution – where it did occur
  1. Dramatic decrease in welfare rolls
  2. Second order devolution
  3. Third order devolution

E. Congressional preemption
   1. Express preemption
   2. Implied preemption

IX. Congress and federalism: nation far from wholly centralized
   A. Members of Congress still *local* representatives
   B. Members of Congress represent different constituencies from the same localities
   C. Link to local political groups eroded
   D. Differences of opinion over which level of government works best

KEY TERMS MATCH

Match the following terms and descriptions:

1. Governmental concerns considered to be primarily the responsibility of the central government
2. Governmental concerns considered to be primarily the responsibility of the state governments
3. Allows a violation of a law or a rule that would otherwise apply
4. Individual who shared Hamilton's viewpoint on federalism as a member of the United States Supreme Court
5. Supreme or ultimate political authority
6. A system in which sovereignty is wholly in the hands of the national government
7. A system in which the state governments are sovereign and the national government may do only what the states permit
8. A system in which sovereignty is shared between the national and the state governments
9. Individual who argues the main effect of federalism since the Civil War has been to perpetuate racism
10. The Founders' term for a federation
11. The clause that stipulates that powers not delegated to the United States are reserved to the states or to the people

a. AFDC
b. block grants
c. categorical grants
d. conditions of aid
e. confederation or confederal system
f. devolution
g. dual federalism
h. Daniel J. Elazar
i. federal system
j. federal republic
k. grants-in-aid
l. initiative
m. intergovernmental lobby
n. interstate commerce
o. intrastate commerce
p. land grant colleges
q. James Madison
r. John Marshall
s. *McCulloch* v. *Maryland*
t. mandates
u. Medicaid
v. national interests
w. necessary-and-proper clause
x. nullification

12. A Supreme Court decision embodying the principle of implied powers of the national government
13. The phrase used by the Supreme Court to create the category of implied powers of the national government
14. A doctrine espoused by Calhoun that states could hold certain national policies invalid within their boundaries
15. The doctrine that both state and national governments are supreme in their respective spheres
16. Federal funds provided to states and localities
17. Individual who argues federalism has contributed to political flexibility and individual liberty
18. State educational institutions built with the benefit of federally donated lands
19. A federal grant for a specific purpose, often with accompanying conditions and/or requiring a local match
20. A federal grant that could be used for a variety of purposes, usually with few accompanying restrictions
21. Business that is conducted entirely within one state
22. Federal rules that states must follow, whether they receive federal grants or not
23. Federal rules that states must follow if they choose to receive the federal grants with which the rules are associated
24. An interest group made up of mayors, governors, and other state and local officials who depend on federal funds

y. police powers

z. recall

aa. referendum

bb. revenue sharing

cc. William H. Riker

dd. second-order devolution

ee. sovereignty

ff. states' rights

gg. Tenth Amendment

hh. third-order devolution

ii. unitary system

jj. waiver

25. The Federalist author who said that both state and federal governments "are in fact but different agents and trustees of the people constituted with different powers"

26. Business that is conducted in more than one state

27. Program to distribute welfare benefits that was formerly federally funded then devolved to the states in 1996

28. Federally funded medical care for the poor

29. An effort to shift responsibility for a wide range of domestic programs from Washington to the states

30. Those state laws and regulations not otherwise unconstitutional, that promote health, safety, and morals

31. A procedure whereby voters can remove an elected official from office

32. A procedure that enables voters to reject a measure adopted by the legislature

33. A procedure that allows voters to place legislative measures (and sometimes constitutional amendments) directly on the ballot by getting a specified proportion of voter signatures on a petition

34. Refers to a flow of power and responsibility from the states to local governments

35. A federal grant that requires no matching funds and provides freedom in how to spend it

36. Refers to the increased role of nonprofit organizations and private groups in policy implementation

DATA CHECK

Table 3.1 (Page 63): Federal Grants to State and Local Government (Federal Fiscal Year 2006)

1. What was the total amount of dollars given to state and local government by the federal government in fiscal year 2006?

____

2. What was the total percentage of federal dollars used for education, training, employment and social services?

____

3. What was the total percentage of federal dollars used for transportation?

____

4. What specific government program accounted for the largest percentage of federal dollars?

____

Figure 3.2 (Page 64): The Changing Purposes of Federal Grants to State and Local Governments

5. Where was the highest percentage of grant money spent in 1960 and 2006?

____

6. How did education spending change from 1960 to 2006?

____

7. How did spending on transportation and highways change from 1960 to 2006?

____

PRACTICING FOR EXAMS

TRUE/FALSE QUESTIONS

Read each statement carefully. Mark true statements *T*. If any part of the statement is false, mark it *F*, and write in the space provided a concise explanation of why the statement is false.

1. T F The Supreme Court has allowed a local government to seize private property in order to "promote economic development."

____

2. T F The minimum wage in most states is higher than the federal standard.

____

3. T F Today, an effort is being made to scale back the size and activity of the national government.

____

4. T F Almost every nation in the world has local units of government of some kind.

5. T F The United States, Canada, and France are examples of federal governments.

6. T F The constitution of the former Soviet Union created a federal system in theory.

7. T F In France, education, the police and the use of land are all matters that are directed nationally.

8. T F William Riker and Daniel J. Elazar have remarkably divergent viewpoints on the value of American federalism.

9. T F Federalism was intended by the Founders to operate as a protection for personal liberty.

10. T F If the *Federalist* papers are a guide, the Founders envisioned a system where neither the national nor state government would have supreme authority over the other.

11. T F Federalism was an entirely new plan, for which no historical precedent existed.

12. T F The Constitution makes clear distinctions between inter- and intrastate commerce.

13. T F The Tenth Amendment has rarely had much practical significance.

14. T F Alexander Hamilton thought the national government was the superior and leading force in political affairs.

15. T F James Madison argued for state supremacy at the Constitutional Convention.

16. T F *McCulloch* v. *Maryland* grew out of the refusal of a federal official to deliver a warrant to a duly appointed justice of the peace.

17. T F The word "bank" does not appear in the Constitution.

18. T F States cannot make treaties with foreign nations.

19. T F In *McCulloch*, Chief Justice Marshall concluded that a state could not tax an entity of the federal government.

______

20. T F Nullification first became an issue during the Civil War.

______

21. T F The doctrine of nullification held that a state could refuse to enforce within its boundaries a federal law that exceeded the national government's authority.

______

22. T F Dual federalism implied Congress had the power to regulate interstate commerce.

______

23. T F Professional baseball is not considered to be interstate commerce.

______

24. T F It would be a mistake to think the doctrine of dual federalism is entirely dead.

______

25. T F In 1997, the Supreme Court upheld a law which required local police to conduct background checks on all gun purchasers.

______

26. T F The Eleventh Amendment protects states from lawsuits by citizens of other states and foreign nations.

______

27. T F A referendum allows voters to place legislative measures (and sometimes constitutional amendments) directly on the ballot by getting enough signatures on a petition.

______

28. T F The existence of states is guaranteed by the federal Constitution.

______

29. T F The federal government sometimes finds that the political limitations on its exercise of power over the states are greater than the constitutional limitations.

______

30. T F Federal grants-in-aid began even before the Constitution was adopted.

______

31. T F Cash grants-in-aid began in the late 1950s.

______

32. T F The text suggests that, initially, the most attractive feature of federal grants-in-aid was the fact that there were surpluses in the federal budget.

______

33. T F Most of the federal grant money to state and local governments is used for transportation and highways.

____

34. T F Governors and mayors complained about categorical grants.

____

35. T F Block grants are sometimes called "special revenue sharing."

____

36. T F Distribution of money related to revenue sharing was based on a formula which took into account population.

____

37. T F Members of Congress speak about "local needs" with a single voice in Washington as a result of party strength.

____

MULTIPLE CHOICE QUESTIONS

Circle the letter of the response that best answers the question or completes the statement.

1. The Supreme Court's controversial 2005 decision *Kelo* v. *City of New London* involved
   a. government seizure of private property.
   b. taxation without representation.
   c. judicial oversight of private daycare facilities.
   d. protests outside of abortion clinics and adult bookstores.
   e. private use of drugs for medicinal purposes.
2. The response of many state legislatures to the Court's decision in the *Kelo* case was to
   a. legalize some drugs for medicinal purposes.
   b. remove judges who had violated state codes of ethics.
   c. expand its scope by amendments to state constitutions.
   d. restrict its scope by passage of new laws.
   e. restrict freedom of speech near certain public buildings and private businesses.
3. Today's effort to scale back the size and activities of the national government and shift responsibilities back to the states has become known as
   a. devolution.
   b. anti-federalism.
   c. reverse-federalism.
   d. statism.
   e. repatriation.
4. A system is not federal unless local units of government
   a. are the official distributors of the national government's resources.
   b. exist independently and can make decisions independent of the national government.
   c. answer solely to the national government.
   d. make decisions in conjunction with national goals and needs.
   e. are mere administrative subunits of the national government.

5. The text identifies all of the following has having federal systems *except*
   a. Canada.
   b. Australia.
   c. India.
   d. Germany.
   e. Great Britain.
6. William H. Riker, an American political scientist argued that the "main effect" of federalism since the Civil War has been to
   a. increase ideological conflicts.
   b. increase the tax burden.
   c. fuel economic recessions.
   d. frustrate the efforts of law enforcement.
   e. perpetuate racism.
7. According to the text, the most "obvious" effect of federalism has been to
   a. modify ideological conflicts.
   b. protect the interests of the upper classes.
   c. facilitate the mobilization of political activity.
   d. reverse the democratic tendency in the states.
   e. increase the scope of the president's power.
8. All of the following statements are correct *except*
   a. the Constitution does not spell out the powers that the states are to have.
   b. the delegates at Philadelphia used "federalism" as a synonym for "unitary."
   c. the Tenth Amendment was added at the insistence of the states.
   d. the Founders assumed the federal government would have only those powers given to it by the Constitution.
   e. the Tenth Amendment has rarely had much practical significance.
9. Alexander Hamilton's view of federalism held that
   a. the federal government and the state governments are equals.
   b. state governments were superior to the federal government.
   c. the federal government was superior to the state governments.
   d. the principle threat to the rights of the people would be the federal government.
   e. the government was the product of an agreement among the states.
10. The national supremacy view of the newly formed federal government was powerfully defended by Chief Justice
    a. John Marshall.
    b. James McCulloch.
    c. Roger Taney.
    d. John C. Calhoun.
    e. James Madison.
11. The landmark case *McCulloch* v. *Maryland* determined that
    a. a state had the power to tax the federal government.
    b. the federal government had the power to tax a state.
    c. Congress did not have the power to set up a national bank.
    d. the "necessary and proper clause" allowed for the creation of a bank.
    e. the Constitution was established by the states.

12. Although the doctrine of nullification is commonly associated with John C. Calhoun, the notion is plainly evident in
    a. the Declaration of Independence.
    b. the Articles of Confederation.
    c. Madison's notes at the Constitutional Convention.
    d. the Bill of Rights.
    e. the Virginia and Kentucky Resolutions.
13. After the Civil War the debate about the meaning of federalism focused on the _________ clause of the Constitution.
    a. defense
    b. tax
    c. currency
    d. full faith and credit
    e. commerce
14. The text suggests that, by the 1940s, Supreme Court rulings concerning the commerce clause
    a. centered on a rigorous definition of interstate commerce.
    b. centered on a rigorous definition of intrastate commerce.
    c. almost always distinguished between interstate and intrastate commerce.
    d. abandoned hard distinctions between interstate and intrastate commerce.
    e. consistently struck down federal attempts to regulate commerce.
15. According to the text, federal anti-trust laws do not affect
    a. artists.
    b. morticians.
    c. professional baseball players.
    d. lawyers.
    e. window washers.
16. In the 2000 case *United States* v. *Morrison*, the Supreme Court refused to connect or extend the scope of the commerce clause to
    a. school restrictions on guns.
    b. background checks for gun owners.
    c. copyright law suits.
    d. abortion laws.
    e. violence against women.
17. Which of the following statements regarding state constitutions is *incorrect*?
    a. They tend to be far more detailed than the federal Constitution.
    b. They tend to embody a more expansive view of government responsibilities.
    c. They tend to embody a more expansive view of individual rights.
    d. None of the above.
    e. All of the above.
18. Which procedure allows voters to reject a measure adopted by the legislature?
    a. Referendum
    b. Initiative
    c. Recall
    d. Roll back
    e. Addendum

19. Which procedure allows voters to remove an elected official from office?
    a. Referendum
    b. Initiative
    c. Recall
    d. Roll back
    e. Addendum
20. The Constitution guarantees the existence of
    a. cities.
    b. counties.
    c. municipal governments.
    d. townships.
    e. the states.
21. At first, federal money seemed attractive to state officials because
    a. there were budget surpluses.
    b. the federal income tax was a flexible tool of public finance.
    c. the production and distribution of currency was managed by the federal government.
    d. it seemed to be "free."
    e. All of the above.
22. One odd effect of the fair-share formulas used to determine grants for Homeland Security is
    a. lack of support for major metropolitan areas.
    b. lack of support for activities and materials related to public safety.
    c. a skew in funding toward states and cities with low populations.
    d. confusion of material for personal and public safety.
    e. a reduction in the number of public safety workers.
23. During the 1960s, federal grant programs were increasingly devised on the basis of ________ needs.
    a. local
    b. state
    c. national
    d. regional
    e. A and B
24. In 1960, over 40 percent of all federal grants to state and local government went to
    a. Education.
    b. Medicaid.
    c. Income Security.
    d. transportation and highways.
    e. community and regional development.
25. As of 2006, the largest percentage of federal grant money goes toward
    a. Education.
    b. Medicaid.
    c. Income Security.
    d. transportation and highways.
    e. community and regional development.

26. The requirement that a state or locality match federal money is most common with
    a. categorical grants.
    b. land grants.
    c. share-pay loans.
    d. block grants.
    e. revenue sharing.
27. The Law Enforcement Assistance Act is an example of a
    a. categorical grant.
    b. share-pay loan.
    c. land grant.
    d. nullification.
    e. block grant.
28. Block grants and revenue sharing were efforts to
    a. ensure that state spending was sensitive to federal policies and goals.
    b. reverse trends by allowing states and localities freedom to spend money as they wished.
    c. increase the dependency of state governments on federal money.
    d. accelerate states spending in areas long ignored by Congress.
    e. increase "strings" on money given to state and local officials.
29. Which of the following has (have) grown fastest in recent years?
    a. Categorical grants
    b. Block grants
    c. Revenue sharing
    d. All have grown at about the same rates
    e. None have actually grown
30. Which of the following is (are) not among the coalition that prefers categorical grants to block grants and revenue sharing?
    a. Congress
    b. The federal bureaucracy
    c. Organized labor
    d. Liberal interest groups
    e. State and local officials
31. The intense debate over the manner in which the federal government distributes funds and awards contracts has been precipitated by
    a. the reemergence of the Tenth Amendment in Supreme Court jurisprudence.
    b. the lack of two party competition in a handful of states.
    c. reductions in discretionary spending.
    d. a shift in population to the South, Southwest and Far West.
    e. popular demand for a balanced federal budget.
32. With the advent of grants based on distributional formulas, the ________ has taken on monumental importance.
    a. balance of trade
    b. electoral college
    c. gross national product
    d. crime rate
    e. census

33. Most federal mandates concern
    a. sexual harassment.
    b. civil liberties and civil rights.
    c. civil rights and environmental protection.
    d. waste management.
    e. law enforcement.
34. A 2006 study found that the *highest* number of unfunded mandates could be found in the area of ________ policy.
    a. environmental
    b. education
    c. health
    d. transportation
    e. law enforcement
35. Which of the following statements is correct?
    a. It is difficult to obtain a waiver from an administrative agency with regard to education.
    b. There are a high number of unfunded mandates in education policy.
    c. The government tends to use more mandates in areas where it spends a great deal of money.
    d. The government tends to use more mandates in areas where it spends less money.
    e. Environmental protection waivers are fairly easy to obtain.
36. The text suggests the growth of mandates has been fueled by the fact that
    a. local citizens can use a federal court to change local practices.
    b. Congress has taken a greater interest in busing, state prisons, and police brutality.
    c. few courts have an interest in hearing cases related to mandates.
    d. the Reagan and Bush administrations supported them so enthusiastically.
    e. none of the above.
37. The conditions attached to grants are by far the most important federal restriction on state action because
    a. the Tenth Amendment amplifies their effect.
    b. they can change, depending upon the size of the state.
    c. they are not subject to review in the courts.
    d. state officials play a major role in their interpretation.
    e. the typical state depends for a quarter or more of its budget on federal grants.
38. When the election of 1994 brought Republican majorities in the House and the Senate, the first key issue in the drive to shift important functions back to the states was
    a. the war on drugs.
    b. welfare.
    c. Social Security.
    d. law enforcement.
    e. gender discrimination.
39. The text suggests devolution was actually an "old idea" that acquired "new vitality" because
    a. courts no longer stood in the way of state policies.
    b. state constitutions were modified in accordance with federal policies.
    c. governors and mayors supported the effort.
    d. Congress, rather than the president, was leading the effort.
    e. Democratic leaders spearheaded the effort.

ESSAY QUESTIONS

Practice writing extended answers to the following questions. These test your ability to integrate and express the ideas that you have been studying in this chapter.

1. Explain the differences between political systems which are unitary, confederal or federal.
2. Summarize the views of federalism held by Hamilton and Jefferson. Which view appears to have won out?
3. Summarize the facts of the case which led up to *McCulloch* v. *Maryland* and the Supreme Court's subsequent decision.
4. Explain what "nullification" refers to and note two prominent examples of "nullification" politics in American history.
5. Discuss some recent decisions of the Supreme Court which suggest the doctrine of dual federalism is not completely dead.
6. Identify and explain three ways that states open the door to "direct democracy."
7. What are three reasons federal grants were initially quite attractive to state officials?
8. What are four reasons why block grants and revenue sharing did not attain the goals of "no strings" or fiscal relief?
9. Explain what the terms "second-order" and "third-order" devolution refer to.

ANSWERS TO KEY TERMS MATCH QUESTIONS

1. v
2. ff
3. jj
4. r
5. ee
6. ii
7. e
8. i
9. cc
10. j
11. gg
12. s
13. w
14. x
15. g
16. k
17. h
18. p
19. c
20. b
21. o
22. t
23. d
24. m
25. q
26. n
27. a
28. u
29. f
30. y
31. z
32. aa
33. l

34. dd
35. bb
36. hh

ANSWERS TO DATA CHECK QUESTIONS

1. $449 billion
2. 13.4 percent
3. 10.4 percent
4. Medicaid, 42.8 percent
5. Transportation and highways in 1960, Medicaid in 2006
6. It increased as a percentage, from 8 to 13 percent
7. It decreased as a percentage, from 43 to a mere 10 percent

ANSWERS TO TRUE/FALSE QUESTIONS

1. T
2. F It is higher in over a half a dozen states.
3. T
4. T
5. F France has a unitary system.
6. T
7. T
8. T
9. T
10. T
11. T
12. F The Constitution merely mentions commerce "among the several states" without any clear additional elaboration.
13. T
14. T
15. T
16. F *McCulloch* developed when a state attempted to tax a federal bank.
17. T
18. T
19. T
20. F Nullification was suggested, at least in theory, in the *Federalist* papers and was a prominent feature of the Virginia and Kentucky Resolutons.
21. T

22. T
23. T
24. T
25. F The Court struck down the law, declaring that Congress had overstepped its bounds with respect to the regulation of commerce.
26. T
27. F This is the description of an initiative, not a referendum.
28. T
29. T
30. T
31. F They actually began even before the Constitution was adopted.
32. T
33. F This may have been true in the 1960s. Today, most goes to Medicaid and Income Security.
34. T
35. T
36. T
37. F Parties are weakening and, increasingly, the emphasis is on "national" needs, not local needs.

ANSWERS TO MULTIPLE CHOICE QUESTIONS

1. a
2. d
3. a
4. b
5. e
6. e
7. c
8. b
9. c
10. a
11. d
12. e
13. e
14. d
15. c
16. e

17. d
18. a
19. c
20. e
21. e
22. c
23. c
24. d
25. b
26. a
27. a
28. b
29. a
30. e
31. d
32. e
33. c
34. a
35. d
36. a
37. e
38. b
39. d

CHAPTER 4

American Political Culture

REVIEWING THE CHAPTER

CHAPTER FOCUS

This chapter departs rather sharply from the previous ones, which focused on the legal and historical aspects of American government, and concentrates instead on the somewhat less concrete notion of *political culture,* or the inherited set of beliefs, attitudes, and opinions people (in this case, Americans) have about how their government ought to operate. After reading and reviewing the material in this chapter, you should be able to do each of the following:

1. Define what scholars mean by *political culture,* and list some of the dominant aspects of political culture in the United States.
2. Discuss how U.S. citizens compare with those of other countries in their political attitudes.
3. List the contributions to U.S. political culture made by the Revolution, by the nation's religious heritages, and by the family. Explain the apparent absence of class consciousness in this country.
4. Explain why some observers are quite concerned about the growth of mistrust in government and why others regard this mistrust as normal and healthy.
5. Define internal and external feelings of *political efficacy,* and explain how the level of each of these has varied over the past generation.
6. Explain why a certain level of political tolerance is necessary in the conduct of democratic politics, and review the evidence that indicates just how much political tolerance exists in this country. Agree or disagree with the text's conclusion that no group is truly free of political intolerance.

STUDY OUTLINE

I. Introduction
  - A. Generalizations about countries can vary, even when they are all representative democracies
  - B. Culture counts when it comes to politics and government

II. Political culture
  - A. Constitutional differences
    1. Can be fairly obvious and easy to summarize
    2. Institutions, features of government and power relationships vary
  - B. Demographic differences
    1. Also pretty straightforward
    2. Language, race, ethnicity, religion, etc.
  - C. Cultural differences
    1. Distinctive patterned ways of thinking about how political and economic life ought to be carried out
    2. Notions of political and economic equality vary from one nation to the next

3. Sometimes the differences are quite sharp despite constitutional similarities
4. Explanations?
   a) Abundant and fertile soil for democracy to grow
   b) No feudal aristocracy; minimal taxes; few legal restraints
   c) Westward movement; vast territory provided opportunities
   d) Nation of small, independent farmers
   e) Tocqueville: "moral and intellectual characteristics" today called political culture

III. American political culture
- A. Five important elements in the American view of the political system
  1. Liberty
  2. Democracy
  3. Equality
  4. Civic duty
  5. Individual responsibility
- B. Some questions about the U.S. political culture
  1. How do we know people share these beliefs?
     Before polls, beliefs inferred from books, speeches, and so on
  2. How do we explain behavior inconsistent with beliefs?
     Beliefs still important, source of change
  3. Why so much political conflict in U.S. history?
     Conflict occurs even with beliefs in common
  4. Most consistent evidence of political culture
     Use of terms Americanism, un-American
- C. The economic system
  1. Americans support free enterprise but see limits on marketplace freedom
  2. Americans prefer equality of opportunity to equality of result; individualist view
  3. Americans have a shared commitment to economic individualism/self-reliance (see 1924 and 1977 polls)

IV. Comparing citizens of the United States with those of other nations
- A. Political system
  1. Swedes: more deferential than participatory
     a) Defer to government experts and specialists
     b) Rarely challenge governmental decisions
     c) Believe in what is best more than what people want
     d) Value equality over liberty
     e) Value harmony and observe obligations
  2. Japanese
     a) Value good relations with colleagues
     b) Emphasize group decisions and social harmony
     c) Respect authority
  3. Americans
     a) Tend to assert rights
     b) Emphasize individualism, competition, equality, following rules, treating others fairly (compare with the Japanese)
  4. Cultural differences affect political and economic systems
  5. Danger of over generalizing: many diverse groups within a culture
  6. Classic study: U.S. and British citizens in cross-national study
     a) Stronger sense of civic duty, civic competence
     b) Institutional confidence

c) Sense of patriotism

B. Economic system
1. Swedes (contrasted with Americans): Verba and Orren
a) Equal pay and top limit on incomes
b) Less income inequality
2. Cultural differences make a difference in politics: private ownership in United States versus public ownership in European countries

C. The civic role of religion
1. Americans are highly religious compared with Europeans
2. Impact on individual behavior
a) Donation of money to charity
b) Volunteer work
3. Impact on political system and processes
a) Religious movements transformed American politics and fueled the break with England
b) Both liberals and conservatives use the pulpit to promote political change
c) Candidate support for faith based approaches to social ills
d) The Pledge of Allegiance and American political culture

V. The sources of political culture

A. Historical roots
1. Revolution essentially over liberty; preoccupied with asserting rights
2. Adversarial culture the result of distrust of authority and a belief that human nature is depraved
3. Federalist-Jeffersonian transition in 1800 legitimated the role of the opposition party; liberty and political change can coexist

B. Legal-sociological factors
1. Widespread participation permitted by the Constitution
2. Absence of an established national religion
a) Religious diversity a source of cleavage
b) Absence of established religion has facilitated the absence of political orthodoxy
c) Puritan heritage (dominant one) stress on personal achievement
(1) Hard work
(2) Save money
(3) Obey secular law
(4) Do good
(5) Embrace "Protestant ethic"
d) Miniature political systems produced by churches' congregational organization
3. Family instills the ways we think about world and politics
a) Great freedom of children
b) Equality among family members
c) Rights accorded each person
d) Varied interests considered
4. Class consciousness absent
a) Most people consider themselves middle class
b) Message of Horatio Alger stories is still popular

C. The culture war
1. Two cultural classes in America battle over values
a) Orthodox: morality, with rules from God, more important than self-expression
b) Progressive: personal freedom, with rules based on circumstances, more important than tradition

2. Culture war differs from political disputes in three ways
    a) Money is not at stake
    b) Compromises are almost impossible
    c) Conflict is more profound – animated by deep differences in people's beliefs about private and public morality
3. Two views of the culture war
    a) Fiorina – war is myth, political leaders are polarize, but not the public
    b) Abramowitz – war is real, issues matter more and more, political engagement more common

VI. Mistrust of government
- A. What the polls say
    1. Since the 1950s, a steady decline in percentage who say they trust the government in Washington
    2. Important qualifications and considerations
        a) Levels of trust rose briefly during the Reagan administration
        b) Distrust of officials is not the same as distrust for our system of government
        c) Americans remain more supportive of the country and its institutions than most Europeans
- B. Possible causes of apparent decline in confidence
    1. Vietnam
    2. Watergate and Nixon's resignation
    3. Clinton's sex scandals and impeachment
    4. War in Iraq
    5. Levels of support may have been abnormally high in the 1950s
        a) Aftermath of victory in World War II and possession of Atomic bomb
        b) From Depression to currency that dominated international trade
        c) Low expectations of Washington and little reason to be upset/disappointed
    6. 1960s and 1970s may have dramatically increased expectations of government
    7. Decline in patriotism (temporarily affected by the attacks of 9/11)
- C. Other factors that might generally affect trust in the government
    1. Political efficacy
        a) Internal – has not changed much since the 1950s and 1960s
        b) External – fairly steep, steady decline since the 1960s
        c) Still, our sense of efficacy remains higher than it is among Europeans
    2. Social and civic engagement
        a) Putnam: the nation of "joiners" is increasingly "bowling alone"
        b) Less socializing, involvement, volunteering, etc.
        c) Evidence appears mixed

VII. Political tolerance
- A. Crucial to democratic politics
    1. Citizens must be reasonably tolerant
    2. But not necessarily perfectly tolerant
- B. Levels of American political tolerance
    1. Most Americans assent in abstract, but would deny rights in concrete cases
    2. General levels of tolerance appear to be increasing
    3. Some considerations
        a) There may be a thin line between intolerance and civic concern
        b) For most people, there is some group or cause worthy of restriction
    4. Groups less tolerated survive because
        a) Few are willing to act on their beliefs—to restrict the liberties of others

b) No widespread agreement as to which groups should be restricted
c) Courts are sufficiently insulated from public opinion to enforce protections

C. Conclusions
1. Political liberty cannot be taken for granted
2. No group should pretend it is always tolerant
a) Conservatives once targeted professors
b) Later, professors targeted conservatives

KEY TERMS MATCH

Match the following terms and descriptions:

1. A distinctive and patterned way of thinking about how political life ought to be carried out
2. The condition of being relatively free of governmental restraints
3. A belief that one can affect government policies
4. The inclination to believe that one's efforts and rewards in life are to be conducted and enjoyed by oneself, apart from larger social groupings
5. Individual who explained the rise of capitalism in part by what he called the Protestant ethic
6. The condition in which people, although not guaranteed equal rewards, expect to have comparable chances to compete for those rewards
7. Refers to states that vote Democrat
8. Conducted a famous cross-national study of political participation
9. The feeling that one ought to do one's share in community affairs, irrespective of concrete rewards
10. A word used in naming a congressional committee to merge the concepts of acceptance of national values and goodness itself
11. A political party that opposes the majority party but within the context of the legal rules of the game

a. Almond and Verba
b. Americanism
c. blue states
d. civic competence
e. civic duty
f. class consciousness
g. Congregational
h. Erik Erikson
i. equal opportunity
j. Individualism
k. liberty
l. Gunnar Myrdal
m. opposition party
n. orthodox (social)
o. political culture
p. political ideology
q. political tolerance
r. progressive (social)
s. red states
t. un-American
u. Max Weber
v. work ethic

12. Individual who described race relations as "an American dilemma" resulting from a conflict between the "American creed" and "American behavior"
13. A set of values that includes working hard, saving one's money, and obeying the law
14. A persistent word in our vocabulary that indicates Americans are bound by common values and hopes
15. A kind of church in which members control activities, whether erecting a building, hiring a preacher, or managing its finances
16. Refers to those states that vote Republican
17. The willingness to allow people with whom one disagrees to have the full protection of the laws when they express their opinions
18. The awareness of belonging to a particular socioeconomic group whose interests are different from those of others
19. People who believe that moral rules are derived from God, are unchanging, and are more important than individual choice
20. Psychologist who noted distinct traits of American and European families
21. A relatively consistent set of views of the policies government ought to pursue
22. People who believe that moral rules are derived in part from an individual's beliefs and the circumstances of modern life

DATA CHECK

Figure 4.1 (Page 88): External Political Efficacy Index, 1952-2004

1. What year featured the highest external political efficacy score?

2. What year features the lowest external political efficacy score?

3. Which years feature scores below 50?

Figure 4.2 (Page 88): Trust in the Federal Government, 1958-2004

4. In what year did the highest percentage of respondents say they had confidence in the government in Washington "most of the time?

5. Describe the typical percentage of respondents who claim they have confidence in the government in Washington "just about always."

6. Describe the typical percentage of respondents who claim they have confidence in the government in Washington "none of the time."

Figure 4.3 (Page 89): The American Civic Health Index, 1975-2002

7. America's civic health appears to have been most healthy in what year?

8. America's civic health appears to be least healthy in what year?

9. How would you describe America's civic health over the last ten years based on these measures?

PRACTICING FOR EXAMS

TRUE/FALSE QUESTIONS

Read each statement carefully. Mark true statements *T*. If any part of the statement is false, mark it *F*, and write in the space provided a concise explanation of why the statement is false.

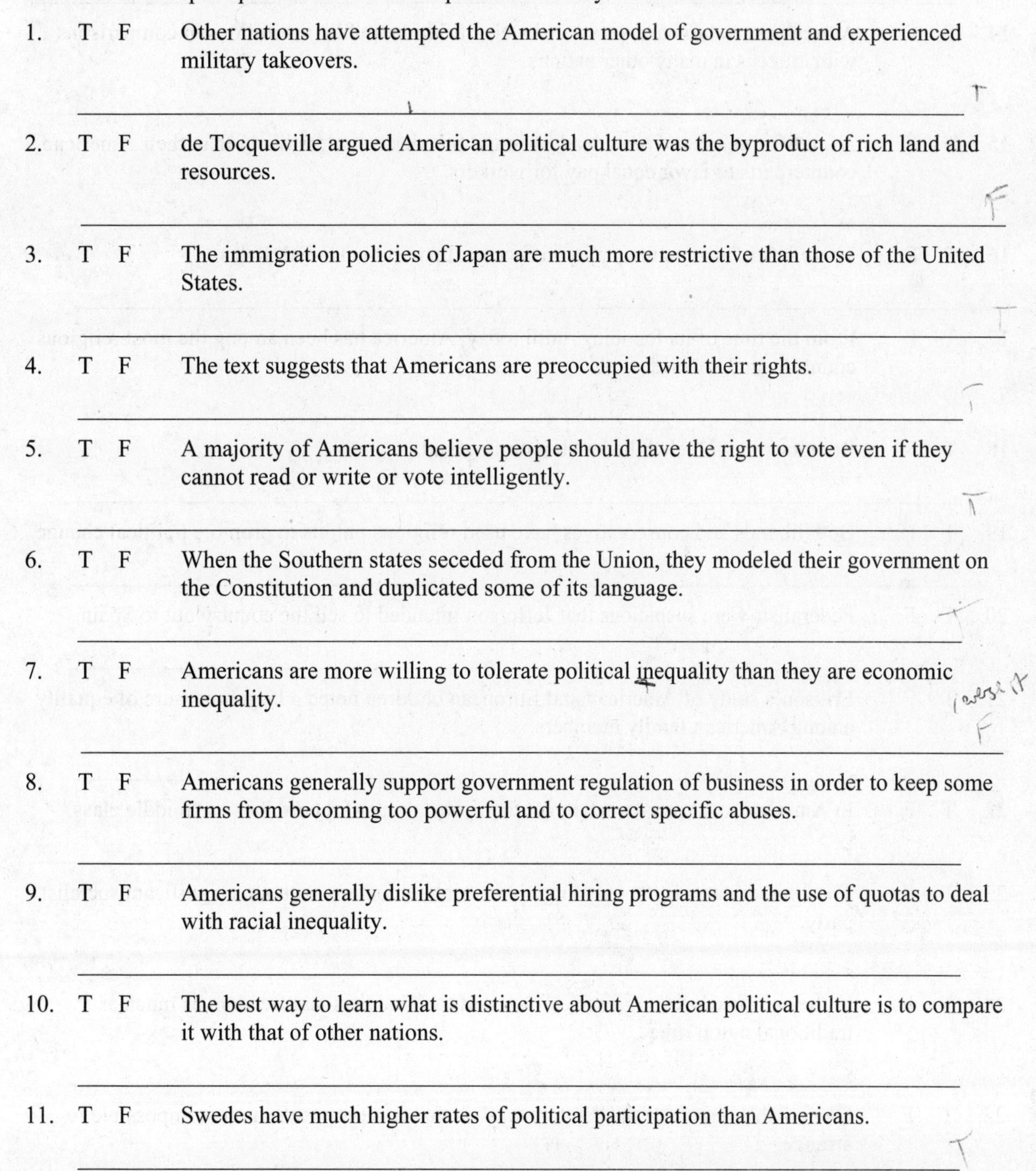

1. T F Other nations have attempted the American model of government and experienced military takeovers.

   ____

2. T F de Tocqueville argued American political culture was the byproduct of rich land and resources.

   ____

3. T F The immigration policies of Japan are much more restrictive than those of the United States.

   ____

4. T F The text suggests that Americans are preoccupied with their rights.

   ____

5. T F A majority of Americans believe people should have the right to vote even if they cannot read or write or vote intelligently.

   ____

6. T F When the Southern states seceded from the Union, they modeled their government on the Constitution and duplicated some of its language.

   ____

7. T F Americans are more willing to tolerate political inequality than they are economic inequality.

   ____

8. T F Americans generally support government regulation of business in order to keep some firms from becoming too powerful and to correct specific abuses.

   ____

9. T F Americans generally dislike preferential hiring programs and the use of quotas to deal with racial inequality.

   ____

10. T F The best way to learn what is distinctive about American political culture is to compare it with that of other nations.

    ____

11. T F Swedes have much higher rates of political participation than Americans.

    ____

12. T F Americans are more interested in reaching decisions through the application of rules than are the Japanese.

____

13. T F Americans tend to have a higher sense of civic confidence than citizens in many other nations.

____

14. T F Americans tend to have very low levels of faith in public institutions in comparisons with citizens in many other nations.

____

15. T F A study of union and party leaders found Swedes were less likely than their American counterparts to favor equal pay for workers.

____

16. T F There is less income inequality in Sweden than in the United States.

____

17. T F From the time of its founding, until today, America has been among the most religious countries in the world.

____

18. T F Religious ideas fueled the break with England.

____

19. T F Both liberals and conservatives have used religious pulpits to promote political change.

____

20. T F Federalists were suspicious that Jefferson intended to sell the country out to Spain.

____

21. T F Erikson's study of American and European children noted a larger measure of equality among American family members.

____

22. T F In America, most people, whatever their jobs, think of themselves as "middle class."

____

23. T F The United States is the only large industrial democracy without a significant socialist party.

____

24. T F In the culture war, "progressives" are said to value personal freedom as much as traditional moral rules.

____

25. T F One notable feature of the "culture war" is that compromise is almost impossible to arrange.

____

26. T F The steady decline in the proportion of Americans who say they trust the government in Washington to do the right thing began in the 1970s.

______

27. T F Levels of public trust in the government in Washington increased briefly during the Reagan administration.

T

______

28. T F Americans are much more supportive of this country and its institutions than Europeans are of theirs.

______

29. T F In immediate aftermath of the attacks of 9/11, Americans' trust in the government further eroded.

______

30. T F Most Americans believe the government is run by "a few big interests."

______

31. T F Since the 1960s, there has been a fairly sharp drop in internal political efficacy in the United States.

______

32. T F The text suggests that, in concrete cases, a good many Americans are not very tolerant of groups they dislike.

______

33. T F The text suggests that most Americans are ready to deny some groups its rights, but simply cannot agree on which group it should be.

______

MULTIPLE CHOICE QUESTIONS

Circle the letter of the response that best answers the question or completes the statement.

1. Compared with people in other democracies, Americans are particularly preoccupied with
   a. elections.
   b. the assertion of rights.
   c. social harmony.
   d. institutions.
   e. equality.
2. Which of the following is *not* among the important elements in the American view of the political system?
   a. Civic duty.
   b. Individualism.
   c. Equality of opportunity.
   d. Democracy.
   e. Equality of condition.

3. Scholars infer the existence of political culture by observing
   a. the kinds of books Americans read.
   b. the political choices Americans make.
   c. the slogans Americans respond to.
   d. the speeches Americans hear.
   e. all of the above.
4. The Civil War provides an illustration of
   a. political behavior inconsistent with personal values.
   b. a radical rejection by the Confederacy of the constitutional order.
   c. how governments cannot last long without internal conflict.
   d. the conflict between existing constitutional values and institutional values.
   e. the persistence of shared beliefs about how a democratic regime ought to be organized.
5. One important piece of evidence that Americans have believed themselves bound by common values and common hopes has been
   a. that free elections could indeed be conducted.
   b. their hostile attitudes toward free speech.
   c. their use of the word *Americanism.*
   d. the importance of the frontier in American history.
   e. their tendency toward idealism.
6. Scholars such as Kinder and Sears worry that the widely shared commitment to economic individualism and personal responsibility might be a kind of camouflage for
   a. symbolic racism.
   b. class centered biases.
   c. anti-Americanism.
   d. ethnic socialization.
   e. partisan groupthink.
7. When a 1924 study in Muncie, Indiana, was repeated in 1977, it found that 1977 respondents
   a. judged those who failed more harshly.
   b. were more sympathetic with failure.
   c. had about the same attitudes as 1924 respondents.
   d. were more critical of those who had great wealth.
   e. were much more desirous of material success.
8. Which of the following statements regarding Swedish political culture is *incorrect*?
   a. It is more deferential than participatory.
   b. Voter turnout is low.
   c. Swedes rarely challenge governmental decisions in court.
   d. Swedes value harmony.
   e. Swedes value equality as much as (or more than) liberty.
9. Compared with Americans, the Japanese are more likely to
   a. emphasize the virtues of individualism and competition in social relations.
   b. reach decisions through discussion rather than the application of rules.
   c. emphasize the virtue of treating others fairly but impersonally, with due regard for their rights.
   d. see conflict as a means of getting to know and understand the psyche of other people.
   e. rely on individual decision-making rather than decisions made by groups.

10. A classic study of political culture in five nations concluded Americans
    a. were generally much like the citizens in four other nations.
    b. exhibited little that could be described as "culture."
    c. had a stronger sense of civic duty than citizens in other nations.
    d. had a stronger sense of civic competence than citizens in other nations.
    e. had a stronger sense of civic duty and civic competence than citizens in other nations.
11. A classic study of political culture in five nations found some degree of similarity between citizens of the United States and citizens of
    a. Germany.
    b. Great Britain.
    c. Italy.
    d. Mexico.
    e. Sweden.
12. Polls suggest Americans have less trust in government than they once did, but it is important to keep in mind that
    a. trust tends to increase when the economy is struggling.
    b. we actually have very little data on the topic.
    c. polls can rarely accurately measure such attitudes and opinions.
    d. levels of trust were never very high to begin with.
    e. confidence in political institutions remains higher than in most places abroad.
13. A 1985 study by Sidney Verba and Gary Orren compared the views of trade union and political party leaders in the United States and
    a. Germany.
    b. Great Britain.
    c. Italy.
    d. Mexico.
    e. Sweden.
14. Which statement is *incorrect*?
    a. In the 1830s, de Tocqueville was amazed at how religious Americans were.
    b. The average American is more likely to believe in God than the average European.
    c. Religious revival movements of the 1700s transformed political life in the colonies.
    d. Today, America is less religious than most European countries.
    e. Candidates for national office in most contemporary democracies rarely mention religion.
15. Research has found that religious persons are
    a. more likely to donate money to charity.
    b. more likely to volunteer time.
    c. more likely to donate their time to nonreligious organizations.
    d. more likely to give money to nonreligious organizations.
    e. all of the above.
16. The unusual degree of concern about religion in the United States was apparent in 2002 when a federal appeals court issued a controversial ruling regarding
    a. the Pledge of Allegiance.
    b. the Salvation Army.
    c. religious paraphernalia in public schools.
    d. Christmas cards.
    e. prayer in legislative chambers.

17. The American preoccupation with assertion and maintenance of rights has imbued the daily conduct of U.S. politics with
    a. irregular sensitivity.
    b. a willingness to compromise at great costs.
    c. a lack of concern about the larger issues of politics.
    d. a kind of adversarial spirit.
    e. confusion.
18. The colonial distrust of British rule was the byproduct of both experience and
    a. dire predictions by sociologists.
    b. the public speeches of European leaders.
    c. folk music in the Southern colonies.
    d. writings of popular novelists.
    e. the religious beliefs of many.
19. While there has been no established religion in the United States, there has certainly been a dominant religious tradition. That tradition can be best described as
    a. Catholicism.
    b. Protestantism.
    c. Protestantism, especially Lutheranism.
    d. Protestantism, especially Puritanism.
    e. none of the above.
20. Max Weber explained the rise of __________, in part, by what he called the "Protestant ethic."
    a. two-party competition
    b. elitism
    c. totalitarianism
    d. democracy
    e. capitalism
21. Erik Erikson, the psychologist, found considerable difference between the __________ of Americans and Europeans.
    a. marital relations
    b. social organizations
    c. religious beliefs
    d. family characteristics
    e. pop icons
22. Which of the following statements about class-consciousness in America is *accurate*?
    a. It has been relatively unimportant.
    b. It has had a powerful effect upon attitudes.
    c. It is particularly salient among the unemployed.
    d. It implies an ideology of class struggle.
    e. It steers the campaigns of most presidential candidates.
23. The terms "progressive" and "orthodox" were first used in the context of a "culture war" by James Davison, a(n)
    a. political scientist.
    b. historian
    c. anthropologist.
    d. economist.
    e. sociologist.

24. According to Davison, a person of "orthodox" beliefs is *not* likely to believe
    a. morality is as important as self-expression.
    b. moral rules derive from the commands of God and the laws of nature.
    c. moral commands and laws are relatively clear.
    d. moral commands and laws are dependent upon individual preferences.
    e. moral commands and laws do not generally change.
25. The culture war is basically a conflict over
    a. economic issues.
    b. foreign affairs.
    c. international norms.
    d. differing religious ideologies.
    e. private and public morality.
26. Morris Fiorina explains the "culture war" as an artifact of
    a. deep divisions in American culture on most policy issues.
    b. the emergence of a politically active middle class.
    c. polarization of political leaders.
    d. media emphasis on so-called "red" and "blue" states.
    e. C and D.
27. The increase in cynicism toward our government has been specifically directed at
    a. government officials.
    b. the system of government itself.
    c. the Constitution.
    d. the Declaration of Independence.
    e. capitalism in America.
28. The authors suggest levels of confidence in government in the 1950s may have been
    a. abnormally high.
    b. abnormally low.
    c. inflated as a result of poor polling techniques.
    d. the byproduct of false responses.
    e. the result of economic stress and a lack of military power and might.
29. When people feel that they have a say in what the government does, that public officials pay attention to them, and they feel that they understand politics, then they are said to have a sense of political
    a. trust.
    b. tolerance.
    c. efficacy.
    d. legitimacy.
    e. reciprocity.
30. Which is a *correct* description of trends in the political efficacy of Americans from the mid-1960s to today?
    a. Internal efficacy has dramatically increased.
    b. External efficacy has dramatically increased.
    c. Internal efficacy and external efficacy have dramatically increased.
    d. Internal efficacy appears to be in decline while external efficacy has remained the same.
    e. Internal efficacy appears to be the same while external efficacy appears to be in decline.

31. The less voters trust political institutions and leaders, the more likely they are to support candidates
    a. who are incumbents.
    b. who are economically liberal.
    c. from the non-incumbent major party or a third party.
    d. who have the highest name recognition.
    e. with little or no experience in politics.
32. Robert D. Putnam's "civic health index" includes measures for which of the following?
    a. Membership in civic groups.
    b. Online "chat."
    c. Trust in the government and other institutions.
    d. Trust in other people.
    e. All of the above.
33. Which of the following statements concerning recent trends in tolerance is most *accurate*?
    a. Female candidates are less tolerated than they once were.
    b. Americans are increasingly less tolerant than they were in the 1950s.
    c. The level of tolerance in America has not changed in the last twenty or thirty years.
    d. Americans appear to be more tolerant than they were twenty or thirty years ago.
    e. Americans are less tolerant of Communists than they once were.
34. Judgments about political tolerance should be made with caution because
    a. Americans rarely have a clear idea of what is meant by the word "tolerance."
    b. there is actually very little reliable data on the topic.
    c. there is so very little intolerance in the world.
    d. no nation is completely tolerant of every kind of political activity.
    e. one person's intolerance is another person's civic "concern."

ESSAY QUESTIONS

Practice writing extended answers to the following questions. These test your ability to integrate and express the ideas that you have been studying in this chapter.

1. Identify and briefly comment on the five elements of American political culture.
2. What are some things that you have learned in this chapter about political culture in Sweden and Japan?
3. Summarize the findings of the classic study of political culture in the United States and citizens in Great Britain, Germany, Italy and Mexico.
4. Discuss some ways that religion has played an important role in American political culture and continued to do so to this day.
5. Discuss 4-5 of the sources of American political culture.
6. Identify the two sides in the culture war and contrast their beliefs. Also note opposing views that notable political scientists (Fiorina and Abramowitz) take on the culture war.
7. What is political efficacy and what is the difference between internal and external political efficacy? What are recent trends in the United States regarding these aspects of public opinion?
8. What are some explanations for why some highly unpopular groups continue to survive in our culture?

ANSWERS TO KEY TERMS MATCH QUESTIONS

1. o
2. k
3. d
4. j
5. u
6. i
7. c
8. a
9. e
10. t
11. m
12. l
13. v
14. b
15. g
16. s
17. q
18. f
19. n
20. h
21. p
22. r

ANSWERS TO DATA CHECK QUESTIONS

1. 1960 (74).
2. 1994 (33).
3. 1986, 1988, 1990, 1994, 1996, 1998, 2000, 2004
4. 1964-1965.
5. It is a percentage which has generally been very small (below 5 percent) but was above 10 percent from the late 1950s to the late 1960s.
6. It is a percentage which has always been very small (below 5 percent).
7. 1974-1975
8. 1993-1994.
9. One might argue that it has been improving, based on these measures.

ANSWERS TO TRUE/FALSE QUESTIONS

1. T
2. F He actually singled out our "moral and intellectual characteristics" as the primary factor in understanding our culture.
3. T
4. T
5. T
6. T
7. F They are more willing to tolerate economic inequality than they are political inequality.
8. T
9. T
10. T
11. T
12. T
13. T
14. F Our faith in institutions tends to be much higher than it is in other nations.
15. F Swedes are much more likely to favor equal pay for workers.
16. T
17. T
18. T
19. T
20. F The concern was that Jefferson would sell us out to France.
21. T
22. T
23. T
24. T
25. T
26. F It actually began in the 1950s.
27. T
28. T
29. F It actually increased a bit, before leveling off and decreasing once again.
30. T
31. F Internal political efficacy has remained about the same. It is external political efficacy which has declined considerably.
32. T
33. T

ANSWERS TO MULTIPLE CHOICE QUESTIONS

1. b
2. e
3. e
4. d
5. c
6. a
7. c
8. b
9. b
10. e
11. b
12. e
13. e
14. d
15. e
16. a
17. d
18. e
19. d
20. e
21. d
22. a
23. e
24. d
25. e
26. e
27. a
28. a
29. c
30. e
31. c
32. e
33. d
34. e

CHAPTER 5

Civil Liberties

REVIEWING THE CHAPTER

CHAPTER FOCUS

This chapter surveys quite a number of pressure points that have developed in the American political system regarding the liberties of individuals and the government's involvement in protecting or restricting those liberties. Included among these pressure points are national security, federal versus state enforcement of rights, First Amendment freedoms, and criminal law. After reading and reviewing the material in this chapter, you should be able to do each of the following:

1. Discuss the relationship of the Bill of Rights to the concept of democratic rule of the majority, and give examples of tension between majority rule and minority rights. Explain how the politics of civil liberties may at times become a mass issue, and offer several examples.
2. Describe the conflicts that have arisen between those who claim First Amendment rights and those who are in favor of sedition laws that might restrict freedom of speech. Explain how the Supreme Court attempts to balance competing interests. Describe the various tests that the Court has applied.
3. Explain how the structure of the federal system affects the application of the Bill of Rights. How has the Supreme Court used the Fourteenth Amendment to expand coverage in the federal system? Discuss changing conceptions of the due process clause of the Fourteenth Amendment.
4. List the categories under which the Supreme Court may classify "speech." Explain the distinction between protected and unprotected speech, and name the various forms of expression that are not protected under the First Amendment. Describe the test used by the Court to decide the circumstances under which freedom of expression may be qualified.
5. State what the Supreme Court decided in *Miranda* v. *Arizona,* and explain why that case illustrates how the Court operates in most such due-process cases.
6. Analyze why the resolution of civil liberties issues involves politics as well as law. Discuss the political factors that influence the Supreme Court when it decides fundamental civil liberties issues.

STUDY OUTLINE

I. The politics of civil liberties
    A. The objectives of the Framers
        1. Limited federal powers
        2. Constitution: a list of dos, not don'ts
        3. Bill of Rights: specific do nots
            a) Not intended to affect states
            b) A limitation on popular rule

B. Civil rights v. civil liberties
1. Liberties: protections against the abuse of government power
2. Rights: protections against discrimination
3. Sometimes the distinction can be blurred

II. Rights in conflict: Bill of Rights contains competing rights
A. *Sheppard* case (free press versus fair trial)
B. *New York Times* and Pentagon Papers (common defense versus free press)
C. Kunz anti-Jewish speeches (free speech versus public order)
D. Struggles over rights show same pattern as interest group politics
1. War is usually the crisis that has resulted in restrictions for some minorities
a) Sedition Act of 1789, during French Revolution
b) Espionage and Sedition Acts of World War I
c) Smith Act of World War II
d) Internal Security Act of 1950, Korean War
e) Community Control Act of 1954, McCarthy era
2. Supreme Court has been called on to decide if limits were proper

III. Culture conflicts
A. Original settlement by white European Protestants produced Americanism
B. Waves of immigration brought new cultures, conflicts
1. Non-Christians offended by government-sponsored crèches at Christmas
2. English speakers prefer monolingual schools
3. Boy Scouts of America exclude homosexuals from being scout leaders
C. Differences even within given cultural traditions

IV. Applying the Bill of Rights to the States
A. Originally, the Bill of Rights applied only to the federal government
1. Affirmed by the Supreme Court in 1883 case
2. Excepting some provisions in Article I, the Constitution was silent on what the states could not do
B. Changes in the post-Civil War era
1. War amendments (13th, 14th and 15th) followed
2. Fourteenth contained two critical clauses
a) The due process clause
b) The equal protection clause
3. Court began (in 1897) to use these clauses to apply certain rights to state government
a) Process known as "incorporation"
(1) Application of some rights (but not all) to the states
(2) No clear answer to which rights are "fundamental"
b) Currently incorporated rights
c) Newly discovered (or created) rights tend to be automatically incorporated

V. Interpreting and applying the First Amendment
A. Speech and national security
1. Original Blackstone view: no prior press censorship
2. Sedition Act of 1789 followed Blackstone view
3. By 1917–1919, Congress defines limits of expression
a) Treason, insurrection, forcible resistance
b) Upheld in *Schenck* via test of "clear and present danger"
c) Justice Holmes dissents, saying test not met
4. The *Gitlow* case elicits "fundamental personal rights"
5. Supreme Court moves toward more free expression after WWI
a) But communists convicted under Smith Act under "gravity of evil"

b) By 1957, test of "calculated to incite"
c) By 1969 (Brandenburg), "imminent" unlawful act
d) 1977 American Nazi march in Skokie, Illinois, held lawful
e) "Hate" speech permissible but not "hate crime"

B. What is speech?
1. Some forms of speech not fully protected; four kinds
2. Libel: written statement defaming another by false statement
a) Oral statement: slander
b) Variable jury awards
c) Malice needed for public figures
3. Obscenity
a) Twelve years of decisions; no lasting definition
b) 1973 definition: patently offensive by community standards of average person
c) Balancing competing claims remains a problem
d) Localities decide whether to tolerate pornography but must comply with strict rules
e) Protection extended: nude dancing only marginally protected
f) Indianapolis statute: pornography degrading but court disagreed
g) Zoning ordinances upheld
h) Regulation of electronic Internet (computer-simulated child pornography)
4. Symbolic speech
a) Acts that convey a political message: flag-burning, draft card burning
b) Not generally protected
c) Exception is flag-burning: restriction of free speech
(1) Public outrage and congressional action
(2) Supreme Court response and the need for an amendment
(3) Reluctance of Congress

VI. Who is a person?
A. Corporations, etc., usually have same rights as individuals
1. Boston bank, antiabortion group, California utility have speech rights
2. More restrictions are allowed, however, on commercial speech
a) Regulation must be narrowly tailored
b) Or it must serve some clear public interest
3. McCain-Feingold campaign finance reform law of 2002
a) Restrictions on "electioneering communications" that refer to candidates within 60 days of an election
b) Restrictions upheld despite legal challenges
4. Young people may have fewer rights; Hazelwood; school newspaper can be restricted

VII. Church and state
A. The free exercise clause: no state interference, similar to speech
1. Law may not impose special burdens on religion
2. But no religious exemptions from laws binding all
3. Some cases difficult to settle
a) Conscientious objection to war, military service
b) Refusal to work Saturdays; unemployment compensation
c) Refusal to send children to school beyond eighth grade

B. The establishment clause
1. Jefferson's view: "wall of separation"
2. Congress at the time: "no national religion"
3. Ambiguous phrasing of First Amendment

4. Supreme Court interpretation: "wall of separation"
    a) 1947 New Jersey case (reimbursements)
        (1) Court: First Amendment applies to the states
        (2) Court: State must be neutral toward religion
    b) Later decisions struck down
        (1) School prayers (voluntary, nonsectarian, delivered by a rabbi or minister or student elected by other students)
        (2) Teaching of creationism
        (3) In-school released-time programs
    c) Public aid to parochial schools particularly controversial
        (1) Allowed: aid for construction of buildings, textbook loans, tax-exempt status, state deductions for tuition, computers, and sign language interpreters
        (2) Disallowed: teacher salary supplements, tuition reimbursements, various school services, money to purchase instructional materials, special districts
        (3) Though the Court can (and does) change its mind on these matters
        (4) Recent controversy: school vouchers in Cleveland, OH
            (a) State offered money to families (especially poor ones) whose students were attending failing schools
            (b) Voucher could be used for another public school or a private school
            (c) Court upheld the program as aid to families, not schools, or religion
    d) Development of a three-part test for constitutional aid
        (1) It has a strictly secular purpose
        (2) It neither advances nor inhibits religion
        (3) It involves no excessive government entanglement
    e) Failure of the Court's test to create certainty in our law
        (1) Nativity scenes, menorahs, and Christmas trees
        (2) Seeming anomalies: prayer in Congress, chaplains in the armed services, "In God We Trust" on currency
        (3) Deep division/confusion among members of the Court

VIII. Crime and due process
  A. The exclusionary rule
    1. Most nations punish police misconduct apart from the criminal trial
    2. United States punishes it by excluding improperly obtained evidence
    3. Supreme Court rulings
        a) 1949: declined to use exclusionary rule
        b) 1961: changed, adopted it in *Mapp* case
  B. Search and seizure
    1. When can "reasonable" searches of individuals be made?
        a) With a properly obtained search warrant with probable cause
        b) Incident to an arrest
    2. What can police search incident to an arrest?
        a) The individual being arrested
        b) Things in plain view
        c) Things under the immediate control of the individual
    3. What of an arrest while driving?
        a) Answer changes almost yearly
            (1) 1979 ruling: cannot search suitcase in car of arrested person
            (2) 1981 ruling: cannot search "closed, opaque container" either

(3) 1982 ruling: can search any place where there is probable cause to suspect the presence of contraband
(4) Further extensions of police power
(a) Can also search things people are carrying in car
(b) Car can be searched if "reasonable suspicion" develops during traffic violation stop
b) Court attempts to protect a "reasonable expectation of privacy"
c) Privacy in body and home but not from government supervisor or private employer

C. Confessions and self-incrimination
1. Constitutional ban originally against torture and "third degree" tactics by police
2. Extension of rights in the 1960s
a) The *Miranda* case
(1) Confessions presumed involuntary unless informed of particular rights
(2) *Miranda* warnings now read by police
b) Applications of *Miranda*
(1) Right to a lawyer in police lineup
(2) Right to a lawyer in mental competence examinations
(3) Exclusion of confessions without lawyer present
(4) Confessions to undercover officer posing as cellmates permitted
(5) Exclusion of confessions which result from questioning before and after *Miranda* warnings are given

D. Relaxing the exclusionary rule
1. Positions taken on the rule
a) Any evidence should be admissible
b) Rule was useful, but had become too technical to be an effective deterrent
c) Rule a vital safeguard to essential liberties
2. Courts have moved to adopt the second position
a) Limiting coverage
b) Allowing for exceptions. Examples:
(1) good faith exception
(2) public safety exception
(3) inevitable discovery exception

E. Terrorism and civil liberties
1. USA Patriot Act
a) Telephone and Internet taps, voice mail seizure
b) Grand jury information exchange
c) Detainment of non-citizens and deportation of aliens
d) Money laundering
e) Crime and punishments
2. Executive order for use of military courts
a) Trial before commission of military officers
(1) May be held in secret
(2) Conviction based on a two-thirds vote of commission members
(3) Appeals to the secretary of defense and president (not civilian courts)
b) Potential uses and associated controversies
(1) Detainees in Guantanamo—Taliban regime, Afghanistan
(2) Detainees in Guantanamo—al Queda terrorist network
3. Legal issues and developments
a) The Second World War position relating to "unlawful combatants"
b) Bush administration issue: neither combatants nor terrorists

c) Supreme Court rulings
   (1) Accepted the legitimacy of the right to make legal challenges
   (2) American citizens are entitled to a hearing before a neutral decision-maker in order to challenge the basis for detention
      (a) 2006 law and military commissions
      (b) Composed of five military officers, selected by the secretary of defense
      (c) Certain fundamental rights applicable to defendants
      (d) Appeals can be made to the D.C. circuit and the Supreme Court
d) Legislation
   (1) Patriot Act renewed with few changes
   (2) 2005 law featuring federal standards for licenses

4. Searches without warrants
   a) Warrantless searches of foreign spies common among presidents of both parties
   b) 1978 FISA required approval by a special court
      (1) Seven judges selected by the Chief Justice
      (2) Would use a lower standard, "probable cause" not required
   c) National newspapers revealed secret NSA program that operated outside FISA
   d) White House changed program despite strong legal position

KEY TERMS MATCH

Match the following terms and descriptions:

1. The government suppression of American leftists after the 1917 Bolshevik Revolution in Russia
2. A Federalist bill of 1789 criminalizing criticism of government
3. A 1940 act criminalizing the advocacy of violent revolution
4. A 1950 act requiring the registration of all communists
5. A 1954 act denying legal rights to the Communist party
6. Term which describes the process whereby the Supreme Court applies provisions of the Bill of Rights to the states
7. A Supreme Court formula to legitimate the abridgement of the right of free speech
8. Harming another by publishing defamatory statements
9. Category of individuals who must show material is false and printed with actual malice to win a libel case

a. actual malice
b. Hugo Black
c. "clear and present danger" test
d. Community Control Act
e. conscientious objector
f. creationism
g. establishment clause
h. exclusionary rule
i. FISA
j. free exercise clause
k. freedom of expression
l. freedom of religion
m. *Giltow* v. *New York*
n. good-faith exception
o. incorporation
p. Internal Security Act
q. Thomas Jefferson
r. least means

10. A government action to prevent rather than punish certain expressions
11. The supposed superiority of rights of expression over other constitutional rights
12. The use of only minimal measures to restrict potentially dangerous expression
13. Case in which the Supreme Court decided to apply the exclusionary rule to state and local law enforcement officers
14. The First Amendment clause guaranteeing religious freedom
15. The First Amendment clause prohibiting an official religion
16. Justice who argued the First Amendment protects all publications, even wholly obscene ones
17. A teaching on the origin of the world found to be religiously inspired
18. A special court that approves electronic eavesdropping on foreign spies
19. A period during the public school day when students get religious instruction
20. The prohibition against the use of illegally obtained evidence in court
21. A written authorization to police officers to conduct a search
22. The legal basis for the issuance of a search warrant
23. A Supreme Court case that led to rules that police officers must follow in warning arrested persons of their rights
24. Individual who first penned the phrase "wall of separation" in a private letter
25. One who refuses military service on religious or ethical grounds
26. Case in which the Supreme Court first applied the First Amendment to the states

s. libel

t. *Mapp* v. *Ohio*

u. *Miranda*

v. preferred position

w. prior restraint

x. probable cause

y. public figures

z. Red scare

aa. released time

bb. search warrant

cc. Sedition Act

dd. Smith Act

ee. symbolic speech

ff. wall-of-separation principle

27. Part of the First Amendment protecting freedom of speech, press, assembly, and the right to petition the government
28. Part of the First Amendment protecting the free exercise of religion and prohibiting an establishment of religion
29. Admission of illegally obtained evidence if illegality results from a technical or minor error
30. Legal term suggesting something was published with reckless disregard for the truth, or with the knowledge that it was false
31. An act that conveys a political message, such as burning a draft card to protest the draft
32. An interpretation of part of the First Amendment that prevents government involvement with religion

DATA CHECK

FIGURE 5.1 (Page 97): Annual Legal Immigration, 1850–2005

1. In approximately what years do the statistics for annual immigration reach their peak?

___

2. What was the apparent impact of World War I on immigration?

___

3. What was the apparent impact of the Immigration and Reform and Control Act of 1986?

___

4. Where does the number of annual immigrants appear to hit its lowest point in the Figure?

___

PRACTICING FOR EXAMS

TRUE/FALSE QUESTIONS

Read each statement carefully. Mark true statements *T.* If any part of the statement is false, mark it *F,* and write in the space provided a concise explanation of why the statement is false.

1. T F In practice, there is no clear line between civil rights and civil liberties.

____

2. T F The Constitution and the Bill of Rights contain a list of competing rights and duties.

____

3. T F The inevitable debates which accompany a time of war have generally been met with expansion in First Amendment liberties by Congress.

____

4. T F The Internal Security Act of 1950 required members of the Communist Party to register with the government.

____

5. T F When legislatures have chosen to restrict freedom of speech, the Supreme Court has had a general tendency to oppose such efforts and defend the First Amendment rights of citizens.

____

6. T F Sedition laws are no longer used today.

____

7. T F The Supreme Court held that the Boy Scouts of America violated federal law when the organization refused to allow homosexuals to be scout leaders.

____

8. T F The process whereby the United States Supreme Court applies amendments to the Bill of Rights is known as "incorporation."

____

9. T F The right to bear arms (Second Amendment) has been applied to the states.

____

10. T F The ban on excessive bail and fines (Eighth Amendment) has not been applied to the states.

____

11. T F Blackstone' *Commentaries* took the position that the press should not be restricted or punished for what it prints.

____

12. T F The Sedition Act of 1798 entrusted judges to convict persons charged under the Act.

____

13. T F None of the convictions under the Sedition Act of 1789 reached the United States Supreme Court by appeal.

____

14. T F Charles T. Schenck was convicted of planting bombs in key government buildings.

____

15. T F Justice Holmes' rule for identification of dangerous speech came to be known as the "clear and probable danger test."

____

16. T F In the *Gitlow* case, the Supreme Court incorporated the freedom of speech and of the press to the states via the due-process clause of the Fourteenth Amendment.

____

17. T F In 1977, the Court upheld the right of leaders in Skokie, Illinois, to ban a group of American Nazis from marching in a street parade.

____

18. T F Nazi swastikas and burning crosses can be banned from public display by state legislatures via "hate crime legislation."

____

19. T F Most Supreme Court justices do not interpret the words "no law" in the First Amendment to literally mean "no law."

____

20. T F If you sue for libel and it turns out the statements in question were true, you cannot win no matter how badly they have harmed you.

____

21. T F In the United States, it is generally very difficult for public figures to win a libel suit.

____

22. T F Nudity and sex are not, by definition, obscenity.

____

23. T F The Court has considered nude dancing a form of "speech" or "expression."

____

24. T F The Court upheld a statute banning total nude dancing.

____

25. T F In 1997, the Court upheld a congressional ban on "virtual " child pornography.

____

26. T F The House and the Senate passed a law banning flag-burning by huge majorities.

____

27. T F The government can place more restrictions on commercial than noncommercial speech.

28. T F When students are in school, they do not have constitutional rights to freedom of speech or expression.

29. T F The Court upheld a Florida city's ban on animal sacrifices that were being made by members of an Afro-Caribbean religion.

30. T F If a person claims membership in an Indian tribe and argues that he/she should be able to use the drug peyote in religious ceremonies, the Supreme Court will uphold their right to do so.

31. T F Draft laws have only recently made exceptions for conscientious objectors.

32. T F The Supreme Court's first attempt at interpreting the Establishment clause was in 1947.

33. T F Recently, the Court declared a school voucher program which especially benefited the poor in Cleveland "unconstitutional."

34. T F The House and the Senate have opened with prayer every session since 1789.

35. T F Initially, the Supreme Court refused to apply the exclusionary rule to the states.

36. T F If you are arrested, the police can search you and things and places under your immediate control without a warrant.

37. T F Private employers have little freedom to search an employee's desk and files.

38. T F The conviction of Ernesto A. Miranda was based upon a written confession.

39. T F Thanks to the Supreme Court, Miranda never served time for the rape and kidnapping for which he was originally convicted.

40. T F Under the USA Patriot Act, the government can tap your telephone and use of the Internet without a court order.

41. T F After the attacks of 9/11, President Bush proclaimed a national emergency and gave military courts jurisdiction over cases involving non-citizens who were suspected terrorists.

____

42. T F Military commissions can operate in secret.

____

43. T F The verdict of a military commission can be appealed to a civilian court.

____

44. T F The Bush administration has taken the position that members of the alQueda terrorist movement can be tried by military tribunals as "unlawful combatants."

____

45. T F More than a few courts have ruled that the president has the inherent authority to conduct warrantless searches to obtain foreign intelligence information.

____

MULTIPLE CHOICE QUESTIONS

Circle the letter of the response that best answers the question or completes the statement.

1. The Framers saw no need for a bill of rights because
   a. in their view, civil liberties were a matter for the states, not for the federal government.
   b. they were convinced that in a democratic republic, public opinion was a sufficient protection.
   c. no one bothered to even bring up the topic at the Convention.
   d. they assumed that the federal government could not do things that it was not explicitly authorized to do.
   e. their chief concern was protecting public order, not guaranteeing rights.
2. The authors suggest that the Founding Fathers would have probably never imagined that the Bill of Rights would
   a. affect what the federal government does.
   b. affect what state governments do.
   c. become so popular with the states.
   d. be ratified with so little debate.
   e. be amended in any way.
3. The leading entrepreneur of the Red scare around the time of World War I was
   a. Joseph McCarthy.
   b. A. Mitchell Palmer.
   c. Kate Richards O'Hare.
   d. Theodore Roosevelt.
   e. Woodrow Wilson.
4. Which of the following statements is *incorrect*?
   a. The Bill of Rights was added many years after the Constitution was signed.
   b. The liberties enumerated in the Bill of Rights applied only to the federal government.
   c. Initially, the Supreme Court refused to apply the first ten amendments to the states.
   d. The first amendments that were applied to the states appeared after the Civil War.
   e. None of the above.

5. Which amendment prohibited the depravation of life, liberty and property without "due process of law?"
   a. Tenth.
   b. Thirteenth.
   c. Fourteenth.
   d. Fifteenth.
   e. Twenty-sixth.
6. In the first case where the Supreme Court began applying certain rights to state governments, the decision involved
   a. freedom of speech.
   b. the taking of private property.
   c. free exercise of religion.
   d. the establishment of religion.
   e. voting rights.
7. In applying (or incorporating) specific rights to the states, the Court has considered whether such rights are
   a. integral.
   b. extremely vital.
   c. secular.
   d. majoritarian.
   e. fundamental.
8. Which of the following sections of the Bill of Rights has been applied in its entirety to the states?
   a. First Amendment.
   b. Second Amendment.
   c. Third Amendment.
   d. Fifth Amendment.
   e. Seventh Amendment.
9. Blackstone argued that the press should be free
   a. from any restrictions whatsoever.
   b. only when it published the truth.
   c. from censorship prior to publication.
   d. from seditious libel restrictions alone.
   e. from libel laws regarding government officers.
10. The debate between the Federalists and the Jeffersonians over the Sedition Act was largely a debate over
   a. the fundamentals of individual liberty.
   b. the role of the press in a democratic republic.
   c. states' rights.
   d. the interpretation of elastic clauses in the Constitution.
   e. the role of government in the economy.
11. The Jeffersonian Republicans believed that the press
   a. should be free from governmental controls.
   b. should be free from governmental controls except when the nation is at war.
   c. should be punished by the federal government for slander and defamation.
   d. could be punished by federal courts but only when malice was shown.
   e. could be punished by the states for slander and defamation.

12. In 1919, the Supreme Court upheld the conviction of Charles T. Schenck, who mailed circulars urging men to resist the draft, on the basis of the _________ test.
    a. bad tendency
    b. clear and probable danger
    c. clear and present danger
    d. articulable suspicion
    e. probable cause
13. The effect of the "clear and present danger" rule seems to have been to
    a. clarify the law but not keep anyone from prison.
    b. greatly clarify and expand the scope of free expression.
    c. increase convictions for sedition and incitement in the states.
    d. make guarantees of freedom of expression as binding on state as on federal officials.
    e. bring the process of incorporation to its logical conclusion.
14. The First Amendment was not made applicable to the states via the Fourteenth Amendment until the
    a. 1920s.
    b. 1930s.
    c. 1940s.
    d. 1950s.
    e. 1970s.
15. The Supreme Court's rulings regarding communists who advocated the overthrow of the government were eventually effected by
    a. presidential rebukes and legislative resolutions.
    b. diminished popular concern about communism.
    c. condemnation from the American Bar Association.
    d. change in the Court's membership.
    e. B and D.
16. The 1969 conviction of KKK leader Clarence Brandenburg was overturned by the Court because the "danger" or "illegal action" that he called for was not
    a. imminent.
    b. properly regulated.
    c. without merit.
    d. patently offensive by contemporary community standards.
    e. B and D.
17. The display of an odious symbol, such as a swastika or a burning cross, has been deemed by the Supreme Court to be
    a. punishable as a hate crime.
    b. punishable as incitement.
    c. an unconstitutional act.
    d. protected by the Constitution.
    e. not a case for Supreme Court review.
18. *Libel* is defined as
    a. stating something untrue about another person.
    b. writing something false about someone without their knowledge.
    c. an oral statement defaming another person.
    d. a written statement defaming another person.
    e. maliciously intending to defame a public official.

19. A successful libel suit is more likely to be filed by
    a. an elected official.
    b. an army general.
    c. a school teacher.
    d. a well-known celebrity.
    e. a famous artist or literary figure.
20. Justice Hugo Black and a few others took the position that obscenity is
    a. protected by the First Amendment.
    b. easy to define, but difficult to punish.
    c. difficult to define, but easy to punish.
    d. subject to federal but not state prosecution.
    e. subject to state but not federal prosecution.
21. The definition of what is obscene and therefore not a form of protected speech
    a. is left almost entirely up to localities.
    b. can be decided by localities but only within narrow limits.
    c. is finely detailed in the Court's decision in the *Roth* case.
    d. has to be decided by the Supreme Court on pretty much a case-by-case basis.
    e. has to be decided by the Supreme Court on the basis of reasonably clear guidelines.
22. Under the current law, the Supreme Court would allow a city to
    a. institute a complete ban on nudity in films and books.
    b. regulate nudity as pornography.
    c. adopt a zoning ordinance restricting where "adult" movie theaters can be located.
    d. define pornography in terms of material that degrades women.
    e. ban the use of the Internet.
23. One controversial rule of the Court is that free expression is not absolute, but occupies a higher position than many other constitutional rights. This is known as the "_______ position" approach to speech.
    a. incorporated
    b. neutrality
    c. least-restrictive means
    d. relaxed
    e. preferred
24. The Supreme Court struck down a 1996 law that addressed the issue of child pornography because it attempted to ban images that were
    a. graphic.
    b. violent.
    c. psychologically harmful.
    d. in the public domain.
    e. computer simulated.
25. The Supreme Court has ruled that one of the following sorts of symbolic speech is protected by the Constitution. Which one?
    a. Burning draft cards.
    b. Burning the flag.
    c. Making obscene gestures toward a police officer.
    d. Sleeping in a public park to draw attention to the plight of the homeless.
    e. Protesting loudly directly outside a court building.

26. Which of the following statements regarding government limitations on commercial and noncommercial speech is correct?
    a. Commercial speech cannot be limited as much.
    b. Commercial speech can be limited more.
    c. Noncommercial speech can be limited more.
    d. Neither can be limited more than the other.
    e. Commercial speech can only be limited in matters regarding public health.
27. Under the McCain –Feingold campaign finance reform law, organizations cannot pay for radio or television spots that refer to candidates for federal office
    a. within sixty days before the election.
    b. more than sixty days before the election.
    c. without consent from the Federal Election Commission.
    d. without a waiver from a court.
    e. in a negative manner.
28. In general, high school students have the same rights as adults. An exception is when
    a. their actions are specifically prohibited by the Constitution.
    b. their actions offend other students.
    c. they exercise these rights as individuals rather than as part of a school-sponsored activity.
    d. some form of symbolic speech is involved.
    e. their exercise of these rights impedes the educational process.
29. The First Amendment states that Congress may not make any law prohibiting the free exercise of religion. It also specifically states that
    a. church and state must be clearly separate.
    b. there will be no official church in the United States.
    c. citizens are exempt from laws binding other citizens when the law goes against their religious beliefs.
    d. Congress may not make any law respecting an establishment of religion.
    e. nonsectarian, voluntary, or limited prayer is permissible in public schools.
30. Conscientious objectors may be excused from participation in war even if they do not believe in a Supreme Being so long as there is evidence that
    a. they are guided by a deeply held moral or ethical code.
    b. they have never been arrested in an anti-war protest.
    c. their parents also objected to war.
    d. ten elected officials support their exclusion from the draft.
    e. they strongly object to particular wars, not all wars in general.
31. A state cannot require you to send your children to public schools beyond the ____ grade.
    a. fifth
    b. sixth
    c. seventh
    d. eighth
    e. tenth
32. The phrase "wall of separation" between church and state comes from
    a. the pen of Thomas Jefferson.
    b. the Bill of Rights.
    c. the debates in the First Congress that drafted the Bill of Rights.
    d. the Fourteenth Amendment.
    e. George Washington's farewell address.

33. Interestingly, the wording of the Establishment clause that was originally debated by Congress was __________ than what finally emerged.
    a. more abstract
    b. longer and even more confusing
    c. more brief
    d. quite different and much plainer
    e. more partial to the federal government
34. The Court has applied the "wall of separation" metaphor to strike down
    a. nonsectarian prayers in public schools.
    b. voluntary prayers in public schools.
    c. invocations given by rabbis or ministers at public school graduation ceremonies.
    d. students, elected by other students, to lead voluntary prayer at public school graduation ceremonies.
    e. all of the above.
35. The Supreme Court's controversial three-part "test" for Establishment clause cases focuses specifically on
    a. whether there is a secular purpose for an action.
    b. the effect of an act advances or inhibits religion.
    c. whether an action fosters excessive governmental entanglement with religion.
    d. all of the above.
    e. none of the above.
36. Instead of using the exclusionary rule, our courts might do as European courts do and
    a. refuse to include illegally obtained evidence at a trial.
    b. ignore the legality or illegality of the method used to obtain the evidence.
    c. levy civil or criminal penalties against law enforcement officers who obtain evidence illegally.
    d. refuse to hear cases tainted with official illegality.
    e. use the rule only when cases do not involve murder.
37. The exclusionary rule was not officially applied to the states until the
    a. 1940s.
    b. 1950s.
    c. 1960s.
    d. 1980s.
    e. 1990s.
38. Some police departments have tried to get around the need for *Miranda* warnings by training their officer to
    a. read the warnings quickly and refuse to answer subsequent questions.
    b. only use the warnings when there is a threat to the safety of the public.
    c. limit the use of warnings to newly hired officers.
    d. question suspects, obtain confessions, read the warnings, then repeat the same questions.
    e. read the warnings and question suspects regardless of their expressed desire not to talk.
39. All of the following are true of the USA Patriot Act (passed in the aftermath of the attack of 9/11) *except*
    a. the penalties for terrorist crimes were increased.
    b. the government can seize voice mail without a court order.
    c. information in secret grand jury hearings can be shared by officials.
    d. non-citizens who pose a national security risk can be detained for up to seven days.
    e. the government can tap Internet communications with a court order.

40. Which statement accurately describes the legal status of complaints concerning the detainment of "unlawful combatants" in Guantanamo Bay?
    a. American courts cannot consider legal challenges regarding the detentions.
    b. American courts can consider legal challenges regarding the detentions.
    c. The Supreme Court has provided lower courts with specific guidelines for petitions.
    d. It is clear that the Supreme Court will rule against the government in these cases.
    e. It is clear that the Supreme Court will rule in favor of the government in these cases.
41. One potentially controversial aspect of a 2005 law regarding Homeland Security might be something like
    a. a national ID card.
    b. optical scanning in airports.
    c. permanent fingerprint files in state drivers' license offices.
    d. armed guards in all public buildings.
    e. loyalty oaths for political office.

ESSAY QUESTIONS

Practice writing extended answers to the following questions. These test your ability to integrate and express the ideas that you have been studying in this chapter.

1. Explain the process whereby the Fourteenth Amendment was utilized to incorporate provisions of the Bill of Rights to the states. Give specific attention to the Supreme Court's decisions in *Gitlow* and *Palko*.
2. Explain the facts of Charles T. Schenck's case, the test that was created by Justice Holmes and the ruling of the Supreme Court.
3. Identify four types of speech which are not automatically granted full constitutional protection.
4. Define libel and explain how libel laws are applied to public figures in the United States.
5. Explain how the issue of flag burning played out in Congress and the Supreme Court.
6. Identify 7-8 practices which the Supreme Court has not allowed under its interpretation of the Establishment clause.
7. What are the considerations featured in the Court's three part test for potential violations of the Establishment clause?
8. What are two ways that court systems can handle the problem of evidence that is seized illegally by law enforcement officers?
9. Summarize the scope of a warrantless police search following an arrest.
10. Summarize the story of Ernesto Miranda and the Supreme Court's decision in his case.
11. Identify some examples of ways in which the Supreme Court has "relaxed" the Exclusionary Rule in recent years.
12. Describe 4-5 provisions in the USA Patriot Act.
13. Discuss the controversy that emerged in 2005 regarding warrantless searches by the government, the FISA and national security.

ANSWERS TO KEY TERMS MATCH QUESTIONS

1. z
2. cc
3. dd
4. p
5. d
6. o
7. c
8. s
9. y
10. w
11. v
12. r
13. t
14. j
15. g
16. b
17. f
18. i
19. aa
20. h
21. bb
22. x
23. u
24. q
25. e
26. m
27. k
28. l
29. n
30. a
31. ee
32. ff

ANSWERS TO DATA CHECK QUESTIONS

1. 1991.
2. Immigration statistics dropped considerably.
3. There was a boom in immigration.
4. 1945 (World War II).

ANSWERS TO TRUE/FALSE QUESTIONS

1. T
2. T
3. F Congress has tended to restrict First Amendment liberties during war.
4. T
5. F To the contrary, courts have tended to uphold the legislatures.
6. F They are still used today, although rarely.
7. F The Court ruled in favor of the Scouts, allowing them to continue to exclude homosexuals from membership.
8. T
9. F It has not.
10. T
11. F Blackstone thought the press should be regulated by subsequent punishment, but not by prior restraints.
12. F The Act was considered an improvement because it entrusted this decision to the jury instead of a judge.
13. T
14. F Schenck merely passed out printed materials calling for resistance to the selective service laws.
15. F It was known as the "clear and present danger" test.
16. T
17. F The Court ruled the Nazi's had the right to assemble peacefully and march.
18. F Such speech may very well be offensive, but it cannot be banned simply for being such.
19. T
20. T
21. T
22. T
23. T
24. T
25. F They ruled against the ban as there were no real children involved, only computer generated, or virtual images.

26. T
27. T
28. F The do have such rights so long as they do not threaten or harm the rights of other students and they do not impede the business of the school.
29. F The Court struck down the ban.
30. F The Court will actually disagree and uphold any criminal punishments which follow.
31. F The draft laws have always exempted conscientious objectors.
32. T
33. F The Court ruled such programs "constitutional" so long as there is "real choice" among private schools.
34. T
35. T
36. T
37. F Private employers have a great deal of freedom to search your desk and files.
38. T
39. F Miranda was retried, convicted and served 9 years in prison.
40. F The government must first obtain a court order to do such.
41. T
42. T
43. F An appeal can be made to the secretary of defense and the president, but not to a civilian court.
44. T
45. T

ANSWERS TO MULTIPLE CHOICE QUESTIONS

1. d
2. b
3. b
4. e
5. c
6. b
7. e
8. a
9. c
10. c
11. e

12. c
13. a
14. a
15. e
16. a
17. d
18. d
19. c
20. a
21. a
22. c
23. e
24. e
25. b
26. b
27. a
28. e
29. d
30. a
31. d
32. a
33. d
34. e
35. d
36. c
37. c
38. d
39. b
40. b
41. a

CHAPTER 6

Civil Rights

REVIEWING THE CHAPTER

CHAPTER FOCUS

This chapter focuses on the two most intense and protracted struggles for civil rights in recent times: that of blacks and that of women. After reading and reviewing the material in this chapter, you should be able to do each of the following:

1. Contrast the experience of economic interest groups with that of black groups in obtaining satisfaction of their interests from the government. Indicate why in most circumstances the black movement involved interest groups rather than client politics. Describe the strategies used by black leaders to overcome their political weaknesses, and explain why the civil rights movement has become more conventional in its strategy in recent years.

2. Summarize the legal struggles of blacks to secure rights under the Fourteenth Amendment, and state how the Court construed that amendment in the civil rights cases and in *Plessy* v. *Ferguson.* Discuss the NAACP strategy of litigation, and indicate why it was suited to the political circumstances. Summarize the rulings in *Brown* v. *Board of Education* and compare them with those in *Plessy* v. *Ferguson.*

3. Discuss the rationale used by the Supreme Court in ordering busing to achieve desegregation. Explain the apparent inconsistency between *Brown* and *Charlotte-Mecklenburg.* State why these decisions are not really inconsistent, and explain why the courts chose busing as an equitable remedy to deal with *de jure* segregation.

4. Trace the campaign launched by blacks for a set of civil rights laws. Explain why they used nonviolent techniques. Discuss the conflict between the agenda-setting and the coalition-building aspects of the movement. Demonstrate how civil rights advocates could overcome sources of resistance in Congress.

5. Describe the differences between the black civil rights movement and the women's movement. List the various standards used by the courts in interpreting the Fourteenth Amendment, and explain how these standards differ depending on whether blacks or women are involved.

6. Summarize the debate over "compensatory action" versus "preferential treatment" and targets versus quotas in affirmative action.

STUDY OUTLINE

I. Introduction
    A. Civil rights issue
        1. Group is denied access to facilities, opportunities, or services available to other groups, usually along ethnic or racial lines
        2. Issue is whether differences in treatment are "reasonable"
            a) Some differences are: progressive taxes

b) Some are not: classification by race subject to "strict scrutiny"

II. The black predicament
  A. Historical context
    1. Stark experience of discrimination was long standing
    2. Tension in both the North and the South
    3. Lynchings shocked whites, but little was done
    4. Little public support for racial equality, integration, civil rights movement
  B. Progress depended on
    1. Finding more white allies or
    2. Shifting policy-making arenas
  C. Civil rights movement followed both strategies
    1. Broadened base by publicizing grievances
    2. Moved legal struggle from Congress to the courts

III. The campaign in the courts
  A. Ambiguities in the Fourteenth Amendment
    1. Broad interpretation: Constitution color-blind
    2. Narrow interpretation: equal legal rights
    3. Supreme court adopted narrow view in *Plessy* case
  B. "Separate but equal"
    1. NAACP campaign objectives in education through courts
      a) Obviously unequal schools
      b) Not so obviously unequal schools
      c) Separate schools inherently unequal
  C. Can separate schools be equal?
    1. Step 1: obvious inequalities
      a) Lloyd Gaines
      b) Ada Lois Sipuel
    2. Step 2: deciding that a separation creates inequality in less obvious cases
      a) Heman Sweatt
      b) George McLaurin
    3. Step 3: making separation inherently unequal; 1950 strategy to go for integration
    4. *Brown* v. *Board of Education* (1954)
      a) Implementation
        (1) Class action suit
        (2) All deliberate speed
      b) Collapse of resistance in the 1970s
    5. The rationale
      a) Detriment to pupils by creating sense of inferiority
      b) Social science used because intent of Fourteenth Amendment unclear; needed unanimous decision
    6. Desegregation versus integration
      a) Ambiguities of *Brown*
        (1) Unrestricted choice or integrated schools?
        (2) *De jure* or *de facto* segregation?
      b) 1968 rejection of "freedom of choice" plan settles matter; mixing
      c) *Charlotte-Mecklenburg*, 1971
        (1) Proof of intent to discriminate
        (2) One-race school creates presumption of intent
        (3) Remedies can include quotas, busing, redrawn lines
        (4) Every school not required to reflect racial composition of school system
      d) Some extensions to intercity busing

e) Busing remains controversial
(1) Some presidents oppose but still implement it
(2) Congress torn in two directions
f) 1992 decision allows busing to end if segregation caused by shifting housing patterns

IV. The campaign in Congress
A. Mobilization of opinion by dramatic event to get on agenda
1. Sit-ins and freedom rides
2. Martin Luther King, Jr.
3. From nonviolence to long, hot summers
B. Mixed results
1. Agenda-setting success
2. Coalition-building setbacks: methods seen as law breaking
C. Legislative politics
1. Opponents' defensive positions
a) Senate Judiciary Committee controlled by southern Democrats
b) House Rules Committee controlled by Howard Smith
c) Senate filibuster threat
d) President Kennedy reluctant
2. Four developments broke deadlock.
a) Change of public opinion
b) Violent white reactions of segregationists became media focus
c) Kennedy assassination
d) 1964 Democratic landslide
3. Five bills pass, 1957–1968
a) 1957, 1960, 1965: voting rights laws
b) 1968: housing discrimination law
4. 1964 civil rights bill: the high point—employment, public accommodations
a) Broad in scope, strong enforcement mechanisms
b) Johnson moves after Kennedy assassinated
c) Discharge petition, cloture invoked
5. Effects since 1964
a) Dramatic rise in black voting
b) Mood of Congress shifted to pro-civil rights; 1988 overturn of Reagan veto of bill that extended federal ban on discrimination in education
D. Racial profiling
1. Profiling refers to increased likelihood of being suspect because of race or ethnicity
2. May be reasonable if members of certain race are, in fact, more likely to commit crime
a) A profiling of young Middle Eastern men might very well have prevented 9/11 attacks
b) But such profiling would inconvenience innocent citizens and attract charges of "racism"

V. Women and equal rights
A. Critical difference from movement to expand the rights of African Americans
1. Laws claimed to protect women (Oregon workday limit)
2. Seneca Falls Convention (1848) and the right to vote
3. Congressional actions
a) Equal pay for equal work
b) Gender discrimination in employment
c) Gender discrimination and schools and universities receiving federal funds
d) Discrimination against pregnant women

B. Supreme Court's position altered after the 1970s
   1. Somewhere between reasonableness and strict-scrutiny standard
   2. Gender-based differences prohibited by courts
      a) Age of adulthood
      b) Drinking age
      c) Arbitrary employee height-weight requirements
      d) Mandatory pregnancy leaves
      e) Little League exclusion
      f) Jaycees exclusion
      g) Unequal retirement benefits
   3. Gender-based differences allowed by courts
      a) All-boy/all-girl schools
      b) Widows' property tax exemption
      c) Delayed promotions in Navy
      d) Statutory rape
   4. Women must be admitted to all-male, state-supported military colleges
C. The military
   1. *Rostker* v. *Goldberg* (1981): Congress may draft men only
   2. Secretary of Defense in 1993 allows women in air and sea combat
D. Sexual harassment
   1. Requesting sexual favors as condition for employment
      a) "*Quid pro quo*" rule
      b) Employer "strictly liable"
   2. Hostile or intimidating work environment
      a) Employer not strictly liable
      b) Employer can be at fault if "negligent"
   3. Almost no federal laws governing it
   4. Vague and inconsistent court and bureaucratic rules tell us what it is
E. Privacy and sex
   1. Police power traditionally extended to laws designated to promote public order and secure the safety and morals of the citizens
   2. The Supreme Court and the right to privacy
      a) 1965 case involving contraceptives and asserting "zones of privacy"
      b) *Roe* v. *Wade* announced a "right to privacy" encompassing a woman's decision whether or not to terminate a pregnancy
         (1) Subsequent controversies over when human life begins
         (2) "Right to life" and "pro-life" v. "right to choose" and "pro-choice"
      c) Congressional attempts to restrict and the Hyde Amendment
      d) Reaffirmation of *Roe* and extension, until the late 1980s
         (1) *Casey* decision (1992) and mandatory twenty-four hour waiting periods, parental consent and provision of information concerning alternatives to abortion
         (2) Decisions which struck down laws requiring married women to obtain consent of husband and forbidding so-called partial birth abortions
         (3) 1997 decision allowed buffer zones around abortion clinics

VI. Affirmative action
   A. Equality of results
      1. Racism and sexism overcome only by taking them into account in designing remedies
      2. Equal rights not enough; people need benefits
      3. Affirmative action should be used in hiring

B. Equality of opportunities
   1. Reverse discrimination to use race or sex as preferential treatment
   2. Laws should be color-blind and sex neutral
   3. Government should only eliminate barriers
C. Targets or quotas?
   1. Issue fought out in courts
      a) No clear direction in Supreme Court decisions
      b) Court is deeply divided; affected by conservative Reagan appointees
      c) Law is complex and confusing
         (1) *Bakke:* numerical minority quotas not permissible
         (2) But Court ruled otherwise in later cases
   2. Emerging standards for quotas and preference systems
      a) Must be "compelling" justification
      b) Must correct pattern of discrimination
      c) Must involve practices that discriminate
      d) Federal quotas are to be given deference
      e) Voluntary preference systems are easier to justify
      f) Not likely to apply to who gets laid off
   3. Congressional efforts to defend affirmative action not yet successful
   4. "Compensatory action" (helping minorities catch up) versus "preferential treatment" (giving minorities preference, applying quotas)
      a) Public supports former but not latter
      b) In line with American political culture
         (1) Support for individualism
         (2) Support for needy
   5. The *Adarand* decision
      a) A low bidder lost a contract because of a government policy favoring racial and ethnic minorities
      b) Court ruled any discrimination based on race must be subject to strict scrutiny
         (1) Must serve a compelling governmental interest
         (2) Must be narrowly tailored to serve that interest
   6. Affirmative action revisited
      a) 1996 California initiative and program at the University of Texas Law School
      b) University of Michigan cases (2003)
         (1) Some applicants given 20 bonus points (of 100 needed) for admission
         (2) Court ruled the policy was not narrowly tailored
         (3) On the other hand, the use of race as a plus factor served a compelling state interest

VII. Gays and the Constitution
A. Originally, state laws could ban homosexual activities
   1. Challenged in *Bowers* v. *Hardwick*
   2. Court ruled the right to privacy protected family, marriage or procreation
B. Court struck down amendment to Colorado state constitution prohibiting laws to protect persons based on their homosexual, lesbian or bisexual orientation
C. *Lawrence* v. *Texas* (2003)
   1. 5-4 decision which overturned Texas law banning sexual conduct between persons of the same sex
   2. Reversed the previous decision in *Bowers*

3. Law was largely irrelevant, but the Court's decision welcomed litigation regarding same sex marriage
    a) Massachusetts Supreme Judicial Court ruled gays and lesbians must be allowed to marry
    b) Mayor of San Francisco issued marriage licenses to gays in defiance of state law
    c) Polls show support for "civil unions"
    d) Constitutionality of the 1996 Defense of Marriage Act may be questioned

D. Private groups can, however, exclude homosexuals from their membership

KEY TERMS MATCH

Match the following terms and descriptions:

1. A legal distinction that the Supreme Court scrutinizes especially closely
2. Post-Civil War era when southern laws protected blacks' freedoms
3. Original litigant in *Roe* who, today, is an outspoken opponent of abortion
4. A Supreme Court decision upholding state-enforced racial segregation
5. The standard under which the Court once upheld racial segregation
6. A black interest group active primarily in the courts
7. A Supreme Court decision declaring segregated schools inherently unequal
8. Document signed by over 100 members of Congress complaining of "abuse of judicial power"
9. Segregation created by law
10. Segregation that exists but that was not created by law
11. A school integration plan mandating no particular racial balance
12. An early nonviolent leader in black civil rights
13. Offering the races an equal chance at desired things
14. Landmark case declaring gender discrimination violates the Equal Protection clause of the Fourteenth Amendment and asserting the reasonableness standard for such discrimination

a. affirmative action
b. aliens
c. *Bakke*
d. *Brown* v. *Board of Education*
e. buffer zone
f. civil rights
g. compensatory action
h. *de facto* segregation
i. *de jure* segregation
j. equality of opportunity
k. equality of results
l. freedom of choice
m. *Griswold* v. *Connecticut*
n. Hyde Amendment
o. *Lawrence v. Texas*
p. Martin Luther King, Jr.
q. NAACP
r. nonviolent civil disobedience
s. Norma McCorvey
t. NOW
u. *Plessy* v. *Ferguson*
v. preferential treatment
w. reasonableness
x. Reconstruction
y. *Reed* v. *Reed*
z. reverse discrimination

15. Distributing desired things equally to the races
16. The standard by which the Court judges gender-based classifications
17. A ruling that held that Congress may draft men but not women
18. A ruling that declared all state laws prohibiting abortion unconstitutional
19. Legislation that barred the use of federal funds for nearly any abortion
20. Declared state laws may not ban sexual relations between same sex partners
21. Landmark case in which the Court first found a "right to privacy" in the Constitution
22. A leading feminist organization
23. A philosophy of peaceful violation of laws considered unjust and accepting punishment for the violation
24. The standard by which the Supreme Court judges classifications based on race: they must have a compelling public purpose
25. The use of race or sex to give preferential treatment to blacks or women
26. Helping disadvantaged people catch up, usually by giving them extra education, training, or services
27. Device used, and upheld by the Court, to address concerns about protestors and abortion clinics
28. Giving minorities preference in hiring, promotions, college admissions, and contracts
29. Designing remedies for overcoming racism and sexism by taking race and sex into account
30. A Supreme Court ruling stating that a college may not use an explicit numerical quota in admitting minorities but could "take race into account"
31. Any persons who are not U.S. citizens

aa. *Roe* v. *Wade*

bb. *Rostker* v. *Goldberg*

cc. separate-but-equal doctrine

dd. Southern Manifesto

ee. strict scrutiny

ff. suspect classification

32. The rights of citizens to vote, receive equal treatment before the law, and share benefits of public facilities

DATA CHECK

Figure 6.1 (Page 133): Changing White Attitudes Toward Differing Levels of School Integration

1. Generalize about the percentage of respondents since 1958 who were willing to accept schools that were integrated with a "few blacks?"

____

2. Generalize about the percentage of respondents since 1958 who were accepting of schools that were integrated with a majority of black students.

____

Figure 6.2 (Page 136): Growing Support Among Southern Democrats in Congress for Civil Rights Bills

3. In which years did less than 25 percent of the Southern Democrats in the House and the Senate support Civil Rights legislation?

____

4. In which years did more than 50 percent of the Southern Democrats in the House and the Senate support Civil Rights legislation?

____

Table 6.1 (Page 136): Increase in Number of Black Elected Officials

5. Which category of elected officials has seen the sharpest increase in the number of black officeholders during the period covered by the table? The next sharpest increase?

____

6. The next sharpest increase?

____

7. In which category of elected officials has the number of black officeholders increased the *least*?

____

PRACTICING FOR EXAMS

TRUE/FALSE QUESTIONS

Read each statement carefully. Mark true statements *T*. If any part of the statement is false, mark it *F*, and write in the space provided a concise explanation of why the statement is false.

1. T F Historians have long debated the intentions of the Congress that proposed the Fourteenth Amendment.

____

2. T F In the 1940s, President Roosevelt approved the army's removal of Japanese Americans from their homes and their placement in "relocation centers."

____

3. T F Civil Rights violations occur when laws and policies make distinctions among people and treat them differently.

____

4. T F The series of test cases that led up to the Court's decision in *Brown* began in the late 1950s.

____

5. T F The Supreme Court's controversial ruling in *Brown* was a 5–4 decision.

____

6. T F *Brown* overruled the Court's previous decision in *Plessy*.

____

7. T F Over one hundred members of Congress signed a declaration that the Court's decision in *Brown* constituted an abuse of judicial power.

____

8. T F By the late 1950s, most southern schools were integrated.

____

9. T F *Brown* ruled the Equal Protection clause of the Fourteenth Amendment rendered the Constitution and state laws "color blind."

____

10. T F De facto segregation is unconstitutional.

____

11. T F Court ordered intercity busing is permissible if there is a demonstration of past discrimination.

____

12. T F The Supreme Court will not allow court-ordered intercity busing.

____

13. T F Recent polls suggest most Americans are supportive of busing.

____

14. T F Presidents Nixon, Ford and Reagan opposed busing.

____

15. T F Early demonstrations of civil disobedience eventually gave way to rioting and the rise of more militant civil rights organizations.

____

16. T F In 1964 and 1968, over two-thirds of whites told pollsters that they thought the civil rights movement was too violent.

____

17. T F John F. Kennedy submitted strong civil rights legislation to Congress, but it was consistently rejected by southern legislators in key leadership positions.

____

18. T F The 1964 Civil Rights Act was not considered by congressional committees.

____

19. T F The text suggests that, today, labeling a bill a civil rights measure almost guarantees its passage.

____

20. T F When Congress passed a law barring discrimination in housing, polls showed a majority of the public supported such a measure.

____

21. T F When an increase in arrests of crack cocaine dealers led to an increase in the arrests of African-American dealers, the Supreme Court found violations of civil rights.

____

22. T F The Court applies the strict scrutiny standard to gender discrimination cases.

____

23. T F Gender discrimination cases rarely reach the United States Supreme Court.

____

24. T F States cannot set different ages at which men and women are allowed to buy beer.

____

25. T F Girls can be barred from Little League baseball teams.

____

26. T F The Virginia Military Institute gender discrimination case came close to employing the strict scrutiny standard.

____

27. T F The Court tends to give little deference to congressional policy related to national defense.

28. T F Ground troop combat positions are reserved for male soldiers.

29. T F There are almost no federal laws governing sexual harassment.

30. T F The right to privacy is nowhere mentioned in the Constitution.

31. T F Constitutional amendments have been introduced to overturn *Roe*.

32. T F The Supreme Court began to uphold state restrictions on abortion in part because of the influence of justices appointed by President Carter.

33. T F The Court struck down a state law requiring that individuals who requested abortions be given pamphlets about alternatives.

34. T F Ironically, the original litigant in *Roe*, Norma McCorvey, has become an outspoken opponent of abortion.

35. T F Aliens cannot vote or run for office, but they must pay taxes.

36. T F Legally admitted aliens are entitled to welfare benefits.

37. T F States cannot bar aliens from serving on juries.

38. T F Affirmative action programs are just about always upheld by the Supreme Court.

39. T F Voluntary preference systems are easier to justify than affirmative action plans that are required by law.

40. T F A 1990 bill limited litigants in employment discrimination cases to back pay.

41. T F President Bush vetoed 1991 legislation which shifted the burden of proof from litigants to employers in employment discrimination cases.

42. T F Colorado's state constitutional amendment disallowing legal protections based on sexual orientation was upheld by the United States Supreme Court.

____

43. T F The Supreme Court's decision in *Lawrence* overruled its decision in *Bowers*.

____

44. T F Many states have passed laws that ban same sex marriages.

____

MULTIPLE CHOICE QUESTIONS

Circle the letter of the response that best answers the question or completes the statement.

1. When Congress, in 1883, passed a law that outlawed racial discrimination in public accommodations such as hotels,
   a. the president exercised the veto power.
   b. the Supreme Court declared the law unconstitutional.
   c. the state legislatures immediately passed similar laws.
   d. governors applauded the legislation as "progressive."
   e. none of the above.
2. The Supreme Court's decision in *Plessy* v. *Ferguson* (whatever its wider implications) directly concerned
   a. segregation on railroad cars.
   b. voting rights for blacks.
   c. interracial marriage.
   d. lynching.
   e. the ability of Congress to regulate race relations in the states.
3. The National Association for the Advancement of Colored People (NAACP) was founded
   a. immediately after the Civil War.
   b. in 1909, in the aftermath of a race riot.
   c. during the presidential election of 1968.
   d. during the Great Depression.
   e. in 1955, following the Montgomery bus boycott.
4. Which of the following statements about *Brown* v. *Board of Education* is *true*?
   a. It was handed down by a divided Court.
   b. It was ultimately rather narrow in its implications.
   c. It explicitly banned *de facto* segregation.
   d. It was almost unnoticed when it was decided.
   e. It was the logical extension of a long line of related cases.
5. In one dramatic test case leading up to *Brown*, the Court considered the case of Ada Sipuel who was
   a. admitted to an all-white law school.
   b. admitted to an all-white law school but relegated to a separate building.
   c. allowed to attend an all-white graduate school, but not allowed to use the library.
   d. separated from other law students by being roped off in a section of the state capitol.
   e. not even allowed to take a law school correspondence course.

6. The federal district court that first considered the case of Linda Brown in Topeka, Kansas concluded
   a. the separate but equal doctrine was unconstitutional.
   b. the separate but equal doctrine no longer applied to schools.
   c. the state could not separate her because the schools for blacks were not really equal.
   d. the state could separate her because the schools for blacks were equal.
   e. she had no standing because she could attend a private school.
7. *Brown* called for the desegregation of public schools
   a. "with all deliberate speed."
   b. as soon as the state legislatures could fund the enterprise.
   c. "in an acceptable amount of time."
   d. "immediately."
   e. immediately following the next school year.
8. In 1954, the Supreme Court ruled that segregation in public schools was "inherently unequal" on the basis of
   a. the fact that black children were not achieving success academically.
   b. the Equal Protection clause of the Fourteenth Amendment.
   c. apparent psychological harm done to black children in separate schools.
   d. inadequate expenditures on black education.
   e. a philosophical understanding of the essentials of equality.
9. According to the text, the authors of the Fourteenth Amendment
   a. intended to outlaw segregated schools in the Washington area.
   b. intended to outlaw segregated schools throughout the United States.
   c. may not have intended to outlaw segregated schools.
   d. were pleased four years later when a civil rights act proposed an end to segregated schools.
   e. thought desegregated schools would cure certain social ills.
10. Segregation maintained by law is labeled
    a. *prima facie*.
    b. *de facto*.
    c. statist.
    d. *de jure*.
    e. *post facto* suspect.
11. In the late 1960s, the Supreme Court rejected a so-called "freedom of choice" plan because
    a. *Brown* had explicitly ruled against such plans.
    b. too many children chose different schools under the plan.
    c. most students chose to stay in the same schools under the plan.
    d. school administrators were not actually allowing students to make a choice.
    e. few people could make up their minds easily about such decisions.
12. Among the remedies for past discrimination in school assignment, the Court will allow
    a. racial quotas in the assignment of teachers.
    b. racial quotas in the assignment of students.
    c. redrawn district lines.
    d. court-ordered busing.
    e. all of the above.

13. The text suggests ________ were at the "leading edge" of changes in attitudes toward integration of public schools.
    a. young, college educated people
    b. older, wealthy persons
    c. Southern legislators
    d. farmers and small business persons
    e. white females
14. The most prominent feature of the five civil rights laws passed between 1957 and 1968 is
    a. housing.
    b. voting.
    c. employment.
    d. education.
    e. public accommodations.
15. The most far reaching civil rights act was passed in
    a. 1957
    b. 1960
    c. 1964
    d. 1965
    e. 1968
16. The landmark 1964 civil rights legislation was passed, in large part, because
    a. President Kennedy supported a discharge petition.
    b. the Senate was dominated by Republicans.
    c. the House was dominated by Republicans.
    d. members of the Supreme Court expressed their support.
    e. consideration by committees was bypassed.
17. The text suggests the great change in the political status of women came with
    a. the Seneca Falls Convention.
    b. the passage of the Nineteenth Amendment.
    c. the need for workers in defense plants during World War II.
    d. the Equal Rights Amendments.
    e. the founding of the National Organization for Women.
18. The Court has generally used the ________________ standard in cases involving gender discrimination.
    a. "strict rationality"
    b. "strict scrutiny"
    c. "substantial relationship"
    d. "suspect"
    e. "reasonableness"
19. Which of the following gender discriminations have been *permitted* by the Supreme Court?
    a. A property tax exemption for widows that is not given to widowers.
    b. Barring girls from Little League baseball teams.
    c. Preference given to men in the appointment of administrators of estates.
    d. Different legal drinking ages for males and females.
    e. Mandatory pregnancy leaves for women.

20. According to the Supreme Court, differences based on sex are *permitted* for
    a. the age at which men and women are allowed to buy beer.
    b. the age at which men and women legally become adults.
    c. allowing women to remain officers longer than men without being promoted in the Navy.
    d. excluding girls from playing on Little League baseball teams.
    e. insisting women pay more for insurance benefits because, on average, they live longer.
21. The Court's 1996 ruling on gender discrimination at the Virginia Military Institute was especially important because
    a. the Court upheld VMI's right to engage in such discrimination.
    b. the Court came close to using the strict scrutiny standard.
    c. the Court upheld VMI's so-called "adversarial method" of training.
    d. the Court ignored the sources of VMI's financial support.
    e. VMI refused to even offer a course at another college.
22. In the 1981 case, *Rostker* v. *Goldberg*, the Court allowed gender discrimination with respect to
    a. draft registration.
    b. vehicle insurance.
    c. nursing schools.
    d. health insurance payments.
    e. the hiring of prison guards.
23. Under the "*quid pro quo*" rule pertaining to sexual harassment
    a. the employer is "strictly liable" even if he/she did not know that sexual harassment was occurring.
    b. the employer cannot be held liable if he/she did not know that sexual harassment was occurring.
    c. an employer is never liable for the sexual harassment of an employee.
    d. a pattern of sexual harassment must be proven before the employer is liable.
    e. the employer is liable but not the employee in sexual harassment cases.
24. The Supreme Court first changed its practice of deference to state police power as it related to the safety and morals of citizens in a case that involved
    a. contraceptives.
    b. nude pictures.
    c. marriage laws.
    d. abortion.
    e. obscenity.
25. The Court has concluded the right of "privacy" can be inferred from _____ cast off by various provisions of the Bill of Rights.
    a. colors
    b. rays of light
    c. firewalls
    d. penumbras
    e. waves
26. *Roe* v. *Wade* held that the state may regulate abortions to protect the health of the mother
    a. in the first trimester.
    b. in the second trimester.
    c. in the third trimester.
    d. at any point in the pregnancy.
    e. in cases involving rape or incest.

27. *Roe* v. *Wade* held that the state may ban abortions
    a. in the first trimester.
    b. in the second trimester.
    c. in the third trimester.
    d. at any point in the pregnancy.
    e. in cases involving rape or incest.
28. The so-called Hyde Amendment
    a. restricts the use of federal funds for abortions.
    b. was upheld by the United States Supreme Court.
    c. has resulted in the denial of Medicaid funds for abortions for low-income women.
    d. all of the above.
    e. was declared unconstitutional by the United States Supreme Court.
29. Which of the following is *not* a statutory qualification for citizenship in the United States?
    a. Good moral character.
    b. Continuous residency since the filing of a petition.
    c. Favorable disposition to the good order and happiness of the United States.
    d. Attachment to constitutional principles.
    e. Employment.
30. The position that the Constitution neither is nor should be color-blind is taken by those who advocate
    a. equality of results.
    b. the incorporation of the Bill of Rights.
    c. the abolition of affirmative action.
    d. freedom-of-education plans.
    e. equal opportunity.
31. In the *Bakke* case the Supreme Court held that a university medical school, in admitting students, may
    a. use quotas for blacks and whites.
    b. use quotas for men, but not women.
    c. use quotas for men and women.
    d. take gender into account.
    e. take race into account.
32. Among the standards that appear to be emerging in the Supreme Court's rulings on quota systems and preference systems are all of the following *except*
    a. such systems must correct a present or past pattern of discrimination.
    b. those systems involving hiring practices are more defensible than those involving layoffs.
    c. those systems created by state law will be given deference to those created by federal law.
    d. there must be compelling justification for such systems.
    e. such systems should be flexible and limited in scope.
33. In the highly publicized cases involving affirmative action programs at the University of Michigan (2003), the Court struck down the use of a ________ but was sympathetic to the use of a so-called ______.
    a. quota … goal
    b. goal … quota
    c. quota guideline … bonus points
    d. racial label … ethnic categorization
    e. fixed quota … plus factor

34. In a 2000 case, the Supreme Court ruled by a vote of 5–4 that the ___________ could prevent gay boys and men from being members.
    a. American Civil Liberties Union
    b. Boy Scouts of America
    c. American Bar Association
    d. Lion's Club
    e. International Brotherhood of Electrical Workers

ESSAY QUESTIONS

Practice writing extended answers to the following questions. These test your ability to integrate and express the ideas that you have been studying in this chapter.

1. Summarize the facts of the case in *Plessy* v. *Ferguson* and the Supreme Court's ruling.
2. Describe some of the test cases that were brought to the Supreme Court leading up to *Brown* v. *Board of Education.*
3. Explain why the rationale of the decision in *Brown* was so unusual and why the Court used that rationale, as opposed to others?
4. Summarize the guidelines for school segregation cases as settled by *Swann* v. *Charlotte-Mecklenburg Board of Education.*
5. What four developments made it possible to break the deadlock in Congress regarding significant civil rights legislation?
6. Identify five provisions of the 1964 Civil Rights Act.
7. Explain the difference between the reasonableness standard and the strict scrutiny standard.
8. Note 6-7 examples of gender discriminations which the Supreme Court has allowed/disallowed under its current interpretation of the law.
9. Explain the two forms of sexual harassment identified by the EEOC and the standards of liability that attend each.
10. Explain the trimester framework asserted in *Roe* v. *Wade* and how the right to privacy was read into the Constitution.
11. Identify some additional regulations and restrictions regarding abortion which have been upheld by the Supreme Court in the aftermath of *Roe*.
12. Identify the five statutory requirements for naturalization.
13. While the Supreme Court's decisions regarding affirmative action are almost evenly divided, a few general standards seem to be emerging. Identify 4-5 of those standards.
14. Summarize the Court's decisions in *Bowers* and *Lawrence*.

ANSWERS TO KEY TERMS MATCH QUESTIONS

1. ff
2. x
3. s
4. u
5. cc
6. q
7. d
8. dd
9. i
10. h
11. l
12. p
13. j
14. y
15. k
16. w
17. bb
18. aa
19. n
20. o
21. m
22. t
23. r
24. ee
25. z
26. g
27. e
28. v
29. a
30. c
31. b
32. f

ANSWERS TO DATA CHECK QUESTIONS

1. The percentage was near 80 and, soon thereafter, rose above that mark.
2. The percentage increases across time, but never seems to rise above 50 percent.
3. 1957, 1960, 1964, 1968.
4. 1965, 1970, 1988, 1991.
5. City and county officials.
6. Boards of education.
7. Congress and state legislatures.

ANSWERS TO TRUE/FALSE QUESTIONS

1. T
2. T
3. F Such violations do not occur when distinctions are being made, but when unreasonable distinctions are being made.
4. F The cases began in the late 1930s.
5. F The vote in the decision was unanimous, 9-0.
6. T
7. T
8. F Most were not integrated until the 1970s.
9. F *Brown* did not rule in this manner because some of the justices did not agree with this position.
10. F *De jure* (or intentional) segregation is illegal.
11. T
12. F The Court will allow such busing if segregation is determined to exist in a central city and suburbs.
13. F The public has generally had an unfavorable view of busing.
14. T
15. T
16. T
17. F Kennedy was reluctant to submit a strong civil rights bill.
18. T
19. T
20. F Only 35 percent supported it.
21. F The Court found no such violation.
22. F The Court applies the reasonableness standard to gender discrimination cases.
23. F Several dozen gender discrimination cases have reached the court.

24. T
25. F Girls cannot be barred from little league baseball teams.
26. T
27. F The Court generally gives great deference to congressional policy in matter related to national defense.
28. T
29. T
30. T
31. T
32. F It was the justices who were appointed by Reagan which encouraged this change.
33. F The Court upheld this law.
34. T
35. T
36. T
37. F States can bar aliens from serving on juries.
38. F The Court has upheld about as many as it has struck down.
39. T
40. F The bill allows for the collection of large damages awards.
41. F He signed the legislation.
42. F The Court declared the amendment unconstitutional.
43. T
44. T

ANSWERS TO MULTIPLE CHOICE QUESTIONS

1. b
2. a
3. b
4. e
5. d
6. a
7. a
8. c
9. c
10. d
11. c
12. e

13. a
14. b
15. c
16. e
17. c
18. e
19. a
20. c
21. b
22. a
23. a
24. a
25. d
26. b
27. c
28. d
29. e
30. a
31. e
32. c
33. e
34. b

PART 1

Classic Statement: *Federalist* No. 39 [1]

INTRODUCTION

The article presented here was written by James Madison to address two questions: first, whether the form of government being proposed in the Constitution was strictly a republican one, and second, whether it was in addition a federal form of government that would preserve the nature of the union between the states that had existed until then.

You will note that his answer to the first question is strongly affirmative, whereas he responds to the second one in a rather more complex fashion.

TO THE PEOPLE OF THE STATE OF NEW YORK:

. . . The first question that offers itself is, whether the general form and aspect of the government be strictly republican. It is evident that no other form would be reconcilable with the genius of the people of America; with the fundamental principles of the revolution; or with that honorable determination which animates every votary of freedom. . . .

What, then, are the distinctive characters of the republican form? . . .

If we resort for a criterion to the different principles on which different forms of government are established, we may define a republic to be, or at least may bestow that name on, a government which derives all its powers directly or indirectly from the great body of the people, and is administered by persons holding their offices during pleasure, for a limited period, or during good behavior. It is *essential* to such a government that it be derived from the great body of the society, not from an inconsiderable proportion, or a favored class of it; otherwise a handful of tyrannical nobles, exercising their oppressions by a delegation of their powers, might aspire to the rank of republicans, and claim for their government the honorable title of republic. It is *sufficient* for such a government that the persons administering it be appointed, either directly or indirectly, by the people; and that they hold their appointments by either of the tenures just specified; otherwise every government that has been or can be well organized or well executed, would be degraded from the republican character. . . .

On comparing the Constitution planned by the convention with the standard here fixed, we perceive at once that it is, in the most rigid sense, conformable to it. The House of Representatives, like that of one branch at least of all the State legislatures, is elected immediately by the great body of the people. The Senate, like the present Congress, and the Senate of Maryland, derives its appointment indirectly from

---

[1] The *Federalist*, sometimes referred to as the Federalist papers, is a series of articles written by Alexander Hamilton, John Jay, and James Madison and addressed to the citizens of New York at the time that the Constitution was being considered for ratification. Because these articles were composed by some of the leading authors of the Constitution, they are widely regarded as an authoritative interpretation of the Constitution and one that spells out in much greater detail the intentions of the authors than is the case with the very brief Constitution itself. A collection of these articles from which the present one is excerpted can be found in the publication of the same name by the Modern Library (New York: Random House, 1941).

the people. The President is indirectly derived from the choice of the people, according to the example in most of the States. Even the judges with all other officers of the Union, will, as in the several States, be the choice, though a remote choice, of the people themselves. The duration of the appointments is equally conformable to the republican standard, and to the model of State constitutions. The House of Representatives is periodically elective, as in all the States; and for the period of two years. . . . The Senate is elective, for the period of six years. . . . The President is to continue in office for the period of four years. . . . In the other States the election is annual. In several of the States, however, no constitutional provision is made for the impeachment of the chief magistrate. . . . The President of the United States is impeachable at any time during his continuance in office. The tenure by which the judges are to hold their places, is, as it unquestionably ought to be, that of good behavior. The tenure of the ministerial offices generally, will be a subject of legal regulation, conformable to the reason of the case and the example of the State constitutions.

Could any further proof be required of the republican complexion of this system, the most decisive one might be found in its absolute prohibition of titles of nobility, both under the federal and the State governments; and in its express guaranty of the republican form to each of the latter.

"But it was not sufficient," say the adversaries of the proposed Constitutions, "for the convention to adhere to the republican form. They ought, with equal care, to have preserved the *federal* form, which regards the Union as a *Confederacy* of sovereign states; instead of which, they have framed a *national* government, which regards the Union as a *consolidation* of the States." And it is asked by which authority this bold and radical innovation was undertaken? The handle which has been made of this objection requires that it should be examined with some precision.

. . . It appears, on one hand, that the Constitution is to be founded on the assent and ratification of the people of America, given by deputies elected for the special purpose; but, on the other, that this assent and ratification is to be given by the people, not as individuals composing one entire nation, but as composing the distinct and independent States to which they respectively belong. It is to be the assent and ratification of the several States, derived from the supreme authority in each State—the authority of the people themselves. The act, therefore, establishing the Constitution, will not be a *national,* but a *federal* act.

. . . It must result from the *unanimous* assent of the several States that are parties to it, differing no otherwise from their ordinary assent than in its being expressed, not by the legislative authority, but by that of the people themselves. . . . Each State, in ratifying the Constitution, is considered as a sovereign body, independent of all others, and only to be bound by its own voluntary act. In this relation, then, the new Constitution will, if established, be a *federal,* and not a *national* constitution.

The next relation is, to the sources from which the ordinary powers of government are to be derived. The House of Representatives will derive its powers from the people of America; and the people will be represented in the same proportion, and on the same principle, as they are in the legislature of a particular State. So far the government is *national,* not *federal.* The Senate, on the other hand, will derive its powers from the States, as political and coequal societies; and these will be represented on the principle of equality in the Senate, as they now are in the existing Congress. So far the government is *federal,* not *national.* The executive power will be derived from a very compound source. The immediate election of the President is to be made by the States in their political characters. The votes allotted to them are in a compound ratio, which considers them partly as distinct and coequal societies, partly as unequal members of the same society. The eventual election, again, is to be made by that branch of the legislature which consists of the national representatives; but in this particular act they are to be thrown into the form of individual delegations, from so many distinct and coequal bodies politic. From this aspect of the government, it appears to be of a mixed character, presenting at least as many *federal* as *national* features.

The difference between a federal and national government, as it relates to the *operation of the government,* is supposed to consist in this, that in the former the powers operate on the political bodies composing the Confederacy, in their political capacities; in the latter, on the individual citizens composing the nation, in their individual capacities. On trying the Constitution by this criterion, it falls under the *national,* not the *federal* character; though perhaps not so completely as has been understood. . . .

But if the government be national with regard to the *operation* of its powers, it changes its aspect again when we contemplate it in relation to the extent of its powers. The idea of a national government involves in it, not only an authority over the individual citizens, but an indefinite supremacy over all persons and things, so far as they are objects of lawful government. Among a people consolidated into one nation, this supremacy is completely vested in the national legislature. Among communities united for particular purposes, it is vested partly in the general and partly in the municipal legislatures. In the former case, all local authorities are subordinate to the supreme; and may be controlled, directed, or abolished by it at pleasure. In the latter, the local or municipal authorities form distinct and independent portions of the supremacy, no more subject, within their respective spheres, to the general authority, than the general authority is subject to them, within its own sphere. In this relation, then, the proposed government cannot be deemed a *national* one; since its jurisdiction extends to certain enumerated objects only, and leaves to the several States a residuary and inviolable sovereignty over all other objects. . . .

If we try the Constitution by its last relation to the authority by which amendments are to be made, we find it neither wholly *ational* nor wholly . Were it wholly national, the supreme and ultimate authority would reside in the *majority* of the people of the Union; and this authority would be competent at all times, like that of a majority of every national society, to alter or abolish its established government. Were it wholly federal, on the other hand, the concurrence of each State in the Union would be essential to every alteration that would be binding on all. The mode provided by the plan of the convention is not founded on either of these principles. In requiring more than a majority, and particularly in computing the proportion by *States,* not by *citizens,* it departs from the *national* and advances towards the *federal* character; in rendering the concurrence of less than the whole number of States sufficient, it loses again the *federal* and partakes of the *national* character.

The proposed Constitution, therefore, is, in strictness, neither a national nor a federal Constitution, but a composition of both. In its foundation it is federal, not national; in the sources from which the ordinary powers of the government are drawn, it is partly federal and partly national; in the operation of these powers, it is national, not federal; in the extent of them, again, it is federal, not national; and, finally, in the authoritative mode of introducing amendments, it is neither wholly federal nor wholly national.

PUBLIUS

QUESTIONS FOR UNDERSTANDING AND DISCUSSION

1. Why, according to Madison, is it altogether necessary that the new government be republican in nature?
2. What would be the difference, in his thinking, between a federal and a national government?
3. Using this distinction, how does Madison describe the following?
    a. the proposed act of establishing a constitution
    b. the composition of Congress and the executive branch
    c. the operation of governmental powers

d. the extent of those governmental powers

e. the process of amending the Constitution

4. He concludes that the proposed constitution is neither federal nor national but a mixture. How do you think the Constitution might have been different if the authors had decided simply on each of the following?

   a. a national government

   b. a federal government

PART II: Opinions, Interests, and Organizations

CHAPTER 7

Public Opinion

REVIEWING THE CHAPTER

CHAPTER FOCUS

The purpose of this chapter is to explore what we mean by *public opinion* and to ask what sorts of effects public opinion has on our supposedly democratic form of government. After reading and reviewing the material in this chapter, you should be able to do each of the following:

1. List the sources of our political attitudes, and indicate which are the most important ones. Assess the influence of various religious traditions on political attitudes.
2. Explain why there is no single cleavage between liberals and conservatives in this country and why there are crosscutting cleavages. Explain the significance of these facts. Assess the significance of race in explaining political attitudes.
3. Define *political ideology* and state why most Americans do not think ideologically. Summarize the liberal positions on the economy, civil rights, and political conduct. Describe the major policy packages in the Democratic Party, and indicate which groups in the Democratic coalition can be identified with each package.
4. Identify which elite groups have become liberal, and compare their current attitudes with the past political preferences of these groups. Discuss the "new class" theory as an explanation for changes in attitudes. Analyze why these changes are causing strain in the political party system.

STUDY OUTLINE

I. Introduction
    A. Lincoln and the Gettysburg Address … "of the people, by the people, for the people"
        1. Yet the federal government's budget is not balanced
        2. Yet the people have opposed busing
        3. Yet the ERA was not ratified
        4. Yet most Americans favor term limits for Congress
    B. Why government policy and public opinion may appear to be at odds
        1. Government not intended to do "what the people want"
            a) Framers of Constitution aimed for substantive goals
            b) Popular rule was only one of several means toward these goals
            c) Large nations feature many "publics" with many "opinions"
                (1) Framers hoped no single opinion would dominate
                (2) Reasonable policies can command support of many factions
        2. Limits on effectiveness of opinion polling; difficult to know public opinion
II. What is public opinion?
    A. Influences and limitations
        1. Position taking on nonexistent legislation, contradictory opinions and inexplicable shifts

2. Political scientists and polling
   a) 1940s: only a small group of citizens appeared to be informed
   b) Later studies: many use limited information (cues) to support candidates, parties and policies that reflect their own personal values

B. How polling works
   1. Sampling techniques
   2. Sampling error
   3. High accuracy rates—in presidential elections

C. How opinions differ
   1. Saliency: some opinions matter more than others
   2. Stability: some opinions are more volatile than others
   3. Policy congruence: some opinions are reflected in government policy more closely than others
   4. Additional observations
      a) Political socialization matters
      b) Elite and mass opinion differ

III. Political socialization

A. The family
   1. Child absorbs party identification of family but becomes more independent with age
   2. Much continuity between generations
   3. Declining ability to pass on identification
      a) Younger voters exhibit less partisanship; more likely to be independent
      b) Meaning of partisanship unclear in most families; less influence on policy preferences
      c) Age related differences in opinions on issues (gay marriage, women's rights, vouchers, etc.)
      d) Few families pass on clear ideologies

B. Religion
   1. Religious traditions affect families
      a) Catholic families somewhat more liberal
      b) Protestant families more conservative
      c) Jewish families decidedly more liberal
   2. Two theories on differences
      a) Social status of religious group
      b) Content of religion's tradition

C. The gender gap
   1. Journalists note women have "deserted" Republican candidates
      a) It would be more correct to say men have "deserted" Democratic candidates
      b) Difference ("gap") in the political views of men and women has existed for a long time
      c) Presents problems for both parties
   2. Females and voting
      a) Turnout
         (1) Right to vote obtained in 1920, Nineteenth Amendment
         (2) Low turnout rate until 1980
      b) Vote choice
         (1) More likely to favor Democratic candidates
         (2) Leaning also evident in mid-term congressional elections
         (3) Reflection of differences in stances on issues
            (a) Banning handguns
            (b) Increased spending on anti-poverty programs

(c) Limiting defense spending
(d) "Issue importance" rankings

D. Schooling and information
1. Much research links college education to liberal attitudes
2. Relationship was especially strong for students at high prestige institutions
3. Increased schooling also correlated with higher levels of voting and political participation
4. Generalizations less applicable today
a) Some evidence to suggest college students are more conservative than they used to be
(1) Concerns about "political correctness"
(2) Conservative students more vocal on campus
(3) Increase in enrollment of religious colleges and universities
b) Political participation among young people is down
c) Decline in reading of newspapers and newsmagazines

IV. Cleavages in public opinion
A. Social class: less important in United States than in Europe
1. More important in 1950s on unemployment, education, housing programs
2. Less important in 1960s on poverty, health insurance, Vietnam, jobs
3. Why the change?
a) Education: occupation depends more on schooling
b) Noneconomic issues now define liberal and conservative

B. Race and ethnicity
1. African Americans: voting patterns and positions on issues
a) African Americans are overwhelmingly Democratic
(1) Younger African Americans are more likely than older ones to identify with the Republican Party
(2) Younger African Americans more likely than older ones to support school vouchers
b) Sharp differences between attitudes of whites and African Americans on public policies
(1) Blacks more likely to support affirmative action
(2) Blacks more likely to think the criminal justice system is biased against them
(3) Blacks more likely to oppose use of military force and less likely to think we should all be willing to fight for our country
(4) Blacks less likely to think believing in God is essential for a person to be moral
c) Areas of agreement
(1) Getting tough on crime
(2) Abortion
(3) Dependency on governmental aid
(4) The power to succeed
2. Latinos and Asians
a) Latinos are the largest minority in America, but there are few studies of their opinions
(1) More likely to be Democrat, although not as much as African Americans
(2) Somewhat more liberal than whites or Asian Americans, although not as liberal as African Americans
(a) Favor big government
(b) Think the Democratic Party cares more about them

(3) Those from Mexico are more Democrat, those from Cuba are more Republican, those from Puerto Rico somewhere in between
(4) Hispanics in Texas are more conservative than Hispanics in California
(5) Differences between native-born and foreign born ones

b) Asians
(1) Asian Americans identify more strongly with the Republican Party than whites
(2) Views on military and welfare programs, prayer in schools, and the death penalty are more similar to those of whites than those of blacks or Hispanics
(3) Japanese Americans are more conservative whereas Korean Americans are more liberal

C. Region
1. Southerners are more conservative than northerners on military and civil rights issues but differences are fading overall
2. Southern lifestyle different
3. Lessening attachment to Democratic Party

V. Political ideology
A. Consistent attitudes
1. Ideology: patterned set of political beliefs about who ought to rule, their principles and policies
2. Measuring ideology
a) Self-identification
b) Searching for "constraint"
3. Recent surveys
a) Moderates are the largest group among Americans
b) Conservatives are second, liberals are the smallest group

B. Concerns about self-identification in surveys
1. Most Americans do not use the words liberal and conservative on their own and many do not have a clear idea of what they mean
2. Inconsistency can be cause by a variety of factors
a) Nature of a problem may have changed
b) Wording of questions may have changed
c) People may have contradictory preferences
3. Some respondents will hide their ideology

C. Mass ideologies: a typology
1. Increasingly, searching for "constraint" is preferred
2. Nine different groups identified by certain key values in one popular survey
a) Liberals and "disadvantaged Democrats" constitute one in three voters and over one quarter of the general public
b) Conservatives and Republican "enterprisers" comprise nearly one in two registered voters and over 40 percent of the general population
c) One in five Americans are "disaffected" or "bystanders"

D. Political elites
1. Definition: those who have a disproportionate amount of some valued resource
2. Elites, or activists, display greater ideological consistency
a) More information than most people
b) Peers reinforce consistency and greater differences of opinion than one finds among average voters
3. Greater ideological consistency of elites can be seen in Congress
a) Democratic members tend to be consistently liberal

b) Republican members tend to be consistently conservative

VI. Political elites, public opinion, and public policy
  A. Elites influence public opinion in three ways
    1. Raise and form political issues
    2. State norms by which to settle issues, defining policy options
    3. Elite views shape mass views
  B. Limits to elite influence on the public
    1. Elites do not define problems
    2. Many elites exist; hence many elite opinions

KEY TERMS MATCH

Match the following terms and descriptions:

1. The political party for which one or one's family usually votes
2. Differences in political views between men and women
3. Differences in political preferences based on more than one variable
4. Term to describe the children of parents who participated in radical movements of the 1960s
5. A coherent and consistent set of beliefs about who ought to rule, what principles rulers should obey, and what policies they ought to pursue
6. People who have a disproportionate amount of political power
7. Researcher who found differences in political opinion were closely associated with occupation in the 1950s
8. Process by which personal and other background traits influence one's views about politics and government
9. Features interviews with voters on election day in a representative sample of districts
10. A standard of right or proper conduct that helps determine the range of acceptable social behavior and policy options
11. Refers to the degree to which a person's opinions are consistent across time, or from one issue to the next at any given point in time

a. crosscutting cleavages
b. exit polling
c. gender gap
d. Barry Goldwater
e. ideological constraint
f. V.O. Key
g. norm
h. party identification
i. political elites
j. political ideology
k. political socialization
l. poll
m. random sample
n. red diaper babies
o. sampling error

12. A survey of public opinion
13. The first major U.S. politician to refer to himself as a "conservative"
14. A sample selected in such a way that any member of the population being surveyed has an equal chance of being interviewed
15. The difference between the results of two surveys or samples

DATA CHECK

Figure 7.1 (Page 157): Opinions Voiced by College Students (2006)

1. What percentage of college students were of the opinion that we should begin to withdraw from Iraq?

____

2. What opinions did these college students express with respect to religion and the moral direction of the country?

____

3. Who would win the votes of college students in a presidential race between Republican John McCain and Democrat Hillary Clinton?

____

Table 7.1 (Page 158): Opinion on School Prayer, By Religion

4. What percentage of the general public strongly agrees with the position that prayer in schools violates the Constitution?

____

5. The majority of which religious group strongly agrees with the position that prayer in schools violates the Constitution?

____

6. How does the American public feel about having a "moment of silence" in schools?

____

Figure 7.2 (Page 159): Gender Gaps on Issue Importance (2006)

7. Who was more likely to see the war in Iraq as an issue of importance, men or women?

____

8. Who was more likely to see Social Security as an issue of importance, men or women?

____

9. Where is the largest gap for issue importance between men and women?

____

Table 7.2 (Page 165): Ideology Typology: Nine Groups and Their Key Values

10. What percentage of registered voters is categorized as "liberals?"

____

11. What percentage of registered voters is some form of "conservative?"

____

Figure 7.3 (Page 167): Policy Preferences Among Registered Voters (2006)

12. Which party's members appear to be closer to the views of all registered voters on the topic of allowing gays and lesbians to marry legally?

____

13. Which party's members are more likely to describe themselves as "conservative Christians?

____

14. Which party's members appear to be closer to the opinions of all registered voters on the topic of whether or not we should have used military force against Iraq?

____

PRACTICING FOR EXAMS

TRUE/FALSE QUESTIONS

Read each statement carefully. Mark true statements *T.* If any part of the statement is false, mark it *F,* and write in the space provided a concise explanation of why the statement is false.

1. T F The public supported the Equal Rights Amendment, but it was not ratified.

____

2. T F The Framers of the Constitution did not try to create a government that would do from day to day "what the people want."

____

3. T F Studies of public opinion in the 1940s found most citizens had high levels of knowledge about government and policy.

____

4. T F Since 1952, the major polls have a modest record with respect to predicting the winner in presidential elections.

____

5. T F The majority of young people identify with their parents' political party.

6. T F The proportion of citizens who consider themselves Democrats or Republicans has steadily increased since the 1950s.

7. T F Younger voters have a weaker sense of partisanship than older ones.

8. T F "Red-diaper babies" are the sons and daughters of 1950s conservatives.

9. T F Studies suggest religious influences on public opinion are most pronounced with respect to economic issues.

10. T F The gender gap is a recent phenomenon in American politics.

11. T F The gender gap is not evident in midterm elections.

12. T F Women are much more likely than men to think that all handguns should be banned.

13. T F Today, there is evidence to suggest that college students are more conservative than they were twenty years ago.

14. T F Today's college students are much more likely to read newspapers and magazines.

15. T F Most blue-collar workers in Great Britain think of themselves as "middle class."

16. T F In the United States, public opinion is less divided by class than it is in Europe.

17. T F Class voting has declined in France, Great Britain and Germany since the 1940s.

18. T F African Americans are overwhelmingly Democrats.

19. T F Asian Americans tend to identify with the Republican Party.

20. T F Korean Americans appear to be more liberal than Japanese Americans.

21. T F Latinos from Mexico are more likely to be Democratic than those from Cuba.

____

22. T F The South has, on the whole, been less accommodating to business enterprises than other regions.

____

23. T F Ronald Reagan was the first presidential candidate to declare himself a "conservative."

____

24. T F Clinton won the presidency in 1992 and 1996 without carrying the South.

____

25. T F The better informed people are about politics and the more interest they take in it, the less likely they are to have consistently liberal or conservative views.

____

26. T F Delegates to presidential nominating conventions tend to be more ideological than the average voter.

____

27. T F According to the text, elites do not define economic problems.

____

MULTIPLE CHOICE QUESTIONS

Circle the letter of the response that best answers the question or completes the statement.

1. Which of the following goals is *not* listed in the Preamble to the Constitution?
   a. Justice.
   b. Domestic tranquility.
   c. The common defense.
   d. Equality.
   e. The general welfare.
2. Which of the following was intended to serve as a check on public opinion?
   a. Representative government.
   b. Federalism.
   c. Separation of powers.
   d. An independent judiciary.
   e. All of the above.
3. The Framers of the Constitution understood that ________ would be the chief source of opinion on most matters.
   a. the general public
   b. elected representatives
   c. factions and interest groups
   d. political theorists and educators
   e. intellectuals

4. The classic research on the Monetary Control Bill suggests we should be cautious in how we think about polling results because, in some instances, respondents will
   a. support measures that are only beneficial to them.
   b. express opinions about things that do not even exist.
   c. favor state over federal legislation.
   d. not answer questions that they feel are "threatening."
   e. share their opinions, but only if they are positive.
5. A properly conducted poll of 250 million people can capture "public opinion" with as few as _________ of them.
   a. 1,500
   b. 2,000
   c. 3,000
   d. 4,500
   e. 5,000
6. Research indicates over half of children identify with the partisan preferences of at least one of their parents by the time they are
   a. in the first grade.
   b. in the fifth grade.
   c. juniors in high school.
   d. seniors in high school.
   e. high school graduates.
7. In adulthood, people whose party identification differs from their parents' usually call themselves
   a. radicals.
   b. independents.
   c. neo-institutionalists.
   d. conservatives.
   e. Democrats.
8. In recent years the influence of the family on party identification has
   a. decreased.
   b. increased.
   c. remained the same.
   d. disappeared.
   e. become too complex to study.
9. Younger Americans are more likely than older Americans to support
   a. gay marriage.
   b. vouchers for private or religious schools.
   c. women's rights.
   d. letting citizens invest some of their Social Security contributions in the stock market.
   e. all of the above.
10. The transfer of political beliefs from generation to generation does not appear in large national studies of political attitudes because
    a. most Americans are quite conservative.
    b. few Americans are either far left or far right of the political spectrum.
    c. polling techniques change radically from one generation to the next.
    d. most Americans are quite liberal.
    e. some generations participate in polls more than others.

11. The "gender gap" refers to the tendency of female voters to __________ in recent elections.
    a. support Democratic candidates
    b. vote Republican
    c. support Independent candidates
    d. refrain from voting
    e. contribute more money
12. The authors suggest the most plausible explanation for the "gender gap" is
    a. the alignment of the policy views of the Democratic party with female voters.
    b. recent efforts by Republicans to attract female voters.
    c. a series of Supreme Court nominations which have alienated female voters.
    d. the lack of support for equal rights in Congress.
    e. the fact that men have "deserted" the Democratic party.
13. Which of the following statements regarding the voting behavior of males and females since 1980 is *correct*?
    a. They have voted at about the same rate.
    b. Females have voted at a somewhat higher rate.
    c. Males have voted at a somewhat higher rate.
    d. Males have voted much at much higher rates than females.
    e. None of the above.
14. There is much research which indicates attending college tends to make people more __________ than the general population.
    a. moderate
    b. conservative
    c. Democratic
    d. Republican
    e. liberal
15. Students attending more prestigious or selective colleges are more __________ than the general population.
    a. liberal
    b. conservative
    c. Democratic
    d. Republican
    e. moderate
16. The political liberalizing effects of college among older Americans were probably attributable to the fact that yesteryear's college graduates
    a. had lower rates of political participation.
    b. watched television.
    c. read newspapers and news magazines.
    d. were influenced by Vietnam and Watergate.
    e. listened to talk radio.
17. In a classic study by V.O. Key in the 1950s, differences in political opinion were closely associated with
    a. occupation.
    b. race.
    c. gender.
    d. ethnicity.
    e. education levels.

18. When political scientists see how accurately they can predict a person's view on one issue based on views on a different issue, then the focus is on
    a. "constraint."
    b. "salience."
    c. "congruence."
    d. "linearity."
    e. "robustness."
19. In a typical ideological self-identification survey, the largest group of Americans will
    a. classify themselves as liberal.
    b. classify themselves as conservative.
    c. classify themselves as moderate.
    d. refuse to classify themselves in any manner.
    e. none of the above.
20. In a typical ideological self-identification survey, the smallest group of Americans will
    a. classify themselves as liberal.
    b. classify themselves as conservative.
    c. classify themselves as moderate.
    d. refuse to classify themselves in any manner.
    e. none of the above.
21. The terms liberal and conservative are ______ political elites.
    a. irrelevant to
    b. somewhat irrelevant to
    c. avoided by
    d. very meaningful for
    e. consistently misunderstood by
22. Which group displays the most consistency in political attitudes?
    a. Average citizens.
    b. Political activists.
    c. Females.
    d. Blacks.
    e. Manual workers.
23. The rate at which governments adopt policies supported by majorities in polls
    a. has increased dramatically.
    b. has increased somewhat.
    c. has remained the same for some time now.
    d. has decreased.
    e. suggests politicians often pander to constituents.
24. Which of the following is an *incorrect* assessment of elite opinion?
    a. Elites influence which issues will capture the public's attention.
    b. Elites are unified in their interests and opinions.
    c. Elites state the norms by which issues should be settled.
    d. Elites raise and frame political issues.
    e. Elites influence how issues are debated and decided.

ESSAY QUESTIONS

Practice writing extended answers to the following questions. These test your ability to integrate and express the ideas that you have been studying in this chapter.

1. What are some explanations for why the American public clearly wants some things, but government policy is very much directed in the opposite direction?
2. What evidence do we have that political socialization takes place in families? What do we know about recent trends in the ability of the family to socialize its members?
3. Explain what the "gender gap" refers to and observe what the authors see as the causes of what we see with respect to men and women in voting and public opinion polls.
4. How have education and political viewpoint been related to each other historically? What might explain current trends with respect to this relationship?
5. Summarize what we know about the role of social class in American politics and recent trends in class voting in America and in Europe.
6. Explain the two ways that political scientists measure political ideology.
7. Why are political scientists increasingly skeptical of polls which ask Americans to identify themselves as liberal or conservative?

ANSWERS TO KEY TERMS MATCH QUESTIONS

1. h
2. c
3. a
4. n
5. j
6. i
7. f
8. k
9. b
10. g
11. e
12. l
13. d
14. m
15. o

ANSWERS TO DATA CHECK QUESTIONS

1. 60 percent.
2. 70 percent said religion was an important part of their life and 54 percent were concerned about the moral direction of the country.
3. The respondents in this survey had the same level of support for both candidates, 40 percent.
4. 21 percent.
5. Jewish (62 percent).
6. 53 percent support the idea.
7. Women.
8. Women.
9. Health care (13 points).
10. 19 percent.
11. 38 percent: Conservative Democrats (15 percent) + Social Conservatives (13 percent) + Pro-Government Conservatives (10 percent).
12. They are both 14 percentage points above or below the figure for all registered voters.
13. Republicans (66 percent).
14. The Democrats appear to be 7 percentage points closer to the opinions of all registered voters.

ANSWERS TO TRUE/FALSE QUESTIONS

1. T
2. T
3. F The vast majority knew next to nothing about government and had only vague notions even on much publicized public policy matters that affected them directly.
4. F Every major poll has correctly picked every winner in such races.
5. T
6. F The proportion of Independents has increased. Democrats and Republicans have decreased.
7. T
8. F They were the sons and daughters of radicals in the 1960s.
9. F Religious influences are most pronounced in social issues.
10. F The gap has been around a long, long time.
11. F It did not assert itself for some time but, today, it is also evident in midterm elections.
12. T
13. T
14. F They are much less likely to read newspapers and magazines.
15. F Most consider themselves "working class."
16. T
17. T
18. T
19. T
20. T
21. T
22. F The South has been more accommodating.
23. F Barry Goldwater was the first.
24. T
25. F With higher levels of information typically comes higher levels of ideological constraint.
26. T
27. T

ANSWERS TO MULTIPLE CHOICE QUESTIONS

1. d
2. e
3. c
4. b
5. a

6. b
7. b
8. a
9. e
10. b
11. a
12. e
13. b
14. e
15. a
16. c
17. a
18. a
19. c
20. a
21. d
22. b
23. d
24. b

CHAPTER 8

Political Participation

REVIEWING THE CHAPTER

CHAPTER FOCUS

This chapter reviews the much-discussed lack of voter turnout and other forms of political participation in the United States, and concludes that individual Americans may not be at fault for their seeming nonparticipation but that other factors may be at work. After reading and reviewing the material in this chapter, you should be able to do each of the following:

1. Explain why the text believes that the description, the analysis, and the proposed remedy for low voter turnout rates in this country are off base.
2. Compare the way turnout statistics are tabulated for this country and for other countries, and explain the significance of these differences.
3. Describe how the control of elections has shifted from the states to the federal government, and explain what effects this shift has had on blacks, women, and youths.
4. State both sides of the debate over whether voter turnout has declined over the past century, and describe those factors that tend to hold down voter turnout in this country.
5. List and explain Nie and Verba's four categories of political participation.
6. Discuss those factors that appear to be associated with high or low political participation.
7. Compare participation rates in various forms of political activity here and in other countries.

STUDY OUTLINE

I. Introduction
   A. 80 percent voter turnout in European countries
   B. Low turnout in America blamed on apathy
   C. Calls for action by government or private groups to mobilize voters
II. A closer look at nonvoting
   A. Alleged problem: low turnout compared with Europeans, but this compares registered voters with the eligible adult population
   B. Common explanation: voter apathy on Election Day, but the real problem is low registration rates
   C. Proposed solution: get-out-the-vote drives
      1. 2004 study found little impact in relation to such efforts
      2. If anything, get-out-the-vote appeals may mobilize those who usually vote in low turnout elections
   D. Apathy not the only cause of nonregistration
      1. Costs here versus no costs in European countries where registration is automatic

2. Motor-voter law of 1993 (which took effect in 1995)
    a) 630,000 new voters in two months
    b) Accounted for almost 40 percent of applications in 2001–2002
    c) Scant evidence of impact on turnout or election outcomes

E. Voting is not the only way of participating

III. The rise of the American electorate

A. From state to federal control
1. Initially, states decided nearly everything
2. This led to wide variation in federal elections
3. Congress has since reduced state prerogatives
    a) 1842 law: House members elected by district
    b) Suffrage to women
    c) Suffrage to blacks
    d) Suffrage to eighteen- to twenty-year-olds
    e) Direct popular election of U.S. senators
4. Black voting rights
    a) Fifteenth Amendment gutted by Supreme Court as not conferring a right to vote
    b) Southern states then use evasive strategies
        (1) Literacy test
        (2) Poll tax
        (3) White primaries
        (4) Grandfather clauses
        (5) Intimidation of black voters
    c) Most of these strategies ruled out by Supreme Court
    d) Major change with 1965 Voting Rights Act; black vote increases
5. Women's voting rights
    a) Western states permit women to vote
    b) Nineteenth Amendment ratified 1920
    c) No dramatic changes in outcomes
6. Youth vote
    a) Voting Rights Act of 1970
    b) Twenty-sixth Amendment ratified 1971
    c) Lower turnout rate initially and no evident party loyalty
    d) Turnout remains lower than that of other age groups although rates of political participation generally are at an all time high
7. National standards now govern most aspects

B. Voting turnout
1. Debate over declining percentages: two theories
    a) The percentages are real and the result of a decline in popular interest in elections and competitiveness of the two parties
        (1) Parties originally worked hard to increase turnout among all voters
        (2) The election of 1896 locked Democrats in the South and Republicans in the North
        (3) Lopsided Republican victories caused citizens to lose interest
        (4) Leadership in the major parties became conservative and resisted mass participation
    b) The percentages represent an apparent decline induced, in part, by more honest ballot counts of today
        (1) Parties once printed ballots
        (2) Ballots cast in public

(3) Parties controlled counting
c) Most scholars see several reasons for some real decline
(1) Registration more difficult: longer residency, educational qualifications, and discrimination
(2) Continuing drop after 1960 cannot be explained
(3) Refinement of VAP data to VEP data also reveals a decline
d) Universal turnout probably would not alter election outcomes

IV. Who participates in politics?
A. Forms of participation
1. Voting the most common, but 8 to 10 percent misreport it
2. Verba and Nie's six types of participants
a) Inactives
b) Voting specialists
c) Campaigners
d) Communalists
e) Parochial participants
f) Complete activists
B. Causes of participation
1. Schooling, or political information, more likely to vote
2. Church-goers vote more
3. Men and women vote same rate
4. Race
a) Black participation lower than that of whites overall
b) But controlling for SES, higher than whites
5. Level of trust in government?
a) Studies show no correlation
6. Difficulty of registering: as turnout declines, registration gets easier
7. Several small factors decrease turnout
a) More youths, blacks, and other minorities
b) Decreasing effectiveness of parties
c) Remaining impediments to registration
d) Voting compulsory in other nations
e) Ethnic minorities encounter language barriers, whereas blacks are involved in nonpolitical institutions
f) May feel that elections do not matter
8. Democrats and Republicans fight over solutions
a) No one really knows who would be helped
b) Nonvoters tend to be poor, black, and so on
c) But an increasing percentage of college graduates are also not voting
d) Hard to be sure that turnout efforts produce gains for either party: Jesse Jackson in 1984
C. The meaning of participation rates
1. Americans vote less but participate more
a) Other forms of activity becoming more common
b) Some forms more common here than in other countries
2. Americans elect more officials than Europeans do and have more elections
3. U.S. turnout rates heavily skewed to higher status; meaning of this is unclear

KEY TERMS MATCH

Match the following terms and descriptions:

1. The lack of interest among the citizenry in participating in elections
2. Those citizens who have filled out the proper forms and are qualified to vote in an election
3. Requirement that voters be able to read; formerly used in the South to disenfranchise blacks
4. Proof of tax payment, to be produced when voting; used to disenfranchise blacks
5. A southern expedient to keep blacks from participating in primary elections
6. Requirement that for an individual to automatically qualify to vote, his or her grandparents had to have voted (excluded former slaves and their descendants)
7. Party supporters that generally favor efforts to make voting easier, suspecting that a higher turnout will benefit them
8. Legislation that made it illegal to exclude potential voters on the basis of race
9. Legislation that extended suffrage to women
10. Legislation that gave eighteen-year-olds the right to vote in federal elections
11. Legislation that gave eighteen-year-olds the right to vote in all U.S. elections
12. A document that is government printed, of uniform size, and cast in secret
13. Those who avoid all forms of political participation
14. Those who restrict their political participation to voting in elections
15. An estimate that results from excluding prisoners, felons and aliens
16. Those who both vote in elections and get involved in campaigns

a. activist
b. Australian ballot
c. campaigners
d. communalists
e. complete activists
f. Democrats
g. Fifteenth Amendment
h. grandfather clauses
i. inactives
j. literacy tests
k. motor-voter law
l. Nineteenth Amendment
m. parochial participants
n. poll tax
o. registered voters
p. Republicans
q. Twenty-sixth Amendment
r. voter apathy
s. voting-age population
t. voting-eligible population
u. Voting Rights Act of 1970
v. voting specialists
w. white primaries

17. Those who join organizations and participate in politics but not in partisan campaigns
18. Those who avoid elections and civic organizations but will contact officials regarding specific problems
19. Those who take part in all forms of political activity
20. An individual who actively promotes a political party, philosophy, or issue she or he cares personally about
21. A bill that requires states to allow voter registration by mail, when applying for a driver's license, and at some state offices that serve the disabled or poor
22. Estimate (based on the census) of the number of citizens who are eligible to vote after reaching a minimum age requirement

DATA CHECK

Table 8.1 (Page 174): Two Ways of Calculating Voter Turnout, 1996–2001 Elections, Selected Countries

1. What percentage of the voting age population in America voted in these elections?

____

2. What percentage of registered voters in America voted in these elections?

____

3. Where is the turnout of the voting age population above 80 percent or higher?

____

4. Where is the turnout of registered voters above 90 percent or higher?

____

Figure 8.1 (Page 175): Sources of Voter Registration Applications, 1999–2004

5. What was the largest source of voter applications in this time period?

____

6. What is the second largest source of voter applications in this time period?

Figure 8.2 (Page 179): Voter Participation in Presidential Elections, 1860–2004

7. How does voter turnout in the twentieth century compare with that of the nineteenth?

8. Identify two time periods of considerable length that are characterized by a steady, general decrease in voter turnout.

9. Describe trends in turnout in the last two elections.

Table 8.3 (Page 181): Two Methods of Calculating Turnout in Presidential Elections, 1948–2000

10. In how many years does the VAP reach 60 percent?

11. In how many years does the VEP reach 60 percent?

12. According to the VEP measure, what percentage of eligible voters participated in the 2004 presidential election?

Figure 8.3 (Page 184): Voter Turnout in Presidential Elections by Age, Schooling, and Race 1964–2000

13. Which age group is least likely to vote in a presidential election?

14. Which group is least likely to vote according to their schooling, or level of education?

15. Describe voter turnout among blacks and Hispanics.

PRACTICING FOR EXAMS

TRUE/FALSE QUESTIONS

Read each statement carefully. Mark true statements *T.* If any part of the statement is false, mark it *F,* and write in the space provided a concise explanation of why the statement is false.

1. T F The percentage of the adult population in America that is registered to vote is remarkably high.

2. T F Research suggests get-out-the-vote drives are generally successful.

3. T F Motor-voter registrants are more likely to vote than other new registrants.

4. T F Low rates of voter registration may indicate people are reasonably well satisfied with how the country is being governed.

5. T F At the time the Constitution was ratified, the only qualifications for voters were that they be white and male.

6. T F At one time, Chinese Americans were widely denied the right to vote.

7. T F According to law, federal elections must be held in even numbered years and on the Tuesday following the first Monday in November.

8. T F The Supreme Court declared grandfather clauses unconstitutional.

9. T F The 1965 Civil Rights Act suspended the use of literacy tests.

10. T F The Nineteenth Amendment nearly doubled the number of eligible voters in the United States.

11. T F When the Voting Rights Act of 1970 extended the right of eighteen-year-olds to vote in state elections, the Supreme Court declared the law unconstitutional.

12. T F Voter turnout for those 18 to 21 has steadily improved since 1972.

13. T F States may not have a residency requirement of more than 60 days.

14. T F Before 1961, residents of the District of Columbia could not vote in presidential elections.

15. T F Turnout in U.S. presidential elections has never been above 70 percent.

16. T F Most scholars believe voter turnout did decrease somewhere around the 1890s.

17. T F Calls to overhaul the nation's voting system were even greater in 2004 than they were in 2000.

18. T F The problem with VEP measures is that they contain a lot of people who cannot vote.

19. T F Voting is by far the most common form of political participation.

20. T F In a typical survey, 20 to 25 percent of Americans misrepresent their voting habits.

21. T F Older persons are more likely than younger persons to misreport their voting habits.

22. T F Political "activists" constitute about 11 percent of the population.

23. T F Parochial participants vote frequently but participate very little in the political process otherwise.

24. T F Research has found little or no correlation between religious involvement and political participation.

25. T F Men and women vote at about the same rate.

26. T F Four states allow voters to register and vote all in the same day.

27. T F Political parties are more effective at mobilizing voters than they once were.

28. T F In Australia and other countries, fines can be levied on nonvoters.

29. T F Democrats usually suspect higher turnout would work to their advantage.

30. T F Nonvoters are more likely to be poor than voters.

____

31. T F Public demonstrations and sit-ins and protest marches are much less common in recent decades.

____

32. T F The kinds of people who vote here are different from the kinds of people who vote abroad.

____

33. T F In the United States, voter turnout is heavily skewed toward higher status persons in professional, managerial and other white-collar occupations.

____

34. T F Blacks are more likely to be members of churches that stimulate political interests, activity, and mobilization than Latinos.

____

MULTIPLE CHOICE QUESTIONS

Circle the letter of the response that best answers the question or completes the statement.

1. In this country about _______ of the voting age population is registered to vote.
   a. one-eighth
   b. one-quarter
   c. one-half
   d. two-thirds
   e. ninety-five percent
2. Which of the following statements about the motor-voter law is *accurate*?
   a. It encouraged about 80 million more people to vote.
   b. It requires states to allow people to register to vote when applying for driver's licenses.
   c. It took effect in 1993.
   d. It has changed the balance of registrants in favor of the Democrats.
   e. It allows illegal aliens and convicted felons to register to vote.
3. A 2001 study found that motor-voter registrants were less likely than other new registrants to
   a. vote.
   b. vote Republican.
   c. vote Democrat.
   d. support Independent candidates.
   e. support incumbents.
4. At the time the Constitution was ratified, voting was limited to
   a. most white males.
   b. most males.
   c. property owners or taxpayers.
   d. the commercial class.
   e. farmers.

5. The most important changes in elections have included all of the following *except*
    a. extension of suffrage to women.
    b. extension of suffrage to African Americans.
    c. extension of suffrage to eighteen-year-olds.
    d. direct popular election of Senators.
    e. direct popular election of Representatives in the House.
6. Which of the following was employed to discriminate against African Americans who wanted to vote?
    a. Literacy tests.
    b. Poll taxes.
    c. Grandfather clauses.
    d. White primaries.
    e. All of the above.
7. Initially, following passage of the Nineteenth Amendment, women
    a. voted as often as men, but generally in the same manner.
    b. voted less often than men, but generally in the same manner.
    c. voted more often than men, but generally in the same manner.
    d. voted more often than men, but quite independently.
    e. voted as often as men, but quite independently.
8. The Voting Rights Act of 1970, which gave eighteen-year-olds the right to vote in state and federal elections
    a. was declared unconstitutional by the Supreme Court.
    b. was vetoed by the president.
    c. was opposed by a large majority of Americans.
    d. was upheld by the Supreme Court but revoked by Congress.
    e. was never considered on the floor of either the House or the Senate.
9. Individuals between the ages of eighteen and twenty-one could vote in a presidential election for the first time in
    a. 1964.
    b. 1968.
    c. 1972.
    d. 1976.
    e. 1980.
10. In the first presidential election where those between eighteen and twenty-one could vote, the turnout rate for the new voters was about
    a. 20 percent.
    b. 30 percent.
    c. 40 percent.
    d. 50 percent.
    e. 60 percent.
11. One explanation for the apparent decline in voter turnout suggests the political parties are no longer attempting to mobilize the mass of voters and are too
    a. conservative.
    b. liberal.
    c. moderate.
    d. disorganized.
    e. ideological.

12. Until about 1890 ballots were printed by the
    a. candidates.
    b. House of Representatives.
    c. state legislatures.
    d. political parties.
    e. local government.
13. Adoption of the Australian ballot enabled United States citizens to vote
    a. early and often.
    b. more easily.
    c. by absentee ballot.
    d. without being informed.
    e. in secret.
14. After the 1890s voter-registration regulations became more burdensome because
    a. they had longer residency requirements.
    b. it became harder for African Americans to vote.
    c. educational qualifications were added in some states.
    d. voters were required to register far in advance of the election.
    e. all of the above.
15. In 2002, Congress passed legislation which did all of the following *except*
    a. required states to have a system in place for counting disputed ballots.
    b. provided federal funds to upgrade voting equipment.
    c. created a uniform national voting system.
    d. provided federal funds for training election officials.
    e. B and D.
16. VEP measures of turnout may have an advantage over VAP measures because
    a. VEP measures attempt to remove ineligible voters from the data.
    b. VEP measures are based on actual census data.
    c. VEP measures include prisoners, but not felons or aliens.
    d. VEP measures include felons, but not prisoners or aliens.
    e. VEP measures are verified by each state legislature.
17. When one refocuses analyses of voter turnout in the last fourteen presidential elections to VEP measures, it is clear that
    a. there never has been anything like a turnout problem in America.
    b. the voter turnout problem disappeared in the most recent elections.
    c. voters are participating more now than ever before.
    d. voter turnout has generally declined in the most recent elections.
    e. voter turnout has generally remained the same.
18. Studies of non-voters suggest that, had they voted in recent presidential elections,
    a. the Democrats would have won more often.
    b. the Republicans would have won more often.
    c. the Democrats would have won more of the elections by "landslides."
    d. the Republicans would have won more of the elections by "landslides."
    e. the outcome of most elections would have been about the same.

19. In surveys, about what percentage of respondents claim to have voted in an election when they did not do so?
    a. 2 to 3 percent
    b. 8 to 10 percent
    c. 20 to 25 percent
    d. 30 to 35 percent
    e. 40 to 50 percent
20. Americans that are ________ are not so likely to misreport voting?
    a. young
    b. low-income
    c. nonwhite
    d. less-educated
    e. elderly
21. About ___ percent of the American population are completely inactive (they rarely discuss politics or vote and are not involved in organizations).
    a. 10
    b. 20
    c. 40
    d. 50
    e. 60
22. Those who are inactive in politics tend to
    a. have lower levels of education.
    b. have lower levels of incomes.
    c. be relatively young.
    d. all of the above.
    e. be extremely liberal or conservative.
23. Those who cast ballots in elections but engage in no other form of political participation are called
    a. voting specialists.
    b. campaigners.
    c. issue belligerents.
    d. communalists.
    e. parochial participants.
24. Those who prefer to participate in politics by forming and joining nonpartisan groups and dealing with various issues in them are referred to as
    a. voting specialists.
    b. campaigners.
    c. communalists.
    d. issue belligerents.
    e. parochial participants.
25. Those who stay out of electoral contests and community organizations but will contact officials to deal with specific problems are called
    a. voting specialists.
    b. campaigners.
    c. communalists.
    d. parochial participants.
    e. issue belligerents.

26. Which of the following are more likely to vote and otherwise take part in politics?
    a. Fans of professional sports.
    b. Midwesterners.
    c. Bowlers.
    d. Regular church goers.
    e. Musicians and poets.
27. Studies show that feelings of distrust toward political leaders have ________ effect on voter turnout.
    a. a stimulating
    b. a depressing
    c. an impressive
    d. no
    e. an unpredictable
28. In states that have instituted same-day voter registration, the effect on voter turnout has been
    a. a major decline.
    b. a slight decline.
    c. a slight increase.
    d. a major increase.
    e. no effect at all.
29. Two careful studies of voter turnout in twenty-four democratic nations found that almost all of the difference in voter turnout could be explained by
    a. the degree of party strength.
    b. the presence or absence of automatic registration.
    c. the presence or absence of compulsory voting laws.
    d. all of the above.
    e. none of the above.
30. Who tends to think that they will benefit from increases in registration and voting?
    a. Democrats
    b. Republicans
    c. Incumbents
    d. State officials
    e. Senators
31. When Jesse Jackson ran for the presidency in 1984,
    a. registration of southern blacks decreased.
    b. registration of southern whites decreased.
    c. registration of southern blacks and whites decreased.
    d. registration of southern blacks and whites increased.
    e. there was no noticeable effect on voter registration.
32. The best evidence suggests Americans
    a. are voting less and participating in politics less.
    b. are voting less and participating in politics more.
    c. are voting and participating in politics at about the same rate.
    d. are voting more and participating less in politics.
    e. are voting more and participating more in politics.

33. Political demonstrations have been used by
    a. antiwar activists.
    b. farmers.
    c. truckers.
    d. civil rights activists.
    e. all of the above.
34. The number of elective offices in the United States, compared with European nations, is
    a. much lower.
    b. slightly lower.
    c. about the same.
    d. slightly higher.
    e. much higher.
35. Compared with Europeans, American voters are offered the opportunity to vote
    a. much less frequently.
    b. slightly less frequently.
    c. more frequently.
    d. just as often.
    e. much less frequently, but their vote counts more.
36. Compared with European turnout, American turnout is more skewed toward ________ persons.
    a. informed
    b. ideological
    c. higher-status
    d. secular
    e. alienated

ESSAY QUESTIONS

Practice writing extended answers to the following questions. These test your ability to integrate and express the ideas that you have been studying in this chapter.

1. Explain what the motor-voter law is. Describe its impact on registration, turnout and election outcomes.
2. What are the four most important changes that have occurred in elections since the founding?
3. Identify some of the ways that African Americans were kept from voting even after ratification of the Fifteenth Amendment.
4. Describe trends in the voting behavior of 18–21 year olds from 1972 to today.
5. Summarize the two major views with respect to the apparent long-term decline in voter turnout in the United States.
6. Explain how Congress addressed the complaints that followed the 2000 presidential election.
7. What is the difference between the VAP and VEP? Explain how these measures may (or may not) affect our thinking about the apparent decline in voter turnout.
8. Summarize the results of the classic study of political participation in the United States by Verba and Nie.
9. How are the kinds of people who typically vote in the United States differ from the types of people who typically vote in Europe?

ANSWERS TO KEY TERMS MATCH QUESTIONS

1. r
2. o
3. j
4. n
5. w
6. h
7. f
8. g
9. l
10. u
11. q
12. b
13. i
14. v
15. t
16. c
17. d
18. m
19. e
20. a
21. k
22. s

ANSWERS TO DATA CHECK QUESTIONS

1. 47.2 percent.
2. 63.4 percent.
3. Australia, Denmark and Belgium.
4. Belgium and Australia.
5. Motor vehicle offices.
6. Mail.
7. It is about 25 percent lower in the twentieth century.
8. 1896 to 1920 / 1960 to 1988.
9. Turnout has increased in the last two presidential elections, although it remains well below pre-1960s levels.
10. Four (1952, 1960, 1964, and 1968).

11. Seven (1952, 1956, 1960, 1964, 1968, 1992 and 2004).
12. 60 percent.
13. 18 to 24.
14. Less than high school.
15. Turnout for blacks and Hispanics is lower than that of whites with Hispanics having the lowest rates for the three groups.

ANSWERS TO TRUE/FALSE QUESTIONS

1. F About 1/3 are not registered.
2. F A 2004 study found the results of such efforts to be small, or nil.
3. F A 2001 study found they are less likely to vote.
4. T
5. F At that point in time, suffrage was extended to white, male property holders.
6. T
7. T
8. T
9. T
10. T
11. T
12. F It started somewhat low and has, for the most part, declined since.
13. F States may not have such requirements longer than 30 days.
14. T
15. F It was very often about 70 percent in the 1800s.
16. T
17. F Calls for reform were almost nonexistence in 2004 because the election was not a close as it was in 2000.
18. F VAP measures contain a lot people who cannot vote, not VEP measures.
19. T
20. F In a typical survey 8–10 percent will misrepresent voting.
21. F Younger persons are more likely to misreport.
22. T
23. F They do not vote, but feel free to contact officials about problems.
24. F Those who are actively involved in religion are much more likely to participate in politics than those who are not.
25. T
26. T

27. F They are much less effective than they used to be at this.
28. T
29. T
30. T
31. F They have become much more common.
32. T
33. T
34. T

ANSWERS TO MULTIPLE CHOICE QUESTIONS

1. d
2. b
3. a
4. c
5. e
6. e
7. b
8. a
9. c
10. c
11. a
12. d
13. e
14. e
15. c
16. a
17. e
18. e
19. b
20. e
21. b
22. d
23. a
24. c
25. d

26. d
27. d
28. c
29. d
30. a
31. d
32. b
33. e
34. e
35. c
36. c

CHAPTER 9

Political Parties

REVIEWING THE CHAPTER

CHAPTER FOCUS

This chapter provides a fairly detailed exploration of one unique aspect of American politics: the two-party system that has evolved in the United States. After reading and reviewing the material in this chapter, you should be able to do each of the following:

1. Define the term *political party* and contrast the structures of the European and American parties, paying particular attention to the federal structure of the American system and the concept of party identification.
2. Trace the development of the party system through its four periods, and offer reasons that parties have been in decline since the New Deal period.
3. Describe the structure of a major party and distinguish powerful from powerless party organs.
4. Define *intraparty democracy* and state its effect on the last few Democratic nominating conventions in the last few contests. Evaluate the relative strengths of state party bosses in recent years, and discuss the increasing importance of primaries in relation to the boss system at conventions.
5. Describe the machine, discuss its functions, and trace its decline. Contrast its structure with that of ideological and reform parties.
6. Offer two explanations for the persistence of the two-party system. Explain why minor parties form, and discuss different kinds of parties. Analyze why they are so rarely successful.
7. Describe some of the issue differences between delegates at Democratic and Republican conventions, and indicate whether there are major differences between the parties. Compare these differences with those between members of the rank and file voters.

STUDY OUTLINE

I. Introduction
   A. Swings in recent elections
      1. Democratic success in 2006 mid-term congressional elections, after years of Republican success
      2. Republican success in 2002
   B. 2006 swings were the result of a general desire for change (as opposed to agreement with the policies of the Democratic Party)
   C. If anything, the relevance of the parties is declining—a serious problem for our representative democracy

II. Parties here and abroad
  A. The American context
    1. A party is a group that seeks to elect candidates to public office by supplying them with a label
    2. American parties: historical development
      a) American parties are the oldest in the world
      b) New parties come and go, but two dominate the process
      c) Do not matter as much as they once did
        (1) They used to mobilize voters
        (2) Identification used to involve a serious commitment
      d) Why the decline?
        (1) Laws and rules
        (2) Voters have lost a sense of commitment
        (3) Decentralization has made the weakening uneven
    3. Relevant arenas
      a) A label in the minds of the voters
      b) Set of leaders in government
      c) Organization recruiting and campaigning
    4. American parties have become weaker in all three arenas
      a) As labels: more independents
      b) As organizations: much weaker since the 1960s
      c) As sets of leaders: the organization of Congress less under their control
  B. Reasons for differences from European parties
    1. Federal system decentralizes power
      a) Early on, most people with political jobs worked for state and local governments
      b) National parties were coalitions of local parties
      c) As political power becomes more centralized, parties become weaker still
    2. Parties closely regulated by state and federal laws
    3. Candidates chosen through primaries, not by party leaders
    4. President elected separately from Congress
    5. Political culture
      a) Parties unimportant in life; Americans do not join or pay dues
      b) Parties separate from other aspects of life
III. The rise and decline of the political party
  A. The Founding (to the 1820s)
    1. Founders' dislike of factions
    2. Emergence of Republicans, Federalists: Jefferson versus Hamilton
      a) Loose caucuses of political notables
      b) Republicans' success and Federalists' demise
    3. No representation of clear economic interests
  B. The Jacksonians (to the Civil War)
    1. Political participation a mass phenomenon
      a) More voters to reach
      b) Party built from the bottom up
      c) Abandonment of presidential caucuses
      d) Beginning of national conventions to allow local control
  C. The Civil War and sectionalism
    1. Jacksonian system unable to survive slavery issue
    2. New Republicans become dominant because of
      a) Civil War and Republicans on Union side

b) Bryan's alienation of northern Democrats in 1896
3. In most states one party predominates
a) Party professionals, or "stalwarts," one faction in GOP
b) Mugwumps, Progressives, or "reformers" another faction
(1) Balance of power at first
(2) Diminished role later
D. The era of reform
1. Progressive push measures to curtail parties
a) Primary elections
b) Nonpartisan elections
c) No party-business alliances
d) Strict voter registration requirements
e) Civil service reform
f) Initiative and referendum elections
2. Effects
a) Reduction in worst forms of political corruption
b) Weakening of all political parties
IV. Party realignments
A. Definition: sharp, lasting shift in the popular coalition supporting one or both parties
B. Occurrences: change in issues
1. 1800: Jeffersonians defeated Federalists
2. 1828: Jacksonian Democrats came to power
3. 1860: Whigs collapsed; Republicans won
4. 1896: Republicans defeated Bryan
5. 1932: FDR Democrats came to power
C. Kinds of realignments
1. Major party disappears and is replaced (1800, 1860)
2. Voters shift from one party to another (1896, 1932)
D. Clearest cases
1. 1860: slavery
2. 1896: economics
3. 1932: depression
E. 1980 not a realignment
1. Expressed dissatisfaction with Carter
2. Also left Congress Democratic
F. 1972–1988: shift in presidential voting patterns in the South
1. Fewer Democrats, more Republicans, more independents
2. Independents vote Republican
3. Now close to fifty-fifty Democratic, Republican
4. Party dealignment, not realignment
G. Party decline; evidence for it
1. Fewer people identify with either party
2. Increase in ticket splitting
V. The national party structure today
A. Parties similar on paper
1. National convention ultimate power; nominates presidential candidate
2. National committee composed of delegates from states
3. Congressional campaign committees
4. National chair manages daily work

B. Party structure diverges in the late 1960s
   1. RNC moves to bureaucratic structure; a well-financed party devoted to electing its candidates
   2. Democrats move to factionalized structure to distribute power
   3. RNC uses computerized mailing lists to raise money
      a) Money used to run political consulting firm
      b) Legal and financial advice, issue research, provide information on voting trends, conduct advertising campaigns, etc.
   4. Democrats copied the Republican strategy and set new records for fund raising
   5. The current competition for soft money and record spending
C. National conventions
   1. National committee sets time and place; issues call setting number of delegates for each state
   2. Formulas used to allocate delegates
      a) Democrats shift the formula away from the South to the North and West
      b) Republicans shift the formula away from the East to the South and Southwest
      c) Result: Democrats move left, Republicans right
   3. Democratic formula rewards large states and Republican-loyal states
   4. Democrats set new rules
      a) In the 1970s the rules changed to weaken party leaders and increase the influence of special interests
      b) Hunt commission in 1981 reverses 1970s rules by increasing the influence of elected officials and by making convention more deliberative
   5. Consequence of reforms: parties represent different set of upper-middle-class voters
      a) Republicans represent traditional middle class
      b) Democrats represent the "new class"
      c) Democrats hurt because the traditional middle class closer in opinions to most citizens
   6. To become more competitive, Democrats adopt rule changes
      a) In 1988 the number of super-delegates increased and special interests decreased
      b) In 1992 three rules: winner-reward system, proportional representation, and states that violate rules are penalized
   7. Conventions today only ratify choices made in primaries

VI. State and local parties
A. The machine
   1. Recruitment via tangible incentives
   2. High degree of leadership control
   3. Abuses
      a) Gradually controlled by reforms
      b) But machines continued
   4. Both self-serving and public regarding
   5. Winning above all else
B. Ideological parties
   1. Principle above all else
   2. Usually outside Democrats and Republicans
   3. But some local reform clubs
   4. Reform clubs replaced by social movements
C. Solidary groups
   1. Most common form of party organization
   2. Members motivated by solidary incentives

3. Advantage: neither corrupt nor inflexible
4. Disadvantage: not very hard working

D. Sponsored parties
1. Created or sustained by another organization
2. Example: Detroit Democrats controlled by UAW
3. Not very common

E. Personal following
1. Examples: Kennedys, Curley, Talmadges, Longs
2. Viability today affected by TV and radio
3. Advantage: vote for the person
4. Disadvantage: takes time to know the person

VII. The two-party system
A. Rarity among nations today
B. Evenly balanced nationally, not locally
C. Why such a permanent feature?
1. Electoral system: winner-take-all and plurality system
2. Opinions of voters: two broad coalitions
a) Most Americans see a difference between Democrats and Republicans
(1) Democrats favored on issues such as poverty, the environment and health care
(2) Republicans favored on issues such as national defense, foreign trade and crime
(3) Parties evenly split on issues such as the economy and taxes
b) Mass perceptions can change (education, national defense, immigration policy, etc.)
3. For many years, the laws of many states

VIII. Minor parties
A. Ideological parties: comprehensive, radical view; most enduring
Examples: Socialist, Communist, Libertarian

B. One-issue parties: address one concern, avoid others
Examples: Free Soil, Know-Nothing, Prohibition

C. Economic protest parties: regional, oppose depressions
Examples: Greenback, Populist

D. Factional parties: from split in a major party
Examples: Bull Moose, Henry Wallace, American Independent

E. Movements *not* producing parties; either slim chance of success or major parties accommodate
Examples: civil rights, antiwar, labor

F. Factional parties have had greatest influence
1. 1992 and 1996, Ross Perot
2. 2000 and 2004, Ralph Nader

IX. Nominating a president
A. Two contrary forces: party's desire to win motivates it to seek an appealing candidate, but its desire to keep dissidents in party forces a compromise to more extreme views
B. Are the delegates representative of the voters?
1. Democratic delegates much more liberal
2. Republican delegates much more conservative

3. Explanation of this disparity not quota rules: quota groups have greater diversity of opinion than do the delegates

C. Who votes in primaries?
1. Primaries now more numerous and more decisive
a) Stevenson and Humphrey never entered a primary
b) By 1992: forty primaries and twenty caucuses
2. Little ideological difference between primary voters and rank-and-file party voters
3. Caucus: meeting of party followers at which delegates are picked
a) Only most-dedicated partisans attend
b) Often choose most ideological candidate: Jackson, Robertson in 1988

D. Who are the new delegates?
1. However chosen, today's delegates a new breed unlikely to resemble average citizen: issue-oriented activists
2. Advantages of new system
a) Increased chance for activists within party
b) Decreased probability of their bolting the party
3. Disadvantage: may nominate presidential candidates unacceptable to voters or rank and file

X. Parties versus voters
A. Democrats: win congressional elections but lose presidential contests
1. Candidates are out of step with average voters on social and tax issues
2. So are delegates, and there's a connection
B. Republicans had the same problem with Goldwater (1964)
C. Rank-and-file Democrats and Republicans differ on many political issues, but the differences are usually small
D. Delegates from two parties differ widely on these same issues
1. 1996 conventions
a) Few conservatives at Democratic convention
b) Few liberals at Republican convention
2. Formula for winning president
a) Nominate candidates with views closer to the average citizen (e.g., 1996 election)
b) Fight campaign over issues agreed on by delegates and voters (e.g., 1992 election)

KEY TERMS MATCH

Match the following terms and descriptions.

1. A group that seeks to elect candidates to public office by supplying them with a label
2. A name applied by some of the Founders to political parties, to connote their tendency toward divisiveness
3. The political party founded and led by Thomas Jefferson
4. The political party founded and led by Alexander Hamilton

a. Anti-Masonic party
b. caucus
c. congressional campaign committee
d. critical (or realigning) period
e. Democratic-Republicans
f. factional parties
g. factions
h. Federalists

5. The arrangement of political parties initiated by Andrew Jackson
6. A name for party professionals, as opposed to volunteers
7. A name for party volunteers who later come to form their own reform movement
8. An election in which candidates for office are not identified by party labels
9. A machine that began as a caucus of well-to-do notables in New York City
10. A party that stresses national organization to raise money and give assistance to local candidates and party units
11. An election in which citizens directly approve or disapprove legislation proposed by the government
12. Political party that held the first convention in American history
13. Features a sharp, lasting shift in the popular coalition supporting one or both parties
14. An election in which citizens can place on the legislative agenda proposals by non-government groups
15. Elected officials who serve as delegates to the national convention
16. An electoral system that gives the only office to the candidate with the largest vote total, rather than apportioning numerous offices by the percentage of the total vote
17. A party unit that recruits members with tangible rewards and that is tightly controlled by the leadership
18. A closed meeting of party leaders to select party candidates
19. Parties that value principle above all else
20. Parties organized around sociability, rather than tangible rewards or ideology
21. Party units established or maintained by outside groups

i. Hatch Act
j. ideological parties
k. initiative
l. machine
m. Mugwumps
n. national (party) chair
o. national committee
p. national convention
q. nonpartisan election
r. office bloc ballot
s. organizational party
t. party column ballot
u. personal following
v. plurality system
w. political machine
x. political party
y. proportional representation
z. referendum
aa. Republican
bb. second-party system
cc. solidary groups
dd. solidary incentives
ee. split ticket voting
ff. sponsored parties
gg. stalwarts
hh. superdelegates
ii. Tammany Hall
jj. two-party system
kk. winner-take-all

22. The practice of voting for one major party's candidate in state or local elections and the other's at the national level
23. Only third party to ever win a presidential election
24. An electoral system that distributes numerous seats to parties on the basis of their percentage of the popular vote
25. Parties formed by a split within one of the major parties
26. Addressed the issue of federal civil service employees taking an active part in political management or campaigns
27. A ballot listing all candidates of a given party together under the name of that party
28. A committee in each party to help elect or reelect members
29. The person elected and paid to manage the day-to-day work of a national political party
30. Delegates from each state who manage party affairs between conventions
31. A meeting of elected party delegates every four years to nominate presidential and vice-presidential candidates and ratify a campaign platform
32. An electoral system with two dominant parties that compete in state and national elections
33. A ballot listing all candidates for a given office under the name of that office
34. An electoral system in which the winner is the person who gets the most votes but not necessarily a majority of votes
35. A party organization that recruits members by dispensing patronage
36. The social rewards that lead people to join political organizations
37. The political support provided to a candidate on the basis of personal popularity and networks

DATA CHECK

Figure 9.1 (Page 192): Decline in Party Identification, 1952–2004

1. Which of the major parties typically has a higher number of "strong" identifiers?

2. In which years has the percentage of "strong" or "weak" Democrats or Republicans risen above 30 percent?

3. In what decade do independent voters first represent at least 30 percent of respondents?

Figure 9.2 (Page 201): Split Ticket Voting for President/House, 1952–2004

4. In what year did split ticket voting occur least often?

5. Generalize about the total amount of split ticket voting since 1972.

6. When does split ticket voting occur more often, when voters are selecting a Democratic or Republican president?

Table 9.1 (Page 205): Who Are the Party Delegates?

7. Which party has a higher percentage of women and blacks among delegates?

8. Which party has a higher percentage of Protestants and born again Christians?

9. Which party has a majority of delegates who are college educated?

10. Which party has more than 40 percent of its delegates with family incomes of $100,000 or more?

Table 9.2 (Page 212): Party Voting in Presidential Elections

11. In which elections did Democratic voters support Democratic candidates at a higher rate than Republican voters supported Republican candidates?

12. What can be concluded with respect to independent votes based on in these five elections?

Table 9.3 (Page 218): Political Opinions of Delegates and Voters, 2004

For each issue the three sets of percentages indicate the proportion of convention delegates and voters who favor the issue. You can compare both differences between Democrats and Republicans and differences between delegates and voters.

13. On what three issues do Democratic and Republican *delegates* appear to differ most widely?

____

14. On what issues do *voters* and Democratic *delegates* appear to differ most widely?

____

15. On what issues do *voters* and Republican *delegates* appear to differ most widely?

____

16. What do these figures indicate?

____

PRACTICING FOR EXAMS

TRUE/FALSE QUESTIONS

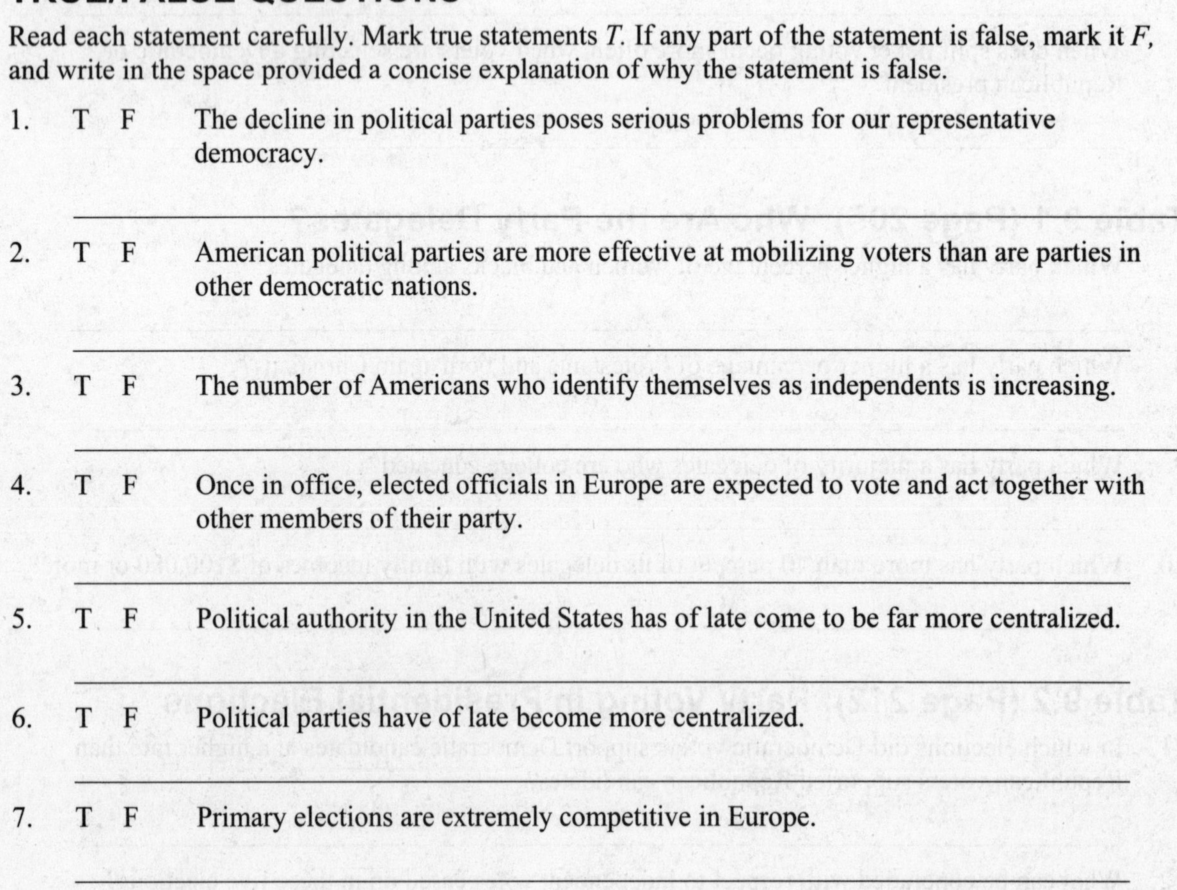

Read each statement carefully. Mark true statements *T*. If any part of the statement is false, mark it *F*, and write in the space provided a concise explanation of why the statement is false.

1. T F The decline in political parties poses serious problems for our representative democracy.

____

2. T F American political parties are more effective at mobilizing voters than are parties in other democratic nations.

____

3. T F The number of Americans who identify themselves as independents is increasing.

____

4. T F Once in office, elected officials in Europe are expected to vote and act together with other members of their party.

____

5. T F Political authority in the United States has of late come to be far more centralized.

____

6. T F Political parties have of late become more centralized.

____

7. T F Primary elections are extremely competitive in Europe.

____

8. T F Most Americans would resent partisanship becoming a conspicuous feature of other organizations to which they belong.

____

9. T F Our nation began without political parties.

____

10. T F The Founders favored parties because they enhanced communication between the government and its citizens.

____

11. T F The followers of Hamilton founded the first political party.

____

12. T F The first political party took for a name "Republicans."

____

13. T F Popular support for the Federalist party was limited to sections of the country and particular classes of Americans.

____

14. T F The convention system was first developed in part as a reform

____

15. T F The modern Republican Party began as a third party.

____

16. T F The Progressives opposed non-partisan elections.

____

17. T F The reforms of the Progressives had the effect of weakening political parties.

____

18. T F An electoral realignment took place in 1860.

____

19. T F Economic issues triggered the alignments of 1896 and 1932.

____

20. T F The text concludes the election of Ronald Reagan clearly signaled a new electoral realignment.

____

21. T F Split ticket voting has been most common in the northeastern United States.

____

22. T F Super-delegates are delegates to the national conventions who are also public officials.

____

23. T F The "reforms" which followed the 1960s resulted in a Democratic national convention that more closely reflected public opinion than the Republican national convention.

____

24. T F Today, national conventions are places where party leaders meet to bargain over the selection of their presidential candidates.

____

25. T F The Hatch Act of 1939 made it illegal for federal civil service employees to work in partisan campaigns.

____

26. T F The text suggests the Hatch Act of 1939 destroyed so-called "political machines."

____

27. T F Elections where party machines were active commonly featured high voter turnout.

____

28. T F Political machines usually supported presidential candidates who had the best chance of winning even if they held contrary policy viewpoints.

____

29. T F Abraham Lincoln and John F. Kennedy benefited from machine politics.

____

30. T F The ideological party values winning above all else.

____

31. T F The most firmly ideological parties have been factions within the Democratic Party.

____

32. T F Solidary groups tend to work harder than others.

____

33. T F David Mayhew suggests the traditional party organization exists in about half of the states.

____

34. T F Most European democracies have strong two party systems like the United States.

____

35. T F In 1992, Bill Clinton won 45 percent of the popular vote in Missouri, but all of the state's electoral votes.

____

36. T F The United States has never experimented with proportional representation.

____

37. T F In the United States, a third party has never won the presidency.

____

38. T F The text suggests no third party is likely to win—or even come close to winning— the presidency any time soon.

____

39. T F For many years, the laws of many states made it difficult, if not impossible, for third parties to get on the ballot.

____

40. T F The minor parties that have endured in American politics have been ideological ones.

____

41. T F The authors conclude that it is striking that we have had so many minor parties.

____

42. T F Today, a larger proportion of party delegates are interested in issues and less amenable to compromise.

____

43. T F Before 1972, party leaders chose most party delegates.

____

44. T F Only about half as many people vote in primaries as in general elections.

____

45. T F Since 1968, the Democratic Party has had no trouble winning congressional elections.

____

46. T F Republican convention delegates appear to be more separated from the opinions of most citizens than Democratic convention delegates.

____

MULTIPLE CHOICE QUESTIONS

Circle the letter of the response that best answers the question or completes the statement.

1. The oldest political parties in the world are currently found in
   a. India.
   b. the United States.
   c. Great Britain.
   d. Germany.
   e. Switzerland.
2. Parties in the United States are relatively weak today mainly because
   a. the laws and rules under which they operate have taken away much of their power.
   b. political leaders have insisted that ballots do not identify the party of candidates.
   c. interest groups are less influential than they were 40 years ago.
   d. many voters have lost their sense of commitment to party identification.
   e. A and D.

3. American political parties have become weaker as
   a. labels in the minds of voters.
   b. a set of political leaders who try to organize and control government.
   c. organizations that recruit candidates.
   d. all of the above.
   e. none of the above.
4. In Europe, candidates for elective office are generally nominated by
   a. local referenda.
   b. aristocrats.
   c. party leaders.
   d. prime ministers.
   e. national primaries.
5. Decentralization of political authority in the United States is chiefly promoted by
   a. the legal community.
   b. federalism.
   c. nationalism.
   d. the church.
   e. the mass media.
6. American political parties, unlike those of most other democratic nations, are closely regulated by
   a. minorities.
   b. the Constitution.
   c. powerful machines.
   d. the executive branch of government.
   e. state and federal laws.
7. The text suggests most Americans would ________ partisanship's becoming a conspicuous feature of other organizations to which they belong.
   a. resent
   b. support
   c. welcome
   d. hardly notice or care about
   e. praise
8. Which of the following is *not* a reason for stronger political parties in Europe?
   a. The greater age of European parties.
   b. The absence of primary elections.
   c. The ability of the legislature to choose the chief executive.
   d. The power of leaders to nominate candidates.
   e. A political culture more favorable to parties.
9. George Washington was critical of political parties most notably in his
   a. Last Will and Testament.
   b. inaugural speech.
   c. messages to Congress.
   d. Farewell Address.
   e. correspondence with Thomas Jefferson.

10. Why should George Washington, among other Founders of our nation, have been so opposed to political parties?
    a. Because the Constitution made clear the dangers of partisanship in government.
    b. Because political parties during the early years of the republic were both strong and centralized.
    c. Because disputes over policies and elections were not easily separated from disputes over governmental legitimacy.
    d. Because political parties during the early years of the Republic represented clear, homogeneous economic interests.
    e. Because Washington was concerned that Hamilton would win the White House as a result of party mobilization.
11. The first political party was organized by
    a. the followers of Hamilton.
    b. the followers of Jefferson.
    c. farmers and Revolutionary War soldiers.
    d. the Danbury Baptists.
    e. Federalist newspapermen.
12. Thomas Jefferson considered his Republican party to be
    a. secret monarchists.
    b. a federalism broker.
    c. antifederalist.
    d. a temporary arrangement.
    e. a permanent organization.
13. Which description of the Jacksonian period of political parties is *incorrect*?
    a. The North and the South became more divided.
    b. The Democrats and the Whigs were fairly evenly balanced.
    c. The number of eligible voters decreased.
    d. The party convention system was invented.
    e. It featured the first truly national system.
14. Up until the Jacksonian period of political parties, presidential candidates were nominated by
    a. the Supreme Court.
    b. state legislatures.
    c. primary voters.
    d. members of Congress.
    e. party leaders.
15. In 1831 the ________ Party held the first American party convention.
    a. Anti-Masonic
    b. Free Soil
    c. Greenback
    d. Whig
    e. Know-Nothing
16. Leading up the Civil War, Republicans generally won
    a. the House.
    b. the Senate.
    c. the House and the Senate.
    d. the Presidency
    e. B and D.

17. The candidacy of William Jennings Bryan strengthened the Republican Party because Bryan
    a. was quite unpopular in the South.
    b. alienated many voters in the populous northeastern states.
    c. called for a strong national government.
    d. alienated rural voters in the Midwest.
    e. represented the narrow interests of industrialists.
18. The Mugwumps were
    a. a political branch of the American Legion.
    b. a faction of the Republican party.
    c. the forerunners of the Ku Klux Klan.
    d. an activist Indian tribe.
    e. Louisiana tobacco farmers who held land near the coast.
19. All of the following were true of the so-called "progressives" *except*
    a. they wanted more strict voter registration requirements.
    b. they pressed for civil service reform.
    c. they called for non-partisan elections at the city level.
    d. they called for non-partisan elections at the state level.
    e. they opposed the use of mass media in the conduct of political debate.
20. Scholars recognize at least ____ periods of critical realignment in American politics.
    a. two
    b. five
    c. fifteen
    d. thirty
    e. thirty-two
21. Even if one questions the validity of the concept of a critical election, it is quite clear that
    a. Ronald Reagan's election in 1980 signaled a realignment.
    b. Ronald Reagan's election in 1984 signaled a realignment.
    c. the South is becoming more supportive of the Democratic Party.
    d. the South is becoming more supportive of the Republican Party.
    e. parties are gaining in strength.
22. Ticket splitting was almost unheard of in the nineteenth century because
    a. voters were not as divided as they are today.
    b. divided government was considered a circumstance worth avoiding.
    c. the parties had little strength and were constantly violating election laws.
    d. ballots were printed by the parties and government ballots featured "party columns."
    e. the party identification of most candidates was unknown.
23. Split ticket voting became less common around the turn of the century when the Progressives instituted the "______ ballot."
    a. office
    b. column
    c. markup
    d. descriptive
    e. institutional

24. As a result of changes made by the parties in the 1960s and 1970s, the Democrats have become more ____________ and the Republican Party has become more ________.
    a. libertarian … liberal
    b. factionalized … bureaucratized
    c. unified … people-oriented
    d. traditional … modern
    e. organized … popular
25. In political jargon, the money given to aid political parties is known as "________ money."
    a. soft
    b. safe
    c. picket
    d. liquid
    e. rock
26. The formulas for apportioning delegates to the national party conventions are such that the Democrats give extra delegates to ______ states and the Republicans give extra delegates to states that are _______.
    a. small … large
    b. Midwestern … heavily populated
    c. large … loyal
    d. Southern … heavily contested
    e. conservative … liberal
27. Under convention rules adopted by Democrats in 1980, there must be an equal number of
    a. lawyers and doctors.
    b. Northerners and Southerners.
    c. rural and suburban dwellers.
    d. whites and nonwhites.
    e. men and women.
28. Under convention rules adopted by Democrats in 1988, most Democratic ______ are automatically delegates.
    a. members of Congress
    b. governors
    c. judges
    d. precinct captains
    e. A and B
29. A political machine is a party organization that recruits its members by the use of
    a. lofty ideals and admirable goals.
    b. ideological sympathy.
    c. community ties.
    d. tangible incentives.
    e. socialization.
30. Political machines are credited with helping elect
    a. Abraham Lincoln.
    b. John F. Kennedy.
    c. Franklin Roosevelt.
    d. Warren G. Harding.
    e. all of the above.

31. At the opposite extreme from the political machine is
    a. the sponsored party.
    b. a personal following.
    c. the ideological party.
    d. the party bundle.
    e. the solidary group.
32. The political action arm of the United Auto Workers (UAW) in Detroit has created a clear example of a(n)
    a. ideological party.
    b. solidary group.
    c. sponsored party.
    d. political machine.
    e. personal following.
33. The text suggests ____________ have become "grand masters" at building personal followings.
    a. southern politicians in one-party states
    b. Democrats
    c. Republicans
    d. governors in states with small populations
    e. U.S. Senators
34. More than half of the delegates at the 1984 Democratic national conventions are
    a. chosen randomly at state conventions.
    b. hand picked by the expected presidential nominee.
    c. females who are candidates in state and local elections.
    d. elected officials who are supported by unions.
    e. drawn from the ranks of the AFL-CIO, the National Education Association and the National Organization for Women.
35. Almost all elections in the United States are based on
    a. the plurality system.
    b. the majority system.
    c. proportional representation.
    d. retention and recall.
    e. a combination of systems.
36. The two-party system has persisted in the United States for all of the following reasons *except*
    a. it is very difficult to form the broad coalitions necessary to win.
    b. the plurality system
    c. the Fourteenth Amendment limits access to the ballot.
    d. party voting is still quite common among American voters.
    e. the laws of many states made it difficult for third parties to exist or win.
37. Which of the following statements concerning the Socialist Party of Eugene Debs is *incorrect*?
    a. It won 6 percent of the vote in the 1912 presidential election.
    b. It elected over a thousand candidates to offices throughout the United States.
    c. It elected almost eighty mayors throughout the United States.
    d. It was outspoken in its criticism of municipal corruption and American entry into World War I.
    e. None of the above.

38. The Free Soil and Know-Nothing Parties are examples of
    a. factional parties.
    b. backlash parties.
    c. ideological parties.
    d. economic protest parties.
    e. one-issue parties.
39. Which type of minor party probably has the *greatest* influence on U.S. public policy?
    a. Factional
    b. Ideological
    c. Economic protest
    d. Backlash
    e. One issue
40. Party activists are *not* likely to
    a. take issues seriously.
    b. resemble the average citizen.
    c. vote with any degree of consistency.
    d. work very hard.
    e. support candidates with strong ideological appeal.
41. The disadvantage to parties of the current system of presidential nomination is that it
    a. affords little opportunity to minorities to voice their concerns.
    b. decreases the chances that a faction will separate itself from the party.
    c. decreases the chances of a realigning election.
    d. increases the chances of nominating a candidate unappealing to the average voter or to the party's rank and file.
    e. increases the chances that a faction will separate itself from the party.
42. To obtain power within a political party, an individual must usually
    a. move toward the center.
    b. move away from the center.
    c. remain above political conflict.
    d. avoid publicity.
    e. reflect the views of the average voter.
43. The text suggests Democrats have had some difficulty in competing for the presidency, in part, because
    a. they have typically had little experience in government.
    b. redistricting which has created an advantage for Republicans.
    c. slanted reporting by media.
    d. of recent changes in electoral laws regarding placement on the ballot.
    e. of the views their candidates have had on social issues and taxation.

ESSAY QUESTIONS

Practice writing extended answers to the following questions. These test your ability to integrate and express the ideas that you have been studying in this chapter.

1. Identify the three political arenas in which political parties exist.
2. Describe how American political culture affects the power of political parties. How do Americans differ in their attitudes about parties from Europeans?
3. Explain why some of the Founding Fathers were so negative about political parties.

4. Describe political parties in the second party (or Jacksonian) system.
5. Identify some of the reforms and causes espoused by the Progressives and assess their impact on political parties.
6. Explain the two types of political realignment and identify the three clearest examples of such alignments in American history.
7. What are the two major explanations scholars employ when they attempt to explain the presence of the two-partysystem in America?

ANSWERS TO KEY TERMS MATCH QUESTIONS

1. x
2. g
3. e
4. h
5. bb
6. gg
7. m
8. q
9. ii
10. s
11. z
12. a
13. d
14. k
15. hh
16. kk
17. l
18. b
19. j
20. cc
21. ff
22. ee
23. aa
24. y
25. f
26. i
27. t
28. c
29. n
30. o
31. p
32. jj
33. r

34. v
35. w
36. dd
37. u

ANSWERS TO DATA CHECK QUESTIONS

1. Democrats.
2. Never.
3. 1960s.
4. 1952 (12 percent).
5. Arguably, it has gone down gradually, from a high of 30 percent (1972) to 17 percent (2004).
6. It seems to have occurred more often when voters are choosing a Republican president and a Democratic House. Although the data for the last three elections are somewhat mixed.
7. Democrats.
8. Republicans.
9. Both parties.
10. Both parties.
11. 1992 and 1996.
12. A higher percentage of independent voters supported the Democrats in three of the five elections represented in the data.
13. Government should do more to solve national problems (70 percent), abortion should be generally available (62 percent) and government's antiterrorism laws restrict civil liberties (62 percent).
14. Government should do more to solve national problems (37 percent).
15. Government should do more to solve national problems (33 percent).
16. That delegates generally take more extreme positions than voters.

ANSWERS TO TRUE/FALSE QUESTIONS

1. T
2. F They are much less effective at this than other parties.
3. T
4. T
5. F It has become more decentralized.
6. F They have also become more decentralized.
7. F There are no primary elections in Europe.
8. T
9. T
10. F They looked down upon parties because factions were viewed with suspicion and distrust.

11. F The followers of Jefferson founded the first party.
12. T
13. T
14. T
15. T
16. F The progressives were great proponents of non-partisan elections.
17. T
18. T
19. T
20. F Reagan's election was not accompanied by Republican control of both chambers of Congress. It was clearly less than anything like a traditional realignment.
21. F It has been most common in the South.
22. T
23. F The Democratic convention appeared to drift further away from public opinion.
24. F Actually, they meet to ratify and confirm the decisions already made by primary participants.
25. T
26. F It did not destroy all of them. Machines continued to exist in Chicago and Philadelphia for example.
27. T
28. T
29. T
30. F The ideological party values principle above all else.
31. F The most firmly ideological have been independent "third parties."
32. F They tend to work less, doing only what is fun, or appealing.
33. F Mayhew sees such competition in only about 8 states.
34. F Most European nations have multi-party systems.
35. T
36. F We have experimented with it in municipal elections in New York City and it is used in Cambridge, Massachusetts.
37. F One has, the Republicans in 1860.
38. T
39. T
40. T
41. F It is striking that we have not had more minor parties.
42. T

43. T
44. T
45. T
46. F The Democratic delegates appear to be more separated

ANSWERS TO MULTIPLE CHOICE QUESTIONS

1. b
2. e
3. d
4. c
5. b
6. e
7. a
8. a
9. d
10. c
11. b
12. d
13. c
14. d
15. a
16. e
17. b
18. b
19. e
20. b
21. d
22. d
23. a
24. b
25. a
26. c
27. e
28. e
29. d

30. e
31. c
32. c
33. a
34. e
35. a
36. c
37. e
38. e
39. a
40. b
41. d
42. b
43. e

CHAPTER 10

Elections and Campaigns

REVIEWING THE CHAPTER

CHAPTER FOCUS

This chapter takes you on a cook's tour of some of the scholarly examinations, the common folklore, and the amazing intricacies of America's most enduring and exciting political institution, the election. Major topics include, but are not limited to, the debate over just how democratic elections are (given a very low voter turnout), the new personalistic nature of campaigning in the latter part of the twentieth century, the role that money plays in determining outcomes, the role of special-interest groups, so-called realigning elections, and the elements of successful coalition building by Democrats and Republicans. After reading and reviewing the material in this chapter, you should be able to do each of the following:

1. Explain why elections in the United States are both more democratic and less democratic than those of other countries.
2. Demonstrate the differences between the party-oriented campaigns of the nineteenth century and the candidate-oriented ones of today, explaining the major elements of a successful campaign for office today.
3. Discuss how important campaign funding is to election outcomes, what the major sources of such funding are under current law, and how successful reform legislation has been in purifying U.S. elections of improper monetary influences.
4. Discuss the partisan effects of campaigns, or why the party with the most registered voters does not always win the election.
5. Define the term *realigning election* and discuss the major examples of such elections in the past, as well as recent debates over whether realignment is again underway.
6. Describe what the Democrats and the Republicans, respectively, must do to put together a successful national coalition to achieve political power in any election.
7. Outline the major arguments on either side of the question of whether elections result in major changes in public policy in the United States.

STUDY OUTLINE

I. Introduction
    A. 2008 presidential race
        1. Over a dozen candidates
        2. Early start
        3. Millions of dollars raised
    B. Comparison with previous elections
        1. 1968, Humphrey won nomination without competing in state primaries

2. 1968, Humphrey raised little money compared to today's also-rans
3. 1988, Bush campaign relatively small scale

II. Campaigns then and now
- A. Key changes relate to parties, media and money
- B. Parties
  1. Once determined, or powerfully influenced who was nominated
  2. Congressional caucuses were replaced by national nominating conventions and local party leaders
  3. Most people voted straight party ticket
  4. Candidates are "on their own" with assistance from
     - a) Media consultants
     - b) Direct mail firms
     - c) Polling firms
     - d) Political technology firms
- C. Media and money
  1. Today's candidates depend—and spend—the most on media
  2. Impact of ads not clear
     - a) No clear relationship between exposure and victory
     - b) Recent study found plurality of ads appealed to voter's fears
     - c) More effective with those interested in politics, with higher levels of information
- D. Better or worse?
  1. Increasing emphasis on polling
     - a) Commonly used to guide ads, communications, positions on issues, speeches and attire
     - b) Also used to shape or change voters' attitudes
     - c) Micro targeting and grass roots campaigns
  2. Increasing dependence on the strategic expertise of political consultants
  3. Campaigning has become synonymous with fundraising

III. Elections here and abroad
- A. Two phases: getting nominated and getting elected
  1. Getting on the ballot is largely an individual effort
  2. An organizational effort in most European nations
  3. Parties play a minor role here
- B. Presidential and congressional campaigns
  1. Presidential races are more competitive
     - a) House races have lately been one-sided for Democrats
     - b) Presidential winner rarely gets more than 55 percent of the vote
     - c) Most House incumbents are reelected (more than 90 percent)
  2. Fewer people vote in congressional elections
     - a) Unless election coincides with presidential election
     - b) Gives greater importance to partisan voters (party regulars)
  3. Congressional incumbents can service their constituents
     - a) Can take credit for governmental grants, programs, and so forth
     - b) President can't: power is not local
  4. Congressional candidates can duck responsibility
     - a) "I didn't do it; the people in Washington did!"
     - b) President is stuck with blame
     - c) But local candidates can suffer when their leader's economic policies fail
  5. Benefit of presidential coattails has declined
     - a) Congressional elections have become largely independent
     - b) Reduces meaning (and importance) of party

C. Running for president
  1. Getting mentioned
    a) Using reporters, trips, speeches, and name recognition
    b) Sponsoring legislation, governing large state
  2. Setting aside time to run
    a) Reagan: six years. Mondale: four years.
    b) May have to resign from office first
  3. Background of candidate can make a difference
    a) Voters seem to prefer those with experience as governor or military heroes
    b) Some members of Congress and former members with experience as vice-president have been elected
  4. Money
    a) Individuals can give $2,000, political action committees (PACs) $5,000
    b) Candidates must raise $5,000 in twenty states to qualify for matching grants to pay for primary
  5. Organization
    a) Need a large (paid) staff
    b) Need volunteers
    c) Need advisers on issues: position papers
  6. Strategy and themes
    a) Incumbent versus challenger: defend or attack?
    b) Setting the tone (positive or negative)
    c) Developing a theme: trust, confidence, and so on
    d) Judging the timing
    e) Choosing a target voter: who's the audience?

D. Getting elected to Congress
  1. Malapportionment and gerrymandering
  2. Establishing the size of the House
  3. Winning the primary
    a) Ballot procedures
    b) Developing a personal following for the "party's" nomination
    c) Incumbent advantage
  4. Sophomore surge
    a) Using the perks of office
    b) Campaigning for/against Congress
  5. Impact of the way we elect individuals to Congress
    a) Legislators closely tied to local concerns
    b) Weak party leadership

IV. Primary versus general campaigns
  A. Kinds of elections and primaries: general versus primary elections and caucuses
  B. Each election or caucus attracts a different mix of voters so strategy must change
    1. Primaries and caucuses
      a) Must mobilize political activists who give money, do volunteer work and are willing to attend caucuses
      b) Such activists are more ideologically stringent than the average voter
        (1) So Democratic candidates need to be more liberal in their tone and theme
        (2) Republican candidates must be more conservative in their tone and theme
    2. Example: the Iowa caucus
      a) Held in February so winner can gain an early advantage in media attention and fund raising efforts

b) Participants are not representative of party members in the state, much less the nation
c) Procedural oddities exist as well

C. The balancing game exists in every state where activists are more ideologically polarized than the average voter
1. Possible result: the "clothespin vote"
2. John Kerry in 2004 and George McGovern in 1972
3. Front runners in early polls rarely prevail

D. Two kinds of campaign issues
1. Position issues
2. Valence issues
3. Trends in recent elections

E. Television, debates, and direct mail
1. Paid advertising (spots)
a) Has little (or a very subtle) effect on outcome: spots tend to cancel each other out
b) Most voters rely on many sources of information
2. News broadcasts (visuals)
a) Cost little
b) May have greater credibility with voters
c) Rely on having TV camera crew around
d) May be less informative than spots
3. Debates
a) Usually an advantage only to the challenger
b) Reagan in 1980: reassured voters
c) Three debates between Bush and Kerry did not seem to have an impact on the results of the election
4. Risk of slips of the tongue on visuals and debates
a) Ford and Poland, Carter and lust, Reagan and trees
b) Forces candidates to rely on stock speeches
c) Sell yourself, not your ideas
5. Free television time to major presidential candidates in 1996
6. The Internet
a) Makes sophisticated direct-mail campaigns possible
b) Allows candidates to address specific voters and solicit contributions
c) Creates increased importance to mailing lists
7. The gap between running a campaign and running the government
a) Party leaders had to worry about reelection
b) Today's political consultants don't

V. Money

A. The sources of campaign money
1. Presidential primaries: part private, part public money
a) Federal matching funds
b) Only match small donors: less than $250; $5,000 in twenty states
c) Gives incentive to raise money from small donors
d) Government also gives lump-sum grants to parties to cover conventions
2. Presidential general elections: all public money
3. Congressional elections: all private money
a) From individuals, PACs, and parties
b) Most from individual small donors ($100 to $200 a person)

B. Campaign finance rules
1. Watergate
a) Dubious and illegal money-raising schemes
b) Democrats and Republicans benefited from unenforceable laws
c) Nixon's resignation and a new campaign finance law
2. Reform law
a) Set limit on individual donations ($2,000 per election)
b) Reaffirmed ban on corporate and union donations, but allowed them to raise money through PACs
c) Set limit on PAC donations ($5,000 per election to individuals, $15,000 per year to a party)
d) Federal tax money made available for primaries and general election campaigns
3. Impact of the law
a) Increase in the amount of money spent on elections
b) Dramatic increase in PAC spending
c) More clever methods of solicitation (direct mail, telephone solicitation, etc.)
d) Additional problems: independent expenditures and soft money
4. A second campaign finance law
a) Reforms can have unintended consequences
b) Bipartisan Campaign Finance Reform Act of 2002
(1) Ban on soft money
(2) Increase on individual contributions (to $2,000 per candidate per election)
(3) Restrictions on independent expenditures
(a) Constitutional challenges as a violation of freedom of speech
(b) Court upheld almost all of the law
c) New sources of money: 527 organizations
(1) Designed to permit soft money expenditures once made by parties
(2) Unlimited expenditure allowed as long as there is no coordination with a candidate and no direct lobbying for that candidate
(3) Over 500 such organizations in 2004

C. Money and winning
1. During peacetime, presidential elections usually decided by three things
a) Political party affiliation
b) State of the economy
c) Character of candidates
2. Money makes a difference in congressional races
a) Challenger must spend to gain recognition
b) Jacobson: big-spending challengers do better
3. Advantages of incumbency
a) Easier to raise money
b) Can provide services for constituency
c) Can use franked mailings
d) Can get free publicity through legislation and such

VI. What decides elections?
A. Party identification, but why don't Democrats always win?
1. Democrats less wedded to their party
2. GOP does better among independents
3. Republicans have higher turnout

B. Issues, especially the economy
   1. V. O. Key: most voters who switch parties do so in their own interests
      a) They know which issues affect them personally
      b) They care strongly about emotional issues (abortion, etc.)
   2. Prospective voting
      a) Know the issues and vote for the best candidate
      b) Most common among activists and special-interest groups
      c) Few voters use prospective voting because it requires information
   3. Retrospective voting
      a) Judge the incumbent's performance and vote accordingly
      b) Have things gotten better or worse, especially economically?
      c) Examples: presidential campaigns of 1980, 1984, 1988, and 1992
      d) Usually helps incumbent unless economy has gotten worse
      e) Most elections decided by retrospective votes
      f) Midterm election: voters turn against president's party
C. The campaign
   1. Campaigns do make a difference
      a) Reawaken voters' partisan loyalties
      b) Let voters see how candidates handle pressure
      c) Let voters judge candidates' characters
   2. Campaigns tend to emphasize themes over details
      a) True throughout American history
      b) What has changed is the importance of primary elections and tone of campaigns
      c) Theme campaigns give more influence to single-issue groups
D. Finding a winning coalition
   1. Ways of looking at various groups
      a) How loyal, or percentage voting for party
      b) How important, or number voting for party
   2. Democratic coalition
      a) Blacks most loyal
      b) Jews slipping somewhat
      c) Hispanics somewhat mixed
      d) Catholics, southerners, unionists departing the coalition lately
   3. Republican coalition
      a) Party of business and professional people
      b) Very loyal, defecting only in 1964
      c) Usually wins vote of poor because of retired, elderly voters
   4. Contribution to Democratic coalition
      a) Blacks loyal but small proportion
      b) Catholics, unionists, and southerners largest part but least dependable

VII. The effect of elections on policy
   A. Political scientists are interested in broad trends in winning and losing
   B. Cynics: public policy remains more or less the same no matter which official or party is in office
      1. Comparison: Great Britain, with parliamentary system and strong parties, often sees marked changes, as in 1945
      2. Reply: evidence indicates that many American elections do make great differences in policy
      3. Why, then, the perception that elections do not matter? Because change alternates with consolidation; most elections are only retrospective judgments

KEY TERMS MATCH

Match the following terms and descriptions.

1. A means of soliciting funds from millions of people
2. Refers to states where the Republican candidate carried the electoral vote
3. Refers to states where the Democratic candidate carried the electoral vote
4. A filmed episode showing a candidate doing something newsworthy
5. Televised pictures showing nothing more than individuals speaking
6. Party that would always win presidential elections if party identification were the only thing that influenced the vote
7. Party that typically gets the greater support from so-called independent voters
8. A voter describing herself or himself as neither a Democrat nor a Republican
9. Can be given to the parties in limitless amounts so long as it is not used to back candidates by name
10. The tendency for newly elected members of Congress to become strong in their districts very quickly
11. A group legally able to solicit campaign contributions from individuals within an organization and, under certain restrictions, to funnel these to candidates for office
12. An election intended to select a party's candidates for elective office
13. A meeting of voters to help choose a candidate for office
14. An election used to fill an elective office
15. A primary election in which voters must first declare to which party they belong
16. A primary in which voters can vote for the candidates of either the Democratic or the Republican party

a. blanket primary
b. blue states
c. caucus (electoral)
d. closed primary
e. Democrats
f. direct mail
g. 527 organizations
h. general election
i. gerrymandering
j. incumbent
k. Independent
l. open primary
m. malapportionment
n. political action committee (PAC)
o. position issue
p. presidential primary
q. primary election
r. prospective voting
s. red states
t. Republican
u. retrospective voting
v. runoff primary
w. soft money
x. sophomore surge
y. spots
z. talking heads
aa. valence issue
bb. visual

17. A primary in which voters can vote for the Democratic candidates, the Republican candidates, or some from each party
18. A primary in which, to be successful, the candidate must receive a majority of all votes cast in that race
19. Organizations that, under an IRS code, raises and spends money to advance political causes
20. The person currently in office
21. The result of having districts of very unequal size
22. Drawing a district in some bizarre or unusual manner in order to create an electoral advantage
23. An issue dividing the electorate on which rival parties adopt different policy positions to attract voters
24. A primary held to select delegates to the presidential nominating conventions of the major parties
25. Voting for a candidate because one favors his or her ideas for addressing issues after the election
26. Voting for the candidate or party in office because one likes or dislikes how things have gone in the recent past
27. Short television advertisements used to promote a candidate for government office
28. An issue on which voters distinguish rival parties by the degree to which they associate each party with conditions or goals that the electorate universally supports or opposes

DATA CHECK

Table 10.1 (Page 230): Changes in State Representation in the House of Representatives

1. Which two states gained the largest number of electoral votes from 1990 to 2000?

____

2. Which two states lost the largest number of electoral votes from 1990 to 2000?

____

Figure 10.2 (Page 240): Growth of PACs

3. How does the recent growth of corporate PACs compare with that of PACs representing labor?

____

Table 10.2 (Page 245): Top Twenty PAC Contributors to Federal Candidates, Democrats and Repuiblicans (2005-2006)

4. What PAC contributed the largest amount of money in 2005-2006?

____

5. Which of the top PACs contributed 90 percent or more of their money to Democrats?

____

____

____

6. Which of the top PACs contributed 70 percent or more to the Republicans?

____

Table 10.3 (Page 248): Percentage of Popular Vote by Groups in Presidential Election, 1960–2004

This table indicates how voters with each set of identifiers (Republicans, Democrats, Independents) claim to have voted in a series of presidential elections. For each year the total percentages for each party equal 100 percent, divided among the various candidates. Columns are read down to see how group support has changed from one election to the next. Columns are read across to see how a candidate won votes, whether he or she built a partisan or bipartisan coalition, and whether she or he won the independent vote. Remember again that these figures are based on how people *said* they voted, not on *how* they voted.

7. In which elections did Republicans give the GOP candidate at least 90 percent of their vote?

____

8. In which elections did Democrats give the Democrats 90 percent or more of their vote?

____

9. What percentage of Republicans claimed to have voted for Ross Perot in 1992 and 1996?

10. What percentage of Democrats claimed to have voted for Ross Perot in 1992 and 1996?

11. Describe the vote of political Independents in the 2004 election.

Table 10.5 (Page 252): Who Likes the Democrats?

Percentages refer to the proportion of the group stating that they voted for the Democratic presidential nominee in the indicated year.

12. Describe the relationship between education and the tendency to vote for Democratic candidates.

13. Which group appears to consistently provide the highest level of support for Democratic candidates?

14. Which group appears to consistently provide the lowest level of support for Democratic candidates?

15. In what years has the difference between male and female support for Democratic candidates been greater than 5 percent?

16. In what years has the difference between Protestants and members of the Jewish faith been greater than 20 percent?

Figure 10.4 (Page 253): Partisan Division of the Presidential Vote in the Nation, 1856–2004

Each of the colored lines represents the percentage of the popular vote received by the major parties in presidential elections. Third parties receiving more than five percent of the popular vote are indicated by green dots.

17. The popular vote for Democratic candidates was higher than 60 percent in which election(s)?

18. The popular vote for Republican candidates was higher than 60 percent in which election(s)?

19. In which elections has popular support for either of the major parties fallen below 30 percent?

20. Which third party has gained the highest percentage of the popular vote in a presidential election?

____

PRACTICING FOR EXAMS

TRUE/FALSE QUESTIONS

Read each statement carefully. Mark true statements *T*. If any part of the statement is false, mark it *F*, and write in the space provided a concise explanation of why the statement is false.

1. T F The 2008 presidential sweepstakes started in 2006.

____

2. T F In 1968 a candidate won his party's nomination to the presidency without competing in a single state primary.

____

3. T F Presidential races are more competitive than races for the House of Representatives.

____

4. T F In a typical House race, the incumbent receives over 60 percent of the vote.

____

5. T F Voter turnout is higher in years when there is no presidential contest.

____

6. T F Increasingly, congressional candidates benefit from the coattails of popular presidential candidates.

____

7. T F Members of Congress can serve for an unlimited number of terms.

____

8. T F The Constitution provides detailed instructions on the selection of representatives.

____

9. T F The Supreme Court decides how many seats a state will have in the House of Representatives.

____

10. T F The Supreme Court requires that a census is taken every ten years.

____

11. T F It is quite unusual for an incumbent to lose a primary.

____

12. T F Congressmen often run for Congress by running against it.

____

13. T F Congressmen who claim the "delegate" role use their best judgment on issues without regard to the preferences of their district.

14. T F "Trustees" seek out committee assignments and projects that will produce benefits for their districts.

15. T F The several thousand Iowans who participate in their parties' caucuses are not representative of the followers of their party in the state.

16. T F The Iowa caucuses are the first real test of candidates vying for the nomination.

17. T F In order to contrast himself with Howard Dean in the early primaries and caucuses, John Kerry claimed he supported the invasion of Iraq.

18. T F The Democratic "frontrunner" in early polls usually gets the nomination.

19. T F Many of the great party realignments have been based on valence issues.

20. T F Valence issues divide both voters and candidates.

21. T F The 2004 campaign relied on both valence and position issues.

22. T F Television advertising probably has a greater impact on primaries.

23. T F There is considerable evidence that the 2004 presidential debates had an impact on the outcome of the election.

24. T F In 1980, Ronald Reagan slipped by suggesting trees cause pollution.

25. T F A PAC must have at least fifty members.

26. T F Most of the money for congressional campaigns comes from big business and PACs.

27. T F Typically, a PAC will donate the maximum amount ($5,000) per election to individual candidates.

28. T F Bush, Dean and Kerry all declined federal matching funds in the 2004 election.

29. T F The reassignment in electoral votes that took place prior to the 2004 election benefited George Bush.

30. T F If the U.S. Supreme Court had allowed the vote count ordered by the Florida Supreme Court to continue, Al Gore would have won.

31. T F If the U.S. Supreme Court had allowed Al Gore's original request for hand counts of votes in Florida counties, he would have won.

32. T F Critics of 2002 campaign finance rules have challenged their constitutionality in the courts.

33. T F The text suggests campaign finance laws are not likely to take money out of politics.

34. T F In good economic times the party holding the White House normally does well.

35. T F The choice a presidential candidate makes for the vice-president slot is critical to winning or losing an election.

36. T F In the general election, one's position on abortion is not likely to be critical.

37. T F Self-proclaimed Democrats are more likely to vote than Republicans.

38. T F Political activists are more likely to be prospective voters.

39. T F Retrospective voters decide elections.

40. T F The Republicans are often described as the party of business and professional people.

41. T F Studies by scholars confirm that elections are often a critical source of policy change.

42. T F Elections in ordinary times are not "critical."

MULTIPLE CHOICE QUESTIONS

Circle the letter of the response that best answers the question or completes the statement.

1. Among the major changes in elections in campaigns are all of the following *except*
   a. money matters more than ever.
   b. parties are less important.
   c. fund raising is a non-stop activity.
   d. media are more important.
   e. debates are more important.
2. Research suggests political ads which ________ wield the greatest influence over voters with the greatest interest in politics.
   a. focus on the issues
   b. appeal to emotion
   c. emphasize the positive characteristics of candidates
   d. employ humor
   e. compare and contrast candidates
3. "Campaigning" has largely become synonymous with
   a. fundraising.
   b. mobilization.
   c. triangulation.
   d. clarification.
   e. polarizing.
4. In America, candidates win party nominations primarily through
   a. convention politics.
   b. the decision-making of state party leaders.
   c. the decision-making of national party leaders.
   d. seniority.
   e. individual effort.
5. A major difference between presidential and congressional campaigns is that
   a. more people vote in congressional elections.
   b. presidential races are generally less competitive.
   c. presidential candidates can more credibly take credit for improvements in a district.
   d. presidential incumbents can better provide services for their constituents.
   e. congressional incumbents can more easily duck responsibility.
6. All of the following statements about presidential and congressional races are true *except*
   a. presidential races are more competitive.
   b. more people vote in presidential elections.
   c. congressional incumbents usually win.
   d. presidents can rarely take credit for improvements in a district.
   e. presidents can distance themselves from the "mess" in Washington.
7. Which statement best reflects the relationship between popular presidential candidates and congressional candidates of the same party?
   a. There is considerable evidence of a coattail effect benefiting congressional candidates.
   b. There is considerable evidence of a coattail effect benefiting presidential candidates.
   c. Congressional candidates increasingly benefit from popular presidential candidates.
   d. There has been a sharp decline in the benefit of presidential coattails for congressional candidates.
   e. Congressional candidates have never benefited from the coattails of popular presidential candidates.

8. Which, according to the text, is probably least likely to be elected president?
   a. A current member of the Senate.
   b. A former member of Congress.
   c. A governor.
   d. A military hero.
   e. A vice-president.
9. Federal law restricts the amount that any single individual can give a candidate to ________ in each election.
   a. $500
   b. $1,000
   c. $1,500
   d. $2,000
   e. $5,000
10. Federal law restricts the amount that a PAC can give a candidate to ________ in each election.
    a. $500
    b. $1,000
    c. $1,500
    d. $2,000
    e. $5,000
11. In the 1992 election, Bill Clinton chose as a theme
    a. trust.
    b. compassionate conservatism.
    c. competence.
    d. stay the course.
    e. we need change.
12. In the 2000 election, George W. Bush chose as a theme
    a. trust.
    b. compassionate conservatism.
    c. competence.
    d. stay the course.
    e. we need change.
13. According to the text, which of the following is a *critical* problem to solve in deciding who gets represented in the House?
    a. Allocating seats in the House among the states.
    b. Determining the shape of districts.
    c. Determining the size of districts.
    d. Establishing the total size of the House.
    e. All of the above.
14. In 1911, Congress fixed the size of the House of Representatives at ______ members.
    a. 50
    b. 100
    c. 435
    d. 535
    e. 537

15. The states did little about malapportionment and gerrymandering until ordered to do so by
    a. the president.
    b. Congress.
    c. the Supreme Court.
    d. political party leaders.
    e. the Justice Department.
16. Which statement about the so-called "sophomore surge" is *correct*?
    a. It has been around since the 1940s.
    b. It usually means an 8 to 10 percent increase in votes.
    c. It benefits members of the Senate more than members of the House.
    d. It does not benefit members of the Senate at all.
    e. It is the result of an increase in trust of the federal government.
17. Former House Speaker Thomas P. "Tip" O'Neill famously said "All politics is ______."
    a. local
    b. contentious
    c. stressful
    d. economic
    e. flexible
18. In order to win the party nomination, candidates need to appear particularly
    a. liberal.
    b. conservative.
    c. void of anything that looks like an ideological disposition.
    d. liberal if Democrats, conservative if Republicans.
    e. conservative if Democrats, liberal if Republicans.
19. Voters at the Iowa Democratic caucuses, compared with other Democrats from Iowa, tend to be
    a. void of anything that looks like an ideological disposition.
    b. more conservative.
    c. more liberal.
    d. younger.
    e. less educated.
20. When a voter casts a "clothespin" vote, he or she picks the
    a. most comfortable, homelike candidate.
    b. candidate most likely to endure.
    c. most familiar candidate.
    d. candidate that appears most reliable in a time of crisis.
    e. least objectionable candidate.
21. Which of the following is a valence issue rather than a position issue?
    a. Legal access to abortion.
    b. Nuclear disarmament.
    c. Civil rights legislation.
    d. All of the above.
    e. Wasted tax dollars.

22. In a(n) ________ primary, voters must declare themselves registered members of a party in advance.
    a. open
    b. closed
    c. blanket
    d. runoff
    e. free love
23. Which of the following statements concerning research on political advertising and television news programs is *correct*?
    a. News programs tend to convey more information.
    b. Paid commercials often contain information seen, remembered and evaluated by the public.
    c. News programs tend to make greater impressions on viewers.
    d. More lengthy presentations (such as televised interviews and debates) provide more information and make greater impressions on voters.
    e. News programs avoid stark visual images and campaign slogans.
24. To a political candidate, the drawback of television visuals and debates is
    a. their expense.
    b. the risk of slipups.
    c. the low audience response.
    d. their lack of credibility.
    e. the complications surrounding choice of back-drops.
25. If one were to argue debates can have considerable impact on the opinions of potential voters, they would most likely point to the case of
    a. Walter Mondale in 1984.
    b. Ross Perot in 1992.
    c. Bill Clinton in 1992.
    d. Bill Clinton in 1996.
    e. George Bush in 2004.
26. Unlike funding for presidential campaigns, the money for congressional campaigns comes from
    a. both private and public sources.
    b. public sources only.
    c. private sources only.
    d. federal matching grants only.
    e. state income taxes.
27. In the general election, the government pays all the costs of each candidate up to a limit set by law. In 2004, that limit was at about ______ million dollars.
    a. 40
    b. 54
    c. 64
    d. 74
    e. 100
28. In 2004, President Bush generally received the votes of all of the following *except*
    a. union members.
    b. military veterans.
    c. whites.
    d. married couples.
    e. conservatives.

29. Which of the following was a consequence of the Bipartisan Campaign Finance Reform Act of 2002?
    a. Impressive levels of spending by so-called 527 organizations.
    b. A decrease in the costs of campaigns.
    c. A reduction in the influence of money in campaigns.
    d. Less restriction on "independent expenditures."
    e. Elimination of the so-called "incumbent advantage."
30. If presidential campaigns were decided simply by party identification,
    a. the Democrats would always win.
    b. the Republicans would always win.
    c. the Democrats would win most of the time.
    d. the Republicans would win most of the time.
    e. there would be no intelligent way to know what the impact would be.
31. In recent presidential elections the independent vote has usually favored
    a. a third party.
    b. the Republicans.
    c. the Democrats.
    d. no one party.
    e. male candidates.
32. Ronald Reagan's 1980 victory over Jimmy Carter particularly suggests the importance of
    a. the personal popularity of Reagan.
    b. the public's broad agreement with Reagan's position on issues.
    c. partisan loyalty in voting decisions.
    d. prospective voting in presidential elections.
    e. retrospective voting in presidential elections.
33. Careful statistical studies based on actual campaigns suggest that negative ads
    a. backfire on the candidates that use them and mobilize support for their opponents.
    b. are a turn-off to voters.
    c. increase the disgust of voters with politics and decrease voter turnout.
    d. work by stimulating voter turnout.
    e. have a major impact on levels of confidence in the political system.
34. With respect to the seemingly "negative" tone of today's campaigns, the authors suggest it
    a. is not a new feature of American politics and it has been much worse.
    b. is not a new feature of American politics, but it is worse now than it has ever been.
    c. is a relatively new feature in American politics.
    d. became a feature of American politics when pro- and antiabortion groups grew in influence.
    e. tends to disappear when the nation is at war.
35. Blacks and Jews have been the most loyal supporters of
    a. the Democrats.
    b. independent candidates.
    c. minor parties.
    d. nonideological candidates.
    e. the Republicans.
36. The text suggests ________ are "a volatile group" and "thus quick to change parties."
    a. businessmen
    b. teachers
    c. lawyers
    d. doctors
    e. farmers

ESSAY QUESTIONS

Practice writing extended answers to the following questions. These test your ability to integrate and express the ideas that you have been studying in this chapter.

1. Identify the ways in which winning a party nomination in the United States is an individual effort.
2. Explain four major ways in which presidential and congressional elections differ.
3. What is the "sophomore surge" and to whom does it typically apply the most?
4. The local orientation of legislators have what three important effects on how policy is made?
5. List the qualifications for members of the House and members of the Senate.
6. Explain the role of ideology in primary elections and in the general election. Why do the authors suggest a candidate has to run two different elections to win?
7. Explain the difference between valence and position issues and generalize about the use of each in recent campaigns.
8. Explain how presidential candidates can qualify for matching funds in primary campaigns.
9. Describe three important changes in the Bipartisan Campaign Finance Reform Act of 2002.
10. The test suggest money does not make much of a difference in who wins or loses the general election because all of the major candidates have it. What are four other things that the text suggests "do not make much of a difference?"
11. What are some ways that campaigns do make a difference?

ANSWERS TO KEY TERMS MATCH QUESTIONS

1. f
2. s
3. b
4. bb
5. z
6. e
7. t
8. k
9. w
10. x
11. n
12. q
13. c
14. h
15. d
16. l
17. a
18. v
19. g
20. j
21. m
22. i
23. o
24. p
25. r
26. u
27. y
28. aa

ANSWERS TO DATA CHECK QUESTIONS

1. Florida and California.
2. New York and Pennsylvania.
3. No comparison; labor PACs have hardly grown at all.
4. National Association of Realtors.

5. International Brotherhood of Electrical Workers, American Association for Justice, United Auto Workers, American Federation of Teachers, American Federation of State County and Municipal Employees and Plumbers and Pipe fitters Union.
6. National Beer Wholesalers Association and National Association of Homebuilders.
7. 1960, 1972, 1984, 1988, 2000, 2004.
8. None.
9. 1992 (17 percent); 1996 (6 percent).
10. 1992 (13 percent); 1996 (5 percent).
11. Independents claimed to have voted at a slightly higher rate (1 percent) for John Kerry.
12. Higher levels of education (grad school) are associated with higher levels of support for Democratic candidates.
13. Probably non-whites, who have an average level of support of 78 percent across ten elections.
14. Probably those in business and professional occupations, who have an average level of support of only 39 percent in the seven elections for which data are available.
15. 1980, 1988, 1996, 2000, and 2004.
16. Every year for which there are available data.
17. 1936 and 1964.
18. 1920 and 1972.
19. 1860 (Democrats), 1912 (Republicans) and 1924 (Democrats).
20. 1912, Bull Moose Party.

ANSWERS TO TRUE/FALSE QUESTIONS

1. T
2. T
3. T
4. T
5. F Voter turnout is much higher in years when there is a presidential election than it is in mid-term elections.
6. F The amount of benefit that congressional candidates receive from the coattails of a popular president has always been in doubt. Today, it is non-existent.
7. T
8. F The Constitution says little on the topic, leaving it up to the states to decide for themselves.
9. F Congress makes this determination after the census.
10. F The Constitution makes this requirement, not the Supreme Court.
11. T
12. T
13. F Delegates attempt to act in manner that they believe would please their constituents.

14. F This describes the behavior of delegates. Trustees seek committee assignments that will enable them to address "larger" questions and issues.
15. T
16. T
17. T
18. F Muskie, Wallace, Kennedy, Hart, Cuomo and Lieberman were all Democratic frontrunners and none of them got their party's nomination.
19. F Since 1860, many have been based on position issues.
20. F Valence issues are issues about which nearly everyone agrees.
21. T
22. T
23. F There is little evidence that they had any impact.
24. T
25. T
26. F Most of it comes from individuals.
27. F In fact, they give very little, often no more than $500.
28. T
29. T
30. F Bush would have still won by 493.
31. F Bush would have still won by 225.
32. T
33. T
34. T
35. F The text suggests there has "rarely" been an election when this choice mattered.
36. T
37. F Self-proclaimed Republicans are more likely to vote than self-proclaimed Democrats.
38. T
39. T
40. T
41. T
42. T

ANSWERS TO MULTIPLE CHOICE QUESTIONS

1. e
2. b
3. a

4. e
5. e
6. e
7. d
8. a
9. d
10. e
11. e
12. b
13. e
14. c
15. c
16. b
17. a
18. d
19. c
20. e
21. e
22. b
23. b
24. b
25. b
26. c
27. d
28. a
29. a
30. a
31. b
32. e
33. d
34. a
35. a
36. e

CHAPTER 11

Interest Groups

REVIEWING THE CHAPTER

CHAPTER FOCUS

The purpose of this chapter is to survey the wide variety of interest groups or lobbies that operate in the United States and to assess the effect they have on the political system of the country. After reading and reviewing the material in this chapter, you should be able to do each of the following:

1. Explain why the characteristics of American society and government encourage a multiplicity of interest groups, and compare the American and British experiences in this regard.
2. Describe the historical conditions under which interest groups are likely to form, and specify the kinds of organizations Americans are most likely to join.
3. Describe relations between leaders and rank-and-file members of groups, including why the sentiments of members may not determine the actions of leaders.
4. Describe several methods that interest groups use to formulate and carry out their political objectives, especially the lobbying techniques used to gain public support. Explain why courts have become an important forum for public-interest groups.
5. List the laws regulating conflict of interest, and describe the problems involved with "revolving door" government employment. Describe the provisions of the 1978 conflict-of-interest law. Explain the suggestions that have been made for stricter laws. Describe the balance between the First Amendment's freedom of expression and the need to prevent corruption in the political system.

STUDY OUTLINE

I. Explaining proliferation: why interest groups are common in the United States
    A. Many kinds of cleavage in the country
    B. Constitution makes for many access points
    C. Public laws favor the non-profit sector
    D. Political parties are weak
II. The birth of interest groups
    A. Periods of rapid growth
        1. Since 1960, 70 percent have established an office in Washington, D.C.
        2. 1770s, independence groups
        3. 1830s and 1840s, religious, antislavery groups
        4. 1860s, craft unions
        5. 1880s and 1890s, business associations
        6. 1900s and 1910, most major lobbies of today

- B. Factors explaining the rise of interest groups
  - 1. Broad economic developments create new interests
    - a) Farmers produce cash crops
    - b) Mass production industries begin
  - 2. Government policy itself
    - a) Created veterans' groups—wars
    - b) Encouraged formation of Farm Bureau
    - c) Launched Chamber of Commerce
    - d) Favored growth of unions
  - 3. Emergence of strong leaders, usually at certain times
  - 4. Expanding role of government

III. Kinds of organizations

- A. Institutional interests
  - 1. Defined: individuals or organizations representing other organizations
  - 2. Types
    - a) Businesses: example, General Motors
    - b) Trade or governmental associations
  - 3. Concerns—bread-and-butter issues of concern to their clients
    - a) Clearly defined, with homogeneous groups
    - b) Diffuse, with diversified groups
  - 4. Other interests—governments, foundations, universities
- B. Membership interests
  - 1. Americans join some groups more frequently than people in other nations
    - a) Social, business, and so on, same rate as elsewhere
    - b) Unions, less likely to join
    - c) Religious or civic groups, more likely to join
    - d) Greater sense of efficacy and duty explains the tendency to join civic groups
  - 2. Most sympathizers do not join because
    - a) Individuals not that significant
    - b) Benefits flow to nonmembers too
- C. Incentives to join
  - 1. Solidary incentives—pleasure, companionship (League of Women Voters, AARP, NAACP, Rotary, etc.)
  - 2. Material incentives—money, things, services (farm organizations, retired persons, etc.)
  - 3. Purpose of the organization itself—public-interest organizations
    - a) Ideological interest groups' appeal is controversial principles
    - b) Engage in research and bring lawsuits
- D. Influence of the staff
  - 1. Many issues affect different members differently
  - 2. Issues may be irrelevant to those joining for solidary or material benefits
  - 3. Group efforts may reflect opinion of staff more than general membership

IV. Interest groups and social movements

- A. Social movement is a widely shared demand for change
- B. Environmental movement
- C. Feminist movement: three kinds
  - 1. Solidary—LWV and others (widest support)
  - 2. Purposive—NOW, NARAL (strong position on divisive issues)
  - 3. Caucus—WEAL (material benefits)
- D. Union movement
  - 1. Major movement occurred in the 1930s

2. Peak around 1945
3. Steady decline since, today about 10 percent of all workers
4. Explanations for the decline
    a) Shift from industrial production to service delivery
    b) Decline in popular approval of unions
5. Growth in unions composed of government workers

V. Funds for interest groups
  A. Expansion and cutbacks in federal grants affect interest groups
    1. Support for projects undertaken
        a) Largenot-for-profits benefit when grants are awarded for services they provide
        b) Performance audits of independent research evaluations rarely follow
        c) Recipients rarely change
    2. Efforts by Reagan and Bush to cut back and increase funds
    3. Business and federal contracts
  B. Direct mail
    1. Unique to modern interest groups through use of computers
    2. Common cause a classic example
    3. Techniques
        a) Teaser
        b) Emotional arousal
        c) Celebrity endorsement
        d) Personalization of letter

VI. Problem of bias
  A. Reasons for belief in upper-class bias
    1. More affluent more likely to join
    2. Business or professional groups more numerous; better financed
  B. Why these facts do not decide the issue
    1. Describe inputs but not outputs
    2. Business groups often divided among themselves
  C. Important to ask what the bias is
    1. Many conflicts are within upper middle class
    2. Resource differentials are clues, not conclusions

VII. Activities of interest groups
  A. Information
    1. Single most important tactic
        a) Nonpolitical sources insufficient
        b) Provide detailed, current information
    2. Most effective on narrow, technical issues
    3. Officials also need cues; ratings systems
    4. Dissemination of information and cues via fax
  B. Public support: rise of new politics
    1. Outsider strategy replacing insider strategy
    2. New strategy leads to controversy that politicians dislike
    3. Key targets: the undecided
    4. Some groups attack their likely allies to embarrass them
    5. Legislators sometimes buck public opinion, unless issue important
    6. Some groups try for grassroots support
        a) Saccharin issue
        b) "Dirty Dozen" environmental polluters
    7. Few large, well-funded interests are all-powerful (e.g., NRA)

C. Money and PACs
   1. Money is least effective way to influence politicians
   2. Campaign finance reform law of 1973 had two effects
      a) Restricted amount interest groups can give to candidates
      b) Made it legal for corporations and unions to create PACs
   3. Rapid growth in PACs has not led to vote buying
      a) More money is available on all sides
      b) Members of Congress take money but still decide how to vote
   4. Almost any organization can create a PAC
      a) More than half of all PACs sponsored by corporations
      b) Recent increase in ideological PACs; one-third liberal, two-thirds conservative
   5. Ideological PACs raise more but spend less because of cost of raising money
   6. In 2000 unions and business organizations gave most
   7. Incumbents get most PAC money
      a) Business PACs split money between Democrats and Republicans
      b) Democrats get most PAC money
   8. PAC contributions small
   9. No evidence PAC money influences votes in Congress
      a) Most members vote their ideology
      b) When issue of little concern to voters, slight correlation but may be misleading
      c) PAC money may influence in other ways, such as access
      d) PAC money most likely to influence on client politics
D. The revolving door
   1. Individuals leave important jobs in the federal government and go into lucrative positions in private industry
   2. Some become lobbyists and there are concerns
      a) Improper influence
      b) Promise of positions upon leaving government
   3. Some prominent examples, especially in the procurement process
E. Trouble
   1. Disruption always part of American politics
   2. Used by groups of varying ideologies
   3. Better accepted since 1960s
   4. History of proper persons using disruption: suffrage, civil rights, antiwar movements
   5. Officials dread no-win situation

VIII. Regulating interest groups
A. Protection by First Amendment
B. 1946 law accomplished little in requiring registration
C. 1995 lobby act enacted by Congress
   1. Broadens definition of a lobbyist
   2. Lobbyists must report twice annually
      a) The names of clients
      b) Their income and expenditures
      c) The issues on which they worked
   3. Exempts grassroots organizations
   4. No enforcement organization created
D. 2007 reforms by Democrats
   1. Gifts from registered lobbyists or firms that employ them
   2. Reimbursement for travel costs from registered lobbyists or forms that employ them

3. Reimbursements for travel for trips organized or requested by registered lobbyists or firms that employ them

E. Impact of reforms?
1. Rules will probably be enforces "strictly speaking"
2. Exceptions, loopholes and need for clarification
3. Still room for evasion and abuse

F. Significant restraints prior to 1995 still in effect
1. Tax code: threat of losing tax exempt status
2. Campaign finance laws

KEY TERMS MATCH

Match the following terms and descriptions.

1. Any group that seeks to influence public policy
2. Interest groups made up of those who join voluntarily
3. Large not-for-profit firms with trade representatives or lobbyists in Washington who win federal grants and contracts
4. The sense of pleasure, status, or companionship arising from group membership
5. Money, things, or services obtainable from interest group membership
6. The goals of an organization that, if attained, would benefit primarily nongroup members
7. Organizations that attract members mostly by the appeal of their broad, controversial principles
8. Organizations that gather information on consumer topics (first organized by Ralph Nader)
9. The solicitation of funding through letter campaigns
10. The situation that arises when a government agency services as well as regulates a distinct group
11. Argued the latent causes of faction are sown in the nature of man
12. Nonprofit group that lobbies, campaigns and received non-tax deductible donations

a. "beltway bandits"
b. client politics
c. cue (political)
d. direct mail
e. "Dirty Dozen"
f. Federal Regulation of Lobbying Act of 1946
g. *Federalist* 10
h. Section 501(c)(3) organizations
i. Section 501 (c)(4) organizations
j. grassroots support
k. ideological interest groups
l. incentive (political)
m. insider strategy
n. institutional interests
o. interest groups
p. issue public
q. lobbyist
r. material benefit incentives
s. membership interests
t. outsider strategy
u. PACs
v. PIRGs
w. public-interest lobby
x. purposive incentive

13. Backing for a public policy that arises or is created in public opinion
14. A list, compiled by an environmental interest group, of those legislators who voted most frequently against its measures
15. The part of the public that is directly affected by or deeply concerned with a governmental policy
16. Groups that can collect political donations and make campaign contributions to candidates for office
17. The practice of lobbying officials with such promises as employment after their government service
18. Its application restricted to lobbying efforts involving direct contacts with members of Congress
19. A signal to a member of Congress that identifies which values are at stake in a vote
20. Nonprofit group that addresses political matters but cannot lobby or campaign
21. A valued benefit obtained by joining a political organization
22. A person attempting to influence government decisions on behalf of an interest group
23. The sense of satisfaction derived from serving a cause from which one does not benefit personally
24. An assessment of a representative's voting record on issues important to an interest group
25. A widely shared demand for change in some aspect of the social or political order
26. Lobbyists working closely with a few key members of Congress, meeting them privately to exchange information and sometimes favors
27. Plan increasingly used by lobbyists with advent of modern technology and employing grassroots lobbying

y. ratings

z. revolving-door influence

aa. social movement

bb. solidary incentives

PRACTICING FOR EXAMS

TRUE/FALSE QUESTIONS

Read each statement carefully. Mark true statements *T*. If any part of the statement is false, mark it *F*, and write in the space provided a concise explanation of why the statement is false.

1. T F James Madison considered the latent causes of "faction" to be sown in "human nature."

   ____

2. T F The American system features more interest groups than that of Great Britain because there are more points of access and opportunities to influence policy.

   ____

3. T F Section 501(c)(3) organizations are forbidden to lobby government officials or contribute to political campaigns.

   ____

4. T F The number of interest groups has grown rapidly since the 1960s.

   ____

5. T F Political interest groups tend to arise inevitably out of natural social processes.

   ____

6. T F Governmental policies have generally been a roadblock to the creation of interest groups.

   ____

7. T F Europeans are more likely than Americans to think that organized activity is an effective way to influence the national government.

   ____

8. T F The League of Women Voters represents an organization based on solidary incentives.

   ____

9. T F It is probably easier for organizations to form small local chapters in the United States because of the importance of local government.

   ____

10. T F The provision of money and services would constitute solidary incentives for membership.

    ____

11. T F Conservatives have been slow to adopt the public-interest organizational strategy.

    ____

12. T F The text suggests that public-interest lobbies often do best when the government is in the hands of an administration that is hostile to their views.

    ____

13. T F The larger organizations that are spawned by social movements tend to be more passionate and extreme in their position taking than smaller organizations.

    ____

14. T F The League of Women Voters was founded to educate women and organize women to effectively use their newly gained right to vote.

15. T F Women's organizations that rely chiefly on solidary incentives take controversial stands and are constantly embroiled in internal quarrels.

16. T F Membership in unions is steadily increasing.

17. T F Membership in unions composed of government workers is decreasing.

18. T F Businesses receive far more money in federal contracts than non-profit groups.

19. T F The text suggests business-oriented interest groups are rarely divided among themselves.

20. T F Interest groups are an accurate reflection of the high degree of unity that exists among politically active elites.

21. T F When an issue is broad and highly visible, the value of information provided by lobbyists is reduced.

22. T F Interest groups produce "ratings" in order to generate support for, or opposition to, legislators.

23. T F Ratings can be biased by arbitrary determination of what constitutes a liberal or conservative vote.

24. T F Republican activist William Kristol is given credit for creative use of billboards in an effort to defeat President Clinton's education programs.

25. T F Increasingly, interest groups and lobbyists have turned to an "insider strategy."

26. T F Most legislators tend to work with interest groups with whom they agree.

27. T F Members of interest groups tend to work primarily with legislators with whom they agree.

28. T F The text suggests money is probably one of the least effective ways for interest groups to advance their causes.

29. T F Some members of Congress tell PACs what to do rather than take orders from them.

30. T F Members of Congress are not allowed to set up their own PACs.

31. T F Almost 80 percent of all PACs are sponsored by corporations.

32. T F In recent years, there has been little interest in the creation of ideological PACs.

33. T F Ideological PACs tend to raise more money and to contribute more to candidates.

34. T F Both parties are dependent upon PAC money.

35. T F Even with all of the loopholes, the laws regulating lobbying are tighter than ever.

36. T F The Sierra Club lost its tax exempt status because of its extensive lobbying activities.

MULTIPLE CHOICE QUESTIONS

Circle the letter of the response that best answers the question or completes the statement.

1. In the *Federalist* papers, Madison took the position that the causes of faction can be found in
   a. constitutional arrangements.
   b. self-serving interest groups.
   c. ambitious politicians.
   d. the nature of man.
   e. notions of rights and responsibilities.
2. Where political parties are strong, interest groups are likely to be
   a. stronger.
   b. independent.
   c. weak.
   d. more numerous.
   e. nonideological.
3. The "great era of organization building" in America occurred during the years
   a. 1830–1840.
   b. 1900–1920.
   c. 1883–1896.
   d. 1970–1980.
   e. 1940–1960.

4. Large labor unions had no reason to exist until the era of
   a. mass-production industry.
   b. "ill feeling."
   c. "goodwill."
   d. anti-federalism.
   e. consumerism.
5. Professional societies of doctors and lawyers first gained in importance because
   a. their numbers increased more than those of other professions.
   b. more and more legislators came from those professions.
   c. the Supreme Court made several decisions favorable toward their interests.
   d. state governments gave them authority to decide qualifications for their professions.
   e. the Tenth Amendment was ignored by most state governments.
6. The great majority of "public-interest" lobbies were established
   a. after 1960.
   b. after 1970.
   c. after 1980.
   d. after 1990.
   e. after 1995.
7. In the landmark case *U.S.* v. *Harris* (1954), the Supreme Court ruled the government can
   a. require information from groups that try to influence legislation.
   b. limit the number of groups that try to influence government.
   c. prohibit interest groups from lobbying on government property.
   d. prohibit government officials from contributing to interest groups.
   e. declare some interest groups more "qualified" than others.
8. It is often said that Americans are a nation of
   a. linkers.
   b. combinationists.
   c. relaters.
   d. joiners.
   e. aggregationists.
9. Americans are less likely than the British to join
   a. labor unions.
   b. social organizations.
   c. business organizations.
   d. veteran organizations.
   e. professional organizations.
10. Americans have an unusually high rate of membership in
   a. religious organizations.
   b. civic organizations.
   c. business organizations.
   d. political associations.
   e. A, B and D.
11. Solidary incentives involve
   a. employment opportunities in government agencies.
   b. the appeal of a stated goal.
   c. a sense of pleasure, status or companionship.
   d. money, or things and services readily valued in monetary terms.
   e. assurances that partisanship will play no part in an organization's decision-making.

12. When the Illinois Farm Bureau offers its members discount prices and the chance to purchase low-cost insurance, it is providing _________ incentives.
    a. solidary
    b. material
    c. purposive
    d. both solidary and purposive
    e. ideological
13. Purposive incentives involve
    a. employment opportunities in government agencies.
    b. the appeal of a stated goal.
    c. a sense of pleasure, status or companionship.
    d. money, or things and services readily valued in monetary terms.
    e. assurances that partisanship will play no part in an organization's decision-making.
14. Ralph Nader rose to national prominence on the issue of
    a. school busing.
    b. abortion.
    c. auto safety.
    d. nuclear power.
    e. discrimination.
15. Membership organizations that rely on purposive incentives tend to be shaped by
    a. economic trends.
    b. social policy.
    c. the mood of the times.
    d. legal developments.
    e. demographic shifts.
16. All of the following are examples of liberal public-interest law firms *except* the
    a. American Civil Liberties Union.
    b. Asian American Legal Defense Fund.
    c. NAACP Legal Defense and Education Fund.
    d. Criminal Justice Legal Foundation.
    e. Women's Legal Defense Fund.
17. The Center for Defense Information, the Children's Defense Fund, and the Economic Policy Institute are examples of
    a. liberal public-interest law firms.
    b. nonideological public-interest think tanks.
    c. conservative public-interest law firms.
    d. liberal think tanks.
    e. conservative think tanks.
18. The National Organization for Women and the National Abortion Rights Action League are examples of organizations that feature
    a. solidary incentives.
    b. purposive incentives.
    c. material incentives.
    d. non-partisan incentives.
    e. all of the above.

19. The major union movement in America occurred in the
    a. 1920s.
    b. 1930s.
    c. 1950s.
    d. 1960s.
    e. 1970s.
20. The shift in the nation's economic life toward _______ has contributed to the decline in unions.
    a. industrial production
    b. the development of infrastructure
    c. international trade
    d. service delivery
    e. A and B
21. "Beltway bandits" are
    a. interest groups who actively oppose increases in federal grants.
    b. large national for-profit firms with trade representatives or lobbyists in Washington.
    c. coalitions of interest groups who lobby against applications for federal contracts.
    d. Washington-based lobbyists who obtain grants for small, not-for-profit organizations.
    e. federal employees who oversee the application process for grants and contracts.
22. Which statement is *incorrect*?
    a. Nobody really knows whether the groups that win federal grants and contracts are doing a good job or not.
    b. The organizations that receive the lion's share of grants and contracts are frequently audited and evaluated.
    c. The list of top discretionary grant recipients generally looks the same from year to year.
    d. The organizations that administer social services funded by Washington are typically large.
    e. Ronald Reagan attempted to cut back on federal funds going to nonprofit groups that supposedly lobbied for liberal causes.
23. About ________ percent of the interest groups represented in Washington, D.C., are public-interest groups.
    a. 4
    b. 12
    c. 15
    d. 20
    e. 40
24. Although farmers today have difficulty getting Congress to pass bills in their favor, they are still able to
    a. block bills that they don't like.
    b. appeal to public sentiment.
    c. win court cases.
    d. manipulate prices by withholding their produce.
    e. affect collective bargaining agreements and discourage strikes.
25. Probably the best measure of an interest group's ability to influence legislators and bureaucrats is
    a. the size of the membership.
    b. the dollar amount of its contributions.
    c. the occupational sketch of its members.
    d. its organizational skill.
    e. its contacts.

26. The single most important "tactic" of an interest group is the ability to
    a. provide credible information.
    b. smooth over ideological differences.
    c. mask partisan loyalties.
    d. publicize the decision-making process.
    e. persuade through the use of litigation.
27. Interest-group ratings can be helpful sources of information but can be problematic because of
    a. the costs of obtaining the results.
    b. constant change in group membership.
    c. a lack of participation by members of Congress.
    d. bias in arbitrary measurement and assessment.
    e. lack of public interest.
28. The "Dirty Dozen" refers to members of Congress who one interest group deemed to be
    a. corrupt.
    b. anti-environment.
    c. beleaguered.
    d. free-thinking.
    e. parlor "pinks."
29. The passage of the campaign finance reform law in 1973 led to the rapid growth in
    a. political parties.
    b. interest groups.
    c. PACs.
    d. voter registration.
    e. revenue sharing.
30. Senator Kennedy's observation that we may have "the finest Congress that money can buy" is probably off mark because
    a. individual contributions have never been a major source of congressional campaign funds.
    b. campaign finance reform laws have decreased the influence of money in elections.
    c. large corporations rarely contribute the full amount allowed by law.
    d. incumbents are well funded and do not need money from interest groups.
    e. PACs are so numerous and easy to form.
31. Over half of all PACs are sponsored by
    a. public-interest lobbies.
    b. citizens groups.
    c. ideological groups.
    d. labor unions.
    e. corporations.
32. Scholars have found a "slight statistical correlation" between PAC contributions and congressional votes when votes involve
    a. racial discrimination.
    b. issues which do not interest constituents.
    c. abortion and affirmative action.
    d. issues where positions are not driven by ideology.
    e. B and D.

33. The revolving door between government and business raises the possibility of
    a. poor communications.
    b. revenue sharing.
    c. conflicts of interest.
    d. duplication.
    e. ticket splitting.
34. Former executive-branch employees may *not* appear before an agency for ____ after leaving government service on matters that came before the former employees' official sphere of responsibility.
    a. six months
    b. eight months
    c. one year
    d. two years
    e. five years
35. Laws which restrict the activity of interest groups are always in potential conflict with
    a. the Due Process clause of the Fourteenth Amendment.
    b. the Equal Protection clause of the Fourteenth Amendment.
    c. the Privileges and Immunities clause of the Fourteenth Amendment.
    d. the First Amendment.
    e. the Tenth Amendment.

ESSAY QUESTIONS

Practice writing extended answers to the following questions. These test your ability to integrate and express the ideas that you have been studying in this chapter.

1. Discuss the four reasons identified by the authors for why interest groups are so common in this country.
2. Explain how government policy contributed to the rise of interest groups since the 1960s.
3. Identify some of the defining characteristics of institutional and membership interests.
4. Identify and explain the three types of incentives which mass-membership organizations offer.
5. Describe the three types of feminist organizations.
6. Discuss the rise and fall of the union movement with attention given to causes of decline and recent trends in union membership.
7. Why are federal grants and contracts a topic of interest in relation to interest groups and how have recent administrations attempted to affect the relationship between them?
8. How do interest groups employ "ratings?" What are some examples of groups who employ such devices and why are they also problematic?
9. Summarize what political scientists know about trends in PAC activity and what we know about the influence of PACs on congressional voting.
10. Identify three restrictions on former executive branch employees who want to represent clients before government agencies.
11. What three regulations were placed on lobbyists and lobbying activity in March of 2007?

ANSWERS TO KEY TERMS MATCH QUESTIONS

1. o
2. s
3. a
4. bb
5. r
6. w
7. k
8. v
9. d
10. b
11. g
12. i
13. j
14. e
15. p
16. u
17. z
18. f
19. c
20. h
21. l
22. q
23. x
24. y
25. aa
26. m
27. t

ANSWERS TO TRUE/FALSE QUESTIONS

1. T
2. T
3. T
4. T
5. F In fact, they are created more rapidly in some time periods than in others.

6. F Government policy has helped create interest groups.
7. F Americans are much more likely to hold this opinion.
8. T
9. T
10. F Those would be examples of material incentives. Solidary incentives are derived from a sense of pleasure, status or companionship that arise out of meeting together in groups.
11. T
12. T
13. F As Madison predicted, larger groups tend to be more moderate.
14. T
15. F They tend to support those causes that command the widest support among women generally.
16. F Membership in unions has fallen steadily since 1945.
17. F Unions of this type are becoming the most important part of the union movement.
18. T
19. F Business-oriented groups do not speak with a unified voice, so it is important to be careful about generalizing with respect to the "influence' of the business lobby.
20. F Interest groups are an accurate reflection of the distribution of opinion among political active elites, but that opinion is quite diverse.
21. T
22. T
23. T
24. F Kristol distinguished himself via the use of the fax machine.
25. T
26. T
27. T
28. T
29. T
30. F Members of Congress are allowed to set up PACs and often do, especially the leadership.
31. F It would be more accurate to say "over half" are sponsored by corporations.
32. F The rise of ideological PACs in recent years is the most remarkable development in interest group activity.
33. F They raise more money, but they spend less on campaigns and give less to candidates.
34. T
35. T
36. T

ANSWERS TO MULTIPLE CHOICE QUESTIONS

1. d
2. c
3. b
4. a
5. d
6. a
7. a
8. d
9. a
10. e
11. c
12. b
13. b
14. c
15. c
16. d
17. d
18. b
19. b
20. d
21. b
22. b
23. a
24. a
25. d
26. a
27. d
28. b
29. c
30. e
31. e
32. e
33. c
34. d
35. d

CHAPTER 12

The Media

REVIEWING THE CHAPTER

CHAPTER FOCUS

In this chapter you examine the historical evolution and current status of relations between the government and the news media—how the media affect government and politics and how government seeks to affect the media.

After reading and reviewing the material in this chapter, you should be able to do each of the following:

1. Describe the evolution of journalism in American political history, and describe the differences between the party press and the mass media of today.
2. Demonstrate how the characteristics of the electronic media have affected the actions of public officials and candidates for national office.
3. Describe the effect of the pattern of ownership and control of the media on the dissemination of news, and show how wire services and television networks have affected national news coverage. Discuss the influence of the national press.
4. Describe the rules that govern the media, and contrast the regulation of electronic and print media. Describe the effect of libel laws on freedom of the press and of government rules on broadcasters.
5. Assess the effect of the media on politics, and discuss why it is difficult to find evidence that can be used to make a meaningful and accurate assessment. Explain why the executive branch probably benefits at the expense of Congress.
6. Describe the adversarial press and how reporters use their sources. Describe how an administration can develop tactics to use against the adversarial press.

STUDY OUTLINE

I. Introduction
   A. New media v. the old media
      1. New media: television and the Internet
      2. Old media: newspapers and magazines
      3. New media getting stronger
         a) 60 Minutes story on Bush and the National Guard
         b) Bloggers rebuttal
         c) Young people and the Internet
   B. Media and public officials
      1. Love-hate relationship
         a) The media advance careers and causes
         b) But the media also criticize, expose and destroy

2. Relationship shaped by laws and understandings that accord tremendous degree of freedom for the media
    a) Cross national study of freedom of press
        (1) Comparisons with Great Britain
            (a) Libel law in Great Britain
            (b) Official Secrets Act (Great Britain)
            (c) Freedom of Information Act (United States)
            (d) Government regulation of press in other nations (Austria, France, Italy)
    b) The media landscape in the United States
        (1) Long tradition of private ownership
        (2) No licensing for newspapers
        (3) Licenses and F.C.C. regulation for radio and television
        (4) Potential limits to freedom
            (a) The need for profit
            (b) Media bias

II. Journalism in American political history
  A. The party press
    1. Parties created and subsidized various newspapers
    2. Circulation was small, newspapers expensive, advertisers few
    3. Newspapers circulated among political and commercial elites
  B. The popular press
    1. Changes in society and technology made the press self-supporting and able to reach mass readership
        a) High-speed press
        b) Telegraph
        c) Associated Press, 1848; objective reporting
        d) Urbanization allowed large numbers to support paper
        e) Government Printing Office; end of subsidies in 1860
    2. Influence of publishers, editors created partisan bias
        a) "Yellow journalism" to attract readers
        b) Hearst foments war against Spain
    3. Emergence of a common national culture
  C. Magazines of opinion
    1. Middle class favors new, progressive periodicals
        a) *Nation*, *Atlantic*, *Harper's* in 1850s and 1860s on behalf of certain issues
        b) *McClure's*, *Scribner's*, *Cosmopolitan* later on
    2. Individual writers gain national followings through investigative reporting
    3. Number of competing newspapers declines, as does sensationalism
    4. Today the number of national magazines focusing on politics accounts for a small and declining fraction of magazines
  D. Electronic journalism
    1. Radio arrives in the 1920s, television in the 1940s
    2. Politicians could address voters directly but people could easily ignore them
    3. But fewer politicians could be covered.
        a) President routinely covered
        b) Others must use bold tactics
    4. Recent rise in the talk show as a political forum has increased politicians' access to electronic media
        a) Big Three networks have made it harder for candidates by shortening sound bites

b) But politicians have more sources: cable, early morning news, news magazine shows
c) These new sources feature lengthy interviews
5. No research on consequences of two changes:
a) Recent access of politicians to electronic media
b) "Narrowcasting," which targets segmented audiences
6. Politicians continue to seek visuals even after they are elected

E. The Internet
1. Ultimate free market in political news
2. Increasingly important role in politics
a) Fund raising efforts
b) Blogs, discussion and criticism
c) Candidate web sites
3. Voters and political activists can now communicate with each other

III. The structure of the media
A. Degree of competition
1. Newspapers
a) Number of daily newspapers has declined significantly
b) Number of cities with multiple papers has declined
(1) 60 percent of cities had competing newspapers in 1900
(2) Only 4 percent in 1972
(3) Joint Operating Agreements allow same company to own the major papers of different cities
c) Newspaper circulation has fallen in recent years
d) Most people now get most of their news from television
e) Age and newspaper readership
(1) Made little difference in the 1940s and 1950s
(2) Radical change by the 1970s
2. Radio and television
a) Intensely competitive, becoming more so
b) Composed mostly of locally owned and managed enterprises, unlike Europe
c) Orientation to local market
d) Limitations by FCC; widespread ownership created

B. The national media
1. Existence somewhat offsets local orientation
2. Consists of
a) Wire services
b) National magazines
c) Television networks—some with news around the clock
d) Newspapers with national standing and readership because
(1) They sell many copies
(2) They are closely followed by political elites
(3) Radio and television often consult such papers in their own reporting
(4) They provided background, investigative, or interpretive stories about issues and politics
3. Roles played
a) Gatekeeper: what is news, for how long
(1) Auto safety
(2) Water pollution
(3) Prescription drugs
(4) Crime rates

b) Scorekeeper: who is winning or losing
   (1) Attention to Iowa, New Hampshire
   (2) Free publicity for winners and momentum for subsequent primaries
c) Watchdog: investigate personalities and expose scandals
   (1) Hart's relationship with Donna Rice in 1987
   (2) Watergate (Woodward and Bernstein)

IV. Rules governing the media
- A. Newspapers versus electronic media
  1. Newspapers almost entirely free from government regulation; prosecutions only after the fact and limited: libel, obscenity, incitement
  2. Radio and television licensed, regulated
- B. Confidentiality of sources
  1. Reporters want right to keep sources confidential
  2. Most states and federal government disagree
  3. Supreme Court allows government to compel reporters to divulge information in court if it bears on a crime
  4. Myron Farber jailed for contempt
  5. Police search of newspaper office upheld
- C. Regulating broadcasting
  1. FCC licensing
     a) Seven years for radio
     b) Five years for television
     c) Stations must serve "community needs"
     d) Public service, other aspects can be regulated
  2. Recent movement to deregulate
     a) License renewal by postcard
     b) No hearing unless opposed
     c) Relaxation of rule enforcement
  3. Radio broadcasting deregulated the most
     a) Telecommunications Act of 1996 permits one company to own as many as eight stations in large markets (five in smaller ones)
     b) Results:
        (1) Few large companies now own most of the big-market radio stations
        (2) Greater variety of opinion and shows on radio
  4. Deregulation and the content of broadcasting
     a) Fairness Doctrine (eventually abandoned)
     b) Equal Time Rule
- D. Campaigning
  1. Equal time rule applies
     a) Equal access for all candidates
     b) Rates no higher than least expensive commercial rate
     c) Debates formerly had to include all candidates
        (1) Reagan-Carter debate sponsored by LWV as a "news event"
        (2) Now stations and networks can sponsor
  2. Efficiency in reaching voters
     a) Works well when market and boundaries of state or district overlap
     b) More Senate than House candidates buy TV time

V. Are the national media biased?
- A. What are the views of members of the national media?
  1. More self-described liberals than in the general public
  2. Higher voting for Democratic candidates than in the general public

3. More secular
4. Some evidence that levels of liberalism are increasing
5. Public perception of a liberal bias
6. Existence of conservative media outlets—talk radio
   a) Rapid growth
   b) Explanations for conservative dominance
      (1) High ratings
      (2) More self-described conservatives than liberals in this country
      (3) Conservatives do not feel other media outlets reflect their views
      (4) Liberal audience is divided into racial and ethnic groups which are loyal to media outlets which are more narrow in their orientation

B. Do the beliefs of the national media affect how they report the news?
1. American ideal of neutrality and objectivity
2. Opportunity for bias varies with the type of story reported
   a) Routine stories
   b) Feature stories
   c) Inside stories
3. Trends in American history
   a) Early newspapers emphasized opinion
   b) With technological change (telephone, telegraph, AP) came emphasis on routine stories
   c) With radio, television and round the clock news came an emphasis on feature and insider stories
4. Research on media beliefs and reporting
   a) *Times* and *Post* stories covering 12 years
      (1) Conservatives much more likely to be identified as such
      (2) Ideological labeling might influence readers
   b) Study of *Time* and *Newsweek* magazine
      (1) Focus on stories concerning nuclear power
      (2) Scientists and engineers in the field were avoided
      (3) Magazines were opponents of nuclear power
   c) Coverage of economic news by top ten newspapers
      (1) Varied depending on whether a Democrat or Republican was in office of the presidency
      (2) Headlines were more positive with Democratic presidents
   d) Assessment of the *Times* by its public editor

C. Does what the media write or say influence how their readers and viewers think?
1. Selective attention complicates our understanding
2. Study of 60 Senate contests over five year period
   a) Newspapers that endorsed incumbents gave them more positive coverage
   b) Voters were more positive about endorsed incumbents
3. Study of the impact of FOX news aired at different times in different cities
4. CN and NC studies showing influence of media on public beliefs about issues
   a) Influence may be mitigated by personal experience—unemployment, crime, gasoline prices, etc.
   b) Where there is lack of personal knowledge, influence may be greater—American foreign policy, the environment, etc.
5. Best evidence of media impact: name recognition and popularity and support
   a) Estes Kefauver
   b) Importance of a media presence
   c) Impact on television commentary on presidential popularity

VI. Government and the news
 A. Prominence of the president
  1. Theodore Roosevelt: systematic cultivation of the press
  2. Franklin Roosevelt: press secretary a major instrument for cultivating press
  3. Press secretary today: large staff, many functions
  4. White House press corps is the focus of press secretary
  5. Unparalleled personalization of government
 B. Coverage of Congress
  1. Never equal to that of president; members resentful
  2. House quite restrictive
   a) No cameras on the floor until 1978
   b) Sometimes refused to permit coverage of committees
   c) Gavel-to-gavel coverage of proceedings since 1979
  3. Senate more open
   a) Hearings since Kefauver; TV coverage of sessions in 1986
   b) Incubator for presidential contenders through committee hearings
 C. Why do we have so many news leaks?
  1. *Constitution*: separation of powers
   a) Power is shared, decentralized
   b) Branches of government compete
   c) Not illegal to print most secrets
  2. Adversarial nature of the press since Vietnam War, Watergate
   a) Press and politicians distrust each other
   b) Media are eager to embarrass officials
  3. Cynicism created era of attack journalism
   a) Many people do not like this kind of news
   b) People believe media slant coverage
   c) Public support for idea of licensing journalists or fines to discourage biased reporting
  4. Public confidence in big business down and now media are big business.
  5. Drive for market share forces media to use theme of corruption
  6. Increased use of negative advertising
 D. Sensationalism in the media
  1. Prior to 1980, sexual escapades of political figures not reported
  2. Since 1980, sex and politics extensively covered
  3. Reasons for change
   a) Sensationalism gets attention in a market of intense competition
   b) Sensational stories are often cheaper than expert analysis and/or investigation of stories about policy or substantive issues
   c) Journalists have become distrusting adversaries of government
   d) Journalists are much more likely to rely on unnamed sources today and, as a result, are more easily manipulated
  4. Impact of 9/11
   a) Public interest in national news
   b) Greater confidence and trust in news organizations, for about a year
 E. Government constraints on journalists
  1. Reporters must strike a balance between
   a) Expression of views
   b) Retaining sources
  2. Abundance of congressional staffers makes it easier

3. Governmental tools to fight back
    a) Numerous press officers and press releases (canned news)
    b) Controlling form of communication
        (1) On the record
        (2) Off the record
        (3) On background
        (4) On deep background
    c) Skipping over national media and going local

KEY TERMS MATCH

Match the following terms and descriptions:

1. British legislation to punish officials who divulge private government business
2. U.S. legislation guaranteeing citizens access to certain government documents
3. Role of the media which involves influencing what subjects become national political issues and for how long
4. An organization founded for the telegraphic dissemination of news in 1848
5. Sensationalized news reporting
6. Filmed stories for evening television news
7. The government agency charged with regulating the electronic media
8. A series, or log, of discussion items on a page of the World Wide Web
9. Information from a government official who can be quoted by name
10. Information from an official that cannot be printed
11. Information from an official that can be printed but not attributed to the official by name
12. Information from an official that can be printed but not attributed at all
13. The tendency of the national media to be suspicious of officials and eager to reveal unflattering stories about them
14. A court standard for finding the media guilty of libeling officials

a. adversarial press
b. Associated Press
c. attack journalism
d. blog
e. canned news
f. community needs
g. equal time rule
h. fairness doctrine
i. FCC
j. feature stories
k. Freedom of Information Act*t*
l. Gatekeeper
m. insider stories
n. loaded language
o. market (television)
p. Official Secrets Act
q. off the record
r. on background
s. on deep background
t. on the record
u. reckless disregard
v. routine stories
w. Scorekeeper
x. selective attention
y. sound bite

15. An official criterion for the renewal of broadcast licenses
16. A principle that formerly obligated broadcasters to present both sides of an issue
17. An obligation for broadcasters to give all candidates equal access to the media
18. An area easily reached by one television signal
19. The tendency of people to see what they like and ignore what they do not like
20. Reporters regularly assigned to cover the president
21. Role of the media which concerns the making of political reputations by providing coverage and mentioning candidates
22. Public events regularly covered by reporters
23. Public events not regularly covered by reporters
24. Events that become public only if revealed to reporters
25. Press releases or other news items prepared for reporters
26. Journalism that seizes on information that might question the character or qualifications of a public official
27. Words that reflect a value judgment, used to persuade the listener without making an argument
28. A brief statement no longer than a few seconds used on a radio or television broadcast
29. Information provided to the media by an anonymous source as a way of testing the reaction to a potential policy or appointment
30. Allows one company to own as many as eight radio stations in large markets (five in smaller ones) and as many as it wishes nationally

z. Telecommunication Act of 1996

aa. trial balloon

bb. visuals

cc. White House Press Corps

dd. "yellow journalism"

PRACTICING FOR EXAMS

TRUE/FALSE QUESTIONS

Read each statement carefully. Mark true statements *T*. If any part of the statement is false, mark it *F*, and write in the space provided a concise explanation of why the statement is false.

1. T F Our media enjoy a greater degree of freedom than that found in almost any other nation.

2. T F It is more difficult for politicians to sue newspapers for libel in Great Britain than it is in America.

3. T F Leaks are punished in Great Britain via the Official Secrets Act.

4. T F America has a long tradition of privately owned media.

5. T F In the early years of the Republic, newspapers were relatively unbiased and placed a premium on reporting "just the facts."

6. T F Randolph Hearst used his newspapers to agitate for war.

7. T F The majority of today's magazines focus on entertainment and leisure activities.

8. T F In 1992, Ross Perot declared his willingness to run for the presidency on the television program "Meet the Press."

9. T F The text suggests one way to capture the media spotlight is to be supportive of the president.

10. T F When Howard Dean ran for the presidency in 2004, most of the money he raised was from Internet appeals.

11. T F Due to the lack of regulation, there has been an increase in the number of daily newspapers that serve large communities.

12. T F The typical American newspaper has more local than national news in it.

13. T F The wire services provide most of the national news that local papers publish.

14. T F Newspaper reporters have less freedom to develop their own stories than radio and television reporters.

15. T F Newspapers and magazines need no license to publish in the United States.

16. T F In general, your name and picture can be printed without your consent if they are part of a news story of some conceivable public interest.

17. T F If a paper attacks you in print, it has a legal obligation to allow you space to reply.

18. T F Licenses for radio stations must be renewed every seven years.

19. T F Licenses for television stations must be renewed every five years.

20. T F Television broadcasting has been deregulated more than radio.

21. T F A few large corporations now own most of the big-market radio stations.

22. T F Today, stations and networks can sponsor debates, but they must invite all candidates.

23. T F Members of the House are more likely to use television ads than members of the Senate.

24. T F Members of the media are more likely to support Democratic candidates for President.

25. T F The public perception is that the news media are conservative.

26. T F Talk radio is predominately conservative.

27. T F In France and Great Britain, newspapers often identify with one party or another.

28. T F A study of the *Times* and the *Post* revealed liberal members of Congress were much more likely to be labeled "liberal" than conservative members were to be labeled "conservative."

29. T F Public distrust of the media has grown.

30. T F What the press covers affects the policy issues that people think are important.

31. T F Congress did not allow live coverage of committee hearings until the House considered the impeachment of Richard Nixon.

32. T F American government is one of the least leakiest in the world.

33. T F There are fewer leaks to members of the media where governments are more decentralized.

34. T F Today, journalists are far less willing to accept at face value the statements of elected officials.

35. T F Most Americans oppose the idea of imposing fines for inaccurate or "biased" reporting.

36. T F The texts suggests "negative" attack ads are used because they work.

37. T F Research indicates "negative" ads are associated with increased voter turnout.

38. T F Newspapers knew that Franklin Roosevelt had a romantic affair in the 1930s but did not report it.

MULTIPLE CHOICE QUESTIONS

Circle the letter of the response that best answers the question or completes the statement.

1. When *CBS News* ran a story claiming President Bush performed poorly during his time in the National Guard, _________ produced evidenced that the documents underlying the report were forgeries.
   a. NBC
   b. Fox News
   c. White House lawyers
   d. Republican media consultants
   e. bloggers

2. Politicians have become more heavily dependent on the media as
   a. the public has become better educated.
   b. the federal bureaucracy has enlarged itself.
   c. public affairs have become much more complex.
   d. the scope of government has expanded.
   e. political party organizations have declined.
3. Which of the following was a milestone in the development of a reasonably nonpartisan and unbiased press?
   a. The establishment of the *Gazette of the United States* during the Washington administration
   b. The establishment of the Associated Press in 1848
   c. The creation of the *National Intelligence* by Jacksonian Democrats
   d. The rise of magazines of opinion in the late 1800s
   e. The rise of competition from radio in the 1920s
4. Which of the following was *not* among the achievements of the mass-based press, exemplified by Hearst and Pulitzer?
   a. Instituting responsible and unbiased journalism
   b. Beginning the creation of a national political culture
   c. Proving the feasibility of a press free of government subsidy or control
   d. Revealing public scandal
   e. Criticizing public policy
5. The invention of radio was a politically important media development because it
   a. allowed public officials to reach the public in a less-filtered manner.
   b. gave rise to the era of mass politics and a large electorate.
   c. rendered image more important than substance in seeking political office.
   d. more than doubled the number of persons who followed politics with interest.
   e. reinforced the influence of political parties when it was first introduced.
6. In 2000, the average sound bite of a presidential contender was __________ the average sound bite of such contenders in 1968.
   a. considerably longer than
   b. about the same length as
   c. considerably shorter than
   d. more controversial than
   e. less complex than
7. Politicians wishing to make news are well advised to criticize
   a. the president.
   b. Congress
   c. the Supreme Court.
   d. the federal bureaucracy.
   e. state government.
8. Joint Operating Agreements are important to consider when assessing the competition and diversity of viewpoint among newspapers because they
   a. encourage the hiring of minorities.
   b. have increased the sales of newspapers in major metropolitan areas.
   c. are usually biased in a conservative direction.
   d. allow businesses to own more than one paper in a large city.
   e. do not allow the expression of political opinion without prior consent.

9. Research suggests _____ especially have turned their interests away from political news.
   a. those living in rural America
   b. religious persons
   c. professionals
   d. college educated persons
   e. young people
10. Which of the following statements concerning national newspapers is *incorrect*?
    a. They distribute millions of copies on a daily basis.
    b. They are carefully followed by political elites.
    c. Radio and television stations look to such papers for cues on reporting.
    d. The reporters for such papers have higher levels of education than their local counterparts.
    e. none of the above.
11. One of Jimmy Carter's signal achievements in dealing with the press in the 1976 primary campaign was
    a. keeping a low profile.
    b. taking newsworthy positions on important issues.
    c. defusing an initial bias against him among reporters.
    d. refusing to buckle under the pressure of special interests.
    e. getting himself mentioned with great frequency.
12. The emphasis the media places on its role as "scorekeeper" might come at the cost of attention to
    a. which candidates are not viable.
    b. which candidates might be gaining momentum.
    c. who is actually ahead.
    d. the horse race.
    e. policies.
13. In the late 1980s the "watchdog" function of the media was notable in the case of the front-running Democratic presidential nominee, Gary Hart, who was accused of
    a. having an extra marital affair.
    b. using illegal drugs.
    c. income tax evasion.
    d. lying to congressional committees.
    e. falsifying draft registration records.
14. An irony concerning government regulation of the news media is that
    a. American media are less regulated than foreign media despite the greater need for regulation here.
    b. legislation designed to intimidate the media has in fact made them more hostile toward officials.
    c. the least competitive part of the media is almost entirely unregulated, whereas the most competitive part is substantially regulated.
    d. the most influential media, the broadcast media, show highly concentrated patterns of ownership by a few large corporations.
    e. all of the above.
15. Once something is published, a newspaper may be sued or prosecuted if the material
    a. is libelous.
    b. is obscene.
    c. incites someone to commit an illegal act.
    d. all of the above.
    e. none of the above.

16. For a public official in the United States to win a libel suit against the press, he or she must prove that
    a. what was printed was untrue.
    b. the material was untrue and was printed maliciously.
    c. the material caused "emotional duress."
    d. his or her privacy was violated.
    e. the printing of the material in question has done "substantial harm" to the public interest.
17. In general, the Supreme Court has upheld the right of government to compel reporters to divulge information as part of a properly conducted criminal investigation if
    a. the president has pardoned a defendant for contempt of court.
    b. a jury is unable to reach a decision.
    c. it has not been reported publicly.
    d. it has been reported publicly.
    e. it bears on the commission of a crime.
18. The text suggests that, if the Fairness Doctrine had stayed in place,
    a. there would be more competition among radio and television stations.
    b. political advertising would be available to all candidates regardless of party or viewpoint.
    c. there would be no Rush Limbaugh.
    d. Congress would have developed the law on libel more meticulously.
    e. the Supreme Court would have received more news coverage.
19. Since the 1980s, studies of media bias have reached the same conclusion, that members of the national press are
    a. more liberal than the average member of the public.
    b. more conservative than the average member of the public.
    c. more moderate than the average member of the public.
    d. generally objective, and without political bias.
    e. without noticeable, systematic bias.
20. Research suggests members of the national news media are generally more _______ than the average member of the public.
    a. conservative
    b. alienated
    c. secular
    d. moderate
    e. patriotic
21. Conservative dominance in talk radio can be best explained by the fact that
    a. liberal hosts have never had big corporate sponsors.
    b. conservatives flooded the market first and left little room for competition.
    c. the Fairness Doctrine gave an advantage to conservatives.
    d. media owners are not tolerant of liberal viewpoints.
    e. liberal hosts have never attained high ratings.
22. Early in American history, newspapers had virtually no _________ stories.
    a. routine
    b. feature
    c. insider
    d. opinion-based
    e. editorial-driven

23. A study of the top ten newspapers and the Associated Press found news items concerning _______ were more likely to be interpreted in a negative fashion when there was a Republican president.
    a. Supreme Court decisions
    b. social issues
    c. government economic reports
    d. immigration
    e. mid-term elections
24. The potential impact of the media coverage is certainly well illustrated by the case of Estes Kefauver who, in the 1950s, became a "household name" by
    a. leading members of the House and Senate in a protest march through the White House.
    b. chairing a Senate committee investigating organized crime.
    c. submitting a law which attempted to eliminate the influence of interest groups in elections.
    d. dropping thousands of leaflets from a plane while flying over the White House.
    e. refusing to give up his Senate seat, even after having lost his bid for re-election.
25. The first president to engage in the systematic cultivation of news reporters was
    a. Theodore Roosevelt.
    b. Franklin Roosevelt.
    c. Woodrow Wilson.
    d. John F. Kennedy.
    e. Richard Nixon.
26. Which of the following presidents first made his press secretary a major instrument for dealing with the press?
    a. Herbert Hoover
    b. Franklin Roosevelt
    c. Dwight Eisenhower
    d. John F. Kennedy
    e. Ronald Reagan
27. The president of the United States is unlike the chief executive of other nations with regard to the
    a. hostility with which he is normally treated by the press.
    b. use of the press secretary as an instrument for dealing with the press.
    c. extreme difficulty that the press experiences in covering his activities.
    d. close physical proximity between the press and the center of government.
    e. manner in which he is required to conduct press conferences.
28. In an age in which the media are very important, who of the following is best positioned to run for president?
    a. A House member
    b. An innovative person with a business background
    c. A senator
    d. A state governor
    e. A big-city mayor
29. The text suggests American government is the "leakiest" in the world, in large part, because of
    a. the centralized nature of power in the federal system.
    b. cordial relations between media and most government officials.
    c. the rise of cable news networks.
    d. the emergence of the Internet.
    e. the separation of powers.

30. The adversarial nature of the modern press has probably made __________ more socially acceptable.
    a. negative campaign advertising
    b. political corruption
    c. frivolous campaigns
    d. bipartisan coalitions
    e. fruitless congressional investigations
31. Which of the following does the text suggest is one of the consequences of intense competition in media today?
    a. Reporters are more easily manipulated by sources than once was the case.
    b. The requirements for citation of sources are more rigorous than ever.
    c. There are few incentives to rely on sensational news stories.
    d. Reporters are less confrontational with public officials than they once were.
    e. None of the above.

ESSAY QUESTIONS

Practice writing extended answers to the following questions. These test your ability to integrate and express the ideas that you have been studying in this chapter.

1. What events and circumstances enabled the transition from the party press of the Early Republic to the popular press?
2. Describe competition in the newspaper industry and in radio and television.
3. What are some reasons why papers like the *New York Times* and the *Wall Street Journal* have national standing?
4. Identify and explain the three roles that are played by the national news media.
5. Summarize the rules government the publication and content of newspapers and magazines.
6. Discuss how the Supreme Court has ruled on the issue of confidentiality of sources with references to the specifics of particular cases.
7. What explanations does William G. Mayer give for why conservative talk shows are so common on radio?
8. What evidence might one emphasize to make the argument that the liberal beliefs of members of the national news media are reflected in their work?
9. Summarize what we know about the actual influence that the media have on voting, approval ratings, concern with issues and name recognition.
10. How has television coverage differed in the House and the Senate and what particular events in American politics have played a role in that coverage?
11. Explain why American government is the leakiest in the world.

ANSWERS TO KEY TERMS MATCH QUESTIONS

1. p
2. k
3. l
4. b
5. dd
6. bb
7. i
8. d
9. t
10. q
11. r
12. s
13. a
14. u
15. f
16. h
17. g
18. o
19. x
20. cc
21. w
22. v
23. j
24. m
25. e
26. c
27. n
28. y
29. aa
30. z

ANSWERS TO TRUE/FALSE QUESTIONS

1. T
2. F It is easier for public officials to sue for libel in Great Britain and they win with some frequency.
3. T
4. T
5. F The early papers were sponsored by parties and politicians. Objectivity was not a goal.
6. T
7. T
8. F Perot declared his candidacy on the Larry King show.
9. F Actually, the individual who wants media attention is advised to be critical of the president as he is the constant focus of news and news reports.
10. T
11. F There has been a significant decrease in the number of newspapers and the number of competing newspapers in big cities.
12. T
13. T
14. F Newspaper reporters have much greater freedom in this regard.
15. T
16. T
17. F It has no such obligation.
18. F Such licenses much be renewed every 5 years.
19. T
20. F Radio has regulated much less, even though there is less competition in that environment.
21. T
22. F They do not have to invite all candidates. They can invite only "major" candidates.
23. F Members of the Senate are more likely to use television because the decision of a House member might be shaped by complex considerations of "the market."
24. T
25. F The public generally perceives the media as being liberal.
26. T
27. T
28. F Conservative members of Congress are much more likely to be labeled "conservative" than are liberal members.
29. T
30. T

31. T
32. F We are actually one of the leakiest governments in the world because of separation of powers, freedom of press and the adversarial nature of the press.
33. F Decentralization tends to increase the opportunities for leaks.
34. T
35. F 70 percent favor such punishment.
36. T
37. F Negative ads are associated with a decrease in vote turnout.
38. T

ANSWERS TO MULTIPLE CHOICE QUESTIONS

1. e
2. e
3. b
4. a
5. a
6. c
7. a
8. d
9. e
10. e
11. e
12. e
13. a
14. c
15. d
16. b
17. e
18. c
19. a
20. c
21. a
22. a
23. c
24. b
25. a

26. a
27. d
28. c
29. e
30. a
31. a

PART 2

Classic Statement: "The Omnipotence of the Majority in the United States and Its Effects," from *Democracy in America*, by Alexis de Tocqueville[1]

INTRODUCTION

Alexis de Tocqueville's classic book on American democracy is in many ways an admiring work: Tocqueville was particularly taken with the spirit of equality and energy he met from his first days in the United States in the 1830s. But he also discerned flaws and dangers in the world's newest democracy, and some of these were, in his view, very much bound up with the nation's strengths.

Nowhere is this more true than in his discussion of the will of the majority. Although the principle of majority rule is inseparable from the workings of a democratic system, majority rule can, if not challenged or limited, lead to tyranny and to the undoing of the democratic experiment. More than a century and a half later, see whether you find that any of Tocqueville's thoughts on this subject still ring true.

The absolute sovereignty of the will of the majority is the essence of democratic government, for in democracies there is nothing outside the majority capable of resisting it.

Most American constitutions have sought further artificially to increase this natural strength of the majority.

Of all political powers, the legislature is the one most ready to obey the wishes of the majority. The Americans wanted the members of the legislatures to be appointed *directly* by the people and for a *very short* term of office so that they should be obliged to submit only to the general views but also to the passing passions of their constituents.

In America several particular circumstances also tend to make the power of the majority not only predominant but irresistible.

The moral authority of the majority is partly based on the notion that there is more enlightenment and wisdom in a numerous assembly than in a single man, and the number of the legislators is more important than how they are chosen. It is the theory of equality applied to brains. This doctrine attacks the last asylum of human pride; for that reason the minority is reluctant in admitting it and takes a long time to get used to it.

---

[1] *Democracy in America* was published as a result of the French author's trip to America in 1831 to observe the workings of this New World democracy. His observations from the early days of Jacksonian democracy, published in two separate volumes, would be hailed as "the greatest book ever written on America." The excerpts presented here are taken from Volume I, Part II, Chapter 7, as presented in *Democracy in America* (New York: Harper and Row, 1966).

The idea that the majority has a right based on enlightenment to govern society was brought to the United States by its first inhabitants; and this idea, which would of itself be enough to create a free nation, has by now passed into mores and affects even the smallest habits of life.

The moral authority of the majority is also founded on the principle that the interest of the greatest number should be preferred to that of those who are fewer. Now, it is easy to understand that the respect professed for this right of the greatest number naturally grows or shrinks according to the state of the parties. When a nation is divided between several great irreconcilable interests, the privilege of the majority is often disregarded, for it would be too unpleasant to submit to it.

Hence the majority in the United States has immense actual power and a power of opinion which is almost as great. When once its mind is made up on any question, there are, so to say, no obstacles which can retard, much less halt, its progress and give it time to hear the wails of those it crushes as it passes.

The consequences of this state of affairs are fate-laden and dangerous for the future.

I have spoken before of the vices natural to democratic government, and every single one of them increases with the growing power of the majority.

To begin with the most obvious of all:

Legislative instability is an ill inherent in democratic government because it is the nature of democracies to bring new men to power. But this ill is greater or less according to the power and means of action accorded to the legislator.

In America the lawmaking authority has been given sovereign power. This authority can carry out anything it desires quickly and irresistibly, and its representatives change annually. That it is to say, just that combination has been chosen which most encourages democratic instability and allows the changing wishes of democracy to be applied to the most important matters.

Thus American laws have a shorter duration than those of any other country in the world today. Almost all American constitutions have been amended within the last thirty years, and so there is no American state which has not modified the basis of its laws within that period.

As for the laws themselves, it is enough to glance at the archives of the various states of the Union to realize that in America the legislator's activity never slows down. Not that American democracy is by nature more unstable than any other, but it has been given the means to carry the natural instability of its inclinations into the making of laws.

The omnipotence of the majority and the rapid as well as absolute manner in which its decisions are executed in the United States not only make the law unstable but have a like effect on the execution of the law and on public administrative activity.

My greatest complaint against democratic government as organized in the United States is not, as many Europeans make out, its weakness, but rather its irresistible strength. What I find most repulsive in America is not the extreme freedom reigning there but the shortage of guarantees against tyranny.

When a man or a party suffers an injustice in the United States, to whom can he turn? To public opinion? That is what forms the majority. To the legislative body? It represents the majority and obeys it blindly. To the executive power? It is appointed by the majority and serves as its passive instrument. To the police? They are nothing but the majority under arms. A jury? The jury is the majority vested with the right to pronounce judgment; even the judges in certain states are elected by the majority. So, however iniquitous or unreasonable the measure which hurts you, you must submit.

But suppose you were to have a legislative body so composed that it represented the majority without being necessarily the slave of its passions, an executive power having a strength of its own, and a judicial power independent of the other two authorities; then you would still have a democratic government, but there would be hardly any remaining risk of tyranny.

I am not asserting that at the present time in America there are frequent acts of tyranny. I do say that one can find no guarantee against it there and that the reasons for the government's gentleness must be sought in circumstances and in mores rather than in the laws.

It is when one comes to look into the use made of thought in the United States that one most clearly sees how far the power of the majority goes beyond all powers known to us in Europe.

Thought is an invisible power and one almost impossible to lay hands on, which makes sport of all tyrannies. In our day the most absolute sovereigns in Europe cannot prevent certain thoughts hostile to their power from silently circulating in their states and even in their own courts. It is not like that in America; while the majority is in doubt, one talks; but when it has irrevocably pronounced, everyone is silent, and friends and enemies alike seem to make for its bandwagon. The reason is simple: no monarch is so absolute that he can hold all the forces of society in his hands and overcome all resistance, as a majority invested with the right to make the laws and to execute them can do.

I know no country in which, speaking generally, there is less independence of mind and true freedom of discussion than in America.

There is no religious or political theory which one cannot preach freely in the constitutional states of Europe or which does not penetrate into the others, for there is no country in Europe so subject to a single power that he who wishes to speak the truth cannot find support enough to protect him against the consequences of his independence. If he is unlucky enough to live under an absolute government, he often has the people with him; if he lives in a free country, he may at need find shelter behind the royal authority. In democratic countries the aristocracy may support him, and in other lands the democracy. But in a democracy organized on the model of the United States there is only one authority, one source of strength and of success, and nothing outside it.

In America the majority has enclosed thought within a formidable fence. A writer is free inside that area, but woe to the man who goes beyond it. Not that he stands in fear of an *auto-da-fé*, but he must face all kinds of unpleasantness and everyday persecution. A career in politics is closed to him, for he has offended the only power that holds the keys. He is denied everything, including renown. Before he goes into print, he believes he has supporters; but he feels that he has them no more once he stands revealed to all, for those who condemn him express their views loudly, while those who think as he does, but without his courage, retreat into silence as if ashamed of having told the truth.

Formerly tyranny used the clumsy weapons of chains and hangmen; nowadays even despotism, though it seemed to have nothing more to learn, has been perfected by civilization. . . .

The influence of what I have been talking about is as yet only weakly felt in political society, but its ill effects on the national character are already apparent. I think that the rareness now of outstanding men on the political scene is due to the ever-increasing despotism of the American majority.

Governments ordinarily break down either through impotence or through tyranny. In the first case power slips from their grasp, whereas in the second it is taken from them.

Many people, seeing democratic states fall into anarchy, have supposed that government in such states was by nature weak and impotent. The truth is that once war has broken out between the parties, government influence over society ceases. But I do not think a lack of strength or resources is part of the nature of democratic authority; on the contrary, I believe that it is almost always the abuse of that strength and the ill use of those resources which bring it down. Anarchy is almost always a consequence either of the tyranny or of the inability of democracy, but not of its impotence.

One must not confuse stability with strength or a thing's size with its duration. In democratic republics the power directing society is not stable, for both its personnel and its aims change often. But wherever it is brought to bear, its strength is almost irresistible.

The government of the American republics seems to me as centralized and more energetic than the absolute monarchies of Europe. So I do not think that it will collapse from weakness.

If ever freedom is lost in America, that will be due to the omnipotence of the majority driving the minorities to desperation and forcing them to appeal to physical force. We may then see anarchy, but it will have come as the result of despotism.

QUESTIONS FOR UNDERSTANDING AND DISCUSSION

1. What did various American states and the federal Constitution do to make legislative bodies even more responsive to the wishes of the majority than the basic principle of democracy might demand?
2. Why are Americans, more than members of more traditional societies, likely to recognize the rights of the majority?
3. On what grounds does Tocqueville expect to find greater legislative instability in the United States than in other countries?
4. Explain why the author, unlike others, is more fearful of the power of democratic regimes than of their weakness.
5. How do you react to Tocqueville's assertion that there is more mind control in this country than in any other?
6. What is his explanation for his observation that few truly outstanding individuals seek political office in this country?
7. How, according to Tocqueville, might the "omnipotence" of the majority lead to anarchy?
8. Of the various observations presented here by Tocqueville, which ones seem to you particularly relevant today? Why?

PART III: Institutions of Government

CHAPTER 13

Congress

REVIEWING THE CHAPTER

CHAPTER FOCUS

The central purpose of this chapter is to describe the Framers' understanding of the role of Congress and to describe the role and organization of Congress today. You should pay particular attention to the effects of organizational characteristics on the behavior of members of Congress and on the way that the House and the Senate perform their functions. After reading and reviewing the material in this chapter, you should be able to do each of the following:

1. Explain the differences between Congress and Parliament.
2. Delineate the role that the Framers expected Congress to play.
3. Pinpoint the significant eras in the evolution of Congress.
4. Describe the characteristics of members of Congress.
5. Discuss the relationship between ideology and civility in Congress in recent years.
6. Identify the factors that help to explain why a member of Congress votes as she or he does.
7. Outline the process for electing members of Congress.
8. Identify the functions of party affiliation in the organization of Congress.
9. Explain the effect of committee reform on the organization of Congress.
10. Describe the formal process by which a bill becomes a law.
11. Explain the ethical problems confronting Congress.

STUDY OUTLINE

I. Introduction
  A. Congress: the least popular branch
  B. Heavily emphasized in the text of the Constitution
  C. An independent and powerful institution
II. Congress versus Parliament
  A. Parliamentary candidates are selected by party
    1. Members of Parliament select the prime minister and other leaders
    2. Party members vote together on most issues
    3. Renomination depends on loyalty to party
    4. Principal work is debating national issues
    5. Very little power, very little pay
  B. Congressional candidates run in a primary election, with little party control
    1. Vote is for the man or woman, not the party

2. Result is a body of independent representatives
3. Members do not choose the president
4. Principal work is representation and action
5. Great deal of power, high pay; parties cannot discipline members

C. Congress a decentralized institution
1. Members more concerned with their views and the views of their constituents
2. Members less concerned with organized parties and program proposals of president

D. Congress can be unpopular with voters

III. The evolution of Congress

A. Intent of the Framers
1. To oppose concentration of power in a single institution
2. To balance large and small states: bicameralism

B. Traditional criticism: Congress is too slow
1. Centralization needed for quick and decisive action
2. Decentralization needed if congressional constituency interests are to be dominant

C. Development of the House
1. Always powerful but varied in organization and leadership
   a) Powerful Speakers
   b) Powerful committee chairmen
   c) Powerful individual members
2. Ongoing dilemmas
   a) Increases in size have lead to the need for centralization and less individual influence
   b) Desire for individual influence has led to institutional weakness

D. Development of the Senate
1. Structural advantages over the House
   a) Small enough to be run without giving authority to small group of leaders
   b) Interests more carefully balanced
   c) No time limits on speakers or committee control of debate
   d) Senators not elected by voters until twentieth century
      (1) Chosen by state legislators
      (2) Often leaders of local party organizations
2. Major changes
   a) Demand for direct popular election
      (1) Intense political maneuvering and the Millionaire's Club
      (2) Senate opposition and the threat of a constitutional convention
      (3) Seventeenth Amendment approved in 1913
   b) Filibuster restricted by Rule 22—though tradition of unlimited debate remains

IV. Who is in Congress?

A. The beliefs and interests of members of Congress can affect policy

B. Sex and race
1. House has become less male and less white
2. Senate has been slower to change, but several blacks and Hispanics hold powerful positions

C. Incumbency
1. Low turnover rates and safe districts common in Congress before 1980s
2. Incumbents increasingly viewed as professional politicians and out of touch with the people by the 1980s
3. Call for term limits; however, natural forces were doing what term limits were designed to do by the mid-1990s
4. Influx of new members should not distort incumbents' advantage

D. Party
  1. Democratic control of Congress post-1933 and possible explanations
    a) Democratic legislatures redraw district lines to favor Democratic candidates: higher percentage of seats obtained than the percentage of actual votes
      (1) Striking anecdotal evidence (Texas and California)
      (2) By 2006, things evened out nationally
      (3) Conditions for partisan gerrymandering do not exist in most states
    b) Democrats tend to do better in low turnout districts
    c) Another explanation: incumbent advantage is increasing
      (1) Worth 6 to 8 points today
      (2) Although Republicans have enjoyed the same advantages
  2. Recent Republican surges in the House and Senate and possible explanations
    a) Advantages of incumbency can become disadvantages
      (1) Dislike of professional politicians
      (2) Perceptions that Washington was a "mess"
      (3) Congressional scandals
      (4) Decline in public confidence in Congress
    b) Democrats were in power when the above trends set in

V. Do members represent their voters?
  A. Representational view
    1. Assumes that members vote to please their constituents
    2. Constituents must have a clear opinion of the issue
      a) Very strong correlation on civil rights and social welfare bills
      b) Very weak correlation on foreign policy
    3. May be conflict between legislator and constituency on certain measures: gun control, Panama Canal treaty, abortion
    4. Constituency influence more important in Senate votes
    5. Members in marginal districts as independent as those in safe districts
    6. Weakness of representational explanation: no clear opinion in the constituency
  B. Organizational view
    1. Assumes members of Congress vote to please colleagues
    2. Organizational cues
      a) Party
      b) Ideology
    3. Problem is that party and other organizations do not have a clear position on all issues
    4. On minor votes most members influenced by party members on sponsoring committees
  C. Attitudinal view
    1. Assumes that ideology affects a legislator's vote
    2. House members tend more than senators to have opinions similar to those of the public
      a) 1970s: senators more liberal
      b) 1980s: senators more conservative
    3. Prior to 1990s, southern Democrats often aligned with Republicans to form a conservative coalition
    4. Conservative coalition no longer as important since most southerners are Republicans
  D. A polarized Congress
    1. Members of Congress more sharply divided ideologically than they once were
    2. New members of Congress are more ideological
    3. Members of Congress more polarized than voters
      a) Democrats more liberal/Republicans more conservative
      b) Voters closer to center of political spectrum

4. Members of Congress (especially the House) do not get along as well as they once did

VI. The organization of Congress: parties and caucuses
   A. Party organization of the Senate
      1. President pro tempore presides; member with most seniority in majority party
      2. Leaders are the majority leader and the minority leader, elected by their respective party members
      3. Party whips keep leaders informed, round up votes, count noses
      4. Policy Committee schedules Senate business
      5. Committee assignments
         a) Democratic Steering Committee
         b) Republican Committee on Committees
         c) Emphasize ideological and regional balance
         d) Other factors: popularity, effectiveness on television, favors owed
   B. Party structure in the House
      1. Speaker of the House as leader of majority party; presides over House
         a) Decides whom to recognize to speak on the floor
         b) Rules of germaneness of motions
         c) Decides to which committee bills go to
         d) Appoints members of special and select committees
         e) Has some patronage power
      2. Majority leader and minority leader
      3. Party whip organizations
      4. Democratic Steering and Policy Committee, chaired by Speaker
         a) Makes committee assignments
         b) Schedules legislation
      5. Republican Committee on Committees; makes committee assignments
      6. Republican Policy Committee; discusses policy
      7. Democratic and Republican congressional campaign committees
   C. The strength of party structure
      1. Loose measure is ability of leaders to determine party rules and organization
      2. Tested in 103d Congress: 110 new members
         a) Ran as outsiders
         b) Yet reelected entire leadership and committee chairs
      3. Senate different since transformed by changes in norms, not rules: now less party centered, less leader oriented, more hospitable to new members
   D. Party unity
      1. Recent trends
         a) Party unity voting higher between 1953 and 1965 and lower between 1966 and 1982
         b) Party unity voting increased since 1983, and was norm in the 1990s
         c) Party unity voting lower today than in the 1800s and early 1900s
         d) Party splits today may reflect sharp ideological differences between parties (or at least their respective leaders)
      2. Such strong differences in opinion are not so obvious among the public
         a) Impeachment vote did not reflect public opinion
         b) Congressional Democrats and Republicans also more sharply divided on abortion
      3. Why are congressional Democrats and Republicans so liberal and conservative?
         a) Most districts are drawn to protect partisan interests
            (1) Few are truly competitive
            (2) Primary elections count for more and ideological voters are more common in such a low turnout environment

b) Voters may be taking cues from the liberal and conservative votes of members of Congress
c) Committee chairs are typically chosen on the basis of seniority
(1) They are also usually from safe districts
(2) And hold views shaped by lifetime dedication to the cause of their party
(3) Although extent of leadership influence is difficult to document

E. Caucuses: rivals to parties in policy formulation
1. Rapid growth, to about 290 today
2. Reports that they would be abolished
3. Some are more influential than others (Congressional Black Caucus)

VII. The organization of Congress: committees
A. Legislative committees—most important organizational feature of Congress
1. Consider bills or legislative proposals
2. Maintain oversight of executive agencies
3. Conduct investigations

B. Types of committees
1. Select committees—groups appointed for a limited purpose and limited duration
2. Joint committees—those on which both representatives and senators serve
3. Conference committee—a joint committee appointed to resolve differences in the Senate and House versions of the same piece of legislation before final passage
4. Standing committees—most important type of committee
a) Majority party has majority of seats on the committees
b) Each member usually serves on two standing committees
c) Chairs are elected, but usually the most senior member of the committee is elected by the majority party
d) Subcommittee "bill of rights" of 1970s changed several traditions
(1) Opened more meetings to the public
(2) Allowed television coverage of meetings
(3) Effort to reduce number of committees in 1995–1996

C. Committee styles
1. Decentralization has increased individual member's influence
a) Less control by chairs
b) More amendments proposed and adopted
2. Ideological orientations of committees vary, depending on attitudes of members
3. Certain committees tend to attract particular types of legislators
a) Policy-oriented members
b) Constituency-oriented members

VIII. The organization of Congress: staffs and specialized offices
A. Tasks of staff members
1. Constituency service: major task of staff
2. Legislative functions: monitoring hearings, devising proposals, drafting reports, meeting with lobbyists
3. Staff members consider themselves advocates of their employers

B. Growth and influence of staff
1. Rapid growth: a large staff itself requires a large staff
2. Larger staff generates more legislative work
3. Members of Congress can no longer keep up with increased legislative work and so must rely on staff
4. Results in a more individualistic Congress

C. Staff agencies offer specialized information
1. Congressional Research Service (CRS)

2. General Accounting Office (GAO)
3. Office of Technology Assessment (OTA)
4. Congressional Budget Office (CBO)

IX. How a bill becomes law
  A. Bills travel through Congress at different speeds
    1. Bills to spend money or to tax or regulate business move slowly
    2. Bills with a clear, appealing idea move fast
      a) Examples: "Stop drugs," "End scandal"
  B. Introducing a bill
    1. Introduced by a member of Congress: hopper in House, recognized in Senate
    2. Most legislation has been initiated in Congress
    3. Presidentially-drafted legislation is shaped by Congress
    4. Resolutions
      a) Simple—passed by one house affecting that house
      b) Concurrent—passed by both houses affecting both
      c) Joint—passed by both houses, signed by president (except for constitutional amendments)
  C. Study by committees
    1. Bill is referred to a committee for consideration by either Speaker or presiding officer
    2. Revenue bills must originate in the House
    3. Most bills die in committee
    4. Hearings are often conducted by several subcommittees: multiple referrals (replaced by sequential referral system in 1995)
    5. Markup of bills—bills are revised by committees
    6. Committee reports a bill out to the House or Senate
      a) If bill is not reported out, the House can use the discharge petition
      b) If bill is not reported out, the Senate can pass a discharge motion
    7. House Rules Committee sets the rules for consideration
      a) Closed rule: sets time limit on debate and restricts amendments
      b) Open rule: permits amendments from the floor
      c) Restrictive rule: permits only some amendments
      d) Use of closed and restrictive rules growing
      e) Rules can be bypassed by the House
      f) No direct equivalent in Senate
  D. Floor debate, House
    1. Committee of the Whole—procedural device for expediting House consideration of bills but cannot pass bills
    2. Committee sponsor of bill organizes the discussion
  E. Floor debate, Senate
    1. No rule limiting debate or germaneness
    2. Entire committee hearing process can be bypassed by a senator
    3. Cloture—sets time limit on debate—three-fifths of Senate must vote for a cloture petition
    4. Both filibusters and cloture votes becoming more common
      a) Easier now to stage filibuster
      b) Roll calls are replacing long speeches
      c) But can be curtailed by "double tracking"—disputed bill is shelved temporarily—making filibuster less costly
  F. Methods of voting
    1. To investigate voting behavior one must know how a legislator voted on amendments as well as on the bill itself

2. Procedures for voting in the House
   a) Voice vote
   b) Division vote
   c) Teller vote
   d) Roll call vote
3. Senate voting is the same except no teller vote
4. Differences in Senate and House versions of a bill
   a) If minor, last house to act merely sends bill to the other house, which accepts the changes
   b) If major, a conference committee is appointed
      (1) Decisions are made by a majority of each delegation; Senate version favored
      (2) Conference reports back to each house for acceptance or rejection
5. Bill, in final form, goes to the president
   a) President may sign it
   b) If president vetoes it, it returns to the house of origin
      (1) Either house may override the president by a vote of two-thirds of those present
      (2) If both override, the bill becomes law without the president's signature

X. Reducing power and perks
   A. Many proposals made to "reform" and "improve" Congress
   B. Common perception it is overstaffed and self-indulgent
      1. Quick to regulate others, but not itself
      2. Quick to pass pork barrel legislation but slow to address controversial questions of national policy
      3. Use of franking privilege to subsidize personal campaigns
         a) Proposals to abolish it
         b) Proposals for restrictions on timing of mailings and a taxpayer "notice"
   C. Congressional Accountability Act of 1995
      1. For years Congress routinely exempted itself from many of the laws it passed
      2. Concern for enforcement (by Executive branch) and separation of powers
      3. 1995 Act
         a) Obliged Congress to obey eleven major laws
         b) Created the Office of Compliance
         c) Established an employee grievance procedure
   D. Trimming the pork
      1. Main cause of deficit is entitlement programs, not pork
      2. Some spending in districts represents needed projects
      3. Members supposed to advocate interests of district
      4. Price of citizen-oriented Congress is pork

XI. The Post-September 11 Congress
   A. Standard criticism: Congress cannot act quickly or change to meet new challenges
   B. Important consideration: Framers preferred deliberation over dispatch and boldness only when
      1. Backed by a persistent popular majority
      2. There is broad consensus among leaders
      3. Or both of the conditions mentioned above

C. Congress and terrorism
   1. 9/11 Commission recommended fundamental changes in oversight of intelligence gathering and counter-terrorism activities
      a) Concern over fracturing of executive management by divided congressional oversight
      b) Recognition that committee jurisdiction and prerogatives are difficult to change
   2. Reluctance of Congress to pass legislation implementing the Commission's recommendations
   3. Reorganization is likely to take years

KEY TERMS MATCH

Set 1

Match the following terms and descriptions:

4. The system under which committee chairs are awarded to members who have the longest continuous service on the committee
5. An assembly of party representatives that chooses a government and discusses major national issues
6. Explanation of congressional voting which suggests members of Congress respond primarily to cues provided by their colleagues
7. An alliance of conservative Democrats with Republicans for voting purposes
8. Indicated by votes in which a majority of voting Democrats oppose a majority of voting Republicans
9. A rule issued by the Rules Committee that does not allow a bill to be amended on the House floor
10. Resolution used for matters such as establishing the rules under which each body will operate
11. Resolution used for settling housekeeping and procedural matters that affect both houses
12. Resolution that is essentially the same as a law and is used to propose constitutional amendments

a. attitudinal view
b. bicameral legislature
c. closed rule
d. cloture rule
e. Committee on Committees
f. concurrent resolution
g. congressional caucus
h. conservative coalition
i. discharge petition
j. filibuster
k. House Rules Committee
l. joint resolution
m. marginal districts
n. markup
o. Millionaire's Club
p. multiple referral
q. organizational view
r. Parliament
s. party caucus
t. party polarization
u. party vote
v. party whip

13. A means by which senators can extend debate on a bill in order to prevent or delay its consideration
14. Explanation of congressional voting which emphasizes the impact of personal ideology and party identification as a voting cue
15. A Senate rule offering a means for stopping a filibuster
16. A rule issued by the Rules Committee that permits some amendments to a bill but not to others
17. Committee revisions of a bill
18. An association of members of Congress created to advocate a political ideology or a regional or economic interest
19. An individual who assists the party leader in staying abreast of the concerns and voting intentions of the party members
20. Assigns Republicans to standing committees in the Senate
21. Explanation of congressional voting that is based on the assumption that members want to get reelected and vote to please their constituents
22. The group that decides what business comes up for a vote and what the limitations on debate should be
23. A means by which the House can remove a bill stalled in committee
24. The process through which a bill is referred to several committees that simultaneously consider it in whole or in part
25. Assigns Democrats to standing committees in the Senate
26. A meeting of the members of a political party to decide questions of policy
27. The extent to which members of a party vote together in the House or the Senate

w. representational view

x. restrictive rule

y. riders

z. safe districts

aa. seniority

bb. sequential referral

cc. simple resolution

dd. Steering Committee

28. A lawmaking body composed of two chambers or parts
29. Districts in which the winner got less than 55 percent of the vote
30. Unrelated amendments added to a bill
31. Districts in which the winner got more than 55 percent of the vote
32. The process through which a bill is referred to second committee after the first is finished acting
33. A traditional, pejorative name for the United States Senate

Set 2

Match the following terms and descriptions:

1. The legislative leader elected by party members holding the majority of seats in the House or Senate
2. Congressional committees appointed for a limited time period and purpose
3. The ability of members of Congress to mail letters to their constituents free of charge
4. A congressional voting procedure that consists of members answering yea or nay to their names
5. The legislative leader elected by party members holding a minority of seats in the House or Senate
6. A committee on which both representatives and senators serve
7. Legislation that deals with matters of general concern
8. An order from the Rules Committee in the House that permits a bill to be amended on the legislative floor
9. A method of voting used in both houses in which members vote by shouting yea or nay

a. Christmas tree bill
b. conference committees
c. division vote
d. double tracking
e. franking privilege
f. joint committee
g. majority leader
h. minority leader
i. open rule
j. pork barrel legislation
k. private bill
l. public bill
m. quorum call
n. roll call vote
o. select committees
p. standing committees
q. teller vote
r. voice vote

10. A congressional voting procedure in which members pass between two tellers, first the yeas and then the nays
11. A procedure to keep the Senate going during a filibuster; the disputed bill is shelved temporarily
12. A special type of joint committee appointed to resolve differences in the House and Senate versions of a piece of legislation
13. A bill that has many riders
14. A congressional voting procedure in which members stand and are counted
15. The permanent committees of each house with the power to report bills
16. Legislation that deals only with specific matters rather than with general legislative affairs
17. Legislation that gives tangible benefits to constituents in the hope of winning their votes
18. A calling of the role in either house of Congress to determine whether the number of members in attendance meets the minimum number required to conduct official business

DATA CHECK

Table 13.1 (Page 323): Blacks, Hispanics, and Women in Congress, 1971–2008

1. Which chamber generally features a greater number of blacks, Hispanics, and women?

____

2. Which Congress featured the greatest number of blacks in the House of Representatives?

____

3. Which Congress featured the greatest number of women in the House of Representatives?

____

4. Which Congress featured the greatest number of women in the Senate?

____

Figure 13.1 (Page 325): Percentage of Incumbents Reelected to Congress

5. Generalize about the percentage of House members who have been reelected in elections from 1952 to 2004.

____

6. Generalize about the percentage of Senate members who have been reelected in elections from 1952 to 2004.

____

7. Which members of Congress tend to win with 60 percent or more of the vote?

____

PRACTICING FOR EXAMS

TRUE/FALSE QUESTIONS

Read each statement carefully. Mark true statements *T*. If any part of the statement is false, mark it *F*, and write in the space provided a concise explanation of why the statement is false.

1. T F Congress derives from a Latin term that means "a coming together."

____

2. T F In the United States, political parties exercise considerable control over the choice of who is nominated to run for congressional office.

____

3. T F The critical decision for a member of parliament is whether or not to support the government.

____

4. T F Political parties cannot discipline members of Congress who fail to support the party leadership.

____

5. T F Members of the British House of Commons are poorly paid and have no offices of their own.

____

6. T F Members of Congress are more concerned with their own constituencies than they are with the interests of any organized party.

____

7. T F Congress was designed by the Founders in ways that almost inevitably make it popular with voters.

____

8. T F The House has 335 members.

____

9. T F By the end of the nineteenth century, the House was known as the "Millionaires' Club."

____

10. T F The Senate eventually agreed to a constitutional amendment that changed the manner in which its members were elected.

____

11. T F The text suggests conservatives in the Senate monopolized the use of the filibuster for both lofty and self-serving purposes.

____

12. T F The tradition of unlimited debate remains strong in the Senate.

____

13. T F Congress has become less male and white.

____

14. T F Serving in Congress had become a career by the 1930s.

____

15. T F The Supreme Court struck down an effort by a state to impose term limits on its own members of Congress.

____

16. T F Senators are more likely to lose bids for reelection than members of the House.

____

17. T F In every election from 1968 to 1992, Republicans have gathered a higher percentage of the popular vote than they have the percentage of seats in the House of Representatives.

____

18. T F Democrats tend to do exceptionally well in low-turnout districts.

____

19. T F Studies suggest the incumbency advantage is worth about two to three points in an election today.

____

20. T F During the 1980s, about forty members of Congress were charged with misconduct.

____

21. T F The Conservative Coalition consisted of Republicans and certain Southern Democrats.

____

22. T F A member's final vote on a bill may conceal as much as it reveals.

____

23. T F Members of Congress who win in close races are usually eager to vote the way their constituents want.

____

24. T F Senators are often less in tune with public opinion than members of the House.

25. T F The Senate highlights the fact that the Republican Party is more deeply divided than the Democratic Party.

26. T F Congress has become an increasingly ideological organization.

27. T F The organizational explanation of how members of Congress vote has increased in importance.

28. T F Today, members of the House are more likely to investigate and denounce each other.

29. T F Leadership carries more power in the Senate than in the House.

30. T F The votes of Republicans on the four impeachment articles against President Clinton did not even represent the views of their districts.

31. T F Most congressional districts are not competitive.

32. T F Members of the majority party could, in theory, occupy all of the seats on all of the committees.

33. T F The Democratic Caucus changed the rules of Congress so that House chairmen were elected by secret ballot in party caucus.

34. T F Republicans in Congress also implemented term limits for committee chairmen.

35. T F In 1995, Republicans increased the number of committees in Congress.

36. T F In a typical Congress, several hundred bills are introduced.

37. T F Members of Congress are more likely to deal with one another through staff intermediaries than personally.

38. T F Bills which feature the spending of a lot of money tend to move through Congress more quickly than others.

39. T F Pending legislation does not carry over from one Congress to the next.

____

40. T F Most bills die in committee and they are often introduced only to get publicity for a member of Congress.

____

41. T F Sequential referrals have slowed down the business of Congress considerably.

____

42. T F Today, most bills are considered under strict time limits and no possibility of amendment from the floor.

____

43. T F What the filibuster means in practice is that neither political party can control the Senate unless it has at least sixty votes.

____

44. T F Most bills require a conference of committees from each house.

____

45. T F Conferences tend to report bills that favor the Senate version.

____

46. T F In most instances, the conference report on a bill is accepted by the respective chambers.

____

47. T F The text suggests that the only way to get rid of congressional "pork" is to eliminate Congress altogether and replace it with a tightly controlled parliament.

____

MULTIPLE CHOICE QUESTIONS

Circle the letter of the response that best answers the question or completes the statement.

1. A person ordinarily becomes a candidate for representative or senator by
   a. appealing to party leaders.
   b. serving first in the state legislature.
   c. serving in the state judiciary.
   d. running in a primary election.
   e. serving first in a government agency.
2. Whereas the principal work of a parliament is debate, that of a congress is
   a. representation and action.
   b. oversight and assessment.
   c. administration.
   d. investigation and reorganization.
   e. discussion.

3. Contemporary critics of Congress disagree with the Framers' vision of Congress in that the critics
   a. believe that Congress should normally proceed slowly in its deliberations.
   b. believe that Congress should rarely act without guidance from the executive branch.
   c. view Congress as designed to check and balance strong leaders in the executive branch.
   d. wish to end policy gridlock by making Congress capable of speedily adopting sweeping changes in national policies.
   e. wish to make changes to prevent the American political system from resembling a parliamentary system.
4. In the twentieth century, the trend in congressional decision-making has been toward
   a. centralization.
   b. increasing the power of the Speaker.
   c. increasing the power of party leaders.
   d. increasing the power of the president.
   e. decentralization.
5. Until 1913 senators were
   a. popularly elected.
   b. picked by state legislatures.
   c. appointed by state governors.
   d. selected by the state judiciaries.
   e. elected by the electoral college.
6. Which amendment changed the manner in which U.S. Senators are selected?
   a. Tenth.
   b. Fourteenth.
   c. Fifteenth.
   d. Seventeenth.
   e. Twenty-first.
7. Originally, filibusterers were sixteenth century
   a. auctioneers.
   b. lawyers.
   c. salesmen.
   d. cavalrymen.
   e. pirates.
8. The typical representative or senator is
   a. white.
   b. male.
   c. Protestant.
   d. a lawyer.
   e. all of the above.
9. In 1994, Native American Ben Nighthorse Campbell
   a. was elected to the Senate.
   b. was elected to the House.
   c. used radio programs to argue persuasively in favor of term limits.
   d. was allowed to fill a congressional seat as the result of a resignation.
   e. ran for seats in the House and the Senate simultaneously.

10. In the 1860s, being a congressman was not regarded as a "career" because
    a. the federal government was not very important.
    b. travel to Washington, D.C., was difficult.
    c. the job did not pay well.
    d. Washington was not generally considered a pleasant place to live.
    e. all of the above.
11. Serving in Congress became a career by the
    a. 1920s.
    b. 1940s.
    c. 1950s.
    d. 1970s.
    e. 1990s.
12. When a state attempted to impose term limits on its own members of Congress
    a. four other states did the same.
    b. a majority of states did the same.
    c. Congress outlawed the practice.
    d. the Supreme Court struck down the effort.
    e. a majority of incumbents nationwide announced they would not seek reelection.
13. Political scientists define a "safe" district as one where the incumbent received ___ percent or more of the vote in the previous election.
    a. 50
    b. 55
    c. 60
    d. 65
    e. 80
14. A new Congress convenes every ____ years.
    a. 2
    b. 3
    c. 4
    d. 6
    e. 10
15. The evidence that the electoral fortunes of members of Congress are shaped by the redrawing of congressional districts is
    a. compelling.
    b. striking, but anecdotal.
    c. long-standing.
    d. irrefutable.
    e. somewhat mixed, but convincing.
16. Today, few congressional votes feature the so-called "conservative coalition" because
    a. congressmen are increasingly facing strong challengers in their bid for reelection.
    b. members of Congress have generally become more moderate in terms of ideology.
    c. very few votes have an ideological dimension.
    d. the Republicans deeply offended Southern Democrats during the Carter administration.
    e. almost all of the conservatives are now in the Republican party.

17. Studies have found correlations between constituency opinion and congressional roll-call votes on bills related to
    a. civil rights.
    b. foreign policy.
    c. social welfare.
    d. international trade
    e. A and C.
18. When voting on matters where constituency interests or opinion are not vitally at stake, members of Congress respond primarily to voting cues provided by
    a. their colleagues.
    b. judicial rulings.
    c. interest groups.
    d. PACs.
    e. administrative agencies.
19. During the 1950s and 1960s, the Senate was dominated by
    a. northern senators.
    b. liberal senators.
    c. conservative Republicans.
    d. southern senators.
    e. freshman senators.
20. Beginning in the mid-1960s, ________ rose steadily in number, seniority and influence.
    a. northern senators
    b. liberal senators
    c. conservative Republicans
    d. southern senators
    e. freshman senators
21. Beginning in the late 1970s, ________ began to regain seats in the Senate.
    a. northern senators
    b. liberal senators
    c. conservative Republicans
    d. southern senators
    e. freshman senators
22. The increasingly ideological nature of the House means today's members are more likely to
    a. consult with campaign managers before voting.
    b. be influenced by PAC contributions when they vote.
    c. serve on low-profile committees.
    d. investigate and denounce each other.
    e. sponsor legislation written by interest groups.
23. The real leadership in the Senate rests with the
    a. majority leader.
    b. president pro tempore.
    c. managers.
    d. vice president.
    e. Senate whip.

24. In the House, the most important position is the
    a. majority leader.
    b. manager.
    c. Speaker.
    d. president pro tempore.
    e. floor leader.
25. In recent years, the Senate has become more hospitable to
    a. lawyers.
    b. ideologues.
    c. partisans.
    d. state legislators.
    e. freshmen.
26. An extreme example of party voting was the response to Clinton's 1993 budget plan in which every Republican in the
    a. House voted against it.
    b. Senate voted for it.
    c. House and Senate voted against it.
    d. House and Senate voted for it.
    e. House and Senate refused to vote on the matter at all.
27. The text suggests ____________ are "a growing rival to the parties as a source of policy leadership."
    a. senior leadership councils
    b. PAC-based think tanks
    c. regional alliances
    d. executive liaisons
    e. congressional caucuses
28. The most important organizational feature of Congress is the
    a. party caucus.
    b. floor leader.
    c. committee structure.
    d. legislative leadership program.
    e. congressional campaign committee.
29. Each member of the House usually serves on ___ standing committees.
    a. 2
    b. 3
    c. 4
    d. 6
    e. 7
30. The text suggests that closed rules, proxy voting and strong committee chairmen
    a. were desired by Democrats, but not the Republicans.
    b. were a major campaign issue in 1976.
    c. reduced the number of bills that were introduced in Congress.
    d. made it easier to get things done.
    e. enhanced the public reputation of Congress.

31. Which of the following is signed by the president and has the force of law?
    a. Simple resolution.
    b. Concurrent resolution.
    c. Parallel resolution.
    d. Joint resolution.
    e. A and B.
32. Which of the following is required in order to propose a constitutional amendment?
    a. Simple resolution.
    b. Concurrent resolution.
    c. Parallel resolution.
    d. Joint resolution.
    e. A and B.
33. The Constitution requires that "all bills for raising revenue shall …
    a. originate in the House of Representatives."
    b. originate in the Senate."
    c. originate in Conference Committee."
    d. require a unanimous vote."
    e. be exempt from the veto of the President."
34. In the House, a stalled bill can be extracted from a committee and brought to the floor by means of
    a. a discharge petition.
    b. an extraction bill.
    c. a committee rule.
    d. cloture.
    e. a unanimous consent vote.
35. The "Committee of the Whole" refers to
    a. a collection of committee chairs in the House.
    b. the senior sponsors of a piece of legislation.
    c. freshmen members of both the House and the Senate.
    d. members of the House who happen to be on the floor when a bill is discussed.
    e. none of the above.
36. The practical advantage of the "Committee of the Whole" is that
    a. committee chairs have greater understanding of parliamentary procedure.
    b. senior members of Congress are probably more enthusiastic supporters of legislation.
    c. new members of Congress are made to feel more welcomed in chambers.
    d. it requires a much smaller number of members to hold quorum.
    e. none of the above.
37. In recent years, the filibuster has occurred more frequently because
    a. the Senate has increased in size.
    b. Republicans have gained seats in the Senate.
    c. Democrats have gained seats in the Senate.
    d. participants are guaranteed media exposure.
    e. it is easier to stage one.

38. Bills which contain a large number of "riders" are known as "__________ bills."
    a. Loaded
    b. Constituency
    c. Valentine
    d. Dry Ice
    e. Christmas Tree
39. The process of "double tracking" allows
    a. committees to consider recently rejected legislation within a limited time frame.
    b. members of the House to filibuster two bills at the same time.
    c. the president to influence congressional votes at the beginning and end of the legislative session.
    d. members of the Senate to focus on other business during a filibuster.
    e. freshmen members of Congress two chances to pass their first piece of legislation.
40. For years Congress defended the manner in which it exempted itself from many of its own laws by reference to
    a. federalism.
    b. bicameralism.
    c. the separation of powers.
    d. legislative supremacy.
    e. the committee structure.
41. According to the text, most categories of pork spending have _______ in the last ten or fifteen years.
    a. decreased
    b. remained at approximately the same levels
    c. increased
    d. slightly increased
    e. dramatically increased

ESSAY QUESTIONS

Practice writing extended answers to the following questions. These test your ability to integrate and express the ideas that you have been studying in this chapter.

1. Compare and contrast membership in Parliament with membership in the U.S. Congress.
2. Explain what a "filibuster" is and how "Rule 22" applies to filibusters.
3. Generalize about the social background characteristics of the typical member of Congress and describe recent trends in membership.
4. What are some explanations that scholars provide for why congressional seats have become less marginal?
5. Identify and explain the three views of congressional voting.
6. Why are members of Congress strong liberals and conservatives while the American people are usually somewhere in the center?
7. Explain the three types of resolutions that Congress can pass.
8. Explain the four procedures for voting in Congress.
9. Identify 5-6 rules with respect to Congressional ethics.

ANSWERS TO KEY TERMS MATCH QUESTIONS

Set 1

1. aa
2. r
3. q
4. h
5. t
6. c
7. cc
8. f
9. l
10. j
11. a
12. d
13. x
14. n
15. g
16. v
17. e
18. w
19. k
20. i
21. p
22. dd
23. s
24. u
25. b
26. m
27. y
28. z
29. bb
30. o

Set 2

1. g
2. o
3. e
4. n
5. h
6. f
7. l
8. i
9. r
10. q
11. d
12. b
13. a
14. c
15. p
16. k
17. j
18. m

ANSWERS TO DATA CHECK QUESTIONS

1. The House.
2. 106th and 108th (with 39).
3. 110th (with 74).
4. 110th (with 16).
5. The number has varied to some degree, but generally hangs around the 90 percent mark. It has never fallen below 70 percent.
6. The number has varied considerably compared to the number for the House. It has fluctuated between 55 and 95 percent, but generally remains about the 70 percent mark.
7. House members are more likely to gather 60 percent or more of the vote.

ANSWERS TO TRUE/FALSE QUESTIONS

1. T
2. F Although parties do play a role in the process, attaining the nomination is largely an individual effort in the United States.
3. T
4. T

5. T
6. T
7. F It was designed in a way that would inevitably make it slow moving and unpopular.
8. F The House has 435 members.
9. T
10. T
11. F This has been the case with respect to both liberals and conservatives in the Senate.
12. T
13. T
14. F It did not become a career until the 1950s.
15. T
16. T
17. T
18. T
19. F It is worth 6 to 8 points today.
20. T
21. T
22. T
23. F Amazingly, there is no evidence of this. Perhaps it is because opinion is so divided in a marginal district that it isn't possible (or smart to even try to) please everyone.
24. T
25. F The Democratic party is more deeply divided (the split occurring between Northern and Southern Democrats).
26. T
27. F The attitudinal explanation has increased in importance as Congress has become more ideological.
28. T
29. F Leadership carries much more power in the House.
30. T
31. T
32. T
33. T
34. T
35. F They actually decreased the number.
36. F It would be more accurate to say five to six thousand are introduced.
37. T

38. F The more money involved in a bill, the slower it moves through the process.

39. T

40. T

41. F They are a device that could possibly slow down the process, to be sure, but there is as of yet, no evidence that they do.

42. T

43. T

44. F Most bills do not require the attention of such a committee.

45. T

46. T

47. T

ANSWERS TO MULTIPLE CHOICE QUESTIONS

1. d
2. a
3. d
4. e
5. b
6. d
7. e
8. e
9. a
10. e
11. c
12. d
13. b
14. a
15. b
16. e
17. a
18. a
19. d
20. b
21. c
22. d
23. a

24. c
25. e
26. c
27. e
28. c
29. a
30. d
31. d
32. d
33. a
34. a
35. d
36. d
37. e
38. e
39. d
40. c
41. a

CHAPTER 14

The Presidency

REVIEWING THE CHAPTER

CHAPTER FOCUS

This chapter introduces you to the institution that has become the hub of American government during its two centuries of history: the presidency. The chapter demonstrates that this institution is unique or at least significantly different from other positions of government leadership. It also surveys the changes that have occurred in the office from the original, limited position intended by the Founders, through historical evolution, and down to the office of the president as we know it today. After reading and reviewing the material in this chapter, you should be able to do each of the following:

1. Explain the differences between the positions of president and prime minister.
2. Discuss the approach of the Founders toward executive power.
3. Sketch the evolution of the presidency from 1789 to the present.
4. List and describe the various offices that make up the office of the president.
5. Review discussions of presidential character and how these relate to the achievements in office of various presidents.
6. Enumerate and discuss the various facets—formal and informal—of presidential power.

STUDY OUTLINE

I. Presidents and prime ministers
   A. Characteristics of parliaments
      1. Parliamentary system twice as common
      2. Chief executive chosen by legislature
      3. Cabinet ministers chosen from among members of parliament
      4. Prime minister remains in power as long as his or her party or coalition maintains a majority in the legislature
   B. Differences
      1. Presidents are often outsiders; prime ministers are always insiders, chosen by party members in parliament
      2. Presidents choose their cabinet from outside Congress; prime ministers choose members of parliament
      3. Presidents have no guaranteed majority in the legislature; prime ministers always have a majority. The United States usually has a divided government
      4. Presidents and the legislature often work at cross-purposes
         a) Even when one party controls both branches
         b) A consequence of separation of powers
         c) Only Roosevelt and Johnson had much luck with Congress

5. Presidents and prime ministers at war
    a) Bush had to cajole a Congress controlled by his own property, Blair encountered no meaningful resistance in parliament
    b) When public opinion turned against Bush's position, he remained in office. When public opinion turned against Blair, he announced his resignation

II. Divided Government
  A. Divided versus unified government
    1. Fifteen of twenty-two congressional/presidential elections since 1952 produced divided government
    2. Americans dislike divided government because it can lead to gridlock
  B. Does gridlock matter?
    1. But divided government enacts as many important laws as a unified government
    2. Reason: Unified government is something of a myth in U.S.
  C. Is policy gridlock bad?
    1. Unclear whether gridlock is always bad; it is a necessary consequence of representative democracy
    2. Representative democracy opposite direct democracy

III. The evolution of the presidency
  A. Delegates feared both anarchy and monarchy
    1. Idea of a plural executive
    2. Idea of an executive checked by a council
  B. Concerns of the Founders
    1. Fear of military power of president who could overpower states
    2. Fear of presidential corruption of Senate
    3. Fear of presidential bribery to ensure reelection
  C. The electoral college
    1. Each state to choose own method for selecting electors
    2. Electors to meet in own capital to vote for president and vice president
    3. If no majority, House would decide
  D. The president's term of office
    1. Precedent of George Washington and two terms
    2. Twenty-second Amendment in 1951 limits to two terms
    3. Problem of establishing the legitimacy of the office
    4. Provision for orderly transfer of power
  E. The first presidents
    1. Prominent men helped provide legitimacy
    2. Minimal activism of early government contributed to lessening fear of the presidency
    3. Appointed people of stature in the community (rule of fitness)
    4. Relations with Congress were reserved; few vetoes, no advice
  F. The Jacksonians
    1. Jackson sought to maximize powers of presidency
    2. Vigorous use of veto for policy reasons
    3. Challenged Congress
  G. The reemergence of Congress
    1. With brief exceptions the next hundred years was a period of congressional ascendancy
    2. Intensely divided public opinion
    3. Only Lincoln expanded presidential power
      a) Asserted "implied powers" and power of commander-in-chief
      b) Justified by emergency conditions
    4. President mostly a negative force to Congress until the New Deal

5. Since the 1930s power has been institutionalized in the presidency
6. Popular conception of the president as the center of government contradicts reality; Congress often policy leader

IV. The powers of the president
- A. Formal powers found in Article II
  1. Not a large number of explicit powers
  2. Potential for power found in ambiguous clauses of the Constitution, such as power as commander in chief and duty to "take care that laws be faithfully executed"
- B. Greatest source of power lies in politics and public opinion
  1. Increase in broad statutory authority
  2. Expectation of presidential leadership from the public

V. The office of the president
- A. The White House Office
  1. Contains the president's closest assistants
  2. Three types of organization
     - a) Circular
     - b) Pyramid
     - c) *Ad hoc*
  3. Staff typically worked on the campaign: a few are experts
  4. Relative influence of staff depends on how close one's office is to the president's
- B. The Executive Office of the President
  1. Composed of agencies that report directly to the president
  2. Appointments must receive Senate confirmation
  3. Office of Management and Budget most important
     - a) Assembles the budget
     - b) Develops reorganization plans
     - c) Reviews legislative proposals of agencies
- C. The cabinet
  1. Largely a fiction, not mentioned in Constitution
  2. President appoints or controls more members of cabinet than does prime minister
  3. Secretaries become preoccupied and defensive about their own departments
- D. Independent agencies, commissions, and judgeships
  1. President appoints members of agencies that have a quasi-independent status
  2. Agency heads serve a fixed term and can be removed only "for cause"
  3. Judges can be removed only by impeachment

VI. Who gets appointed
- A. President knows few appointees personally
- B. Most appointees have had federal experience
  1. "In-and-outers"; alternate federal and private sector jobs
  2. No longer have political followings but picked for expertise
- C. Need to consider important interest groups when making appointments
- D. Rivalry between department heads and White House staff

VII. Presidential character
- A. Eisenhower: orderly
- B. Kennedy: improviser
- C. Johnson: dealmaker
- D. Nixon: mistrustful
- E. Ford: genial
- F. Carter: outsider
- G. Reagan: communicator
- H. Bush: hands-on manager

I. Clinton: focus on details
J. Bush: a different kind of outsider

VIII. The power to persuade
A. Formal opportunities for persuasion
B. The three audiences
1. Other politicians and leaders in Washington, D.C.; reputation very important
2. Party activists and officials inside Washington
3. The various publics
4. Trends in informal remarks, press conferences, and formal speeches (the bully pulpit)
C. Popularity and influence
1. Presidents try to transform popularity into support in Congress
2. Little effect of presidential coattails
3. Members of Congress believe it is politically risky to challenge a popular president
4. Popularity is unpredictable and influenced by factors beyond the president's control
D. The decline in popularity
1. Popularity highest immediately after an election
2. Declines by midterm after honeymoon period

IX. The power to say no
A. Veto
1. Veto message
2. Pocket veto (only before end of Congress)
3. Congress rarely overrode vetoes in 1996
B. Executive privilege
1. Confidential communications between president and advisers
2. Justification
a) Separation of powers
b) Need for candid advice
3. *U.S.* v. *Nixon* (1973) rejects claim of absolute executive privilege
C. Impoundment of funds
1. Defined: presidential refusal to spend funds appropriated by Congress
2. Countered by Budget Reform Act of 1974
a) Requires president to notify Congress of funds he does not intend to spend
b) Congress must agree in forty-five days
D. Signing statements
1. Issued when a president signs legislation
2. Have a variety of purposes
a) express attitudes about a law
b) tell executive branch how to implement law
c) discuss some aspect considered unconstitutional
3. Common among twentieth century presidents
4. Not very popular with Congress
5. Supreme Court has not addressed the constitutional significance of such statements

X. The president's program
A. Putting together a program
1. President can try to have a policy on everything (Carter).
2. President can concentrate on a small number of initiatives (Reagan)
3. Constraints
a) Public reaction may be adverse
b) Limited time and attention span
c) Unexpected crises
d) Programs can be changed only marginally

4. Need for president to be selective about what he wants
5. Heavy reliance on opinion polls
6. Impact of dramatic events and prolonged crises

B. Attempts to reorganize the executive branch
1. An item on presidential agendas since the administration of Herbert Hoover
2. Bush and the Department of Homeland Defense
   a) White House Office of Homeland Security created in aftermath of terrorist attack of 9/11
      (1) Small staff
      (2) Little budgetary authority
      (3) No ability to enforce decisions
   b) Bush's call for a reorganization
      (1) Creation of third largest cabinet department encompassing twenty-two federal agencies
      (2) 170,000 employees and an annual budget of almost $40 million
   c) Fate of proposal is pending, but it is neither the first of its kind nor the largest.
3. Reasons for reorganizing
   a) Large number of agencies
   b) Easier to change policy through reorganization
4. Reorganization outside the White House staff must be by law

XI. Presidential transition

A. Few presidents serve two terms

B. The vice president
1. May succeed on death of president
   a) Has happened eight times
   b) John Tyler defined status of ascending vice president: president in title and in powers
2. Rarely are vice presidents elected president
   a) Unless they first took over for a president who died
   b) Only five instances otherwise: Adams, Jefferson, Van Buren, Nixon, and Bush
3. "A rather empty job"
   a) Candidates still pursue it
   b) Preside over Senate and vote in case of a tie
   c) Leadership powers in Senate are weak

C. Problems of succession
1. What if the president falls ill?
   a) Examples: Garfield, Wilson
2. If vice president steps up, who becomes vice president?
   a) Succession Act (1886): designated secretary of state as next in line
   b) Amended in 1947 to designate Speaker of the House
3. Twenty-fifth Amendment resolved both issues
   a) Allows vice president to serve as "acting president" if president is disabled; decided by president, by vice president and cabinet, or by two-thirds vote of Congress
   b) Requires vice president who ascends to office on death or resignation of the president to name a vice president
      (1) Must be confirmed by both houses
      (2) Examples: Agnew and Nixon resignations

D. Impeachment
1. Judges most frequent targets of impeachment
2. Indictment by the House, conviction by the Senate

XII. How powerful is the president?
  A. Both president and Congress are constrained
  B. Reasons for constraints
    1. Complexity of issues
    2. Scrutiny of the media
    3. Power of interest groups

KEY TERMS MATCH

Match the following terms and descriptions:

1. A constitutional procedure by which federal judges and civil officers can be removed from office before their terms expire
2. Legislation that specifies the conditions and order of succession to the presidency and vice presidency when the president leaves office before completion of his term
3. People who alternate between jobs in the federal government and employment in the private sector
4. Presidential staff who oversee the policy interests of the president
5. A statement sent to Congress by the president giving the reasons for vetoing a bill
6. The president's use of his prestige and visibility to guide or enthuse the American public
7. The chief executive in a parliamentary system who is chosen by the legislature
8. Reveals what the president thinks about a new law and how it ought to be enforced
9. The presidential assertion of the right to withhold certain information from Congress
10. The organization responsible for preparing the federal budget and for central clearance of legislative proposals from federal agencies
11. Agencies headed by appointees who serve for fixed terms and can be removed only "for cause"
12. A presidential refusal to spend money appropriated by Congress
13. Term used to describe the early months of the presidential term when popularity ratings tend to be relatively high
14. Agencies that perform staff services for the president but are not part of the White House

a. *ad hoc* structure
b. Article II
c. bully pulpit
d. cabinet
e. circular structure
f. delegate
g. direct democracy
h. divided government
i. electoral college
j. Executive Office of the President
k. Executive privilege
l. gridlock
m. honeymoon
n. impeachment
o. impoundment of funds
p. "in-and-outers"
q. independent agencies
r. lame duck
s. legislative veto
t. line-item veto
u. Office of Management and Budget
v. perks
w. pocket veto
x. prime minister
y. pyramid structure
z. representative democracy
aa. signing statement

15. View of presidential decision-making which stresses what the public wants
16. The power of some governors (and the president in a limited way between 1996 and 1998) to veto portions of a bill instead of having to veto the entire bill
17. Andrew Jackson's view of his role as president of the United States
18. A legal system by which states select electors who then vote for the president and vice president
19. A statement that defines the constitutional powers of the president
20. Term used to express concern over inefficacy in government which might result from Congress and the Presidency being controlled by members of different parties
21. A method of organizing a president's staff in which several task forces, committees, and informal groups deal directly with the president
22. A president's council of advisers
23. A method of organizing a president's staff in which several presidential assistants report directly to the president
24. View of presidential decision making which stresses what the public interest requires
25. A political system in which all or most citizens participate directly by either holding office or making policy
26. A government in which one party controls the White House and another party controls one or both houses of Congress
27. A politician who is still in office after having lost a reelection bid
28. The rejection of a presidential or administrative action by a vote of one or both houses of Congress without the consent of the president
29. The fringe benefits of holding an office
30. A form of veto in which the president fails to sign a bill passed by both houses within ten days and Congress has adjourned during that time
31. A method of organizing a president's staff in which most presidential assistants report through a hierarchy to the president's chief of staff

bb. Tribune of the People

cc. trustee

dd. Twenty-fifth Amendment

ee. unified government

ff. veto message

gg. White House Office

32. A political system in which leaders and representatives acquire political power by means of a competitive struggle for the people's vote

33. A government in which the same party controls the White House and both houses of Congress

DATA CHECK

Table 14.1 (Page 378): The Cabinet Department

1. Which cabinet departments are the oldest?

2. Which cabinet department is the newest?

3. Which cabinet department has the largest number of employees?

4. How many of the cabinet departments have been created since 1960?

Table 14.2 (Page 384): Partisan Gains or Losses in Congress in Presidential Election Years

5. What hypothesis underlies the table?

6. What does the 1956 election suggest about the popularity of Eisenhower (who won 57% of the popular vote) and the popularity of the Republican party as an institution?

7. In which election was the greatest number of seats gained by the president's party in the House of Representatives?

8. In which election was the greatest number of seats gained by the president's party in the Senate?

9. In which two elections were the greatest number of seats lost by the president's party in the House of Representatives?

Figure 14.1 (Pages 386–7): Presidential Popularity

10. What question was asked of respondents in order to collect the data presented in this Figure?

11. In which terms was it quite clear that the president was not as popular at the end of his term as he was at the very beginning?

12. What do the terms that do not exhibit the trend identified in the previous question have in common?

Table 14.3 (Page 387): Partisan Gains or Losses in Congress in Off-Year Elections

13. What does Table 14.4 tell us generally?

14. In which election(s) did the party of the president lose more than fifty seats in the House?

15. In which election(s) did the party of the president lose more than ten seats in the Senate?

16. In which two elections did a president *gain* seats in *both* the House and the Senate?

PRACTICING FOR EXAMS

TRUE/FALSE QUESTIONS

Read each statement carefully. Mark true statements *T.* If any part of the statement is false, mark it *F,* and write in the space provided a concise explanation of why the statement is false.

1. T F Democratic president Jimmy Cater could not get the Democratic-controlled Senate to ratify his strategic arms limitation treaty.

2. T F The popularly elected president is an American invention.

3. T F Divided government has been the result of most national elections since 1952.

4. T F Research suggests divided governments do not ratify significant treaties or pass important laws.

5. T F We may have had a truly unified government in 1933 and 1965.

6. T F In a typical presidential election, one half of all voters will vote for one party's candidate for president and the other party's candidate for Congress.

7. T F The general assumption of the Framers of the Constitution was that George Washington would be the first president.

____

8. T F Presidential elections have never been decided by the House of Representatives.

____

9. T F George Washington limited himself to two terms.

____

10. T F George Washington was a strong supporter of political parties.

____

11. T F Congress decided no president's image would appear on currency until after his death.

____

12. T F The Nation's early presidents made extensive use of the veto power.

____

13. T F Although he had been elected as a military hero, Andrew Jackson had also been a member of both the House and the Senate.

____

14. T F Abraham Lincoln praised Andrew Jackson's exceptional use of executive authority.

____

15. T F Lincoln raised an army and spent money without prior approval of Congress.

____

16. T F Lincoln issued the Emancipation Proclamation Act without prior congressional approval.

____

17. T F From the Eisenhower years through the Reagan administration, Congress often took the lead in setting the legislative agenda.

____

18. T F The Clean Air Act (1990) and the Welfare Reform Act (1996) were both bills deigned by Congress, not by the president.

____

19. T F Grover Cleveland used federal troops to break a labor strike in the 1890s.

____

20. T F President Carter employed the pyramid structure for organization of personal staff.

____

21. T F Typically, senior White House staff members are drawn from the ranks of the president's campaign staff.

____

22. T F There are ten major executive departments headed by cabinet officers.

____

23. T F A president rarely knows more than a few of the people that he appoints.

____

24. T F According to the text, much of Eisenhower's bumbling, incoherent manner of speaking was a strategic "public disguise."

____

25. T F Richard Nixon thrived on personal confrontation and face-to-face encounters with other politicians.

____

26. T F Presidents have made fewer and fewer impromptu remarks in the years since Franklin Roosevelt held office.

____

27. T F President Roosevelt failed to "purge" members of Congress who opposed his program.

____

28. T F Some presidents have not experienced a "honeymoon" in the sense of initially high levels of public support and congressional compliance.

____

29. T F Most state governors possess the power of the line-item veto.

____

30. T F In 1996, Congress effectively gave the president the power of the line item veto with the introduction of the "enhanced rescission."

____

31. T F The Supreme Court upheld the power of the president to carve up legislation, retaining only those parts with which he is in agreement.

____

32. T F The Constitution specifically requires the president to divulge private communications between himself and his principal advisors if a congressional investigation demands such information.

____

33. T F For most of our nation's history, there was no serious challenge to the claim of presidential confidentiality.

____

34. T F The Constitution specifically requires the president to spend money that is appropriated by Congress.

____

35. T F Signing statements were the creation of presidents in the early 1900s.

____

36. T F Members of Congress have encouraged presidents to accompany legislation with signing statements.

______

37. T F The text suggests that a sixty-hour workweek is typical for a president.

______

38. T F The Supreme Court has declared so-called legislative vetoes unconstitutional.

______

39. T F Presidents routinely complain of what they feel is the limited scope of their power.

______

40. T F In 1841, John Tyler became the first vice president to become president because of the death of his predecessor.

______

41. T F The only official task of the vice president is to preside over the Senate and to vote in case of a tie.

______

42. T F The Twenty-fifth Amendment to the Constitution addresses the problem of presidential succession.

______

43. T F Only two presidents have ever been impeached.

______

MULTIPLE CHOICE QUESTIONS

Circle the letter of the response that best answers the question or completes the statement.

1. In a parliamentary system the prime minister is chosen by the
   a. people.
   b. signatories.
   c. electors.
   d. legislature.
   e. monarch.
2. Which of the following statements is *true* of U.S. presidents but not of British prime ministers?
   a. Presidents and the legislature often work at cross-purposes.
   b. Presidents are selected by the legislature.
   c. Presidents have more strict control over members of their party.
   d. Presidents are most often government insiders.
   e. Presidents generally choose their cabinets from among members of Congress.
3. The text suggests that policy gridlock is a necessary consequence of
   a. representative democracy.
   b. big government.
   c. direct democracy.
   d. divided government.
   e. unified government.

4. Who called for something like an elective monarchy here in the United States?
   a. George Washington
   b. John Adams
   c. Thomas Jefferson
   d. John Jay
   e. Alexander Hamilton
5. The Framers first considered having _________ select the president.
   a. the Supreme Court
   b. Congress
   c. the state legislatures
   d. the various governors
   e. the large states
6. Which amendment formally limited presidents to two terms?
   a. 9th
   b. 10th
   c. 17th
   d. 22nd
   e. 26th
7. Establishing the legitimacy of the presidency in the early years was made easier by the fact that the national government
   a. was both efficient and popular.
   b. acted cautiously because it was in debt.
   c. had relatively little to do.
   d. kept the Treasury Department weak.
   e. was dominated by one political faction.
8. Andrew Jackson's use of the veto power was conspicuous because
   a. he rarely used it.
   b. he used it more than all of the presidents before him combined.
   c. all of his vetoes were overridden.
   d. he would not use the power unless he thought legislation was unconstitutional.
   e. he would not use the veto simply because of a policy disagreement.
9. Jackson's view of a strong and independent presidency
   a. was forsaken after two years in office.
   b. has not been adopted by any other president.
   c. was only adopted by Abraham Lincoln.
   d. emerged as the norm a century later.
   e. has been adopted by the Democratic Party.
10. Which of the following actions did Abraham Lincoln take without prior congressional approval?
    a. Raised an army.
    b. Spent money.
    c. Blockaded Southern ports.
    d. Suspended *habeas corpus.*
    e. all of the above.
11. Today, winning the presidency means a candidate must get ____ electoral votes.
    a. 100
    b. 170
    c. 250
    d. 270
    e. 538

12. The elimination of the Electoral College might have the effect of
    a. encouraging third parties.
    b. reducing vote turnout.
    c. increasing the importance of less populous states.
    d. reducing the importance of independent candidates.
    e. expediting the results of presidential elections.
13. Which of the following presidential powers is not a shared power?
    a. Treaty making
    b. Appointment of ambassadors
    c. Approval of legislation
    d. The pardoning power
    e. Appointment of judges and high officials
14. The greatest source of presidential power is found in
    a. the Constitution.
    b. Congress.
    c. public communication.
    d. the bureaucracy.
    e. politics and public opinion.
15. The text suggests that the ability of a presidential assistant to influence the president is governed by the rule of
    a. reason.
    b. propinquity.
    c. law.
    d. integrity.
    e. Congress.
16. Which organizational structure runs the risk of isolating or misinforming the president?
    a. pyramid
    b. circular
    c. ad hoc
    d. titular
    e. vertical
17. Which organizational structure lends itself to confusion and conflict?
    a. pyramid
    b. circular
    c. ad hoc
    d. titular
    e. vertical
18. The Office of Management and Budget both assembles the president's budget and
    a. manages the departments.
    b. reviews departmental legislative proposals.
    c. manages federal personnel.
    d. organizes presidential cabinet meetings.
    e. reviews the Senior Executive Service.

19. Which modern president is almost the only one given credit for coming close to making his cabinet a truly deliberative body?
    a. Harry Truman
    b. Calvin Coolidge
    c. John F. Kennedy
    d. Dwight Eisenhower
    e. Bill Clinton
20. The main difference between a presidential agency and an independent agency is that heads of the former
    a. cannot have their salaries reduced.
    b. serve at the president's discretion.
    c. can only be removed "for cause."
    d. cannot sponsor legislation.
    e. serve at Congress's pleasure.
21. All of the following statements regarding "acting appointments" are correct *except*:
    a. Such appointees hold office until the Senate acts on their nomination.
    b. Such appointees have been known to hold office for months without confirmation.
    c. Senators generally favor such appointees because of their heavy nomination workload.
    d. Presidents see the allowance of such appointees as a necessity.
    e. The existence of such appointees appears to be contrary to the Vacancies Act of 1868.
22. In recent administrations there has been a tendency for presidents to place in their cabinet people known for their
    a. independent political power.
    b. personal wealth.
    c. creativity.
    d. loyalty to Congress.
    e. expertise.
23. Of the three audiences that the president confronts, the one that is most often important for maintaining and exercising power is
    a. other politicians and leaders in Washington.
    b. the mass public throughout the nation.
    c. party activists.
    d. foreign leaders.
    e. officeholders outside Washington.
24. There is a noticeable decline in the number of __________ by recent presidents.
    a. public appearances made
    b. public speeches given
    c. press conferences held
    d. cabinet meetings called
    e. State of the Union addresses given
25. The personal popularity of the president affects which of the following most directly?
    a. How Congress treats presidential legislative proposals
    b. How members of the president's party do in House elections
    c. How members of the president's party do in Senate elections
    d. The president's ability to conduct foreign affairs
    e. b and d

26. Which of the following statements about George W. Bush's approval ratings is *incorrect*?
    a. His initial ratings were comparable to those of President Clinton's in 1993.
    b. His disapproval rating was the highest of any president since polling began.
    c. His approval rating for the first six months was fairly typical for modern presidents.
    d. His approval ratings after the September 11 attack were the highest ever recorded.
    e. none of the above.
27. Once in office a president can expect to see his popularity
    a. increase over time.
    b. remain about the same.
    c. fluctuate in a manner that admits of no generalization.
    d. decline over time.
    e. be dependent on the actions of Congress.
28. Which of the following statements is true of a bill that is not signed or vetoed within ten days while Congress is still in session?
    a. It is considered to have received a pocket veto.
    b. It is returned to Congress.
    c. It must be given a veto message.
    d. It becomes a law until the next session of Congress.
    e. It becomes law automatically.
29. From George Washington to Bill Clinton, about ____ percent of over 2,500 presidential vetoes have been overridden.
    a. 4
    b. 15
    c. 20
    d. 25
    e. 30
30. Which statement best describes George W. Bush's use of the veto power?
    a. He has used it about as much as most recent presidents.
    b. He has used it more often than recent presidents.
    c. He has used it slightly less than recent presidents.
    d. He has hardly used the power at all.
    e. He has vetoed more legislation than any modern president.
31. The doctrine of executive privilege is based on separation of powers and on the
    a. constitutional requirements for secrecy.
    b. War Powers Act.
    c. president's need for confidential advice.
    d. White House *Sourcebook*.
    e. integrity of each branch of government.
32. The issue of executive privilege was not directly addressed by the Supreme Court until
    a. John F. Kennedy was reported to have had dealings with organized crime.
    b. Harry Truman refused to provide testimony in regard to some controversial last minute pardons.
    c. George Bush interfered with Iran-Contra prosecutions.
    d. Richard Nixon attempted to withhold tape recordings from a special prosecutor.
    e. Gerald Ford pardoned Richard Nixon.

33. In *Clinton* v.. *Jones* (1997) the Supreme Court ruled that the president can be sued
    a. while in office.
    b. for actions taken before he became president.
    c. in state and federal court.
    d. by non-U.S. citizens.
    e. A and D.
34. Which of the following factors is emphasized by the text as placing considerable constraint on a president's ability to plan a program?
    a. The president's personal ideology
    b. The limits of the president's time and attention
    c. The need to campaign
    d. The leaders in his own party
    e. The mass media
35. During an average year, Congress passes ________ bills.
    a. between 50 and 100
    b. between 200 and 300
    c. between 400 and 600
    d. over one thousand
    e. over six thousand
36. ______________ was the last president *not* to use public opinion polls.
    a. Woodrow Wilson
    b. Herbert Hoover
    c. John F. Kennedy
    d. Franklin Roosevelt
    e. Harry Truman
37. The text reports Bill Clinton actually used public opinion polls to determine
    a. how to decorate the inside of the White House.
    b. what to name his pets.
    c. how he should answer the question of marijuana use.
    d. what color his saxophone should be.
    e. where he should go on vacation.
38. The phrase "mend it but don't end it" was poll-tested by Bill Clinton for use in discussions concerning
    a. affirmative action.
    b. sexual harassment.
    c. our relationship with Israel.
    d. his relationship with Republicans after impeachment.
    e. Social Security.
39. One item on the presidential agenda for almost every president since Herbert Hoover has been
    a. reduction in the separation of powers
    b. expanding legislative power
    c. reforming the federal judiciary
    d. lowering taxes.
    e. reorganization of the executive branch.

40. A president suffers a stroke that leaves him or her partially paralyzed. The vice president, with the support of a majority of the cabinet, declares that the president is unable to discharge the duties of the office, but the president disagrees. What happens next?
    a. Congress decides who is president.
    b. Because the vice president has the support of a majority of the cabinet, the vice president assumes the presidency.
    c. Because the president is still alive, he or she remains president.
    d. Because the president and vice president disagree, a new election is held, allowing the people to decide who should be president.
    e. The Supreme Court decides who is president.
41. Which of the following statements is *incorrect*?
    a. Sixteen persons have been impeached by the House.
    b. Seven persons have been convicted by the Senate.
    c. No federal judge has ever been removed by impeachment.
    d. The impeachment case against Andrew Johnson was "flimsy."
    e. Clinton's impeachment led to the expiration of the office of independent council.

ESSAY QUESTIONS

Practice writing extended answers to the following questions. These test your ability to integrate and express the ideas that you have been studying in this chapter.

1. Compare and contrast presidents and prime ministers.
2. What do the authors offer as the cause of divided government and what do they have to say with respect to curing the supposed ills of opposite party control of the presidency and Congress?
3. Explain why Andrew Jackson's use of the veto power was so unique.
4. Identify some actions which Abraham Lincoln took without the authorization of Congress.
5. Explain how the electoral college works, how many votes are needed win and what happens if no candidate receives a majority of electoral college votes.
6. Identify 5–6 powers of the president.
7. Describe the three ways that presidents can organize his personal staff. In doing so, address the strengths and weaknesses of each approach.
8. What are the "three audiences" that are identified by presidential scholar Richard Neustadt?
9. Explain why presidential success scores in Congress should be used with caution.
10. Summarize the two basic arguments supporting the notion of executive privilege and how the Supreme Court has ruled on this issue.
11. What are "signing statements" and what are the arguments both for and against their use?
12. What do the authors identify as the major constraints on the president's program?
13. Describe how the impeachment of Bill Clinton differed from the impeachment of Andrew Johnson.

ANSWERS TO KEY TERMS MATCH QUESTIONS

1. n
2. dd
3. p
4. d
5. ff
6. c
7. x
8. aa
9. k
10. u
11. q
12. o
13. m
14. j
15. f
16. t
17. bb
18. i
19. b
20. l
21. a
22. gg
23. e
24. cc
25. g
26. h
27. r
28. s
29. v
30. w
31. y
32. z
33. ee

ANSWERS TO DATA CHECK QUESTIONS

1. State and Treasury.
2. Homeland Security.
3. Defense (670,790)
4. 6.
5. There is a chance that individuals running for the House and the Senate who are of the same party as the individual who is elected presidency will win at a higher rate. That is, they will ride the president's coattails into office.
6. The relationship between the presidential candidate's popularity and the popularity of the party is not easy to detect.
7. 1932, Roosevelt, 90 seats.
8. 1980, Reagan, 12 seats.
9. 1960 Kennedy (-20 seats) and 1992 Clinton (-9 seats).
10. "Do you approve of the way ___ is handling his job as president?"
11. Every administration except Eisenhower, Reagan, Clinton.
12. In each case, they are the first terms of two-term administrations.
13. The president's party usually loses seats in the House and the Senate during the mid-term elections.
14. 1942, 1946, 1994.
15. 1946 and 1958.
16. 1934 (Roosevelt), 2002 (Bush)

ANSWERS TO TRUE/FALSE QUESTIONS

1. T
2. T
3. T
4. F Research suggests divided governments ratify important treaties and pass important legislation about as much as any other kind of government.
5. T
6. F It would be more accurate to say that about 1/4 of voters will do this.
7. T
8. F They have gone to the House twice, 1800 and 1824.
9. T
10. F Washington opposed the formation of political parties and condemned them often.
11. T
12. F The nation's early president used the power rarely, and only when they thought a law violated the letter or the spirit of the Constitution.

13. T
14. F Ironically, Lincoln condemended Jackson's use of the war power.
15. T
16. T
17. T
18. T
19. T
20. F Carter employed the circular structure.
21. T
22. F There are 14 major cabinet departments.
23. T
24. T
25. F Nixon disliked persona confrontations and tended to shield himself behind an elaborate staff.
26. T
27. T
28. T
29. T
30. T
31. F The Supreme Court struck down the enhanced rescission created by Congress in 1996.
32. F The Constitution does not address this topic at all.
33. T
34. F The Constitution is silent on whether the president must spend the money that Congress appropriates.
35. F Signing statements date back to at least the administration of James Monroe.
36. F Members of Congress oppose such statements suspecting they can amount to a veto that cannot be formally overridden.
37. F A 90 hour week is typical.
38. T
39. T
40. T
41. T
42. T
43. T

ANSWERS TO MULTIPLE CHOICE QUESTIONS

1. d
2. a
3. a
4. e
5. b
6. d
7. c
8. b
9. d
10. e
11. d
12. a
13. d
14. e
15. b
16. a
17. b
18. b
19. d
20. b
21. c
22. e
23. a
24. c
25. a
26. e
27. d
28. e
29. a
30. d
31. c
32. d
33. b
34. b

35. c
36. b
37. e
38. a
39. e
40. a
41. c

CHAPTER 15

The Bureaucracy

REVIEWING THE CHAPTER

CHAPTER FOCUS

This chapter introduces you to what is big about big government: the bureaucracy. Both the distinctiveness and the size of the federal government bureaucracy are reviewed, along with the various roles that have been assigned to it throughout its history. Significant aspects of the bureaucracy today include the extent and character of its authority, how members are recruited, and other factors that help explain the conduct of bureaucrats in office. Finally, the chapter looks at the ways in which Congress attempts to control the behavior of bureaucrats and at various "pathologies" of various large bureaucracies. After reading and reviewing the material in this chapter, you should be able to do each of the following:

1. Compare and contrast the American and British models of government bureaucracy.
2. Sketch the history of the growth of bureaucracy in this country and the different uses to which it has been put.
3. Show how bureaucracy continues to grow today, although the number of persons directly employed by government has not greatly increased lately.
4. Discuss the recruitment, retention, and personal characteristics of federal bureaucrats.
5. Show how the roles and missions of the agencies are affected by both internal and external factors.
6. Review congressional measures to control the bureaucracy, and evaluate their effectiveness.
7. List the "pathologies" that may affect bureaucracies, and discuss whether they are relevant to the federal government bureaucracy today.
8. Discuss why it is so difficult to reform the bureaucracy.

STUDY OUTLINE

I. Distinctiveness of the American bureaucracy
   A. Constitutional system and traditions
      1. Supervision shared
      2. A federalist structure shares functions
      3. Adversary culture leads to defense of rights and lawsuits
   B. Scope of bureaucracy
      1. Little public ownership of industry in the United States
      2. High degree of regulation in the United States of private industries
   C. Proxy government
      1. Bureaucrats have others do work for them: state and local governments, business firms and nonprofit organizations

2. Examples: Social Security, Medicare, much environmental protection, collecting income taxes, many military duties and FEMA
3. Points of debate
   a) Concerns about how third parties use the money we give them
   b) Congress and the president like to keep the bureaucracy small
   c) Defenders highlight flexibility, principles of federalism and good use of private and nonprofit skills

II. The growth of the bureaucracy
   A. The early controversies
      1. Senate consent to removal of officials is challenged by supporters of a strong president
      2. President is given sole removal power but Congress funds and investigates
   B. The appointment of officials
      1. Officials affect how laws are interpreted, the tone of their administration, and their effectiveness
      2. Use of patronage in the nineteenth and early twentieth centuries to reward supporters
      3. Civil War a watershed in bureaucratic growth; showed the weakness of federal government
   C. A service role
      1. 1861–1901: shift in role from regulation to service
      2. Reflects desire for limited government, laissez-faire beliefs, and the Constitution's silence
   D. A change in role
      1. Depression and World War II lead to a role of government activism
      2. Introduction of heavy income taxes supports a large bureaucracy
      3. Impact of 9/11 terrorist attacks
         a) Creation of the Department of Homeland Security
         b) Consolidation of federal agencies
         c) Authority over dozens of intergovernmental grant-making agencies
         d) Further consolidation and a new National Intelligence Director

III. The federal bureaucracy today
   A. Direct and indirect growth
      1. Modest increase in the number of government employees
      2. Indirect increase through the use of private contractors much greater
      3. Most federal executive departments have reduced workforce – major exception being the Federal Bureau of Prisons in the U.S. Department of Justice
   B. Growth in discretionary authority
      1. Delegation of undefined authority by Congress
      2. Primary areas of delegation
         a) Subsidies to groups
         b) Grant-in-aid programs
         c) Enforcement of regulations
   C. Factors explaining behavior of officials
      1. Recruitment and retention
         a) The competitive service: most bureaucrats compete for jobs through OPM
            (1) Appointment by merit based on a written exam
            (2) Decreased to less than 54 percent of federal government work force
         b) The excepted service: most are appointed by other agencies on the basis of qualifications approved by OPM
            (1) Fastest growing sector of federal government employment
            (2) Examples: postal service employees and FBI agents

(3) But president can also appoint employees: presidential appointments, Schedule C jobs, and NEA jobs
(4) Pendleton Act (1883): transferred basis of government jobs from patronage to merit
(5) Merit system protects president from pressure and protects patronage appointees from new presidents ("blanketing in")

c) The buddy system
(1) Name-request job: filled by a person whom an agency has already identified for middle- and upper-level jobs
(2) Job description may be tailored for person
(3) Circumvents usual search process
(4) But also encourages "issue networks" based on shared policy views

d) Firing a bureaucrat
(1) Most bureaucrats cannot be fired
(2) Exception: Senior Executive Service (SES)
(3) SES managers receive cash bonuses for good performance
(4) But very few SES members have been fired or even transferred

e) The agencies' point of view
(1) Agencies are dominated by lifetime bureaucrats who have worked for no other agency
(2) System assures continuity and expertise
(3) But also gives subordinates power over new bosses: can work behind boss's back through sabotage, delaying, and so on

2. Personal attributes
a) Allegations of critics
(1) Higher civil servants are elitists
(2) Career bureaucrats are more likely to hold liberal views, vote Democrat and trust government
b) Correlation between type of agency and attitudes of employees: activist versus traditional
c) Professional values of officials

3. Do bureaucrats sabotage their political bosses?
a) If so, such sabotage hurts conservatives more than liberals; bureaucrats tend to be liberal
b) But loyalty to bosses runs strong—despite the power of bureaucrats to obstruct or complain
(1) Whistleblower Protection Act (1989) created Office of Special Counsel
(2) "Cooperation is the nature of a bureaucrat's job."
c) Most civil servants: highly structured roles make them relatively immune to personal attitudes
d) Professionals such as lawyers and economists in the FTC: loosely structured roles may be much influenced by personal attitudes, professional values help explain how power is used

4. Culture and careers
a) Each agency has its own culture
b) Jobs with an agency can be career enhancing or not
c) Strong agency culture motivates employees but makes agencies resistant to change

5. Constraints
a) Biggest difference between a government agency and a business: hiring, firing, pay, procedures, and so forth

- b) General constraints
  - (1) Administrative Procedure Act (1946)
  - (2) Freedom of Information Act (1966)
  - (3) National Environmental Policy Act (1969)
  - (4) Privacy Act (1974)
  - (5) Open Meeting Law (1976)
  - (6) Assignment of single jobs to several agencies
- c) Effects of constraints
  - (1) Government moves slowly
  - (2) Government acts inconsistently
  - (3) Easier to block than to take action
  - (4) Reluctant decision-making by lower-ranking employees
  - (5) Red tape

6. Why so many constraints?
   - a) Constraints come from us
   - b) They are an agency's response to our demands for openness, honesty, fairness, and so on
7. Agency allies
   - a) Agencies often seek alliances with congressional committees or interest groups: "iron triangle"
   - b) Far less common today; politics has become too complicated
     - (1) More interest groups, more congressional subcommittees, and easier access for individuals
     - (2) Far more competing forces than ever given access by courts
   - c) "Issue networks": groups that regularly debate government policy on certain issues
     - (1) Contentious and partisan
     - (2) New president often recruits from networks

IV. Congressional oversight

A. Forms of congressional supervision
1. Approval necessary for creation
2. Statutes influence agency behavior (sometimes precisely)
3. Authorization of money, either permanent or fixed number of years
4. Appropriation of money allows spending

B. Congressional oversight and "homeland security"
1. Lieberman's call for Department of Homeland Defense after 9/11 attack
2. President Bush's creation of Office of Homeland Security
   - a) Appointment of Governor Ridge and the blueprint for homeland security
   - b) Congressional calls for testimony about strategies
   - c) Need to coordinate personnel and budgets
3. Proposal of a Department of Homeland Security
   - a) Consolidation, reorganization and transformation
   - b) Need for Congress to reorganize itself to make the bureaucracy work
     - (1) Immediate protests about committee and subcommittee jurisdiction
     - (2) Congress' historical tendency to resist streamlining

C. The Appropriations Committee and legislative committees
1. Appropriations Committee most powerful
   - a) Most expenditure recommendations are approved by House
   - b) Has power to lower agency's expenditure request
   - c) Has power to influence an agency's policies by marking up an agency's budget

d) But becoming less powerful because of
(1) Trust funds: Social Security
(2) Annual authorizations
(3) Meeting target spending limits
2. Legislative committees are important when
a) A law is first passed
b) An agency is first created
c) An agency is subject to annual authorization
3. Informal congressional controls over agencies
a) Individual members of Congress can seek privileges for constituents
b) Congressional committees may seek committee clearance: right to pass on certain agency decisions
c) Committee heads may ask to be consulted
D. The legislative veto
1. Declared unconstitutional by Supreme Court in *Chadha* (1983)
2. Weakens traditional legislative oversight but Congress continues creating such vetoes
E. Congressional investigations
1. Power inferred from power to legislate
2. Means for checking agency discretion
3. Means for limiting presidential control
V. Bureaucratic "pathologies"
A. Red tape—complex and sometimes conflicting rules among agencies
B. Conflict—agencies work at cross-purposes
C. Duplication—two or more agencies seem to do the same thing
D. Imperialism—tendency of agencies to grow, irrespective of benefits and costs of programs
E. Waste—spending more than is necessary to buy some product or service
VI. Reforming the bureaucracy
A. Numerous attempts to make bureaucracy work better for less money
1. Eleven attempts to reform in the twentieth century alone
2. National Performance Review (NPR) in 1993 designed to reinvent government
a) Differs from previous reforms that sought to increase presidential control
b) Emphasizes customer satisfaction by bringing citizens in contact with agencies
3. NPR calls for innovation and quality consciousness by
a) Less-centralized management
b) More employee initiatives
c) Customer satisfaction
B. Bureaucratic reform always difficult to accomplish
1. Most rules and red tape result from the struggle between the president and Congress
2. This struggle makes bureaucrats nervous about irritating either
3. Periods of divided government exacerbate matters, especially in implementing policy
a) Republican presidents seek to increase political control (executive micromanagement)
b) Democratic Congresses respond by increasing investigations and rules (legislative micromanagement).

KEY TERMS MATCH

Match the following terms and descriptions:

1. A freely competitive economy
2. Appointment of officials not based on the criteria specified by OPM
3. Ruled the legislative veto unconstitutional
4. A requirement that an executive decision lie before Congress for a specified period before it takes effect
5. A 1993 effort, led by Vice President Al Gore, to make the bureaucracy work better and cost less
6. Refers to the tendency of agencies to grow without regard to the benefits their programs confer or the costs they entail
7. Top-ranking civil servants who can be hired, fired, and rewarded in a more flexible manner than can ordinary bureaucrats
8. A large, complex organization composed of appointed officials
9. Appointment of officials based on selection criteria devised by the employing agency and OPM
10. Legislation that began the federal merit system
11. Governmental appointments made on the basis of political considerations
12. The right of committees to disapprove of certain agency actions
13. The ability of officials to make policies that are not spelled out in advance by laws
14. Groups that regularly debate governmental policy on subjects such as health care or auto safety
15. Government jobs having a confidential or policy-making character
16. When state and local government are hired to staff and administer federal programs

a. annual authorizations
b. appropriation
c. authorization legislation
d. bureaucracy
e. bureaucratic imperialism
f. *Chadha*
g. Civil Service Reform Act
h. committee clearance
i. competitive service
j. Department of Homeland Security
k. discretionary authority
l. excepted service
m. government by proxy
n. iron triangle
o. issue networks
p. laissez-faire
q. legislative veto
r. name-request job
s. National Performance Review
t. patronage
u. Pendleton Act
v. red tape
w. schedule C
x. Senior Executive Service
y. trust funds
z. Whistle Blower Protection Act

17. Created the Senior Executive Service and recognized the need for flexibility in recruiting, assigning and salary
18. Funds such as that of Social Security that operate outside the government budget
19. A proposal by President Bush in 2002 which would consolidate 22 federal agencies and nearly 170,000 federal employees
20. The mutually advantageous relationship among an agency, a committee, and an interest group
21. Monies that are budgeted on a yearly basis; for example Congress may set yearly limits on what agencies can spend
22. Created the Office of Special Counsel to investigate complaints from bureaucrats that they were punished after reporting to Congress about waste, fraud, or abuse in their agencies
23. A legislative grant of money to finance a government program
24. Legislative permission to begin or continue a government program or agency
25. A job to be filled by a person whom a government agency has identified by name
26. Complex bureaucratic rules and procedures that must be followed to get something done

DATA CHECK

Table 15.1 (Page 409) Federal Civilian Employment, 1990-2005

1. How has the total civil employment for all executive departments changed from 1990 to 2005?

____

2. Which two departments experienced the greatest growth in the number of employees?

____

3. Which two departments experienced the greatest reductions in the number of employees?

____

Figure 15.1 (Page 415): Characteristics of Federal Civilian Employees, 1960 and 2004

4. In 1960 what percentage of federal civilian employees were female?

____

5. In 2004 what percentage of federal civilian employees were female?

____

6. In 2004 what percentage of federal civilian employees were racial minorities?

____

PRACTICING FOR EXAMS

TRUE/FALSE QUESTIONS

Read each statement carefully. Mark true statements *T.* If any part of the statement is false, mark it *F,* and write in the space provided a concise explanation of why the statement is false.

1. T F Most of the agencies of the federal government share their functions with related agencies in state and local government.

____

2. T F Government agencies in this country operate under closer public scrutiny than in almost any other nation.

____

3. T F Most of the help that FEMA would provide in the aftermath of Hurricanes Katrina and Rita was actually provided by "partners."

____

4. T F The president's power to remove (fire) governmental officers was heatedly debated by the First Congress.

____

5. T F It was decided early on that cabinet departments would be run by people removable only by the president.

____

6. T F The text suggests the creation of the Interstate Commerce Commission (ICC) further enhanced the service role of the federal bureaucracy.

____

7. T F During World War I, Congress authorized President Wilson to operate the railroads and even control the distribution of food.

____

8. T F As president, Richard Nixon set up a system of price and wage controls.

9. T F World War II was the first occasion during which the government made heavy use of federal income taxes to finance its activities.

10. T F For every single person who earns a living from the federal government there is one person who works indirectly for Washington.

11. T F Those who belong to the competitive service are appointed only after they have passed a written examination.

12. T F In recent years, the percentage of federal employees who belong to the competitive service has decreased.

13. T F The text concludes that a standardized, centralized system governs the federal service.

14. T F Blue collar employment has risen in the federal civil service.

15. T F "Schedule C" appointments involve jobs with a confidential or policy-determining character.

16. T F When Grover Cleveland became president in 1885, he replaced forty thousand Republican postal employees with Democrats.

17. T F Presidents adamantly opposed the merit system.

18. T F The text suggests that the buddy system does not necessarily produce poor employees.

19. T F Unsatisfactory ratings of federal bureaucrats increased sharply after the creation of the Senior Executive Service (SES).

20. T F A federal employee cannot appeal the decision of the Merit Systems Protection Board if it upholds his/her firing.

21. T F The federal civil service as a whole looks very much like a cross section of American society in the education, sex, and race of its members.

22. T F African Americans and other minorities are most likely to be heavily represented in the lower grades of the federal bureaucracy.

____

23. T F Employees of the Environmental Protection Agency are more likely to be liberal than employees of the Department of Commerce.

____

24. T F People with conservative viewpoints tend to be overrepresented in defense agencies.

____

25. T F Economists with the Federal Trade Commission prefer to bring cases against business firms that have done something clearly illegal.

____

26. T F Lawyers with the Federal Trade Commission favor the litigation of "big" or "blockbuster" cases.

____

27. T F In bureaucratic lingo, an NCE job enhances one's career within an agency.

____

28. T F Congress rarely gives any job to a single agency.

____

29. T F One of the effects of the constraints on bureaucracy is that lower-ranking employees will tend to make decisions on their own.

____

30. T F Bureaucratic red tape comes from us, the people.

____

31. T F Ronald Reagan attempted to abolish the Small Business Administration.

____

32. T F Iron triangles are much less common today than once was the case.

____

33. T F Issue networks are made of persons in and out of Washington who regularly debate government policy on certain subjects.

____

34. T F The legislative veto was declared constitutional by the Supreme Court in 1983.

____

35. T F The congressional power to investigate is not mentioned in the Constitution.

____

36. T F Congress can compel a person to attend an investigation by issuing a subpoena.

____

37. T F Of the five major bureaucratic pathologies mentioned in the text, duplication is probably the biggest criticism that people have of the bureaucracy.

38. T F Al Gore's National Performance Review called for more specific rules to guide the federal bureaucracy and the creation of a centralized enforcement mechanism to enhance overall efficiency.

MULTIPLE CHOICE QUESTIONS

Circle the letter of the response that best answers the question or completes the statement.

1. American bureaucracy is complex because
   a. federalism encourages the abuse of power.
   b. it is heavily dependent on career employees.
   c. the Constitution determines its structure and function.
   d. authority is divided among several managing institutions.
   e. civil servants are immune from firing.
2. In contrast to the United States, public enterprises in France account for what percentage of all employment?
   a. 1 percent
   b. 3 percent
   c. 6 percent
   d. 12 percent
   e. 20 percent
3. Government by proxy results when _________ are hired by federal bureaucrats to do work.
   a. local governments
   b. state governments
   c. business firms
   d. nonprofit organizations
   e. all of the above
4. Government by proxy is evident in the administration of
   a. Social Security.
   b. Medicare.
   c. environmental policy.
   d. the collection of income taxes.
   e. all of the above.
5. The political ideology of a presidential appointee is important because she or he
   a. must often work with radical groups.
   b. affects how the laws are interpreted.
   c. is usually bound by specific directives.
   d. is aligned with congressional ideology.
   e. typically has strong party ties.

6. The basis of appointments to the bureaucracy during most of the nineteenth century and the early part of the twentieth century was
   a. financial.
   b. patronage.
   c. nepotism.
   d. technical expertise.
   e. support for the president's policies.
7. The dramatic increase in the number of federal employees from 1816 to 1861 was the direct result of
   a. the need for Secret Service agents in the White House.
   b. expansion in the size of congressional staff.
   c. an increase in the demands on government, especially the Post Office.
   d. the Hatch Act.
   e. President Grant's concern over the Whiskey Ring scandal.
8. When first established, the Departments of Agriculture, Labor, and Commerce had one thing in common:
   a. their secretaries were not appointees.
   b. they all sought to regulate their clienteles.
   c. they were primarily service-oriented.
   d. they all avoided contacts with the public.
   e. they jealously guarded states' rights.
9. Which statement best describes how the text of the Constitution addresses the issue of granting regulatory power to bureaucrats?
   a. It is silent on the matter.
   b. It prohibits transfer of congressional power.
   c. It allows transfer of congressional power with presidential approval.
   d. It allows transfer of congressional power during a declared war.
   e. It prohibits transfer of congressional power during a declared war.
10. As late as 1935 the Supreme Court held that
    a. the legislature may not delegate its powers to any administrative agency.
    b. a regulatory agency was necessary to control interstate commerce.
    c. regulatory agencies could exercise wide discretion.
    d. an agency must be staffed by individuals of different parties.
    e. the creation of new agencies must be approved by Congress.
11. Wars have generally caused the federal bureaucracy to
    a. become more decentralized.
    b. shrink in size, but increase in efficiency.
    c. respond more quickly, but make inefficient decisions.
    d. increase in size.
    e. neutralize the power of Congress.
12. The bureaucracy of American government today is largely a product of which two events?
    a. The Depression and World War II.
    b. World War I and World War II.
    c. World War II and the Korean War.
    d. The Korean War and the Vietnam War.
    e. The Vietnam War and Watergate.

13. The number of civilians working for the federal government, excluding postal workers, is
    a. about 2 million.
    b. about the same as it was in 1960.
    c. less than it was during World War II.
    d. is higher than it has ever been.
    e. A, B and C.
14. In recent years, there has been a sharp increase in the number of employees in the Department of
    a. Justice.
    b. Treasury.
    c. Agriculture.
    d. Transportation.
    e. Education.
15. Which of the following is the *most* important consideration in evaluating the power of a bureaucracy?
    a. The number of employees in it.
    b. The importance of its functions.
    c. The extent to which its actions are supported by the public.
    d. The social status of its leaders.
    e. The amount of discretionary authority that its officials have.
16. Congress has delegated substantial authority to administrative agencies in what three areas?
    a. Grants-in-aid, law enforcement, national defense.
    b. Law enforcement, social services, resource management.
    c. Grants-in-aid, subsidy payments, enforcement of regulations.
    d. Grants-in-aid, subsidy payments, law enforcement.
    e. Social services, law enforcement, national defense.
17. The decentralization of the competitive service system and decrease in the use of examinations was prompted, in part, by
    a. controversies concerning the scoring of exams.
    b. controversies concerning arbitrary rankings.
    c. political pressure by members of Congress to hire influential constituents.
    d. Supreme Court decisions which declared OPM policies unconstitutional.
    e. pressure by Civil Rights groups to make the racial composition of the bureaucracy more representative.
18. What percentage of all federal employees is part of the excepted service?
    a. About 20 percent.
    b. About 30 percent.
    c. About 40 percent.
    d. About 50 percent.
    e. About 80 percent.
19. A steady transfer of federal jobs from the patronage to the merit system was initiated by the passage of the
    a. Seventeenth Amendment.
    b. Eighteenth Amendment.
    c. Pendleton Act.
    d. Hatch Act.
    e. Civil Service Reform Act.

20. The emergence of the merit system was, in part, prompted by
    a. the Whiskey Ring scandal of the Grant administration.
    b. the assassination of James Garfield.
    c. persistent robbery of the federal mails.
    d. scandals involving relatives of presidents who were in critical positions in government.
    e. all of the above.
21. If an agency carefully crafts a job description with a specific person in mind and, afterward, provides the name of that person to the OPM, it is a ______ job.
    a. name-request job
    b. itemized specialty
    c. schedule C
    d. NEA
    e. SES
22. A 1987 study found that _______ of federal employees who had completed their probationary period were fired for misconduct or poor performance.
    a. less than 1 percent
    b. 2 percent
    c. 5 percent
    d. 10 percent
    e. 22 percent
23. Which of the following statements concerning the Senior Executive Service is *incorrect*?
    a. It was created by the Civil Service Reform Act of 1978.
    b. It consists of eight thousand top federal managers who, in theory, can be fired more easily than ordinary civil servants.
    c. It consists of eight thousand top federal managers who, in theory, can be transferred more easily than ordinary civil servants.
    d. Its members are eligible for substantial cash bonuses if they perform their duties well.
    e. None of the above.
24. Which of the following is *not* among the procedures for firing or demoting a member of the competitive civil service?
    a. Written notice of thirty days.
    b. Statement of reasons for dismissal.
    c. Right to a hearing.
    d. Right to an attorney.
    e. Review by the OPM.
25. Surveys find that career bureaucrats are more likely than other people to
    a. favor limited government.
    b. hold liberal views.
    c. trust government.
    d. vote for Democrats.
    e. B, C and D.
26. The powers of obstruction available to aggrieved bureaucrats are
    a. formidable.
    b. unimpressive.
    c. quite limited.
    d. easily countered.
    e. largely symbolic and without consequence.

27. Personal attitudes probably have the greatest influence on
    a. civil servants performing routinized tasks.
    b. civil servants performing tasks which are closely monitored by others.
    c. tasks performed by professionals in federal agencies.
    d. civil servants performing tasks closely defined by laws.
    e. civil servants performing tasks closely defined by rules.
28. The Federal Trade Commission (FTC) tends to employ
    a. lawyers.
    b. doctors.
    c. engineers.
    d. economists.
    e. A and D.
29. The Administrative Procedure Act of 1946 required that
    a. every part of agency meetings be open to the public.
    b. government files about individuals be kept confidential.
    c. environmental impact statements be issued before undertaking major actions.
    d. agencies give notice before they adopt new rules, hold hearings, and solicit comments.
    e. citizens be allowed to inspect certain government records.
30. One effect of the constraints on federal agencies is that lower-ranking employees will tend to
    a. retain sole responsibility for a job.
    b. perform tasks in a prompt, timely fashion.
    c. act with greater consistency.
    d. complain about red tape.
    e. let their bosses make decisions.
31. All of the following statements concerning the legislative veto are correct *except*
    a. Congress made frequent use of it for many decades.
    b. it required an executive decision to lie before Congress for a specified period of time.
    c. resolutions of disapproval could be passed by either or both houses.
    d. the Supreme Court ruled such vetoes unconstitutional.
    e. Congress has not passed a law containing a legislative veto since the Court considered its constitutionality in 1983.
32. Bureaucratic conflict and duplication occur because
    a. large organizations must ensure one part of the organization does not operate out of step.
    b. Congress often wants to achieve a number of different, partially inconsistent goals.
    c. Congress can be unclear as to exactly what it wants an agency to do.
    d. of the need to satisfy political requirements.
    e. of the need to satisfy legal requirements.
33. Bureaucratic imperialism occurs because
    a. large organizations must ensure one part of the organization does not operate out of step.
    b. Congress often wants to achieve a number of different, partially inconsistent goals.
    c. Congress can be unclear as to exactly what it wants an agency to do.
    d. of the need to satisfy political requirements.
    e. of the need to satisfy legal requirements.

34. The text suggests many of the "horror stories" one hears about high-priced items that are purchased at the government's expense are
    a. concocted by critics of the Hatch Act.
    b. more accurate than public officials would like to admit.
    c. documented in *Congressional Quarterly*.
    d. the by-product of bureaucratic imperialism.
    e. either exaggerated or unusual occurrences.
35. The National Performance Review attempts to reform the bureaucracy by stressing
    a. efficiency.
    b. rigidity.
    c. accountability.
    d. customer satisfaction.
    e. consistent policies.

ESSAY QUESTIONS

Practice writing extended answers to the following questions. These test your ability to integrate and express the ideas that you have been studying in this chapter.

1. What are the three aspects of our constitutional system and political traditions that give our bureaucracy a distinctive character?
2. Explain what "government by proxy" means and what are the arguments for and against this method of providing services?
3. Summarize the debate which took place with respect to presidential appointments in the First Congress (1789). What was the outcome of the conflict?
4. Why did federal agencies primarily perform a service role before 1900?
5. Identify the three areas in which Congress has delegated substantial authority to administrative agencies.
6. Generalize about the 3 percent of the excepted service employees who are appointed on grounds other than or in addition to merit.
7. Summarize the process whereby a federal bureaucrat can be fired.
8. Discuss how lawyers and economists who work for the FTC differ in their attitudes, opinions and decision-making.
9. Identify 3-4 effects of the constraints that are placed on agency behavior.
10. Explain why iron triangles are much less common today than they used to be.
11. Identify and explain the five major bureaucratic pathologies and summarize what the author's provide as an explanation for their existence in our system of government.
12. Discuss the approach to reform of the federal bureaucracy that is employed by the National Performance Review (NPR).

ANSWERS TO KEY TERMS MATCH QUESTIONS

1. p
2. l
3. f
4. q
5. s
6. e
7. x
8. d
9. i
10. u
11. t
12. h
13. k
14. o
15. w
16. m
17. g
18. y
19. j
20. n
21. a
22. z
23. b
24. c
25. r
26. v

ANSWERS TO DATA CHECK QUESTIONS

1. It has decreased 18.2 percent.
2. State (33.7 percent) and Justice (25.2 percent).
3. Commerce (-44.3 percent) and Defense (-35.1 percent)
4. 25 percent.
5. 44 percent.
6. 31 percent.

ANSWERS TO TRUE/FALSE QUESTIONS

1. T
2. T
3. T
4. T
5. T
6. F The creation of the I.C.C. marked an important transition from a service role to a regulatory role.
7. T
8. T
9. T
10. F For every one person working directly for the government, there are almost three working indirectly for Washington.
11. T
12. T
13. F It is very much decentralized and features a variety of standards.
14. F Blue-collar employment has fallen.
15. T
16. T
17. F Presidents were satisfied enough with the merit system because the demands of patronage were impossible to satisfy.
18. T
19. F Two years after its creation, less than one percent received such ratings.
20. F Such a decision can be appealed to a U.S. court of appeals which can hold a new hearing.
21. T
22. T
23. T
24. T
25. F This would be a better description of the factors which influence the decision-making of lawyers that work for the Commission.
26. F They actually try to avoid such cases because they are expensive, time-consuming and difficult to prove in court.
27. F NCE stands for "not career enhancing."
28. T
29. F In fact they will tend to be quite reluctant to make decisions on their own, leaving their bosses to make decisions and, if necessary, take the heat (responsibility).

30. T
31. T
32. T
33. T
34. T
35. T
36. T
37. F Waste probably brings the most criticism.
38. F NPR argued bureaucracy was too rule-bound and centralized.

ANSWERS TO MULTIPLE CHOICE QUESTIONS

1. d
2. d
3. e
4. e
5. b
6. b
7. c
8. c
9. a
10. a
11. d
12. a
13. a
14. a
15. e
16. c
17. e
18. d
19. c
20. b
21. a
22. a
23. e
24. e

25. c
26. a
27. c
28. e
29. d
30. e
31. e
32. b
33. c
34. e
35. d

CHAPTER 16

The Judiciary

REVIEWING THE CHAPTER

CHAPTER FOCUS

This chapter introduces you to the final and perhaps most unusual branch of American government: the courts. The chapter explains how courts, particularly the Supreme Court, came to play a uniquely powerful role in forming public policy in this country and how that role has been played to very different effects at different stages of history. Other important considerations include how justices are selected, the jurisdictions of the various courts, and the steps that a case must go through on its way to Supreme Court review. The chapter concludes with an assessment of the power courts have in politics today, the limitations on that power, and why judicial activism seems to be on the increase. After reading and reviewing the material in this chapter, you should be able to do each of the following:

1. Explain what judicial review is, and trace its origin in this country to *Marbury* v. *Madison.*
2. List and comment on the three eras of varying Supreme Court influences on national policy from the days of slavery to the present.
3. Explain what is meant by a dual court system, and describe the effects it has on how cases are handled and appealed.
4. List the various steps that cases go through to be appealed to the Supreme Court, and explain the considerations involved at each level.
5. Discuss the dimensions of power exercised today by the Supreme Court and the opposing viewpoints on the desirability of activism by that court.
6. Develop arguments for and against an activist Supreme Court.

STUDY OUTLINE

I. Introduction
    A. Little public interest in judicial nominations but considerable congressional interest
        1. As the power of the federal government has increased, so has the power of the federal courts
        2. Expansion in federal policy has led to increased opportunities for federal judges to interpret such policies
        3. Recent Supreme Court nominations -Thomas and Bork
        4. The Nuclear Option and the Gang of Fourteen
    B. Only in the United States do judges play so large a role in policy-making
        1. Judicial review: right to rule on laws and executive acts on basis of constitutionality; chief judicial weapon in system of checks and balances
        2. In Great Britain, Parliament is supreme
        3. In other countries, judicial review means little
            a) Exceptions: Australia, Canada, West Germany, India, and a few others

C. Debate is over how the Constitution should be interpreted
   1. Strict constructionist (interpretivist) approach: judges are bound by the wording of the Constitution
   2. Activist (legislative) approach: judges should look to the underlying principles of the Constitution
   3. Not a matter of liberal versus conservative
      a) A judge can be both conservative and activist, or vice versa
      b) Today most activists tend to be liberal, most strict constructionists conservative

II. The development of the federal courts
A. Founders' view
   1. Most Founders probably expected judicial review but not its large role in policy-making
   2. Traditional view: judges find and apply existing law
   3. Activist judges would later respond that judges make law
   4. Traditional view made it easy for Founders to justify judicial review
   5. Hamilton: courts least dangerous branch
   6. But federal judiciary evolved toward judicial activism
B. National supremacy and slavery: 1789–1861
   1. *McCulloch* v. *Maryland:* federal law declared supreme over state law
   2. Interstate commerce clause is placed under the authority of federal law; conflicting state law void
   3. *Dred Scott* v. *Sandford:* Negroes were not and could not become free citizens of the United States; a direct cause of the Civil War
C. Government and the economy: Civil War to 1936
   1. Dominant issue of the period: whether the economy could be regulated by state and federal governments
   2. Private property held to be protected by the Fourteenth Amendment
   3. States seek to protect local businesses and employees from the predatory activities of national monopolies; judicial activism
   4. The Supreme Court determines what is "reasonable" regulation
   5. The Court interprets the Fourteenth and Fifteenth Amendments narrowly as applied to blacks
D. Government and political liberty: 1936 to the present
   1. Court establishes tradition of deferring to the legislature in economic cases
   2. Court shifts attention to personal liberties and becomes active in defining rights
E. The revival of state sovereignty
   1. Supreme Court rules that states have right to resist some forms of federal action
   2. Hint at some real limits to the supremacy of the federal government

III. The structure of the federal courts
A. Two kinds of federal courts
   1. Constitutional courts
      a) Created under Article III
      b) Judges serve during good behavior
      c) Salaries not reduced while in office
      d) Examples: District Courts (ninety-four), Courts of Appeals (twelve)
   2. Legislative courts
      a) Created by Congress for specialized purposes
      b) Judges have fixed terms
      c) No salary protection
B. Selecting judges
   1. Party background makes a difference in judicial behavior (decisions)

2. Senatorial courtesy: judges for U.S. district courts must be approved by that state's senators
3. The litmus test
   a) Presidential successes in selecting compatible judges
   b) Concern this emphasis might downplay the importance of professional qualifications
   c) Increasing importance of ideology
      (1) Sharp drop in the confirmation rates of appeals court nominees
      (2) Even more important with respect to Supreme Court appointments

IV. The jurisdiction of the federal courts
A. Dual court system
1. One state, one federal
2. Federal cases listed in Article III and the Eleventh Amendment of the Constitution
   a) Federal question cases: involving U.S. matters
   b) Diversity cases: involving citizens of different states
   c) All others are left to state courts
3. Some cases can be tried in either court
   a) Example: if both federal and state laws have been broken (dual sovereignty)
   b) Justified: each government has right to enact laws, and neither can block prosecution out of sympathy for the accused
4. State cases sometimes can be appealed to Supreme Court
5. Exclusive federal jurisdiction over federal criminal laws, appeals from federal regulatory agencies, bankruptcy, and controversies between two states

B. Route to the Supreme Court
1. Most federal cases begin in U.S. district courts, are straightforward, and do not lead to new public policy
2. The Supreme Court picks the cases it wants to hear on appeal
   a) Uses *writ of certiorari* ("*cert*")
   b) Requires agreement of four justices to hear case
   c) Usually deals with significant federal or constitutional question
      (1) Conflicting decisions by circuit courts
      (2) State court decisions involving the Constitution
   d) Only 3 to 4 percent of appeals are granted *certiorari*
   e) Others are left to lower courts; this results in a diversity of constitutional interpretation

V. Getting to court
A. Deterrents
1. The Court rejects 95 percent of applications for *certiorari*
2. Costs of appeal are high
   a) But these can be lowered by
      (1) *In forma pauperis*: plaintiff heard as pauper, with costs paid by the government
      (2) Payment by interest groups who have something to gain (American Civil Liberties Union)
   b) Each party must pay its own way except for cases in which it is decided
      (1) That losing defendant will pay (fee shifting)
      (2) Section 1983 suits
3. Standing: guidelines
   a) Must be controversy between adversaries
   b) Personal harm must be demonstrated
   c) Being taxpayer not entitlement for suit

            d) Sovereign immunity
    B. Class action suits
        1. Brought on behalf of all similarly situated
        2. Financial incentives to bring suit
        3. Need to notify all members of the class since 1974 to limit such suits
VI. The Supreme Court in action
    A. Oral arguments by lawyers after briefs submitted
        1. Questions by justices cut down to thirty minutes
        2. Role of solicitor general
        3. *Amicus curiae* briefs
        4. Many sources of influence on justices, such as law journals
    B. Conference procedures
        1. Role of chief justice: speaking first, voting last
        2. Selection of opinion writer: concurring and dissenting opinions
    C. Strategic retirements from the U.S. Supreme Court
        1. There has been a sharp increase in the rate of retirements (*contra* deaths)
        2. Early duties were physically onerous, adverse to one's health.
        3. More recently, retirements occur when justices and presidents share party identification
VII. The power of the federal courts
    A. The power to make policy
        1. By interpretation
        2. By extending reach of existing law
        3. By designing remedies
    B. Measures of power
        1. Number of laws declared unconstitutional (more than 120)
        2. Number of prior cases overturned; not following *stare decisis*
        3. Deference to the legislative branch (political questions)
        4. Kinds of remedies imposed; judges go beyond what justice requires
        5. Basis for sweeping orders from either the Constitution or interpretation of federal laws
    C. Views of judicial activism
        1. Supporters
            a) Courts should correct injustices
            b) Courts are last resort
        2. Critics
            a) Judges lack expertise
            b) Courts not accountable; judges not elected
        3. Various reasons for activism
            a) Too many lawyers; but real cause adversary culture
            b) Easier to get standing in courts
    D. Legislation and courts
        1. Laws and the Constitution are filled with vague language
            a) Ambiguity gives courts opportunities to design remedies
            b) Courts can interpret language in different ways
        2. Federal government is increasingly on the defensive in court cases; laws induce litigation
        3. The attitudes of federal judges affect their decisions
VIII. Checks on judicial power
    A. Judges are not immune to politics or public opinion
        1. Effects will vary from case to case
        2. Decisions can be ignored
            a) Examples: school prayer, segregated schools

b) Usually if register is not highly visible

B. Congress and the courts
1. Confirmation and impeachment proceedings alter the composition of the courts
2. Changing the number of judges
3. Revising legislation declared unconstitutional
4. Altering jurisdiction of the courts and restricting remedies
5. Constitutional amendment

C. Public opinion and the courts
1. Defying public opinion, especially elite opinion, frontally is dangerous
2. Opinion in realigning eras may energize court
3. Public confidence in court since 1966 has varied
4. Change caused by changes of personnel and what government is doing

D. Reasons for increased activism
1. Growth of government
2. Activist ethos of judges

KEY TERMS MATCH

Match the following terms and descriptions:

1. A pattern of voting behavior of two or more justices
2. Agreed to block filibusters unless there were "extraordinary circumstances"
3. Rules defining relationships among private citizens
4. A signed opinion which agrees with the majority view but for different reasons
5. The party that initiates a law suit
6. A ruling that declared that Negroes could not be federal citizens
7. An examination of the political ideology of a nominated judge
8. An individual who represents the federal government before the Supreme Court
9. An unsigned and typically brief court opinion
10. The practice, authorized by statutes, under which the plaintiff is enabled to collect costs from the defendant if the latter loses
11. The meeting at which the justices vote on cases that they have recently heard

a. activist approach
b. *amicus curiae*
c. appellate jurisdiction
d. bloc voting
e. civil law
f. class action suit
g. concurring opinion
h. constitutional court
i. criminal law
j. diversity case
k. *Dred Scott* v. *Sandford*
l. fee shifting
m. Friday conference
n. Gang of Fourteen
o. *In forma pauperis*
p. judicial restraint
q. judicial review
r. litmus test
s. *per curiam* opinion
t. plaintiff

12. A means by which one who has an interest in a case but is not directly involved can present arguments in favor of one side
13. A judicial order enforcing a right or redressing a wrong
14. A means by which one who has been injured can bring action on behalf of all similarly situated
15. A method whereby a poor person can have his or her case heard in federal court without charge
16. The power of the courts to determine the constitutionality of legislative and executive acts
17. The scope of authority by which a higher court reviews a case from a lower court
18. An issue the Court refuses to consider, believing the Constitution intends another branch to make the decision
19. The rule that a citizen cannot sue the government without the government's consent
20. A requirement that must be satisfied before a plaintiff can have a case heard on its merits
21. A tradition under which the Senate will defer to the judgment of a senator of the president's party when determining the suitability of candidates for federal judgeships from the senator's state
22. The body of rules defining offenses that are considered to be offenses against society as a whole
23. Litigation in which a citizen of one state sues a citizen of another state and the amount of money in dispute is more than $50,000
24. A court established under Article III of the Constitution

u. political question
v. remedy
w. senatorial courtesy
x. solicitor general
y. sovereign immunity
z. standing
aa. *stare decisis*
bb. *writ of certiorari*

25. A decision that permits a case to be heard by the Supreme Court when four justices approve
26. The rule of precedent
27. The idea that judges should amplify the vague language of the Constitution on the basis of their moral or economic philosophy and apply it to the case before them
28. The idea that judges should confine themselves to applying those rules stated in or clearly implied by the language of the Constitution

DATA CHECK

Figure 16.1 (Page 442): Female and Minority Judicial Appointments, 1963–2004

1. Did the highest total percentage of female and black judicial appointments take place during a Democratic or Republican presidency, and who was that president?

____

2. Did the highest total percentage of Hispanic judicial appointments take place during a Democratic or Republican presidency, and who was that president?

____

3. Did the lowest total percentage of female and Hispanic judicial appointments take place during a Democratic or Republican presidency, and who was that president?

____

4. Did the lowest total percentage of black judicial appointments take place during a Democratic or Republican presidency, and who was that president?

____

Table 16.2 (Page 449): Supreme Court Justices in Order of Seniority, 2004

5. What is the most commonly represented prior experience of the nine justices of the Court?

____

6. How many justices were appointed by Republican presidents?

____

7. Which justices have come to the Court without previous judicial experience?

____

8. If age is a reasonable predictor of who will retire/resign from the Court next, who should we expect to retire / resign next?

____

9. Who is the youngest member of the Court?

____

PRACTICING FOR EXAMS

TRUE/FALSE QUESTIONS

Read each statement carefully. Mark true statements *T.* If any part of the statement is false, mark it *F,* and write in the space provided a concise explanation of why the statement is false.

1. T F The Supreme Court has declared thousands of federal laws to be unconstitutional since 1789.

____

2. T F Judicial review is not mentioned in the Constitution.

____

3. T F John Marshall and the Supreme Court struck down a license the State of New York gave to Robert Fulton to navigate waterways.

____

4. T F In the immediate aftermath of the *Marbury* decision, the Court began exercising judicial review with great frequency.

____

5. T F Franklin Roosevelt was unable to alter the composition of the Supreme Court in his first term as president.

____

6. T F If implemented, Roosevelt's reorganization plan for the Court would have allowed him to make two new appointments.

____

7. T F Roosevelt actually left the presidency without ever having the opportunity to make a Supreme Court appointment.

____

8. T F The only federal court the Constitution requires is the Supreme Court.

____

9. T F The Constitution sets the number of justices on the Court at nine.

____

10. T F As judges, Democrats are more likely to make conservative decisions than Republican ones.

____

11. T F The tradition of senatorial courtesy gives great weight to the preferences of the senators from the states where judges on the U.S. Courts of Appeals are to serve.

____

12. T F The litmus test issue is not as important when selecting Supreme Court justices.

____

13. T F In recent years, Supreme Court nominations have usually been confirmed by the Senate.

____

14. T F Defendants may not be tried in both state and federal courts for the same offense.

____

15. T F Under some circumstances, a criminal case involving only a violation of state law can be appealed to the United States Supreme Court.

____

16. T F The text suggests that the typical district court case holds marvelous potential for broad policy-making.

____

17. T F The Supreme Court does not have to hear any appeal it does not want to hear.

____

18. T F In a typical year, the Supreme Court may consider over seven thousand petitions.

____

19. T F The influence of law clerks on the selection of the Supreme Court's cases and the rendering of its decisions is considerable.

____

20. T F In this country, each party to a lawsuit must pay its own costs.

____

21. T F Taxpayers automatically have standing and can challenge the constitutionality of a federal government action.

____

22. T F If the government kills your cow while testing a new cannon, you automatically have standing to sue the government.

____

23. T F A taxpayer brought a lawsuit in order to require the CIA to make its budget public and won.

____

24. T F The Supreme Court has made the rules governing class actions suits more lenient in recent years.

____

25. T F The Supreme Court begins each term in the month of August.

____

26. T F Interest groups politely "lobby" the Supreme Court through the use of *amicus* briefs.

____

27. T F In conference, the Chief Justice speaks first, followed by the other justices in order of seniority.

____

28. T F If a tie vote occurs on the Supreme Court, the case is held over for the next term.

____

29. T F The Court tends to overturn its own precedents more frequently than it exercises judicial review of federal legislation.

____

30. T F One valid explanation for increasing judicial activism is the dramatic increase in the number of lawyers in the United States.

____

31. T F The vague language in congressional statutes provide additional opportunities for courts to exercise power.

____

32. T F One president has gone on to become a Supreme Court justice.

____

33. T F The text suggests that schools all over the country were allowing prayers long after the Supreme Court ruled such activities were not allowed in public schools.

____

34. T F No federal judge has ever been impeached.

____

35. T F Congress can change the number of members who are allowed to sit on the Supreme Court.

____

36. T F Judicial review can be exercised in France, but only on the request of a government official.

____

37. T F Congress cannot alter the jurisdiction of district courts and appellate jurisdiction of the Supreme Court.

____

38. T F The most activist periods of the Court's history have coincided with time when the political system was calm and, by all measures, stable.

____

39. T F The conservative Court of Chief Justice Rehnquist has overturned most of the critical decisions that came out of the more liberal Court, headed by Chief Justice Warren.

____

40. T F Courts have come to play a larger role in our lives because Congress, the bureaucracy and the president have come to play a larger ones.

____

41. T F The text suggests that there has been an increase in politically conservative judges who accept the activist view of the function of courts.

____

MULTIPLE CHOICE QUESTIONS

Circle the letter of the response that best answers the question or completes the statement.

1. With respect to a recent controversy regarding judicial appointments, the "nuclear option" focused on the possibility of
   a. requiring all judicial nominees to have federal experience.
   b. forcing all Supreme Court nominees to appear before the Senate Judiciary Committee.
   c. revising Senate rules to block filibusters.
   d. allowing "voice votes" on judicial nominations.
   e. requiring 60 votes of support to confirm judicial nominations.
2. The dramatic and sometimes bitter conflict surrounding some Supreme Court nominations can only be explained by the fact that
   a. there are only nine people on the Court at any given point in time.
   b. the Court plays such a large role in making public policy.
   c. the partisan balance of the Court is quite skewed.
   d. Presidents rarely seek the "advice" of the Senate.
   e. nominees are rarely qualified for the job.
3. In theory, restraint oriented judges differ from activist judges in that they are more likely to
   a. adopt a liberal viewpoint on such issues as states' rights and birth control.
   b. apply rules that are clearly stated in the Constitution.
   c. see, and take advantage of, opportunities in the law for the exercise of discretion.
   d. believe in the application of judicial review to criminal matters.
   e. look for and apply the general principles underlying the Constitution.
4. Seventy years ago judicial activists tended to be
   a. strict constructionists.
   b. liberals.
   c. conservatives.
   d. moderates.
   e. radicals.
5. In *Federalist* 78, Alexander Hamilton described the judicial branch as the _____ branch.
   a. most corrupt
   b. least political
   c. reliable
   d. existential
   e. least dangerous

6. Which of the following statements about *McCulloch* v. *Maryland* is correct?
   a. It established judicial review.
   b. It ruled a national bank unconstitutional.
   c. It restricted the scope of congressional power.
   d. It allowed states to tax federal agencies.
   e. It established the supremacy of national laws over state laws.
7. Who was defiant of Supreme Court rulings and supposedly taunted the Chief Justice to go and "enforce" one of its decisions?
   a. The Mayor of New York City.
   b. The Governor of New York.
   c. The Cherokee Indians of Georgia.
   d. Robert Fulton.
   e. President Andrew Jackson.
8. Roger B. Taney was deliberately chosen for the Supreme Court because he
   a. opposed the invention of the steamboat.
   b. opposed the creation of a national bank.
   c. favored a strong national government.
   d. was an advocate of states' rights.
   e. opposed slavery.
9. During the period from the end of the Civil War to the beginning of the New Deal, the dominant issue that the Supreme Court faced was that of
   a. government regulation of the economy.
   b. rights of privacy.
   c. states' rights versus federal supremacy.
   d. slavery.
   e. government regulation of interstate commerce.
10. The text suggests "judicial activism" was born in the
    a. 1970s.
    b. 1960s.
    c. 1950s.
    d. 1930s.
    e. 1890s.
11. From 1937 to 1974, the Supreme Court did not declare a single federal law dealing with _______ unconstitutional.
    a. freedom of speech
    b. communists
    c. regulation of business
    d. citizenship
    e. government benefits
12. FDR's court-packing bill is an example of a presidential action designed to
    a. help the Court reduce its backlog.
    b. influence the way in which the Court decided its cases.
    c. make the Court more impartial.
    d. discourage the Court from rendering decisions on major economic questions.
    e. allow the Court to grow with society.

13. Franklin Roosevelt's plan to reorganize the Supreme Court called for
    a. the Court to meet once every other year.
    b. the total number of justices to be increased according to the age of sitting justices.
    c. the president to select justices without senatorial confirmation.
    d. the Senate to have the power to remove justices from the Court at will.
    e. all New Deal legislation to be removed from the Court's jurisdiction.
14. Owen Roberts' change of view was a clear concession to
    a. established precedent.
    b. public opinion.
    c. his legal training.
    d. Roosevelt's court-packing plan.
    e. the Chief Justice.
15. A dramatic change in a long standing trends began in the early 1990s, when the Court struck down a congressional statute on the premise that ______did not affect interstate commerce.
    a. nude dancing
    b. racial discrimination
    c. carrying a gun
    d. commercial advertising
    e. the trucking industry
16. The two kinds of lower federal courts created to handle cases that need not be decided by the Supreme Court are
    a. constitutional and district.
    b. appeals and limited jurisdiction.
    c. district and appeals.
    d. appeals and legislative.
    e. constitutional and legislative.
17. There are ____ U.S. District Courts.
    a. 11
    b. 12
    c. 13
    d. 50
    e. 94
18. The Court of Military Appeals is an example of a(n) _________ court.
    a. district
    b. appellate
    c. legislative
    d. general jurisdiction
    e. second level appellate
19. Which of the following statements about the selection of federal judges is *correct*?
    a. The principle of senatorial courtesy applies to the selection of Supreme Court justices.
    b. Presidents generally appoint judges whose political views reflect their own.
    c. Since personal attitudes and opinions have little impact in judicial decision-making, presidents are usually not too concerned about who they nominate.
    d. Nominees for district judgeships often face tough confirmation battles in the Senate.
    e. The application of political litmus tests to Supreme Court nominees is no longer legal.

20. When politicians complain about the use of "litmus tests" in judicial nominations, they are probably
    a. Democrats.
    b. Republicans.
    c. Liberals.
    d. Conservatives.
    e. not part of the group that is currently in power.
21. The increasing importance of a political litmus test is evident in the dramatic drop in the confirmation rates of nominees to
    a. the U.S. District Courts.
    b. the U.S. Courts of Appeal.
    c. the Supreme Court.
    d. the trial courts of limited jurisdiction in the federal system.
    e. all of the above.
22. If citizens of different states wish to sue one another in a matter involving more than $75,000, they can do so in
    a. either a federal or a state court.
    b. a court in the plaintiff's state only.
    c. an intermediate court of appeals.
    d. a court in the defendant's state only.
    e. a federal court only.
23. If you wish to declare bankruptcy, you must do so in
    a. a court in the state in which you reside.
    b. a state appellate court.
    c. a federal appellate court.
    d. the U.S. Supreme Court.
    e. a federal district court.
24. *Certiorari* is a Latin word meaning, roughly,
    a. "certified."
    b. "made more certain."
    c. "without certainty."
    d. "appealed."
    e. "judicial."
25. *Cert* is issued and a case is scheduled for a hearing if ______ justices agree to hear it.
    a. 2
    b. 3
    c. 4
    d. 8
    e. all nine of the
26. What percentage of appeals court cases are rejected by the Supreme Court?
    a. 1 or 2 percent
    b. 20 percent
    c. 30 percent
    d. 50 percent
    e. 99 percent

27. Fee shifting enables the plaintiff to
    a. get paid by the Department of Justice.
    b. split costs with the court.
    c. have taxpayers pay his or her costs.
    d. split the costs with the defendant.
    e. collect costs from the defendant if the defendant loses.
28. To bring suit in a court, a plaintiff must first show that
    a. there is a defendant.
    b. the defendant is a real person.
    c. there is no true case and controversy.
    d. the defendant is a citizen of the United States.
    e. he/she has standing.
29. The doctrine of sovereign immunity prevents citizens from suing the government unless the government
    a. consents to be sued.
    b. has violated a state law.
    c. has violated both a state and federal law.
    d. is exempt from having to pay fees.
    e. has clearly been involved in manipulation of evidence.
30. In 1974, the Supreme Court discouraged class action suits by requiring
    a. lawyers to provide at least 20 *amicus* briefs supporting their claims.
    b. a special panel of judges to review all such suits.
    c. such suits to impact at least 300,000 persons.
    d. all fees in such suits be initially shifted to plaintiffs.
    e. every ascertainable member of a class be individually notified of a suit.
31. In a typical term, the federal government is party to __________ the cases that the Supreme Court hears.
    a. very few of
    b. thirty percent of
    c. about half of
    d. almost all of
    e. a limit of two of
32. The solicitor general has the job of
    a. serving as liaison between the Department of Justice and the president.
    b. deciding whether to sue large corporations.
    c. deciding who is eligible for the Supreme Court.
    d. deciding which cases the government will appeal from the lower courts.
    e. deciding which cases the Supreme Court will hear.
33. *Amicus curiae* is generally translated as meaning
    a. "friend of the court."
    b. "amicable but curious."
    c. "let the decision stand."
    d. "to reveal."
    e. none of the above.

34. Which type of opinion is typically brief and unsigned?
    a. Opinion of the Court.
    b. Majority opinion.
    c. Plurality opinion.
    d. *Per curiam* opinion.
    e. Dissenting opinion.
35. If a justice agrees with the conclusion of the Court's decision, but disagrees with the logic of the opinion of the Court, he/she would probably write a
    a. concurring opinion.
    b. majority opinion.
    c. plurality opinion.
    d. *per curiam* opinion.
    e. dissenting opinion.
36. *Stare decisis* is generally translated as meaning
    a. "friend of the court."
    b. "amicable but curious."
    c. "let the decision stand."
    d. "to reveal."
    e. none of the above.
37. The principle of precedent is not always so clear because
    a. lawyers are gifted at showing cases are different in some relevant way.
    b. records of judicial decisions are not particularly well organized.
    c. most appellate decisions are not accompanied by written decisions.
    d. the Court rarely gets a case that is at all similar to a previous case.
    e. Justices are notable for insisting that their work be original.
38. A political question is a matter
    a. involving voters.
    b. that the Constitution has left to another branch of government.
    c. that an elected state judge has dealt with.
    d. that causes conflict among average voters.
    e. that must first be acted on by Congress.
39. According to the text, the most powerful indicator of judicial power is probably
    a. the use of judicial review.
    b. the extent to which precedent is followed.
    c. the types of political questions courts are willing to handle.
    d. the kinds of remedies that courts will impose.
    e. the use of *per curiam* opinions.
40. Common criticisms of judicial activism include all of the following *except*
    a. judicial activism only works when laws are devoid of ambiguous language.
    b. judges usually have no expertise in designing complex institutions.
    c. judges are not elected and are therefore immune to popular control.
    d. judicial activism often fails to account for the costs of implementing activist rulings.
    e. judges usually have no expertise in managing complex institutions.

41. Which of the following is a major restraint on the influence of federal judges?
    a. Politics, especially the results of recent elections.
    b. Rule 17.
    c. The lack of effective enforcement power.
    d. The veto power of the president.
    e. International law.
42. Which of the following statements regarding judicial impeachments is *incorrect*?
    a. Fifteen federal judges have been impeached.
    b. Some judges have resigned in the face of probable impeachment.
    c. Seven impeached judges were acquitted.
    d. The most recent conviction of a federal judge occurred in 1989.
    e. The possibility of impeachment is an important influence on judicial policy making.
43. The 1868, case of Mississippi newspaper editor William McCardle was extraordinary because
    a. the Supreme Court accepted his appeal before it was formally filed.
    b. it seems almost certain that he would have remained in jail for the rest of his natural life despite having committed the most trivial of offenses.
    c. a federal district court insisted that he be released from jail after Congress issued a proclamation demanding such.
    d. Congress took away the Court's power to consider the case in the middle of his appeal.
    e. a unanimous Court declared Reconstruction policy (under which he was convicted) unconstitutional.
44. A major reason that the courts play a greater role in American society today than they did earlier in the century is that
    a. government plays a greater role generally.
    b. lawyers are more influential than ever.
    c. public opinion is less focused.
    d. judges are better trained.
    e. the courts are more representative of American society.

ESSAY QUESTIONS

Practice writing extended answers to the following questions. These test your ability to integrate and express the ideas that you have been studying in this chapter.

1. Explain the difference between judicial activism and restraint.
2. Summarize the point of view of the Founders with respect to courts.
3. Summarize the facts which led up to the case *Marbury* v. *Madison* and the Supreme Court's ruling in that landmark case.
4. Describe Franklin D. Roosevelt's so-called "court packing" plan.
5. Provide some examples of recent Supreme Court decisions which suggest there is something of a revival of state sovereignty in that institution.
6. Explain the difference between a constitutional and legislative court.
7. Explain how "senatorial courtesy" affects federal court nominations.
8. Generalize about the number of successful and unsuccessful nominations to the United States Supreme Court and provide some explanations for why some nominations have failed.
9. What are two circumstances where the Supreme Court will often grant *certiorari*?

10. Summarize the requirements for standing.
11. Identify and explain the difference between the types of opinions that Supreme Court justices can write and sign.
12. Discuss four manifestations of judicial power. Which is identified by the authors as "the most powerful indicator" of the power of courts to shape policy?
13. Write an essay on judicial activism in which you present arguments for and against this approach and provide an explanation for why we have activist courts.
14. Identify some ways in which Congress can check the judicial branch and identify those which appear to be the most practical and effective.

ANSWERS TO KEY TERMS MATCH QUESTIONS

1. d
2. n
3. e
4. g
5. t
6. k
7. r
8. x
9. s
10. l
11. m
12. b
13. v
14. f
15. o
16. q
17. c
18. u
19. y
20. z
21. w
22. i
23. j
24. h
25. bb
26. aa
27. a
28. p

ANSWERS TO DATA CHECK QUESTIONS

1. Democrat, Clinton.
2. Republican, Bush.
3. Republican, Nixon.
4. Republican, Reagan.

5. Judicial experience, especially federal.
6. Seven.
7. None. They all arrived with some judicial experience.
8. John Paul Stevens.
9. John G. Roberts.

ANSWERS TO TRUE/FALSE QUESTIONS

1. F The Court has declared about 160 federal laws unconstitutional.
2. T
3. T
4. F The Court did not exercise judicial review again until its decision in the *Dred Scott* case and did so very little afterward for many years.
5. T
6. F The plan would have allowed Roosevelt to expand the Court to as many as 15 members.
7. F Roosevelt was able to make 7 appointments to the Court before leaving office.
8. T
9. F The Constitution supplies no such number. Congress decides.
10. F Democrats are more likely to render liberal decisions.
11. F Senatorial Courtesy is a major factor in the appointment of U.S. district court judges and is much less important in appointments to the U.S. Courts of Appeal.
12. F The litmus test is most important in Supreme Court nominations.
13. T
14. F Under the dual sovereignty doctrine, state and federal authorities can prosecute the same person for the same conduct.
15. T
16. F The typical case involves straightforward applications of federal law.
17. T
18. T
19. T
20. T
21. F Taxpayers do not automatically have standing as taxpayers. You must, for example, show personal harm has been done to you before you can bring suit.
22. F Under the doctrine of sovereign immunity, one can only sue the government if it allows them to do so.
23. F The Supreme Court ruled against the taxpayer, saying that he did not have proper standing to bring the suit.

24. F In 1974, the Court drastically tightened the rules, requiring formal notice to all potential beneficiaries of such suits.

25. F The term begins in October.

26. T

27. T

28. F If a tie vote occurs, the decision of the last court to consider the case stands as the final outcome.

29. T

30. F The text says a more plausible reason is that we have made it easier for people to have standing and to bring class-action suits.

31. T

32. T

33. T

34. F Fifteen federal judges have been impeached.

35. T

36. T

37. F Congress can alter both jurisdictions.

38. F The most active periods have been those where the political system has undergone profound and lasting changes.

39. F As of yet, there has been no wholesale retreat from the positions staked out by the Warren Court.

40. T

41. T

ANSWERS TO MULTIPLE CHOICE QUESTIONS

1. c
2. b
3. b
4. c
5. e
6. e
7. e
8. d
9. a
10. e
11. c
12. b

13. b
14. b
15. c
16. e
17. e
18. c
19. b
20. e
21. b
22. a
23. e
24. b
25. c
26. e
27. e
28. e
29. a
30. e
31. c
32. d
33. a
34. d
35. a
36. c
37. a
38. b
39. d
40. a
41. c
42. e
43. d
44. a

PART 3

Classic Statement: "Bureaucracy," from Max Weber: *Essays in Sociology*[1]

INTRODUCTION

Although Weber's essay on bureaucracy certainly does not focus specifically on American government, it does deal with the way in which both governments and all large private enterprises in the modern world organize themselves and operate. It is thus relevant to our study not only of the power of the executive branch of government but also of the powers of the other branches, the political parties, and privately incorporated businesses.

*Weber compares the organization of the major activities of human life in traditional society and in our own times—*gemeinshaft *and* gesellshaft*, in his terminology. Face-to-face interactions based on personal loyalties give way to large, impersonal organizations run by abstract rules and loyalty to the organization itself, whether private or public.*

CHARACTERISTICS OF BUREAUCRACY

Modern officialdom functions in the following specific manner:

I. There is the principle of fixed and official jurisdictional areas, which are generally ordered by rules, that is, by laws or administrative regulations.
   A. The regular activities required for the purposes of the bureaucratically governed structure are distributed in a fixed way as official duties.
   B. The authority to give commands required for the discharge of these duties is distributed in a stable way and is strictly delimited by rules concerning the coercive means, physical, sacerdotal, or otherwise, which may be placed at the disposal of officials.
   C. Methodological provision is made for the regular and continuous fulfillment of these duties and for the execution of the corresponding rights; only persons who have the generally regulated qualifications to serve are employed.

II. The principles of office hierarchy and of levels of graded authority mean a firmly ordered system of super- and subordination in which there is a supervision of the lower offices by the higher ones. Such a system offers the governed the possibility of appealing the decision of a lower office to its higher authority, in a definitely regulated manner. With the full development of the bureaucratic type, the office hierarchy is monocratically organized. The principle of hierarchical office authority is found in all bureaucratic structures: in state and ecclesiastical structures as well as in large party organizations and private enterprises. It does not matter for the character of bureaucracy whether its authority is called "private" or "public."

---

[1] Max Weber, a German scholar, is widely referred to as the father of sociology, yet his writings cover a variety of different fields and have been influential in many of them—political science being no exception. His essay on bureaucracy, from which this selection is taken, comes from *From Max Weber: Essays in Sociology*, edited and translated by H. H. Gerth and C. Wright Mills (New York: Oxford University Press, 1946).

When the principle of jurisdictional "competency" is fully carried through, hierarchical subordination—at least in public office—does not mean that the "higher" authority is simply authorized to take over the business of the "lower." Indeed, the opposite is the rule. Once established and having fulfilled its task, an office tends to continue in existence and be held by another incumbent.

III. The management of the modern office is based upon written documents ("the files"), which are preserved in their original or draught form. There is, therefore, a staff of subaltern officials and scribes of all sorts. The body of officials actively engaged in a "public" office, along with the respective apparatus of material implements and the files, make up a "bureau." In private enterprise, "the bureau" is often called "the office."

IV. Office management, at least all specialized office management—and such management is distinctly modern—usually presupposes thorough and expert training. This increasingly holds for the modern executive and employee of private enterprises, in the same manner as it holds for the state official.

V. When the office is fully developed, official activity demands the full working capacity of the official, irrespective of the fact that his obligatory time in the bureau may be firmly delimited. In the normal case, this is only the product of a long development, in the public as well as in the private office. Formerly, in all cases, the normal state of affairs was reversed: official business was discharged as a secondary activity.

VI. The management of the office follows general rules, which are more or less stable, more or less exhaustive, and which can be learned. Knowledge of these rules represents a special technical learning, which the officials possess. It involves jurisprudence, or administrative or business management.

The reduction of modern office management to rules is deeply embedded in its very nature. The theory of modern public administration, for instance, assumes that the authority to order certain matters by decree—which has been legally granted to public authorities—does not entitle the bureau to regulate the matter by commands given for each case, but only to regulate the matter abstractly. This stands in extreme contrast to the regulation of all relationships through individual privileges and bestowals of favor, which is absolutely dominant in patrimonialism, at least in so far as such relationships are not fixed by sacred tradition.

THE LEVELING OF SOCIAL DIFFERENCES

Bureaucratic organization has usually come into power on the basis of a leveling of economic and social differences. This leveling has been at least relative, and has concerned the significance of social and economic differences for the assumption of administrative functions.

Bureaucracy inevitably accompanies modern *mass democracy* in contrast to the democratic self-government of small homogeneous units. This results from the characteristic principle of bureaucracy: the abstract regularity of the execution of authority, which is a result of the demand for "equality before the law" in the personal and functional sense—hence, of the horror of "privilege," and the principled rejection of doing business "from case to case." Such regularity also follows from the social preconditions of the origin of bureaucracies. The nonbureaucratic administration of any large social structure rests in some way upon the fact that existing social, material, or honorific preferences and ranks are connected with administrative functions and duties. This usually means that a direct or indirect economic exploitation or a "social" exploitation of position, which every sort of administrative activity gives to its bearers, is equivalent to the assumption of administrative functions.

We must expressly recall at this point that the political concept of democracy, deduced from the "equal rights" of the governed, includes these postulates: (1) prevention of the development of a closed status group of officials in the interest of a universal accessibility of office, and (2) minimization of the authority of officialdom in the interest of expanding the sphere of influence on "public opinion" as far as practicable. Hence, wherever possible, political democracy strives to shorten the term of office by election and recall and by not binding the candidate to a special expertness. Thereby democracy inevitably comes into conflict with the bureaucratic tendencies which, by its fight against notable rule, democracy has produced. The generally loose term "democratization" cannot be used here, in so far as it is understood to mean the minimization of the civil servants' ruling power in favor of the greatest possible "direct" rule of the *demos*, which in practice means the respective party leaders of the *demos*. The most decisive thing here—indeed it is rather exclusively so—is the *leveling of the governed* in opposition to the ruling and bureaucratically articulated group, which in its turn may occupy a quite autocratic position, both in fact and in form.

THE PERMANENT CHARACTER OF THE BUREAUCRATIC MACHINE

Once it is fully established, bureaucracy is among those social structures which are the hardest to destroy. Bureaucracy is *the* means of carrying "community action" over into rationally ordered "societal action." Therefore, as an instrument for societalizing" relations of power, bureaucracy has been and is a power instrument of the first order—for one who controls the bureaucratic apparatus.

The individual bureaucrat cannot squirm out of the apparatus in which he is harnessed. In contrast to the honorific or avocational "notable," the professional bureaucrat is chained to his activity by his entire material and ideal existence. In the great majority of cases, he is only a single cog in an ever-moving mechanism which prescribes to him an essentially fixed route of march. The official is entrusted with specialized tasks and normally the mechanism cannot be put into motion or arrested by him, but only from the very top. The individual bureaucrat is thus forged to the community of all the functionaries who are integrated into the mechanism. They have a common interest in seeing that the mechanism continues its functions and that the societally exercised authorities carries on.

The ruled, for their part, cannot dispense with or replace the bureaucratic apparatus of authority once it exists. For this bureaucracy rests upon expert training, a functional specialization of work, and an attitude set for habitual and virtuoso-like mastery of single yet methodically integrated functions. If the official stops working, or if his work is forcefully interrupted, chaos results, and it is difficult to improvise replacements from among the governed who are fit to master such chaos. More and more the material fate of the masses depends upon the steady and correct functioning of the increasingly bureaucratic organizations of private capitalism. The idea of eliminating these organizations becomes more and more utopian.

The discipline of officialdom refers to the attitude-set of the official for precise obedience within his *habitual* activity, in public as well as in private organizations. Such compliance has been conditioned into the officials, on the one hand, and, on the other hand, into the governed. If such an appeal is successful it brings, as it were, the disturbed mechanism into gear again.

The objective indispensability of the once-existing apparatus, with its peculiar, "impersonal" character, means that the mechanism—in contrast to feudal orders based upon personal piety—is easily made to work for anybody who knows how to gain control over it. A rationally ordered system of officials continues to function smoothly after the enemy has occupied the area; he merely needs to change the top officials. This body of officials continues to operate because it is to the vital interest of everyone concerned.

Such a machine makes "revolution," in the sense of the forceful creation of entirely new formations of authority, technically more and more impossible, especially when the apparatus controls the modern means of communication (telegraph, et cetera) and also by virtue of its internal rationalized structure. In classic fashion, France has demonstrated how this process has substituted *coups d'état* for "revolutions": all successful transformations in France have amounted to *coups d'état.*

QUESTIONS FOR UNDERSTANDING AND DISCUSSION

1. What are the key characteristics of modern officialdom?
2. What relationship does Weber say exists between democratization and bureaucracy?
3. Why, according to Weber, does bureaucracy tend to become permanent, and what does this do to the prospects for social or political revolution?

PART IV: The Politics of Public Policy

CHAPTER 17

The Policy-Making Process

REVIEWING THE CHAPTER

CHAPTER FOCUS

In this chapter we move from the study of political and governmental institutions (president, Congress, courts, etc.) to the study of the policies that all those institutions have produced. The purpose of this chapter is to provide you with a set of categories (majoritarian, interest group, client, and entrepreneurial politics) to help you better understand politics in general and the remainder of the book in particular. After reading and reviewing the material in this chapter, you should be able to do each of the following:

1. Explain how certain issues at certain times get placed on the public agenda for action.
2. Identify the terms *costs, benefits,* and *perceived* as used in this chapter.
3. Use these terms to define the four types of politics presented in the text—majoritarian, interest group, client, and entrepreneurial—giving examples of each.
4. Review the history of business regulation in this country, using it to exemplify these four types of politics.
5. Discuss the roles played in the process of public policy formation by people's perceptions, beliefs, interests, and values.

STUDY OUTLINE

I. Setting the agenda
  A. Most important decision affecting policy-making is deciding what belongs on the political agenda
    1. Shared beliefs determine what is legitimate
    2. Legitimacy affected by
      a) Shared political values
      b) Weight of custom and tradition
      c) Changes in way political elites think about politics
  B. The legitimate scope of government action
    1. Always gets larger
      a) Changes in public's attitudes
      b) Influence of events
    2. May be enlarged without public demand even when conditions improving
    3. Groups: a motivating force in adding new issues
      a) May be organized (corporations) or disorganized (urban minorities)
      b) May react to sense of relative deprivation—people's feeling that they are worse off than they expected to be
         Example: Riots of the 1960s

c) May produce an expansion of government agenda
Example: New commissions and laws

d) May change the values and beliefs of others
Example: White response to urban riots

4. Institutions a second force adding new issues
   a) Major institutions: courts, bureaucracy, Senate, national media
   b) Courts
      (1) Make decisions that force action by other branches: school desegregation, abortion
      (2) Change the political agenda
   c) Bureaucracy
      (1) Source of political innovation: size and expertise
      (2) Thinks up problems to solve
      (3) Forms alliances with senators and their staffs
   d) Senate
      (1) Once a slow moving, status quo club
      (2) Influx of liberal activist Senators in the 1960s
      (3) Now—contrary to the intent of the Framers—a major source of change
   e) Media
      (1) Help place issues on political agenda
      (2) Publicize those issues raised by others, such as safety standards proposed by Senate
5. Action by the states
   a) Sometimes laws are pioneered in states
   b) State attorneys general can file suits against businesses that result in settlements binding throughout the country
6. Evolution of political agenda
   a) Changes in popular attitudes that result in gradual revision of the agenda
   b) Critical events, spurring rapid changes in attitudes
   c) Elite attitudes and government actions, occasioning volatile and interdependent change

II. Making a decision
   A. Nature of issue
      1. Affects politicking
      2. Affects intensity of political conflict
   B. Costs and benefits of proposed policy a way to understand how issue affects political power
      1. Cost: any burden, monetary or nonmonetary
      2. Benefit: any satisfaction, monetary or nonmonetary
      3. Two aspects of costs and benefits important:
         a) Perception affects politics
         b) People consider whether it is legitimate for a group to benefit
      4. Politics a process of settling disputes about who benefits and who ought to benefit
      5. People prefer programs that provide benefits at low cost
      6. Perceived distribution of costs and benefits shapes the kinds of political coalitions that form but not who wins.

III. Majoritarian politics: distributed benefits, distributed costs
   A. Gives benefits to large numbers
   B. Distributes costs to large numbers
   C. Initial debate in ideological or cost terms, for example, military budgets

IV. Interest group politics: concentrated benefits, concentrated costs
   A. Gives benefits to relatively small group
   B. Costs imposed on another small group
   C. Debate carried on by interest groups (labor unions versus businesses)

V. Client politics: concentrated benefits, distributed costs
   A. Relatively small group benefits; group has incentive to organize
   B. Costs distributed widely
   C. Most people unaware of costs, sometimes in form of pork barrel projects

VI. Entrepreneurial politics: distributed benefits, concentrated costs
   A. Gives benefits to large numbers
   B. Costs imposed on small group
   C. Success may depend on people who work on behalf of unorganized majorities
   D. Legitimacy of client claims is important, for example, the Superfund

VII. The case of business regulation
   A. The question of wealth and power
      1. One view: economic power dominates political power
      2. Another view: political power a threat to a market economy
      3. Text cautious; weighs variables
   B. Majoritarian politics
      1. Antitrust legislation in the 1890s
         a) Public indignation strong but unfocused
         b) Legislation vague; no specific enforcement agency
      2. Antitrust legislation in the twentieth century strengthened
         a) Presidents take initiative in encouraging enforcement
         b) Politicians, business leaders committed to firm antitrust policy
         c) Federal Trade Commission created in 1914
         d) Enforcement determined primarily by ideology and personal convictions
   C. Interest group politics
      1. Labor-management conflict
         a) 1935: labor unions seek government protection for their rights: businesses oppose
            (1) Unions win
            (2) Wagner Act creates NLRB
         b) 1947: Taft-Hartley Act a victory for management
         c) 1959: Landrum-Griffin Act another victory for management
      2. Politics of the conflict
         a) Highly publicized struggle
         b) Winners and losers determined by partisan composition of Congress
         c) Between enactment of laws, conflict continues in NLRB
      3. Similar pattern found in Occupational Safety and Health Act of 1970
         a) Reflects a labor victory
         b) Agency established
   D. Client politics
      1. Agency capture likely
      2. Licensing of attorneys, barbers, and so on
         a) Prevents fraud, malpractice, and safety hazards
         b) Also restricts entry into occupation or profession; allows members to charge higher prices
         c) Little opposition since:
            (1) People believe regulations protect them
            (2) Costs are not obvious

3. Regulation of milk industry
    a) Regulation prevents price competition, keeping price up
    b) Public unaware of inflated prices
    c) Consumers have little incentive to organize
4. Sugar quotas also benefit sugar producers
5. Attempts to change regulations and cut subsidies and quotas
    a) 1996 bill replaced crop subsidies with direct cash payments
    b) Subsidies continued to increase
    c) 2002 law replaced 1996 law, and new subsidies were authorized
    d) Subsidies: the result of history and politics
6. Client politics for "special interests" seems to be on decline
    a) Importance of appearing to be "deserving"
    b) Regulation can also serve to hurt a client (e.g., FCC and radio broadcasters/telephone companies)

E. Entrepreneurial politics; relies on entrepreneurs to galvanize
1. 1906: Pure Food and Drug Act protected consumers
2. 1960s and 1970s: large number of consumer and environmental protection statutes passed (Clear Air Act, Toxic Substance Control Act)
3. Policy entrepreneur usually associated with such measures (Ralph Nader, Edmund Muskie)
    a) Often assisted by crisis or scandal
    b) Debate becomes moralistic and extreme
4. Risk of such programs: agency may be "captured" by the regulated industry
5. Newer agencies less vulnerable
    a) Standards specific, timetables strict
    b) Usually regulate many different industries; thus do not face unified opposition
    c) Their existence has strengthened public-interest lobbies.
    d) Allies in the media may attack agencies with pro-business bias
    e) Public-interest groups can use courts to bring pressure on regulatory agencies

VIII. Perceptions, beliefs, interests, and values

A. Problem of definition
1. Costs and benefits not completely defined in money terms
2. Cost or benefit a matter of perception
3. Political conflict largely a struggle to make one set of beliefs about costs and benefits prevail over another

B. Types of arguments used
1. "Here-and-now" argument
2. Cost argument

C. Role of values
1. Values: our conceptions of what is good for our community or our country
2. Emphasis on self-interest
3. Ideas as decisive forces

D. Deregulation
1. Example: airline fares, long-distance telephone rates, trucking
2. A challenge to "iron triangles" and client politics
3. Explanation: the power of ideas
    a) Idea: government regulation was bad
    b) Started with academic economists
    c) They were powerless but convinced politicians
    d) Politicians acted for different reasons
        (1) Had support of regulatory agencies and consumers

(2) Industries being deregulated were unpopular
4. Presidents since Ford have sought to review government regulation
5. Many groups oppose deregulation
   a) Dispute focuses mostly on how deregulation occurs
   b) "Process regulation" can be good or bad
6. The limit of ideas
   a) Some clients are just too powerful, for example, dairy farmers, agricultural supports
   b) But trend is toward weaker client politics

KEY TERMS MATCH

Match the following terms and descriptions:

1. A business that will not employ non-union workers
2. A situation in which government bureaucracy thinks up problems for government to solve
3. Political activity in which both benefits and costs are widely distributed
4. Deciding what belongs on the political agenda
5. Individual who noted the government big enough to give you everything you want is also big enough to take away everything you have
6. Political activity in which one group benefits at the expense of many other people
7. Intended to force industries to clean up their own toxic wastes, but a good illustration of entrepreneurial politics
8. Political activity in which benefits are distributed, costs are concentrated
9. Political activity in which benefits are conferred on a distinct group and costs on another distinct group
10. A sense of being worse off than one thinks one ought to be
11. Example of legislation pioneered in the states and replicated by the federal government
12. A situation in which people are more sensitive to what they might lose than to what they might gain

a. agenda setting
b. benefit
c. boycott
d. client politics
e. closed shop
f. cost
g. cost argument
h. Do Not Call Law
i. entrepreneurial politics
j. Gerald Ford
k. the Grange
l. interest-group politics
m. logrolling
n. majoritarian politics
o. policy entrepreneurs
p. political agenda
q. pork-barrel projects
r. process regulation
s. professionalization of reform
t. relative deprivation
u. Theodore Roosevelt
v. secondary boycott
w. Sherman Antitrust Act
x. Superfund

13. People in and out of government who find ways of creating a legislative majority on behalf of interests not well-represented in government
14. A boycott by workers of a company other than the one against which the strike is directed
15. A law passed in 1890 making monopolies illegal
16. An organization of farmers especially outspoken in its criticism of large corporations
17. Any satisfaction that people believe they will derive if a policy is adopted
18. A concerted effort to get people to stop buying from a company in order to punish and to coerce a policy change
19. Individual who persuaded Congress to fund five full time lawyers to prosecute antitrust violations
20. The perceived burden to be borne if a policy is adopted
21. Mutual aid among politicians, whereby one legislator supports another's pet project in return for the latter's support
22. A set of issues thought by the public or those in power to merit action by government
23. Legislation that gives tangible benefits to constituents in the hope of winning their votes
24. Rules regulating manufacturing or industrial processes, usually aimed at improving consumer or worker safety and reducing environmental damage

PRACTICING FOR EXAMS

TRUE/FALSE QUESTIONS

Read each statement carefully. Mark true statements *T.* If any part of the statement is false, mark it *F,* and write in the space provided a concise explanation of why the statement is false.

1. T F The expansion of government has been the result, fundamentally, of a non-partisan process.

   ____

2. T F There was no public demand for government action to make automobiles safer before 1966.

   ____

3. T F Congressional action has been the preferred vehicle for advocates of unpopular causes.

   ____

4. T F The bureaucracy reacts to policy, but is not a source of policy.

   ____

5. T F Somewhat contrary to the intent of the Framers, the House of Representatives has become a source of significant political change.

   ____

6. T F Increasingly, the actions of state governments are irrelevant to national policy-making.

   ____

7. T F Conflicts between rival interest groups are not nearly so important in majoritarian politics.

   ____

8. T F Interest-group politics often produce decisions about which the public is uninformed.

   ____

9. T F The Brady Bill requires background checks on gun buyers before they can purchase a firearm.

   ____

10. T F The Founders deliberately arranged things so that it would be difficult to pass a new law.

    ____

11. T F Policy entrepreneurs are outside of government.

    ____

12. T F Ralph Nader is a well known example of a policy entrepreneur.

    ____

13. T F Entrepreneurial politics cannot occur without the leadership of a policy entrepreneur.

14. T F Superfund is a good example of entrepreneurial politics.

15. T F In part, the decentralization of Congress is responsible for the prominence of entrepreneurial politics.

16. T F Much of the antitrust legislation that was passed in this country was the result of entrepreneurial politics.

17. T F The Grange was an association of small businessmen who were sharply critical of business monopolies and large corporations generally.

18. T F Anti-trust sentiment was strong in the late 1800s and early 1900s, but it was not focused on any single industry.

19. T F The Sherman Act (1890) spelled out rules for restraining monopolies and created and enforcement mechanism.

20. T F Theodore Roosevelt was influential in prompting more prosecutions for violations of antitrust laws.

21. T F Our antitrust policy is perhaps the strongest found in any industrial nation.

22. T F Antitrust enforcement in any particular administration is largely determined by the amount of interest-group pressure that is applied.

23. T F In the labor conflicts of the 1940s and 1950s, Republicans and southern Democrats tended to support the interests of businesses.

24. T F Each president has tried to tilt the National Labor Relations Board (NLRB) in one direction or the other by means of appointments.

25. T F Between 1996 and 2001 subsidies for farmers decreased.

26. T F Farm subsidies are a legacy of the Great Depression.

27. T F Client politics appear to be on the increase in the United States.

____

28. T F Radio broadcasters strongly opposed the creation of the Federal Communications Commission (FCC).

____

29. T F Upton Sinclair's book *The Jungle* dramatized the frightening conditions in steel mills.

____

30. T F Newer consumer- and environmental-protection agencies are more vulnerable to capture than other agencies.

____

31. T F It has become more difficult for groups to use the federal courts to put pressure on regulatory agencies.

____

32. T F Wages paid to airline pilots and truck drivers are no longer protected by federal rules.

____

MULTIPLE CHOICE QUESTIONS

Circle the letter of the response that best answers the question or completes the statement.

1. The most important decision that affects policy-making (and least noticed) is the decision to
   a. enact the policy agenda.
   b. determine what to make policy about.
   c. enforce the policy agenda.
   d. fund the policy agenda.
   e. fund and enforce the policy agenda.
2. The national policy agenda was quite short until the
   a. 1790s
   b. 1870s
   c. 1890s
   d. 1930s
   e. 1980s
3. The text suggests that, at any given time, what is considered legitimate (proper, right) for the government to do is affected by
   a. shared political values.
   b. the weight of custom.
   c. the impact of events.
   d. changes in the way political elites think.
   e. all of the above.
4. What, according to the text, is "always getting larger"?
   a. the scope of legitimate governmental action.
   b. the scope of what is illegitimate for government to do.
   c. the number of legislative proposals restricting the scope of governmental power.
   d. the number of debates about the legitimacy of government programs.
   e. B and D.

5. Who noted that the government "big enough to give you everything you want" is also the government "big enough to take away everything you have?"
   a. Richard Nixon
   b. Gerald Ford
   c. Dwight Eisenhower
   d. Jimmy Carter
   e. Ralph Nader
6. The fact that there were impressive displays of expansion of governmental power in the administrations of Richard Nixon, Dwight Eisenhower and Ronald Reagan suggests
   a. expansion is, fundamentally, the byproduct of liberalism.
   b. expansion is, fundamentally, the result of Democratic politics.
   c. expansion is, fundamentally, the byproduct of Republican politics.
   d. expansion is, fundamentally, a non-partisan process.
   e. A and B.
7. The Occupational Safety and Health Act of 1970 was passed at a time when
   a. the number of industrial deaths had increased steadily for a decade.
   b. the number of industrial deaths had been dropping steadily for twenty years.
   c. industrial fatalities had remained the same for several years.
   d. data on industrial fatalities were unavailable to Congress.
   e. data on industrial fatalities were unreliable.
8. The text's explanation for the urban riots in the 1960s centers on
   a. white radicals who mobilized blacks.
   b. organized special-interest groups in urban areas.
   c. followers of Marcus Garvey.
   d. blacks' sense of relative deprivation.
   e. the Black Panther movement.
9. The text identifies which of the following institutions as "especially important" in influencing agenda setting?
   a. The Senate
   b. The courts
   c. The bureaucracy.
   d. All of the above.
   e. The House of Representatives
10. Despite his dislike of using force against local government, Dwight Eisenhower used federal troops to
    a. run steel mills.
    b. assist with school desegregation.
    c. collect federal taxes.
    d. regulate speed limits on interstate highways.
    e. distribute social welfare benefits.
11. Which of the following statements *best* describes government bureaucracy today?
    a. It is a tool of big business.
    b. It is a major source of policy proposals.
    c. It is an impartial institution.
    d. It is an appendage of the political parties.
    e. It is without significant influence in the policy-making process.

12. Senate proposals for new safety standards for industry, coal mines and automobiles were closely correlated with
    a. the number of registered lobbyists interested in those topics.
    b. PAC money.
    c. statistics on fatalities.
    d. focus on those topics in the pages of the *New York Times*.
    e. television nightly news.
13. The text observes states can play a particularly impressive role in national policy-making when
    a. governors are supportive of federal regulations.
    b. legislatures impose strict limits on liability suits.
    c. courts interpret their own constitutions narrowly.
    d. attorneys general settle suits with businesses that bind industries throughout the country.
    e. they have low tax rate, stimulating economic vitality.
14. The nature of the issue on the current political agenda has its greatest influence on
    a. presidential policy.
    b. the prevailing ideas of society at large.
    c. congressional monitoring.
    d. prevailing media opinion.
    e. the kinds of groups that get politically involved.
15. An example of a policy characterized by distributed benefits and distributed costs is
    a. a tariff on bicycle chains.
    b. farm subsidies.
    c. dairy subsidies.
    d. the construction of a dam.
    e. increased Social Security benefits.
16. An example of a widely distributed benefit is
    a. the reduction of factory pollution.
    b. dairy subsidies.
    c. farm subsidies.
    d. the protection of a business from competition.
    e. a dissident group's freedom to speak.
17. If you receive benefits from a policy achieved by a group to which you do not belong, you are
    a. a majoritarian.
    b. a policy entrepreneur.
    c. a free rider.
    d. a neo-institutionalist.
    e. a secondary entrepreneur.
18. Majoritarian policies tend to reflect
    a. interest-group activity.
    b. interest-group conglomerations.
    c. matters of cost or ideology.
    d. the times.
    e. political party activity.

19. When pork-barrel projects are conglomerated to the point that a majority coalition is formed, the process of building that coalition is known as
    a. group facilitation.
    b. favor empowerment.
    c. legislative monopoly.
    d. pork piling.
    e. logrolling.
20. An example of client politics is
    a. social welfare.
    b. labor legislation.
    c. licensing of barbers.
    d. antitrust legislation.
    e. all of the above.
21. An example of entrepreneurial politics would be
    a. agricultural price supports.
    b. Social Security.
    c. a tariff on imported cars.
    d. requirements for antipollution and safety devices on cars.
    e. none of the above.
22. It is somewhat remarkable that policies which are the product of entrepreneurial politics are ever passed because
    a. Courts rarely rule in a counter-majoritarian fashion.
    b. the Founders made it so hard to pass laws to begin with.
    c. power in Congress is so centralized.
    d. policy entrepreneurs are outside of government.
    e. there are few incentives for anyone to be interested in such legislation.
23. Policies with distributed benefits and concentrated costs are
    a. opposed by policy entrepreneurs.
    b. are not affected by the media.
    c. are very rarely adopted.
    d. adopted less and less.
    e. adopted with increasing frequency.
24. The Superfund program was born in
    a. 1950
    b. 1960
    c. 1970
    d. 1980
    e. 1990
25. The Superfund was intended to force
    a. the automobile industry to manufacture cars that were more safe.
    b. industries to clean up their own toxic waste sites.
    c. the coal mining industry to reduce hours and increase wages.
    d. paper mills to reduce the emission of air pollutants.
    e. Congress to protect the rights of consumers.

26. The theory that the political system always operates to serve corporate interests is
    a. Weberian.
    b. pluralist.
    c. Freudian.
    d. Marxist.
    e. sociological.
27. A policy that did *not* pit a majority against a hostile business community was the
    a. antitrust policy.
    b. farm subsidy policy.
    c. space policy.
    d. labor policy.
    e. all of the above.
28. The president notable for persuading Congress to provide money for lawyers to enforce anti-trust legislation was
    a. Theodore Roosevelt
    b. Herbert Hoover
    c. William H. Taft
    d. Woodrow Wilson
    e. Grover Cleveland
29. Over the years enforcement of antitrust policy has been
    a. quite lax.
    b. generally quite successful.
    c. variable, depending on the president and the chief administrator.
    d. consistently favorable to big business.
    e. consistently biased against big business.
30. The Reagan administration ended its prosecution of _________ because it seemed the costs far outweighed the benefits.
    a. IBM
    b. Standard Oil
    c. AT&T
    d. Microsoft
    e. Northern Songs Ltd.
31. The Reagan administration broke up ________ forcing it to compete with other companies of its kind.
    a. IBM
    b. Standard Oil
    c. AT&T
    d. Microsoft
    e. Northern Songs Ltd.
32. The Clinton administration was notable for its antitrust suit against
    a. IBM.
    b. Standard Oil.
    c. AT&T.
    d. Microsoft.
    e. Northern Songs Ltd.

33. Upton Sinclair's book *The Jungle* helped pave the wave for legislation regulating
    a. meatpacking.
    b. automobile safety.
    c. the stock market.
    d. drug laws.
    e. weapons in public schools.
34. The type of politics that often takes on a moralistic tone, with opponents portrayed as devils and compromises strongly resisted, is
    a. interest-group politics.
    b. majoritarian politics.
    c. client politics.
    d. entrepreneurial politics.
    e. neo-institutional politics.
35. The passage of the auto safety law in 1966 made it easier to
    a. pass a coal mine safety bill in 1969.
    b. pass an occupational safety and health bill in 1970.
    c. portray subsequent legislation as frivolous duplication.
    d. condemn other attempts at regulation as "cheap imitations."
    e. a and b.
36. One reason that the newer consumer protection agencies may not be so vulnerable to capture is that
    a. older interest groups support them.
    b. they do not impose very large costs on industry.
    c. they impose a very large cost on industry.
    d. their regulations are obviously beneficial.
    e. they regulate several industries and so do not face a single, unified opponent.
37. The text speaks of the "power of ideas" as a key force in the deregulation of several industries that has occurred over the past two decades. Where did these ideas most often originate?
    a. With academic economists
    b. With the courts, especially the Supreme Court
    c. With broadcasters in local news stations
    d. With the national media
    e. With Congress, especially the Senate

ESSAY QUESTIONS

Practice writing extended answers to the following questions. These test your ability to integrate and express the ideas that you have been studying in this chapter.

1. Identify the factors which appear to affect the sense that a government action is legitimate.
2. Discuss some examples of enlargement of government policy in absence of crises or widespread public demand.
3. What is relative depravation and how is it relevant to mobilization of group efforts?
4. Explain the role that bureaucracy has played in policy formation in recent years.
5. Describe two ways that states have increasingly played a role in the formation of national policy.
6. Provide some examples of government policy which feature costs and benefits which are widely distributed and narrowly concentrated.

7. Explain why majoritarian politics can be controversial and why they do not feature the pulling and hauling among rival interest groups.
8. Compare and contrast client and entrepreneurial politics.
9. Discuss how anti-trust laws were strengthened from the administration of Theodore Roosevelt forward.
10. Why are the newer consumer and environmental protection agencies less vulnerable to capture?
11. What is the "here and now" argument and how does it impact the decision making of politicians?

ANSWERS TO KEY TERMS MATCH QUESTIONS

1. e
2. s
3. n
4. a
5. j
6. d
7. x
8. i
9. l
10. t
11. h
12. g
13. o
14. v
15. w
16. k
17. b
18. c
19. u
20. f
21. m
22. p
23. q
24. r

ANSWERS TO TRUE/FALSE QUESTIONS

1. T
2. T
3. F The courts are the preferred vehicle for unpopular causes.
4. F Increasingly, the bureaucracy is a major source of policy innovation.
5. F The Framers would have been pleased to see the House have a major role in policy formation. But, today, the Senate has taken on this role. The Framers envisioned the Senate, instead, as a moderating influence, resistant to change.

6. F National policy is increasingly made by the actions of state governments via laws which the federal government copies from the states and settlements by states attorneys general which are binding across state lines.
7. T
8. T
9. T
10. T
11. F They can be in or outside of government.
12. T
13. F It can occur with or without such leadership.
14. T
15. T
16. F Much of this legislation was the result of majoritarian politics.
17. F The Grange was an association of farmers.
18. T
19. F The *Act* did not define terms or create a regulatory agency.
20. T
21. T
22. F Such enforcement is determined more by the ideology and personal convictions of the administration in power.
23. T
24. T
25. F They increased.
26. T
27. F Client politics is becoming harder to practice in this country unless a group is widely thought to be deserving.
28. F They supported the legislation because they thought it would bring order and stability to their industry.
29. F The book focused on practices in meat packing plants.
30. F They are not as vulnerable because they have less discretion, they regulate many different industries, public interest lobbies are stronger and the media are more influential.
31. F Courts have made it easier to apply such pressure.
32. T

ANSWERS TO MULTIPLE CHOICE QUESTIONS

1. b
2. d

3. e
4. a
5. b
6. d
7. b
8. d
9. d
10. b
11. b
12. d
13. d
14. e
15. e
16. a
17. c
18. c
19. e
20. a
21. d
22. b
23. e
24. d
25. b
26. d
27. a
28. a
29. c
30. a
31. c
32. d
33. a
34. d
35. e
36. e
37. a

CHAPTER 18

Economic Policy

REVIEWING THE CHAPTER

CHAPTER FOCUS

The purpose of this chapter is to introduce you to an area of public policy that affects everyone in one way or another: economic policy. The chapter covers both the divided attitudes that voters have toward a "good" economy and the competing theories that economists offer on how to obtain a good economy. The various agencies that participate in formulating government economic policy are reviewed, along with the many stages of producing and implementing the annual federal budget. Finally, the controversial areas of government spending and tax reform are discussed. After reading and reviewing the material in this chapter, you should be able to do each of the following:

1. Show how voters have contradictory attitudes regarding their own and others' economic benefits.
2. List and briefly explain the four competing economic theories discussed in the chapter.
3. Assess the nature and effect of Reaganomics.
4. List the four major federal government agencies involved in setting economic policy, and explain the role of each.
5. Analyze federal fiscal policy in terms of the text's four categories of politics.
6. Trace the history of federal government budgeting practices up to the present day.
7. Comment on the prospects and the desirability of lowering federal spending and reforming the income tax.

STUDY OUTLINE

I. Introduction
    A. Deficit spending, a feature of the government since 1960
    B. National debt is the total of all deficits
    C. Explanations
        1. Economic reason
            a) Debt is a concern only if payments cannot be met
            b) Or the currency is no longer regarded as stable and valuable
            c) Interest on the debt is affordable—8 percent of all federal expenditures
            d) Future economic demands on the government may create a problem
        2. Substantive reason
            a) We don't know what the federal debt is used for
            b) Borrowing continues regardless of what government gets
        3. Political reason
            a) Politicians oppose debt because the public does

b) But they offer opposing remedies
(1) Conservatives want to cut spending
(2) Liberals want to raise taxes
(3) The tension between the positions often leads to no action

D. How reliable are projections about the future?
1. Not very
a) Unforeseen disasters can have an impact
b) Decisions can have a short-term and long-term impact (cutting taxes)
2. Federal agencies and estimates
a) Office of Management and Budget (OMB)
b) Congressional Budget Office (CBO)
3. Scorecard
a) Predicted deficit would be much higher than it actually was from 1993 to 1997
b) Predictions concerning budget surpluses

II. The politics of American economic prosperity
A. Health of American economy creates majoritarian politics
1. Voters influenced by their immediate economic situation
2. Voters worry about the nation as a whole as well as their own situations
3. Voting behavior and economic conditions correlated at the national level but not at the individual level
a) People understand what government can and cannot be held accountable for
b) People see economic conditions as affecting them indirectly, even when they are doing well
B. What politicians try to do
1. Elected officials tempted to take short-term view of the economy
2. Government uses money to influence elections, but government will not always do whatever is necessary
a) Government does not know how to produce desirable outcomes
b) Attempting to cure one economic problem often exacerbates another
3. Ideology plays a large role in determining policy
a) Democrats tend to want to reduce unemployment
b) Republicans tend to want to reduce inflation

III. The politics of taxing and spending
A. Inconsistency in what people want out of majoritarian politics
1. No tax increases
2. No government deficit
3. Continued (or higher) government spending
B. Difficult to make meaningful tax cuts
1. Politicians get reelected by spending money
2. Strategy: raise taxes on "other people"

IV. Economic theories and political needs
A. Monetarism—inflation occurs when there is too much money chasing too few goods (Milton Friedman); advocates increase in money supply about equal to economic growth
B. Keynesianism—government should create right level of demand
1. Assumes that health of economy depends on what fraction of their incomes people save or spend
2. When demand is too low, government should spend more than it collects in taxes by creating public works programs
3. When demand is too high, government should increase taxes

C. Planning—free market too undependable to ensure economic efficiency; therefore government should control it (John Kenneth Galbraith)
   1. Wage-price controls
   2. Industrial policy—government directs investments toward particular industries
D. Supply-side tax cuts—need for less government interference and lower taxes (Arthur Laffer)
   1. Lower taxes would create incentives for investment
   2. Greater productivity would produce more tax revenue
E. Ideology and theory: people embrace an economic theory partly because of their political beliefs
F. Reaganomics
   1. Combination of monetarism, supply-side tax cuts, and domestic budget cutting
   2. Goals not consistent
      a) Reduction in size of federal government
      b) Increase in military strength
   3. Effects
      a) Rate of growth of spending slowed (but not spending itself)
      b) Military spending increased
      c) Money supply controlled
      d) Federal taxes decreased
      e) Large deficits incurred and dramatically increase the size of the national debt
      f) Unemployment decreased

V. The machinery of economic policy making
A. Fragmented policymaking; not under president's full control
   1. Council of Economic Advisers
      a) Members chosen are sympathetic to president's view of economics and are experts
      b) Forecasts economic trends
      c) Prepares annual economic report for president
   2. Office of Management and Budget
      a) Prepares estimates of federal government agencies; negotiates department budgets
      b) Ensures that agencies' legislative proposals are compatible with president's program
   3. Secretary of the Treasury
      a) Reflects point of view of financial community
      b) Provides estimates of government's revenues
      c) Recommends tax changes; represents the nation before bankers and other nations
   4. The Fed (Federal Reserve Board)
      a) Membership, length of term and removal
      b) Independent of both president and Congress
      c) Sets monetary policy by controlling the amount of money and bank deposits and the interest rates charged for money
   5. Congress creates the nation's fiscal policy
      a) Approves taxes and expenditures
      b) Consents to wage and price controls
      c) Can alter Fed policy by threatening to reduce its powers
B. Effects of interest group claims
   1. Usually majoritarian: economic health good for all
   2. Sometimes interest group: free trade (e.g., NAFTA)
C. Globalization
   1. Growing integration of the economies and societies of the world

2. Supporters
 a) Argue it has increased income, literacy and the standard of living around the world
 b) Favor free trade (makes produces cheaper)
3. Opponents
 a) Oppose free trade because it undercuts wages of American workers
 b) See it as being driven by selfish, corporate interests
 c) Note exploitation of people in poor countries
 d) Concerned about cultural imperialism

VI. Spending money
 A. Conflict between majoritarian and client or interest group politics
 B. Sources of conflict reflected in inconsistencies in public opinion
 C. Politicians have incentive to make two kinds of appeals
 1. Keep spending down and cut deficit
 2. Support favorite programs of voters

VII. The budget
 A. Overview
 1. Document that announces
 a) How much the government will collect in taxes
 b) How much the government will spend in revenues
 c) How expenditures will be allocated among various programs
 d) Over the course of the fiscal year (October 1 to September 30)
 2. Spending decisions made with little regard to how much money is available
 B. Earlier practices
 1. Merely adding expenditures before 1921
 2. No unified presidential budget until 1930s
 3. Separate committee reactions after that
 C. Congressional Budget Act of 1974: procedures
 1. President submits budget
 2. House and Senate budget committees analyze budget
 3. Budget resolution in May proposes budget ceilings
 4. Members informed whether or not spending proposals conform to budget resolutions
 5. Committees approve appropriations bills, Congress passes them, and sends them to the president for signature
 6. Hard to make big changes in government spending because of entitlements
 7. Big loophole: Congress not required to tighten government's financial belt
 8. Failures of the process after 1981

VIII. Reducing Spending
 A. Gramm-Rudman Balanced Budget Act (1985) called for
 1. A target cap on the deficit each year, leading to a balanced budget
 2. A spending plan within those targets
 3. If lack of agreement on a spending plan exists, automatic across-the-board percentage budget cuts (a sequester)
 B. "Smoke and mirrors" and failure of the Act
 1. Plan was unpopular, but "necessary"
 2. Congress and president found ways to increase spending about "target" anyway
 C. New strategies
 1. Congress votes for a tax increase
 2. Passage of Budget Enforcement Act of 1990
 a) Set limits on discretionary spending (i.e., nonentitlements)

b) Increases in such spending had to be accompanied by cuts elsewhere or an increase in taxes

IX. Levying taxes
  A. Tax policy reflects blend of majoritarian and client politics
    1. "What is a 'fair' tax law?" (majoritarian)
      a) Tax burden is kept low; Americans pay less than citizens in most other countries
      b) Requires everyone to pay something; Americans cheat less than others
    2. "How much is in it for me?" (client)
      a) Requires the better-off to pay more
      b) Progressiveness is a matter of dispute: hard to calculate
      c) Many loopholes: example of client politics
    3. Client politics (special interests) make tax reform difficult, but Tax Reform Act passed (1986).
  B. The rise of the income tax
    1. Most revenue derived from tariffs until 1913 and ratification of Sixteenth Amendment
    2. Taxes then varied with war (high), peace (low)
      a) High rates offset by many loopholes: compromise
      b) Constituencies organized around loopholes
    3. Tax bills before 1986 dealt more with deductions than with rates
    4. Tax Reform Act of 1986: low rates with smaller deductions
    5. Will Bush tax cuts expire in 2010 or be made permanent?

KEY TERMS MATCH

Match the following terms and descriptions:

1. A group that forecasts economic trends
2. The theory that the health of an economy depends on what fraction of their incomes people save or spend
3. General term for deductions, exemptions and exclusions in the tax code
4. Legislation that authorizes budget ceilings
5. An organization that provides estimates of tax revenues
6. The theory that voters worry about community and national interests
7. The total deficit from the first presidency down to the present
8. The use of the amount of money in bank deposits and the price of money to affect the economy
9. A combination of monetarism, tax cuts, and domestic budget cutting
10. The mechanism that regulates the supply and price of money

a. budget
b. budget resolution
c. budget surplus
d. Congressional Budget Act
e. Council of Economic Advisers
f. deficit
g. discretionary spending
h. economic planning
i. entitlements
j. Federal Reserve System
k. fiscal policy
l. fiscal year (FY)
m. globalization
n. gross domestic product
o. Keynesianism
p. loopholes
q. monetarism

11. The theory that voters are mostly influenced by their own immediate economic situation
12. What occurs when the government in one year spends more money than it takes in from taxes
13. The total of all goods and services produced in the economy during a given year
14. The use of taxes and expenditures to affect the economy
15. The theory that inflation occurs when there is too much money chasing too few goods
16. The theory that government should control wages and prices
17. A document that announces how much the government will collect in taxes and spend in revenues and how those expenditures will be allocated
18. Electoral behavior that regards the condition of the national economy more so than one's own personal finances
19. A recommendation for budget ceilings to guide legislative committees in their spending decisions
20. A situation in which the government takes in more money than it spends
21. An economic philosophy that assumes that the government should plan some part of the country's economic activity
22. The period from October 1 to September 30 for which government appropriations are made and federal books are kept
23. The growing integration of the economies and societies of the world
24. Government regulation of the maximum prices that can be charged and wages that can be paid
25. Automatic, across-the-board cuts in certain federal programs when Congress and the president cannot agree on a spending plan

r. monetary policy
s. national debt
t. other-regarding voter theory
u. planning
v. price and wage control
w. Reaganomics
x. self-regarding voter theory
y. sequester
z. sociotropic voting
aa. supply-side theory
bb. Treasury Department

26. An economic philosophy that holds that sharply cutting taxes would increase the incentive to invest, leading to more tax revenues

27. Spending not required to pay for contracts, interest on the national debt or entitlement programs

28. Mandatory government spending (e.g., Social Security, Medicare, Food Stamps)

DATA CHECK

Figure 18.2 (Page 488): Bad Economic Guesses

1. What is the general impression made by this chart?

2. Can you identify an instance where, for a period of time, the two lines are actually close?

Figure 18.4 (Page 500): Tax Burdens in Democratic Nations

3. What country has the highest tax burden?

4. What country has the lowest tax burden?

5. How does the tax burden of the United States compare with other nations in the Figure?

Figure 18.6 (Page 501): Federal Taxes on Income, Top Percentage Rates, 1913–2002

6. How far back must we go in history to find top-bracket tax rates for individuals that are lower than they were during the Reagan era?

7. How far back must we go in history to find top-bracket corporate tax rates that are lower than they were during the Reagan era?

PRACTICING FOR EXAMS

TRUE/FALSE QUESTIONS

Read each statement carefully. Mark true statements *T.* If any part of the statement is false, mark it *F,* and write in the space provided a concise explanation of why the statement is false.

1. T F In a typical year, the government will spend more on the interest of the national debt than it will on national defense.

____

2. T F President Clinton and the American economy produced budget surpluses between 1998 and 2000.

____

3. T F Low-income people are more likely to vote Democrat.

____

4. T F Higher-income people are more likely to worry about unemployment.

____

5. T F A "sociotropic" voter votes on the basis of his/her own pocketbook.

____

6. T F The text suggests that only recently has the government tried to use money in order to affect elections.

____

7. T F Economics played a role in the defeats of Ford (1976), Carter (1980) and Bush (1992).

____

8. T F Republicans are more likely to attempt to reduce inflation.

____

9. T F Cutting taxes will tend to be more popular than increasing spending.

____

10. T F Most tax issues produce majoritarian politics.

____

11. T F Keynes believed the market would not automatically operate at a full-employment, low-inflation level.

____

12. T F If you are a liberal, monetarism would appeal to you.

____

13. T F If you are a socialist, economic planning would appeal to you.

____

14. T F "Reaganomics" was not dictated by any single economic theory.

____

15. T F Kennedy tended to pick monetarists for the Council of Economic Advisors (CEA).

____

16. T F Members of the Federal Reserve System ("the Fed") serve terms of fourteen years.

____

17. T F No member has ever been removed from the Federal Reserve System ("the Fed").

____

18. T F Bill Clinton reappointed Ronald Reagan's choice for Fed Chairman, Alan Greenspan.

____

19. T F When Congress passes a law governing foreign trade, it is responding to majoritarian politics.

____

20. T F The United States has not extended NAFTA to other countries.

____

21. T F Voters consistently say they want a balanced budget and lower government spending.

____

22. T F Voters consistently say they want increased spending on education and crime control.

____

23. T F Supporters of globalization are generally skeptical of "free trade."

____

24. T F There was no federal budget at all before 1921.

____

25. T F The procedures adopted by Congress affect the policies adopted by Congress.

____

26. T F The Gramm-Rudman Act called for a series of cuts in the federal budget until the deficit disappeared.

____

27. T F The sequester required across-the-board percentage cuts in federal programs if the president and Congress failed to agree on a total spending level.

____

28. T F The text suggests that the Balanced-Budget Act of 1985 was "successful."

____

29. T F Tax policy is a mixture of majoritarian and client politics.

____

30. T F Most other democratic nations have a higher tax rate than the United States.

31. T F There is evidence to suggest Americans evade their income taxes more than citizens in France or Italy.

32. T F Progressive tax rates are not part of the federal income tax scheme.

33. T F The Seventeenth Amendment created the federal income tax.

34. T F If taxes are progressive, those who make more money pay a lower rate than the less affluent.

35. T F Democrats have traditionally accepted loopholes as part of a political compromise.

36. T F In the early years of the federal income tax, high-income people paid a significant amount in income.

37. T F Loophole politics is client politics.

38. T F The big gainers in the Tax Reform Act of 1986 were businesses.

39. T F Presidents Bush (the elder) and Clinton both proposed tax increases.

40. T F Few Democrats voted for George W. Bush's tax-cut plan in 2002.

MULTIPLE CHOICE QUESTIONS

Circle the letter of the response that best answers the question or completes the statement.

1. The total federal debt is around
   a. $1 trillion.
   b. $3 trillion.
   c. $5 trillion.
   d. $8 trillion.
   e. $30 trillon.

2. When we survey the economic guesses of the OMB and the CBO regarding the deficit over the last forty years, we see that such estimates are
   a. quite reliable.
   b. almost perfect, in most instances.
   c. highly accurate in the last two decades.
   d. remarkably close given all of the uncertainties involved.
   e. not very reliable.
3. A sociotropic voter
   a. considers his/her personal economic fortune a major factor in the voting decision.
   b. does not consider economics in his/her voting decision.
   c. votes for incumbents.
   d. considers the economic health of the nation as a whole when voting.
   e. votes against incumbents.
4. The text suggests the massive system of Civil War pensions for Union army veterans and the Social Security system are examples of how
   a. economic decisions tend to be sociotropic.
   b. politicians regard institutional change in economic terms.
   c. the federal deficit has little relation to annual expenditures.
   d. the government has used money to affect elections.
   e. popular governmental programs are rarely held accountable by Congress.
5. Democrats tend to be more worried than Republicans about
   a. inflation.
   b. international politics.
   c. unemployment.
   d. business investment.
   e. recessions.
6. Lower taxes, less debt, and spending on new government programs produce ________ politics.
   a. entrepreneurial
   b. majoritarian
   c. interest group
   d. client
   e. B and D
7. Politicians have a strong tendency to get reelected by
   a. decreasing taxes.
   b. lowering the deficit.
   c. cutting expenditures.
   d. spending money on specific programs that are popular.
   e. raising taxes.
8. Milton Friedman's economic philosophy is called
   a. economic planning.
   b. supply-side theory.
   c. industrial policy.
   d. monetarism.
   e. planning.

9. Friedman takes the position that inflation is caused when
   a. there is too little money chasing too few goods.
   b. there is too much money chasing too many goods.
   c. there is too little money chasing too many goods.
   d. there is too much money chasing too few goods.
   e. the government has a predictable increase in the money supply.
10. Keynesians believe that if people save too much
    a. they will pay too little in taxes.
    b. they will invest too little.
    c. production and money supply will increase.
    d. demand will decrease and production will decline.
    e. demand and production will increase.
11. A follower of Keynes would probably agree with all of the following statements *except*
    a. the government should make sure there is the right level of demand.
    b. the government should take an activist role in the economy.
    c. money should be taken out of the economy when demand is too great.
    d. if demand increases too fast, prices will go up.
    e. the government should balance the budget each and every year.
12. In the economic planning approach of John Kenneth Galbraith, the government should address inflation by
    a. printing more money and lowering taxes.
    b. regulating the maximum prices that can be charged and wages that can be paid.
    c. standing back and allowing the market to adjust itself.
    d. reducing the number of regulations on businesses.
    e. creating public works programs.
13. A key element of the supply-side theory of the economy is the
    a. importance of incentives.
    b. need for careful control of the money supply.
    c. need for a balanced budget.
    d. need for close attention to trade imbalances.
    e. importance of regulations.
14. People are *most* likely to embrace a particular economic theory because of
    a. their race.
    b. the condition of the world economy.
    c. their political beliefs.
    d. their religious beliefs.
    e. the condition of their state's economy.
15. Which of the following statements is *incorrect*?
    a. Conservatives might find monetarism appealing.
    b. Socialists find economic planning appealing.
    c. Liberals find Keynesian economics appealing.
    d. Conservatives might find supply-side economics appealing.
    e. None of the above.

16. All of the following were true under "Reaganomics" *except*
    a. spending on some domestic programs was reduced.
    b. military spending was sharply increased.
    c. there were sharp, across-the-board, cuts in personal income taxes.
    d. business activity decreased.
    e. there was a drop in the unemployment rate.
17. The "troika" that assists the president in making economic policy is composed of the chairman of the Council of Economic Advisers, the director of the Office of Management and Budget, and the
    a. advisory council of the Federal Trade Commission.
    b. Secretary of the Treasury.
    c. Secretary of Labor.
    d. Federal Reserve Board.
    e. head of the Department of Labor.
18. The Office of the Management and Budget has something of a "split personality" because it
    a. makes recommendations, then criticizes its own recommendations.
    b. negotiates budgets with departments, but recruits members from them as well.
    c. prepares spending estimates while discouraging long-range planning.
    d. works with the legislative branch while instituting litigation in the judicial branch.
    e. provides both expert analysis and activist partisan support for the president's programs.
19. The Secretary of Treasury is expected to argue the point of view of
    a. the financial community.
    b. Congress.
    c. the president.
    d. industrial leaders.
    e. taxpayers.
20. Which statement about the Federal Reserve Board is *incorrect*?
    a. It has fifteen members.
    b. Each member is appointed by the president and confirmed by the Senate.
    c. A member's term is fourteen years.
    d. Since its founding in 1913, no member has ever been removed.
    e. The Chairman serves a four-year term.
21. In 2001, the Fed ____________ eleven times in order to help reduce the recession.
    a. sold government securities
    b. increased bank deposits
    c. increased the supply of money
    d. raised interest rates
    e. lowered interest rates
22. The most important part of the economic policy making machinery is the
    a. Federal Reserve Board.
    b. Congress.
    c. Council of Economic Advisers.
    d. General Services Administration.
    e. Secretary of Labor.

23. Republicans tend to support free trade, but George W. Bush imposed sharp increases in taxes on imported steel because
    a. he opposed NAFTA from the beginning.
    b. Democrats in Congress insisted that the steel industry was receiving special treatment.
    c. the automobile industry threatened to strike.
    d. he was interested in electoral support from Ohio and Pennsylvania.
    e. of a lack of compliance with environmental laws.
24. The fiscal year begins
    a. October 1.
    b. October 30.
    c. September 1.
    d. September 30.
    e. None of the above.
25. The Congressional Budget Act of 1974 was intended to
    a. impose some budget discipline on committees.
    b. increase the power of the president.
    c. allow interest groups more access to the budget process.
    d. implement zero-based budgeting.
    e. invite members of Congress to allocate funds in creative ways.
26. Entitlements (that is, mandatory spending) makes up about ____ of what government spends.
    a. one-tenth
    b. one-fourth
    c. one-half
    d. two-thirds
    e. very little
27. The "sequester" featured in the Gramm-Rudman Act (1995) called for what action if the president and Congress could not agree on a total spending level?
    a. Reduction in congressional salaries.
    b. A freeze on congressional salaries.
    c. Across the board cuts in all federal programs
    d. Resubmission of all budget requests with special attention to elimination of programs.
    e. Resubmission of all budget requests with special attention to consolidation of programs.
28. The law enacted by Congress that imposed a cap on discretionary spending (that is, nonentitlement spending) was the
    a. Budget Enforcement Act of 1990.
    b. Balanced-Budget Act of 1985.
    c. Budget and Impoundment Act of 1974.
    d. Budget and Accounting Act of 1921.
    e. Monetary Control Act of 1973.
29. Many other nations rely more heavily on sales taxes than we do because such taxes are
    a. more popular with the public.
    b. easy to raise without opposition and protest.
    c. supported by political elites.
    d. harder to evade.
    e. more traditional and progressive.

30. The text states that tax policy is a blend of majoritarian and client politics. What is an example of the latter?
    a. Progressive taxation.
    b. A low tax burden.
    c. Tax loopholes.
    d. A requirement that everyone pay something.
    e. A and D.
31. Prior to the creation of the income tax, the money that the government needed came mostly from
    a. property taxes.
    b. loans.
    c. state contributions.
    d. tariffs.
    e. highway tolls
32. The ______ Amendment created the federal income tax.
    a. Eleventh
    b. Thirteenth
    c. Sixteenth
    d. Twenty-first
    e. Twenty-second
33. In the first half of the twentieth century, Republicans expressed bitter opposition to
    a. high marginal rates.
    b. tax loopholes.
    c. incentives.
    d. income adjustments.
    e. tax exemptions.
34. Early on, tax loopholes particularly helped
    a. average citizens.
    b. those who were well off.
    c. businesses.
    d. self-employed persons.
    e. farmers.
35. In 1993, President Clinton proposed a law which raised the top tax rate to
    a. 28 percent
    b. 31 percent
    c. 39 percent
    d. 43 percent
    e. 52 percent

ESSAY QUESTIONS

Practice writing extended answers to the following questions. These test your ability to integrate and express the ideas that you have been studying in this chapter.

1. What are three reasons why the government can spend more than it brings in, essentially operating while constantly in debt?

2. Explain the difference between pocketbook and sociotropic voting. How do these approaches affect the outcomes of recent presidential elections?

3. Summarize the economic views of Milton Friedman and monetarists.

4. Explain the relationship between the economy and spending and saving according to John Maynard Keynes.

5. Outline the steps that were taken under the program known as Reaganomics. Detail the impact of these steps on the deficit, the national debt, unemployment, business activity and productivity.

6. Describe the structure and membership of the Fed. Then identify the tools employed by the Fed in order to implement monetary policy.

7. What are some arguments for and against globalization?

8. Discuss loophole politics and the Tax Reform Act of 1986. How did the Act affect rates and deductions and who were the winners and losers?

ANSWERS TO KEY TERMS MATCH QUESTIONS

1. e
2. o
3. p
4. d
5. bb
6. t
7. s
8. r
9. w
10. j
11. x
12. f
13. n
14. k
15. q
16. h
17. a
18. z
19. b
20. c
21. u
22. l
23. m
24. v
25. y
26. aa
27. g
28. i

ANSWERS TO DATA CHECK QUESTIONS

1. The economic guesses of the experts are not always quite so accurate.
2. 1987–1990.
3. Denmark (30.5).
4. Switzerland (8.6).

5. The tax rate in the United States (11.3) is relatively low.
6. 1930s, Hoover administration.
7. 1950s, Truman administration.

ANSWERS TO TRUE/FALSE QUESTIONS

1. F More is spent on social welfare and defense.
2. T
3. T
4. F They are more likely to worry about inflation.
5. F These voters are said to consider the economic health of the nation as a whole, or "the economy" when they cast their vote.
6. F The text notes the role of patronage in the nineteenth century and the government distribution of Civil War pensions as examples of such behavior.
7. T
8. T
9. F Increased spending tends to be more popular than cutting taxes.
10. T
11. T
12. F Monetarism is more likely to appeal to conservatives.
13. T
14. T
15. F Kennedy tried to appoint Keynesians to the CEA.
16. T
17. T
18. T
19. F Such laws would be samples of interest group politics.
20. T
21. T
22. T
23. F Supporters of globalization support free trade because they believe it results in lower prices.
24. T
25. T
26. T
27. T
28. F It failed because, by "smoke and mirrors," Congress and the president found ways to spend higher than the targeted amounts.

29. T

30. T

31. F Americans evade such taxes much less.

32. F Progressive taxation is a part of our system. The only debate surrounds the degree to which our taxes are progressive.

33. T

34. F If taxes are progressive, then those who make more will pay a higher percentage in taxes.

35. T

36. F Only a small percentage of high income people paid any significant amount.

37. T

38. F The big gainers were individuals. Businesses were the big losers.

39. T

40. T Many Democrats and most Republicans voted for it.

ANSWERS TO MULTIPLE CHOICE QUESTIONS

1. d
2. e
3. d
4. d
5. c
6. b
7. d
8. d
9. d
10. d
11. e
12. b
13. a
14. c
15. e
16. a
17. b
18. e
19. a
20. a
21. e

22. b
23. d
24. a
25. a
26. d
27. c
28. a
29. d
30. c
31. d
32. c
33. a
34. a
35. c

CHAPTER 19

Social Welfare

REVIEWING THE CHAPTER

CHAPTER FOCUS

This chapter covers more than fifty years of the political history of efforts to establish, maintain, expand, or cut those major programs that give or claim to give government help to individuals in need. After reading and reviewing the material in this chapter, you should be able to do each of the following:

1. Describe the goals of the American social welfare system, and contrast its programs with those of the British in terms of centralization.
2. Describe the major elements of the American system, including Social Security, Medicare, and AFDC programs.
3. Explain why some welfare policies can be considered majoritarian politics and others client politics. Give examples and indicate the political consequences of each.
4. Discuss recommendations to deal with the rising costs of Social Security and Medicare as well as the Welfare Reform Act of 1996.

STUDY OUTLINE

I. Introduction
  A. Two basic types of welfare programs
    1. First type: benefit most or all people (Examples: Social Security, Medicare)
    2. Second type: help only a small number of them (Food stamps, Medicaid)
  B. Some programs are means tested
    1. First type: are not
    2. Second type: are
  C. Politics associated with each are different
    1. First type: majoritarian politics
    2. Second type: client politics
  D. Problems associated with each are different
    1. First type: Who will pay? And how much?
    2. Second type: Who will benefit? What form will the benefit take?

II. Social welfare in the United States
  A. Who deserves to benefit?
    1. Insistence that it be only those who cannot help themselves
    2. Slow, steady change in deserving/undeserving line
    3. Alternative view: fair share of national income; government redistribute money
    4. Preference to give services, not money, to help deserving poor
  B. Late arrival of welfare policy
    1. Behind twenty-two European nations
    2. Contrast with Great Britain in 1908

C. Influence of federalism
   1. Federal involvement "illegal" until 1930s
   2. Experiments by state governments
      a) Argued against federal involvement because state already providing welfare
      b) Lobbied for federal involvement to help states
D. Administration via grants and contracts to non-governmental institutions
   1. For-profit firms and non-profit organizations
   2. Religious non-profit organizations and small community-based groups
      a) Charitable Choice enjoyed bipartisan support in 1996
      b) Prohibited proselytizing, instruction or worship services
      c) Bush's call for expansion led to a political firestorm
      d) Increases in awards, programs and public support
E. Majoritarian welfare programs
   1. Social Security Act of 1935
      a) Great Depression of 1929: local relief overwhelmed
      b) Elections of 1932: Democrats and Franklin Roosevelt swept in
         (1) Legal and political roadblocks; was direct welfare unconstitutional?
         (2) Fear of more radical movements
            (a) Long's "Share Our Wealth"
            (b) Sinclair's "End Poverty in California"
            (c) Townsend's old-age program
      c) Cabinet Committee's two-part plan
         (1) "Insurance" for unemployed and elderly
         (2) "Assistance" for dependent children, blind, aged
         (3) Federally funded, state-administered program under means test
   2. Medicare Act of 1965
      a) Medical benefits omitted in 1935: controversial but done to ensure passage
      b) Opponents
         (1) AMA
         (2) House Ways and Means Committee under Wilbur Mills
      c) 1964 elections: Democrats' big majority altered Ways and Means
      d) Objections anticipated in plan
         (1) Application only to aged, not everybody
         (2) Only hospital, not doctors', bills covered
      e) Broadened by Ways and Means to include Medicaid for poor; pay doctors' bills for elderly
F. Reforming majoritarian welfare programs
   1. Social Security
      a) Not enough people paying into Social Security
      b) Proposals under consideration
         (1) Raise retirement age
         (2) Reduce benefits for high earners
         (3) Raise payroll taxes
         (4) Increase the wage cap
         (5) Have government make investments
         (6) Let individuals make investments
   2. Medicare
      a) Problems: huge costs and inefficient
      b) Possible solutions
         (1) Get rid of Medicare and have doctors and hospitals work for government
         (2) Elderly take Medicare money and buy health insurance

c) Delaying the inevitable
(1) Clinton and surplus, new benefits
(2) Bush and attempts at new health care measures—Medicare Modernization Act of 2003

G. A client welfare policy: AFDC
1. Scarcely noticed part of Social Security Act
2. Federal government permitted state to
a) Define need
b) Set benefit levels
c) Administer program
3. Federal government increased rules of operation
4. New programs (e.g., Food Stamps, Earned Income Tax Credit, free school meals)
5. Difficult to sustain political support
a) States complained about federal regulations
b) Public opinion turned against program
c) Composition of program participants changed
6. Temporary Assistance to Needy Families (TANF)

III. Majoritarian versus client politics
A. Majoritarian politics: almost everybody pays and benefits, for example, the Social Security Act and the Medicare Act
B. Client politics: everybody pays, relatively few people benefit, for example, the AFDC program
C. Majoritarian politics
1. Programs with widely distributed benefits and costs
a) Beneficiaries must believe they will come out ahead
b) Political elites must believe in legitimacy of program
2. Social Security and Medicare looked like "free lunch"
3. Debate over legitimacy: Social Security (1935)
a) Constitution did not authorize federal welfare (conservatives)
b) But benefits were not really a federal expenditure (liberals)
4. Good politics unless cost to voters exceeds benefits
D. Client politics
1. Programs pass if cost to public not perceived as great and client considered deserving
2. Americans believe today that able-bodied people should work for welfare benefits
3. Americans prefer service strategy to income strategy
a) Charles Murray: high welfare benefits made some young people go on welfare rather than seek jobs
b) No direct evidence supports Murray

KEY TERMS MATCH

Match the following terms and descriptions:

1. First U.S. legislation, in 1935, providing for an income transfer program
2. Federally funded program that provides health care for the poor
3. A feature of Upton Sinclair's gubernatorial platform

a. AFDC
b. almshouses
c. assistance program
d. charitable choice
e. client politics

4. Legislation enacted in 1965 providing medical insurance for the elderly
5. Financial assistance to the poor that replaced the AFDC program
6. Pre-1935 state programs to aid widows with children
7. Pre-1935 state-run or locally run homes for the poor
8. Huey Long's proposal to redistribute income in the United States
9. Refers to religious non-profit organizations that compete for government grants to administer federal welfare-to-work related policies
10. Pre-Social Security proposal that was popular because it aimed to provide financial support to elderly people
11. Benefits paid weekly to laid-off workers unable to find jobs
12. Also known as Social Security
13. Former federally funded program that made payments to poor families with children
14. Cash payments to poor people who are aged, blind, or disabled
15. Vouchers given to the poor to buy food at grocery stores
16. The mechanism by which payments rise automatically when costs do
17. Claimed high welfare benefits made it more attractive for some to go on welfare than to look for a job
18. A proviso that only those below a specified poverty level qualify for a program
19. Policy-making in which almost everybody benefits and almost everybody pays
20. An approach to welfare that aims to give poor people job training or government jobs rather than money
21. Legislation adopted in 1988 to protect the elderly against the costs of long-term medical care; later repealed

f. earned income tax credit
g. End Poverty in California plan
h. food stamps
i. income strategy
j. indexing
k. insurance program
l. majoritarian politics
m. means test
n. Medicaid
o. Medicare
p. Medicare Catastrophic Coverage Act
q. mother's pension
r. Charles Murray
s. Old Age, Survivors, and Disability Insurance
t. service strategy
u. Share Our Wealth plan
v. Social Security Act
w. SSI
x. TANF
y. Townsend plan
z. UI

22. Policy-making in which relatively few people benefit but everybody pays

23. An approach to welfare in which poor people are given money

24. A program financed by income taxes that provides benefits to poor citizens without requiring contributions from them

25. A self-financing program based on contributions that provides benefits to unemployed or retired persons

26. A provision of the 1975 tax law that entitles working families with children to receive money if their incomes fall below a certain level

DATA CHECK

Table 19.2 (Page 516): Post–1970 Government Health Care Spending in Ten Countries

1. What country appears to spend the most on health care?

____

2. How does the United States compare to other nations?

____

PRACTICING FOR EXAMS

TRUE/FALSE QUSTIONS

Read each statement carefully. Mark true statements *T.* If any part of the statement is false, mark it *F,* and write in the space provided a concise explanation of why the statement is false.

1. T F Welfare programs that have no *means* test are available to everyone without regard to income.

____

2. T F Client-based welfare programs are *means* tested.

____

3. T F Client programs are in trouble whenever they lose legitimacy.

____

4. T F The standard measure for welfare payments has been that of a family's fair share of the national income.

5. T F American social welfare policies have generally favored giving people money as opposed to providing them with services.

6. T F Germany was the first nation to create a national social security program.

7. T F Progressives in the United States were less interested in welfare legislation in the early twentieth century than were Labourites in Great Britain.

8. T F The Constitution is silent on whether the Congress has the power to spend money on welfare.

9. T F Religious organizations which receive public funds to provide social services must remove religious art or iconography from buildings where such services are provided.

10. T F President Bush has called for further restrictions and limitations for so called Charitable Choice provisions.

11. T F The New Deal plan for Social Security was a radical departure in the context of the 1930s.

12. T F The Social Security Act passed swiftly and was virtually unchanged by Congress.

13. T F Medical care was left out of the Social Security Act for fear that the Act would not pass if that issue were addressed.

14. T F The most difficult hurdle for the Medicare Act of 1965 was the House Ways and Means Committee.

15. T F Key votes on the Social Security Act pitted a majority of Democrats against a majority of Republicans.

16. T F The key problem for Social Security is that there soon will not be enough people paying Social Security taxes to provide benefits for every retired person.

17. T F The only problem associated with Medicare is its huge costs.

____

18. T F Today, Medicare costs over $300 billion a year.

____

19. T F President Clinton repudiated the findings of a bipartisan commission which was formed in 1997 to study the problem of Medicare.

____

20. T F Americans pay less for health care than do citizens in other western democracies where hospitals work for the government.

____

21. T F One part of the Social Security Act of 1935 created what came to be called Aid to Families with Dependent Children (AFDC).

____

22. T F AFDC began as a noncontroversial client program and was scarcely noticed at the time.

____

23. T F Public suspicions that AFDC recipients were working covertly on the side were unfounded.

____

24. T F As a result of losing political legitimacy the Aid to Families With Dependent Children (AFDC) was abolished.

____

25. T F Social Security is an example of majoritarian politics, while the old AFDC program was an example of client politics.

____

26. T F Today, most Americans believe that able-bodied people on welfare should be made to work for welfare benefits.

____

27. T F Welfare programs that emphasize job training are based on an income strategy.

____

28. T F In welfare policy, a service strategy is strongly preferred to an income strategy.

____

29. T F Charles Murray's position was that social welfare programs actually increased the number of people living in poverty.

____

30. T F Most Republican leaders have opposed plans to give parents school vouchers to pay for private or religious school tuitions.

____

31. T F Democrat Senator Ted Kennedy was a fierce opponent of the No Child Left Behind Act (2002)

____

32. T F The Supreme Court has declared school voucher plans unconstitutional.

____

33. T F Public opinion did not seem to support No Child Left Behind (2002)

____

MULTIPLE CHOICE QUESTIONS

Circle the letter of the response that best answers the question or completes the statement.

1. Welfare programs in which nearly everyone benefits and nearly everyone pays are characterized by
   a. overlapping politics.
   b. minoritarian politics.
   c. club-based politics.
   d. congruent politics.
   e. majoritarian politics.
2. The biggest problem facing majoritarian welfare programs is
   a. their cost.
   b. their legitimacy.
   c. their goals.
   d. who will benefit.
   e. how should clients be served.
3. The biggest problem facing client-oriented welfare programs is
   a. their cost.
   b. their legitimacy.
   c. their goals.
   d. who will pay.
   e. how will costs be determined.
4. A welfare program such as the old Aid to Families with Dependent Children (AFDC) is a good example of
   a. client politics.
   b. club-based politics.
   c. majoritarian politics.
   d. interest-group politics.
   e. entrepreneurial politics.
5. Most of the welfare policies in the United States have attempted to
   a. redistribute income.
   b. change the existing tax structure.
   c. help people with disabilities.
   d. provide everyone with a guaranteed income.
   e. balance the haves and the have-nots.

6. Which of the following beliefs is *not* held by the American people?
   a. Income redistribution is a good thing.
   b. Helping the needy is a good thing.
   c. Assisting those who cannot help themselves is a good thing.
   d. Giving people money will produce a class of welfare chiselers.
   e. Giving people services rather than money is a good thing.
7. In distinct contrast to many other European nations, America's national welfare system
   a. has emphasized the provision of money more than services.
   b. has been a top priority of lawmakers since the 1880s.
   c. is more oriented toward the basic notion of each person's "fair share."
   d. is far less adversarial.
   e. arrived quite late in our history.
8. The experience of England with welfare politics offers a particularly clear contrast in large part because
   a. there was no significant labor party there.
   b. the notion of an activist government was less acceptable there.
   c. authority was centralized there and programs could be administered nationally.
   d. partisanship played no role in the development of policy in England.
   e. Parliament was in constant conflict with the prime minister over policy.
9. By 1935, most states had adopted a ____________ program.
   a. mother's pension
   b. food stamp
   c. unemployment insurance
   d. work training
   e. medicaid
10. The provision which allows religious nonprofit organizations to compete for government funds in order to administer federal welfare-to-work and related policies is known as
    a. welfare plus
    b. the social service rider
    c. charitable choice
    d. Youth Build
    e. TANF
11. George W. Bush has called for an expansion in the role of ____________ in administering federal social programs.
    a. colleges and universities
    b. big business
    c. state government
    d. federal bureaucrats
    e. religious organizations
12. Polling data suggest Americans ________ the administration of social services by faith-based organizations.
    a. know little or nothing about
    b. have no distinct opinions regarding
    c. are somewhat opposed to
    d. are slightly in favor of
    e. are strongly supportive of

13. When Roosevelt created the Committee on Economic Security, there was widespread belief that any direct federal welfare program
    a. could not fund itself.
    b. might be unconstitutional.
    c. had to be supplemented with state taxes.
    d. was consistent with existing programs in the states.
    e. would be rejected by every member of his own party in Congress.
14. Dr. Francis E. Townsend's organization led a nationwide movement that demanded
    a. food stamps for all persons over the age of seventy-five.
    b. government pensions of $200 a month.
    c. health benefits for persons who were both elderly and disabled.
    d. free health insurance for all persons over the age of seventy-five.
    e. government-run hospitals in each state.
15. Which presidents initially supported the idea of having the government pay the medical and hospital bills of the elderly and the poor?
    a. Democrats
    b. Republicans
    c. Both Democrats and Republicans
    d. Those who were chosen in close elections
    e. Those who were former governors
16. The American Medical Association considered the idea of medical support for the elderly and poor to be
    a. "absolutely necessary."
    b. "consistent with the principles of our government."
    c. "a sure way to bankrupt the government."
    d. "incompatible with the rights of patients."
    e. "socialized medicine."
17. By the 1960s, a majority of the House favored a health care plan, but did not expect such legislation to ever reach the floor because
    a. presidents had so roundly condemned the idea.
    b. the Social Security system was unpopular.
    c. it was expected that the Supreme Court would probably rule such a plan unconstitutional.
    d. the Ways and Means Committee adamantly opposed the idea.
    e. all of the above.
18. The text suggests the powerful House Ways and Means Committee chairman Wilbur Mills of Arkansas changed his position with regard to the creation of a health care program because
    a. he realized the bill would pass and he wanted to help shape its form.
    b. the Republicans had gained seats in the House in the recent election.
    c. Republicans outnumbered Democrats on the Ways and Means Committee.
    d. he had a strong sense that he would not be re-elected if he remained in opposition to the program.
    e. Lyndon Johnson promised him a position in the cabinet.
19. The __________ government program provides medical assistance for poor people.
    a. Medicare
    b. Poverty Fund
    c. Medifund
    d. Medicaid
    e. Temporary Assistance to Needy Families (TANF)

20. Under existing law, persons born after 1959 can receive full or partial Social Security benefits when they turn
    a. 60
    b. 65
    c. 67
    d. 70
    e. 75
21. Currently workers pay about ____ percent of their wages to Social Security payroll taxes.
    a. 3.5
    b. 4.7
    c. 5.8
    d. 6.2
    e. 6.7
22. A national advisory commission examined the Social Security crisis and proposed to President Clinton that
    a. the retirement age be raised to eighty-five.
    b. retirement benefits be increased.
    c. Social Security taxes be lowered.
    d. the program be privatized.
    e. citizens be allowed to invest some portion of Social Security taxes in mutual funds.
23. Which of the following options for rescuing Social Security is especially popular with younger voters?
    a. the retirement age be raised to eighty-five.
    b. retirement benefits be increased.
    c. Social Security taxes be lowered.
    d. the program be privatized.
    e. citizens be allowed to invest some portion of Social Security taxes in mutual funds.
24. Which of the following is *not* a problem under Medicare?
    a. Some doctors charge the government for their services.
    b. A lot of people use medical services when they really do not need them.
    c. There is fraud and abuse.
    d. Old people are not generally considered to be "deserving" recipients.
    e. Doctors and hospitals are paid on the basis of a government-approved payment plan.
25. Although AFDC involved giving federal aid to existing state programs, Washington insisted that states
    a. use a federal calculation for applicants' incomes.
    b. establish mandatory job-training programs for many recipients.
    c. provide child-care programs for working AFDC parents.
    d. identify the fathers of the children of recipients.
    e. all of the above.
26. Over the years, AFDC recipients were eligible for what new program?
    a. Medicare
    b. Earned Income Tax Credit
    c. Unemployment compensation
    d. Private School Voucher Program
    e. Workman's compensation

27. By 1994, about _________ of AFDC mothers had been on it for eight years or longer.
    a. one-eighth
    b. one-fourth
    c. one-third
    d. one-half
    e. two-thirds
28. Which statement accurately describes the ultimate fate of AFDC?
    a. It was reformed in 1996 but is scheduled to expire in 2008.
    b. It was abolished in 1996 and replaced by a block grant program, TANF.
    c. It was restructured in a manner that eliminated fraud and increased federal control.
    d. It was supported by so many special interests there was no hope of significant change.
    e. Congress incorporated the program under three categorical grants.
29. Under TANF, welfare caseloads nationally have
    a. decreased significantly.
    b. decreased slightly.
    c. remained about the same as they were under AFDC.
    d. increased slightly from the days of AFDC.
    e. increased significantly from the days of AFDC.
30. Programs such as Social Security and Medicare are the product of
    a. client politics.
    b. association politics.
    c. majoritarian politics.
    d. interest-group politics.
    e. entrepreneurial politics.
31. The big debate in 1935 and 1965 over Social Security and Medicare was over
    a. whether the public wanted them.
    b. whether they were too costly.
    c. whether they constituted unnecessary duplication.
    d. whether they were needed.
    e. whether it was legitimate for government to provide them.
32. Charles Murray argued that social welfare programs
    a. were unconstitutional.
    b. made going on welfare more attractive than to look for a job.
    c. were generally successful in lifting people out of poverty.
    d. discouraged women from having children without being married.
    e. were economically sound but a low priority.
33. In *Zelman* v.*v. Simmons-Harris* (2002), the Supreme Court ruled school voucher programs are constitutional so long as
    a. there is true private choice.
    b. school officials are supportive of applicants.
    c. students are not segregated on the basis of gender.
    d. teachers are educated in secular colleges and universities.
    e. textbooks are purchased by private/ individual funds.

ESSAY QUESTIONS

Practice writing extended answers to the following questions. These test your ability to integrate and express the ideas that you have been studying in this chapter.

1. What are the two general types of social welfare programs in the United States and the biggest problems associated with them?
2. Identify and explain the four factors which have shaped social welfare policy in the United States.
3. Americans tend to think in terms of offering social welfare benefits to those who "deserve" them. Explain the major alternative to this approach that is dominant in other countries.
4. Explain why social welfare policies were much easier to adopt in Great Britain and why such policies appeared there much earlier in history than they did in the United States.
5. Note four examples of social welfare programs which are assistance or "noncontributory" programs and explain what specific assistance they provide.
6. Discuss 4–5 proposals that have been suggested for reforming social security and note which proposals seem to have more public support than others.
7. What are three problems that are created by the Medicare program?
8. Explain two possible solutions to the Medicare program that are presented in the text.
9. How did federal action regarding AFDC created friction between states and the federal government?
10. Explain how the composition of persons accepting AFDC and dependency on the program changed over the years.
11. Discuss the politics of school vouchers. How have the major parties aligned themselves on this issue. How was the issue affected by No Child Left Behind and how has the Supreme Court ruled on the topic?
12. Summarize the controversial position of Charles Murray's *Losing Ground.*

ANSWERS TO KEY TERMS MATCH QUESTIONS

1. v
2. n
3. g
4. o
5. x
6. q
7. b
8. u
9. d
10. y
11. z
12. s
13. a
14. w
15. h
16. j
17. r
18. m
19. l
20. t
21. p
22. e
23. i
24. c
25. k
26. f

ANSWERS TO DATA CHECK QUESTIONS

1. Norway.
2. The United States appears to compare well, topping almost all of the other nations in the Table.

ANSWERS TO TRUE/FALSE QUESTIONS

1. T
2. T

3. T
4. F Americans tend to reject the fair share logic and tend to think in terms of who is deserving of assistance.
5. F Our policies have tended to favor the provision of services and training, as opposed to providing cash.
6. T
7. T
8. T
9. F The government does not require this.
10. F Bush has been a major supporter of Charitable Choice and would like to see the program expanded.
11. F Several alternative—and more radical—plans were being touted by the likes of Huey Long and Upton Sinclair.
12. T
13. T
14. T
15. T
16. T
17. F Its costs are huge and it is an inefficient program as well.
18. T
19. T
20. T
21. T
22. T
23. F At least half of them in several large cities were.
24. T
25. T
26. T
27. F Those programs would represent a service strategy.
28. T
29. T
30. F Republicans, including President Bush, have been the strongest supporters of the program.
31. F Kennedy was one of the Act's' major co-sponsors.
32. F The Court has ruled such plans are constitutional so long as there is a "real choice" among private schools.
33. F The public seemed to support the Act, giving President Bush high marks for its passage.

ANSWERS TO MULTIPLE CHOICE QUESTIONS

1. e
2. a
3. b
4. a
5. c
6. a
7. e
8. c
9. a
10. c
11. e
12. e
13. e
14. b
15. b
16. e
17. d
18. a
19. d
20. c
21. d
22. e
23. e
24. d
25. e
26. b
27. e
28. b
29. a
30. c
31. e
32. b
33. a

CHAPTER 20

Foreign Policy and Military Policy

REVIEWING THE CHAPTER

CHAPTER FOCUS

This chapter presents a survey of selected topics in United States foreign policy (or rather policies), focusing on the political processes involved in arriving at those policies. After reading and reviewing the material in this chapter, you should be able to do each of the following:

1. List the constitutional powers of the president and compare them with the authority of Congress in foreign affairs. Indicate why it is naive to read the Constitution literally in order to determine which institution has the major responsibility to conduct foreign policy. Explain why the president has a larger role than the Framers intended.

2. Compare the president's powers with those of a prime minister in a parliamentary system.

3. Explain why checks on the powers of the national government in foreign affairs are primarily political rather than constitutional.

4. Give reasons for the volatility of public opinion on foreign affairs. Explain the advantages that the president obtains when he acts resolutely in crises. Describe the problems that the president may face, using public opinion on the Vietnam War as an example.

5. Explain the worldview concept, and describe the containment strategy of Mr. X. Summarize essential elements of the Munich–Pearl Harbor and post-Vietnam worldviews. Discuss the revisionist argument that it is the material interests of elites, rather than their principles, that explain American foreign policy. Indicate the potential objections to this view.

6. Explain how the condition of the defense industry makes necessary a follow-up system in the distribution of contracts. Indicate the extent to which client defense politics affects U.S. industry, and compare the performance of defense contractors with that of similar non-defense companies.

7. Explain the events which led up to the War and Iraq and explain how the War has affected public opinion differently than previous wars.

8. Explain why the cost-overrun problem is primarily the result of bureaucratic rather than political factors, and describe proposed reforms of the system.

9. Explain why the 1947 and 1949 Defense Reorganization Acts prevented the merger of services in the Defense Department. Review the current structure of the department, and explain how it contributes to inter-service rivalries. Explain why presidents find it difficult to use the Joint Chiefs of Staff to control defense policy making. Discuss the reforms adopted in 1986.

STUDY OUTLINE

I. Introduction
  A. Effects of the 9/11 attacks
    1. Public consciousness about international terrorism
    2. Outbursts of patriotism
    3. Confidence in government
    4. Emergence of important fundamental questions
      a) How to wage a "war" against terrorism?
      b) How to hold other nations accountable?
      c) How to act when other nations fight terrorism?
      d) Does such a war require military to be redesigned?
    5. Reemergence of classic questions
      a) Do we only support nations that are reasonably free and democratic?
      b) Are we the world's policemen?
  B. Democratic politics and foreign and military policy
    1. Tocqueville and weakness of democracy
    2. Others blame reckless policies of presidents
II. Kinds of foreign policy
  A. Majoritarian politics
    1. Perceived to confer widespread benefits, impose widespread costs
    2. Examples
      a) War
      b) Military alliances
      c) Nuclear test-ban or strategic arms-limitation treaties
      d) Response to Berlin blockade by Soviets
      e) Cuban missile crisis
      f) Covert CIA operations
      g) Diplomatic recognition of People's Republic of China
  B. Interest group politics
    1. Identifiable groups pitted against one another for costs, benefits
    2. Examples
      a) Cyprus policy: Greeks versus Turks
      b) Tariffs: Japanese versus steel
  C. Client politics
    1. Benefits to identifiable group, without apparent costs to any distinct group
    2. Example: Israel policy (transformation to interest-group politics?)
  D. Who has power?
    1. Majoritarian politics: president dominates; public opinion supports but does not guide
    2. Interest group or client politics: larger congressional role
    3. Entrepreneurial politics: Congress the central political arena
III. The constitutional and legal context
  A. The Constitution creates an "invitation to struggle"
    1. President commander in chief but Congress appropriates money
    2. President appoints ambassadors, but Senate confirms
    3. President negotiates treaties, but Senate ratifies
    4. But Americans think president in charge, which history confirms
  B. Presidential box score
    1. Presidents relatively strong in foreign affairs
      a) More successes in Congress on foreign than on domestic affairs

b) Unilateral commitments of troops upheld but stronger than Framers intended

2. Presidents comparatively weak in foreign affairs; other heads of state find U.S. presidents unable to act
   a) Wilson and Franklin Roosevelt unable to ally with Great Britain before World War I and World War II
   b) Wilson unable to lead U.S. into the League of Nations
   c) Reagan criticized on commitments to El Salvador and Lebanon
   d) Bush debated Congress on declaration of Gulf War

C. Evaluating the power of the president
1. Depends on one's agreement/disagreement with policies
2. Supreme Court gives federal government wide powers; reluctant to intervene in Congress-president disputes
   a) Nixon's enlarging of Vietnam War
   b) Lincoln's illegal measures during Civil War
   c) Carter's handling of Iranian assets
   d) Franklin Roosevelt's "relocation" of 100,000 Japanese-Americans

D. Checks on presidential power: political rather than constitutional
1. Congress: control of purse strings
2. Limitations on the president's ability to give military or economic aid to other countries
   a) Arms sales to Turkey
   b) Blockage of intervention in Angola
   c) Legislative veto (previously) on large sale of arms
3. War Powers Act of 1973
   a) Provisions
      (1) Only sixty-day commitment of troops without declaration of war
      (2) All commitments reported within forty-eight hours
      (3) Legislative veto (previously) to bring troops home
   b) Observance
      (1) No president has acknowledged constitutionality
      (2) Ford, Carter, Reagan, Bush, and Clinton sent troops without explicit congressional authorization
   c) Supreme Court action (*Chadha* case)
      (1) Struck down the legislative veto
      (2) Other provisos to be tested
   d) Effect of act doubtful even if upheld
      (1) Brief conflicts not likely to be affected; Congress has not challenged a successful operation
      (2) Even extended hostilities continue: Vietnam and Lebanon
4. Intelligence oversight
   a) Only two committees today, not the previous eight
   b) No authority to disapprove covert action
   c) But "covert" actions less secret after congressional debate
   d) Congress sometimes blocks covert action: Boland Amendment
   e) Congressional concern about CIA after attacks of 9/11
      (1) Creation of the Office of the Director of National Intelligence (DNI)
      (2) Coordinates the work of the CIA, FBI, DIA and the intelligence units of several other government agencies
      (3) Director of DNI is the president's chief advisor

IV. The machinery of foreign policy
  A. Consequences of major power status
    1. President more involved in foreign affairs
    2. More agencies shape foreign policy
  B. Numerous agencies not really coordinated by anyone
  C. Secretary of State unable to coordinate
    1. Job too big for one person
    2. Most agencies owe no political or bureaucratic loyalty
  D. National Security Council created to coordinate
    1. Chaired by president and includes vice president, secretaries of State and Defense, director of CIA, chair of joint chiefs
    2. National security adviser heads staff
    3. Goal of staff is balanced view
    4. Grown in influence since Kennedy but downgraded by Reagan
    5. NSC rivals secretary of state
  E. Consequences of multicentered decision-making machinery
    1. "It's never over" because of rivalries within and between branches
    2. Agency positions influenced by agency interests
    3. CIA and Defense Department leaking information to the press
V. Foreign policy and public opinion
  A. Outlines of foreign policy shaped by public and elite opinion
    1. Before World War II, public opposed U.S. involvement
    2. World War II shifted popular opinion because
      a) Universally popular war
      b) War successful
      c) United States emerged as world's dominant power
    3. Support for active involvement persisted until Vietnam
      a) Growing sense that we should be "independent" of world affairs
      b) Little sense of obligation to help other nations when threatened by communism
    4. 9/11 generated support for war in Afghanistan and addressing the Taliban
    5. Still, the internationalist perspective on foreign policy is mushy and volatile
      a) It is highly general and
      b) Heavily dependent on phrasing of poll questions, opinions of popular leaders, and the impact of world events
  B. Backing the president
    1. Public's tendency to support president in crises
      a) Foreign crises increases presidential level of public approval
      b) Strong support to rally 'round the flag for some but not all foreign military crises
    2. Presidential support does not decrease with casualties
      a) The body bag fallacy
      b) Support for escalation and victory
    3. Most wars have generated some public opposition
      a) Iraq in comparison with Korea and Vietnam
      b) Highest levels of opposition from: Democrats, African Americans, and those with postgraduate degrees
  C. Mass versus elite opinion
    1. Mass opinion
      a) Generally poorly informed
      b) Generally supportive of president
      c) Conservative, less internationalist

2. Elite opinion
    a) Better informed
    b) Opinions change more rapidly (Vietnam)
    c) Protest on moral or philosophical grounds
    d) More liberal and internationalist

VI. Cleavages among foreign policy elites
  A. Foreign policy elite divided
  B. How a worldview shapes foreign policy
    1. Definition of *worldview:* comprehensive mental picture of world issues facing the United States and ways of responding
    2. Example: Mr. X's article on containment of USSR
    3. Not unanimously accepted but consistent with public's mood, events, and experience
  C. Four worldviews
    1. Isolation paradigm
      a) Opposes involvement in European wars
      b) Adopted after World War I because war accomplished little
    2. Appeasement (containment) paradigm
      a) Reaction to appeasement of Hitler in Munich
      b) Pearl Harbor ended isolationism in United States
      c) Postwar policy to resist Soviet expansionism
    3. Disengagement ("Vietnam") paradigm
      a) Reaction to military defeat and political disaster of Vietnam
      b) Crisis interpreted in three ways
        (1) Correct worldview but failed to try hard enough
        (2) Correct worldview but applied in wrong place
        (3) Worldview itself wrong
      c) Critics believed worldview wrong and new one based on new isolationism needed
      d) Elites with disengagement view in Carter administration but were replaced during Reagan and Bush administrations
    4. Human rights
      a) Clinton had a disinterest in foreign policy and his advisors believed in disengagement
      b) Clinton's strongest congressional supporters argued against the Gulf War but advocated military intervention in Kosovo
      c) Change in view explained by concern for human rights and belief that situation in Kosovo amounted to genocide
      d) Conservatives who supported containment in Gulf War urged disengagement in Kosovo
    5. The politics of coalition building
      a) Should the United States act "alone?"
      b) If so, in what circumstances?
    6. Political polarization
      a) Korea
        (1) Produced divisions in Congress
        (2) Exacerbated after the firing of General Douglas MacArthur
        (3) Calls for Truman's impeachment
        (4) But country was not so split along partisan lines
      b) Vietnam
        (1) Divided political elites even more
        (2) Journalists and members of Congress took sharply opposing sides

(3) Democratic and Republican voters were about the same—half thinking the war was a mistake

c) Iraq

(1) Polarization has replaced bipartisanship

(2) Democrats in opposition, Republicans in support

VII. The Use of Military Force

A. Military power more important after collapse of Soviet Union and end of Cold War

1. Military force used to attack Iraq, defend Kosovo, maintain order in Bosnia, and occupy Haiti and Somalia

2. Several nations have long-range rockets and weapons of mass destruction

3. Many nations feel threatened by neighbors

4. Russia still has nuclear weapons

B. Majoritarian view of military

1. Almost all Americans benefit, almost all pay

2. President is the commander-in-chief

3. Congress plays largely a supportive role

C. Client view of military

1. Real beneficiaries of military spending—generals, admirals, big corporations, members of Congress whose districts get fat defense contracts—but everyone pays

2. Military-industrial complex shapes what is spent

D. War in Iraq

1. Prelude to the conflict

a) Iraqi Army under Saddam Hussein invaded Kuwait (1990)

b) United Nations demanded withdrawal and authorized use of force

c) Coalition forces attacked in January 1991

d) Iraqis retreated but Hussein was still in power

e) 12 year no-fly zone and U.N. inspectors (weapons of mass destruction)

f) Hussein expels U.N. inspectors in 1997

2. Invasion, March 2003

a) U.N. did not support the invasion

b) Iraqi army was defeated in six weeks but no WMDs were found

c) Interim parliament, constitution and new government followed

d) Insurgents remained and American support declined

VIII. The defense budget

A. Total spending

1. Small peacetime military until 1950

a) No disarmament after Korea because of Soviet threat

b) Military system designed to repel Soviet invasion of Europe and small-scale invasions

2. Public opinion supports a large military

3. Demise of USSR produced debate

a) Liberals: sharp defense cuts; United States should not serve as world's police officer

b) Conservatives: some cuts but retain well-funded military because world still dangerous

4. Desert Storm and Kosovo campaigns made clear no escaping U.S. need to use military force

5. Kosovo campaign indicated that military had been reduced too much

6. Clinton and Republican Congress called for more military spending

IX. What do we buy with our money?
  A. Changing circumstances make justification of expenditures complex
    1. World War II and Cold War: big armies, artillery, tanks, ships, etc.
    2. War on Terrorism: small groups, special forces, high-tech communications, precision guided bombs, and rockets
    3. Joint operations now also seem more necessary
  B. Secretary of defense
    1. Must transform conventional military for wars on terrorism
    2. Must budget in an atmosphere of debate and pressure from members of both the military and Congress
  C. Debating big new weapons
    1. Washington folks are used to it (B-1, B-2 bombers, MX missiles, M1 tank, etc.)
    2. Strategic Defense Initiative (SDI, or "Star Wars") debate particularly protracted
      a) Major scientific and philosophical quarrels
      b) Reluctance among the military
        (1) Mutually Assured Destruction (MAD) requires more missiles and bombers
        (2) SDI may reduce spending on missiles and bombers
      c) Concern MAD only works against rational leaders

X. What do we get for our money?
  A. Personnel
    1. From draft to all-volunteer force in 1973
    2. Volunteer force improved as result of
      a) Increases in military pay
      b) Rising civilian unemployment
    3. Changes in military
      a) More women in military
      b) Ban of women on combat ships lifted in 1993 but Congress to be consulted if ground combat involved
      c) "Don't ask, don't tell" compromise adopted by Clinton on homosexuals in military
  B. Big-ticket hardware
    1. Main reasons for cost overruns
      a) Unpredictability of cost of new items
      b) Contractor incentives to underestimate at first
      c) Military chiefs want best weapons money can buy
      d) "Sole sourcing" of weapons without competitive bids
      e) Holding down budget by "stretching out" production
    2. Latter four factors can be controlled; first cannot
  C. Readiness, favorite area for short-term budget cutting
    1. Other cuts would hurt constituents
    2. Cuts here show up quickly in money saved
  D. Bases
    1. At one time, a lot of bases opened and few closed
    2. Commission on Base Realignment and Closure created to take client politics out of base closings

XI. Structure of defense decision-making
  A. National Security Act of 1947
    1. Department of Defense
      a) Secretary of Defense (civilian, as are secretaries of the army, navy, and air force)
      b) Joint Chiefs of Staff (military)

2. Reasons for separate uniformed services
   a) Fear that unified military will become too powerful
   b) Desire of services to preserve their autonomy
   c) Interservice rivalries intended by Congress to receive maximum information

B. 1986 defense reorganization plan
1. Joint Chiefs of Staff
   a) Composed of uniformed head of each service with a chair and vice chair appointed by the president and confirmed by the Senate
   b) Chair since 1986 principal military adviser to president
2. Joint Staff
   a) Officers from each service assisting JCS
   b) Since 1986 serves chair; promoted at same rate
3. The services
   a) Each service headed by a civilian secretary responsible for purchasing and public affairs
   b) Senior military officer oversees discipline and training
4. The chain of command
   a) Chair of JCS does not have combat command
   b) Uncertainty whether 1986 changes will work

XII. The New Problem of Terrorism
A. Clarity of policy goals during Cold War is now lost
B. Transition from a bi-polar world to a unipolar world
C. The Bush doctrine (September 2002)
1. Addressing threats before they are fully formed
2. Acting alone if necessary
3. Consideration: doctrine of pre-emption is not new
   a) Standard views of supporters and critics
   b) Positions are often influenced by partisanship and political ideology

D. Support of the United Nations
1. Sought and obtained in Korea (1951) and Kuwait (1991)
2. Not sought in North Vietnam (1950s), Haiti (1994), Bosnia (1994) or Kosovo (1999)
3. Sought, but not obtained for Iraq (2003)

E. Rebuilding nations
1. Positive experiences: Germany and Japan
2. Negative experiences: Somalia and Haiti
3. Making progress: Bosnia and Kosovo
4. New projects: Afghanistan and Iraq
5. Correlates of success (or lessons learned)
   a) Do not leave too quickly
   b) Organize agencies so they can work together and learn from the past
   c) Make certain civilian and military operations are carefully coordinated

KEY TERMS MATCH

Set 1

Match the following terms and descriptions:

1. A policy perceived to confer wide benefits, and impose wide costs
2. A deep and wide conflict over some government policy
3. A policy perceived to confer benefits on one group and costs on another
4. A policy perceived to benefit distinct groups but not to cost others
5. A stoppage by the USSR of Allied access to Germany's capital
6. Case in which the Supreme Court upheld the presidential decision to send Japanese Americans to relocation camps
7. The situation that followed the USSR's installation of hostile missiles in the Caribbean
8. An alleged alliance between military leaders and corporate leaders
9. A cabinet-level body charged with the execution of foreign policy
10. The agency charged with collecting sensitive foreign information
11. The committee appointed by statute that advises the president on foreign policy
12. International agreements submitted to the Senate for approval
13. International agreements not submitted to the Senate for approval
14. When the money actually paid to military suppliers exceeds the estimated costs
15. Schlesinger's depiction of presidential power under Nixon
16. A proviso allowing Congress to overrule the president's actions

a. antiappeasement
b. Berlin blockade
c. *Chadha*
d. CIA
e. client foreign policy
f. cold war
g. commander in chief
h. containment
i. cost overruns
j. Council on Foreign Relations
k. Cuban missile crisis
l. disengagement view
m. domino theory
n. executive agreements
o. gold plating
p. imperial presidency
q. interest-group foreign policy
r. iron curtain
s. isolationism
t. *Korematsu* v. *United States*
u. legislative veto
v. majoritarian foreign policy
w. military-industrial complex
x. multinational corporation
y. Munich
z. NSC
aa. Pearl Harbor
bb. polarization
cc. Rally 'Round the Flag effect

17. Legislation passed in 1973 that attempted to limit the president's power to make war
18. The group of developing nations in Africa, Asia, Latin America, and the Middle East
19. A Supreme Court case voiding the legislative veto in the War Powers Act
20. The constitutional role played by the president in time of war
21. A private but powerful foreign policy think tank funded by the Rockefellers
22. The tendency of Pentagon officials to ask weapons contractors to meet excessively high requirements
23. A relatively consistent picture of the world problems facing the United States
24. The U.S. strategy that has dominated its post-World War II policy on the USSR
25. Weapons of mass destruction
26. Where Neville Chamberlain sought peace through appeasement
27. The site of the Japanese attack on U.S. naval forces in 1941
28. Churchill's view of the barrier separating the Western powers from the USSR-dominated countries after World War II
29. Refers to the tendency of public support for the president to increase in the time of a foreign policy crises
30. A business operating in more than one country
31. The worldview that emerged as a result of World War II and in particular as a reaction to the Munich conference
32. The worldview that emerged in the aftermath of the Vietnam War suggesting that the United States ought to limit foreign intervention

dd. State Department

ee. Third World

ff. treaties

gg. War Powers Act

hh. WMD

ii. worldview

33. The nonmilitary struggle between the United States (and its allies) and the former Soviet Union (and its allies) following World War II

34. The theory that if one nation fell into communist hands, neighboring nations would follow

35. The view that the United States should withdraw from world affairs, limit foreign aid, and avoid involvement in foreign wars

Set 2

Match the following terms and descriptions:

1. Participants in client politics in U.S. defense spending
2. Legislation enacted in 1947 that created the current Department of Defense
3. Competition among the army, navy, air force, and marines
4. Congressional bodies charged with oversight of the military
5. The decision hierarchy, starting with the president at the top and including the Secretary of Defense and various unified and specified commands
6. Money presumably made available for "butter" as a consequence of cuts in military spending
7. A group of several hundred officers from the four services who assist the Joint Chiefs of Staff
8. A committee consisting of the heads of the four military services plus an appointed chair and vice chair
9. The procedure by which new weapons are purchased from a single contractor
10. Controversial defense weapons system
11. The 1991 war in the Persian Gulf involving U.S. troops

a. chain of command
b. defense reorganization plan
c. Desert Storm
d. House Armed Services Committee
e. interservice rivalry
f. Joint Chiefs of Staff
g. Joint Staff
h. military-industrial complex
i. National Security Act
j. peace dividend
k. readiness
l. "sole sourcing"
m. Strategic Defense Initiative (SDI)

12. Training, supplies, munitions, fuel, and food
13. A plan signed in 1986 that increased the power of officers who coordinate the activities of different services

DATA CHECK

Table 20.1 (Page 535): Popular Reactions to Foreign Policy Crises

1. What general conclusion can be drawn regarding the effect of a foreign policy crisis on the president's approval rating?

____

2. Which crisis features the least amount of positive change in the "before" and "after" columns?

____

3. Which two crises are associated with downward trends in the level of public approval?

____

Table 20.2 (Page 537): How the Public and the Elite See Foreign Policy, 2004

Indicate whether the following views would most likely be expressed by the average member of the public or by a foreign policy leader.

4. We should protect the jobs of American workers.

____

5. U.S. troops should support South Korea if North Korea attacks.

____

6. Reducing illegal immigration is very important.

____

Figure 20.1 (Page 544): Trends in Military Spending

7. Which presidents noticeably increased military spending after taking office?

____

8. Which presidents noticeably decreased military spending after taking office?

____

Figure 20.2 (Page 545): Public Sentiment on Defense Spending, 1969–2002

9. What sentiment has been expressed most often by Americans since 1973?

____

PRACTICING FOR EXAMS

TRUE/FALSE QUESTIONS

Read each statement carefully. Mark true statements *T.* If any part of the statement is false, mark it *F,* and write in the space provided a concise explanation of why the statement is false.

1. T F Tocqueville argued that democratic nations were the best adapted to handle foreign affairs.

2. T F Foreign policy decisions are best described as a mix of majoritarian, interest-group and client politics.

3. T F The decision to go to war is a function of majoritarian politics.

4. T F The U.S. policy toward Israel is regarded by the text as an example of majoritarian politics.

5. T F Congress plays a larger role in foreign policy when majoritarian politics is involved.

6. T F The president plays the critical role when foreign policy is shaped by entrepreneurial politics.

7. T F It would be accurate to say the president has the power to "make" war, but Congress has the power to "declare" war.

8. T F The Defense Department is very much under the control of Congress on matters of military strategy.

9. T F Historically, presidents have signed more treaties than they have executive agreements.

10. T F Executive agreements carry the force of law, but do not have to be ratified by the Senate.

11. T F In 1940, President Roosevelt sent fifty destroyers to England to help fight Germany even though we were technically at peace.

12. T F John F. Kennedy waited until Congress issued a declaration of war before sending troops into South Vietnam.

13. T F U.S. presidents have less freedom in foreign affairs than do most other Western heads of state.

____

14. T F Most executive agreements are authorized by Congress in advance.

____

15. T F The Supreme Court has consistently held that the federal government has foreign policy powers beyond those enumerated in the Constitution.

____

16. T F In the World War II era, no Japanese American was ever found guilty of espionage or sabotage.

____

17. T F Congress has yet to use its power to restrict the president's granting military or economic aid to foreign countries.

____

18. T F In *Chadha*, the Supreme Court upheld the constitutionality of the War Powers Act.

____

19. T F The State Department generally favors bold and controversial policies that upset established relationships with other countries.

____

20. T F Before Pearl Harbor, most Americans seemed to oppose U.S. entry into World War II.

____

21. T F If there is an attack on the United States, one should generally expect the approval ratings of the president to fall in a dramatic fashion.

____

22. T F As wars continue, Americans usually become more determined to win them.

____

23. T F The public is poorly informed about foreign affairs.

____

24. T F Public opinion was very much on the side of anti-war protestors at the 1968 Democratic National Convention in Chicago.

____

25. T F Americans want to give less economic aid to other nations.

____

26. T F The world views which guide foreign policy leaders do so irrespective of public opinion.

____

27. T F The antiappeasement approach to foreign policy emerged at the end of the Vietnam War.

____

28. T F The disengagement worldview held that the Munich worldview had not merely been misapplied but was fundamentally wrong.

____

29. T F With respect to the Vietnam conflict, American public opinion did not divide along party lines.

____

30. T F The military-industrial complex theory of defense procurement portrays military spending as an example of majoritarian politics.

____

31. T F The situation in Iraq contributed to the loss of Republican seats in the 2006 congressional election.

____

32. T F The size of the military budget, says the text, is best explained by majoritarian politics.

____

33. T F There has been a steady decline in the percentage of women in the military.

____

34. T F The opening and closing of military bases is a good example of client politics.

____

35. T F The four branches of the military are four separate entities and cannot by law be commanded by a single military officer.

____

36. T F The Joint Chiefs of Staff are charged with the execution of national defense policy.

____

37. T F George Bush's doctrine of preemption was a new approach to international affairs.

____

38. T F Most liberal Democrats opposed our efforts to get Iraq out of Kuwait.

____

39. T F The United States has never sought support from the United Nations, failed to get it, and attacked another nation anyway.

____

40. T F The United States has consistently failed at rebuilding nations after an attack.

____

41. T F The State Department and the Defense Department are usually in agreement and speak with one voice.

____

MULTIPLE CHOICE QUESTIONS

Circle the letter of the response that best answers the question or completes the statement.

1. The division of constitutional authority between the president and Congress is *best* characterized as
   a. congressional dominance.
   b. presidential dominance.
   c. an "invitation to struggle."
   d. "provocative silence."
   e. a true case of controversy.
2. Which statement is *incorrect*?
   a. The president is commander in chief of the armed forces.
   b. Congress must authorize and appropriate money for our armed forces.
   c. The president appoints ambassadors, but they must be confirmed by the Senate.
   d. The president negotiates treaties but they must be ratified by a majority of the Senate.
   e. Only Congress can regulate commerce with other nations.
3. Presidents have asserted the right to send troops aboard on their own authority in more than _____ instances.
   a. 6
   b. 13
   c. 30
   d. 90
   e. 125
4. Of the thirteen major wars fought by this country, ____ have followed a formal declaration of war by Congress.
   a. three
   b. six
   c. ten
   d. twelve
   e. thirteen
5. The Supreme Court has generally held the view that the conduct of foreign affairs
   a. is chiefly a congressional responsibility.
   b. is chiefly a presidential responsibility.
   c. involves important constitutional rights.
   d. is a political question for Congress and the president to work out.
   e. is best handled by the lower federal courts.
6. The most important congressional check on the president in the area of foreign affairs is the power to
   a. impeach.
   b. control the purse strings.
   c. approve ambassadors.
   d. reorganize those federal agencies that make foreign policy—the State Department, the CIA, and so forth.
   e. restrict access to the White House.
7. The War Powers Act of 1973 was designed as a check on the
   a. president.
   b. Courts.
   c. CIA.
   d. Pentagon.
   e. congressional hawks.

8. The War Powers Act calls for Congress to provide a formal declaration or statutory authorization within ________ after troops are sent into a hostile situation.
   a. forty-eight hours
   b. one week
   c. two weeks
   d. sixty days
   e. six months
9. According to the text,
   a. the Director of the CIA authored the War Powers Act.
   b. the Pentagon whole-heartedly supported the War Powers Act.
   c. every president has obeyed the War Powers Act.
   d. every president but Clinton has obeyed the War Powers Act.
   e. no president has acknowledged that the War Powers Act is constitutional.
10. The Boland Amendment attempted to regulate
   a. covert operations.
   b. the gathering of electronic intelligence.
   c. signals intelligence.
   d. U.S. efforts to influence elections in Western Europe.
   e. all of the above.
11. From the administration of George Washington to well into the twentieth century, the ________ generally made and carried out foreign policy.
   a. president
   b. Secretary of State
   c. president's cabinet
   d. foreign ambassadors of the U.S.
   e. vice president
12. When America became a major world power after World War II,
   a. presidents began to put foreign policy at the top of the agenda.
   b. our commitments overseas expanded dramatically.
   c. presidents began to play a larger role in the implementation of foreign policy.
   d. foreign policy began to be shaped by scores of agencies with overseas activities.
   e. all of the above.
13. Attempts by each new secretary of state to "coordinate" or "direct" the foreign policy establishment are generally fruitless because most agencies
   a. are focused on specific tasks and oblivious to broad visions or general directions.
   b. rarely communicate with each other.
   c. are too disorganized to direct in any intelligent way.
   d. owe no political or bureaucratic loyalty to the secretary of state.
   e. are under constant review by Congress.
14. Beginning with the ________ administration, the National Security Council has grown in influence.
   a. Roosevelt
   b. Truman
   c. Kennedy
   d. Eisenhower
   e. Johnson

15. The only war in which public support remained high was
    a. the Korean War.
    b. the Vietnam War.
    c. A and B.
    d. World War II.
    e. World War I.
16. Support for an internationalist American foreign policy is
    a. highly general and heavily dependent on the phrasing of poll questions.
    b. narrowly tailored and specific.
    c. rarely affected by the opinions of popular leaders.
    d. immune to world events.
    e. all of the above.
17. The "rally 'round the flag" effect and boost in presidential approval ratings which typically accompany foreign policy crises were *not* evident when
    a. John F. Kennedy accepted responsibility for the failed invasion of Cuba.
    b. George W. Bush responded to the attack of 9/11.
    c. Ronald Reagan invaded Grenada.
    d. George Bush sent troops to fight Iraq.
    e. Bill Clinton sent forces to Bosnia or launched bombing attacks on Iraq.
18. A careful study of public opinion has concluded that, as American lives are lost during a time of war, the public tends to
    a. desire escalation and swift victory.
    b. seriously rethink the general premises behind our involvement.
    c. withdraw support from its political leaders.
    d. lose faith in our ability to "win."
    e. none of the above.
19. Where foreign policy—particularly declaring and conducting war—is concerned, ________ have the most volatile opinions.
    a. political elites
    b. working-class Americans
    c. women
    d. blacks and other minorities
    e. the elderly
20. Foreign policy leaders are more likely to adopt a ____________ outlook than members of the general public.
    a. nationalistic
    b. liberal and internationalist
    c. conservative
    d. centrist
    e. moderate
21. American elites adopted the isolationist worldview as a result of our experience with
    a. the War Between the States.
    b. World War I.
    c. World War II.
    d. the Korean War.
    e. Vietnam.

22. Containment is also known as
    a. the Vietnam view.
    b. antiappeasement.
    c. the Human Rights view.
    d. preemption.
    e. MADD.
23. The "lessons of Munich," which shaped American foreign policy for a generation, were that
    a. the United States cannot police the world.
    b. nationalism is the predominant force in Third World politics.
    c. aggression could best be met by negotiation and compromise.
    d. aggression should be forcefully opposed.
    e. economic development and foreign aid serve U.S. interests better than military aid.
24. Containment was the policy of
    a. the British and French during the rise of Hitler in Germany.
    b. General Patton.
    c. the United States toward Japan before Pearl Harbor.
    d. Admiral Alfred T. Mahan.
    e. the United States toward Russia after World War II.
25. The disengagement worldview was adopted by younger elites as a result of experience with
    a. the War Between the States.
    b. World War I.
    c. World War II.
    d. the Korean War.
    e. Vietnam.
26. Elites with the __________ worldview played a large role in the Carter administration.
    a. isolationist
    b. containment
    c. disengagement
    d. human rights
    e. antiappeasement
27. Elites with the __________ worldview played a large role in the Reagan administration.
    a. isolationist
    b. containment
    c. disengagement
    d. human rights
    e. antiappeasement
28. When Clinton became president in 1992, he brought with him advisers who were drawn from the ranks of those who believed in
    a. isolationism.
    b. containment.
    c. disengagement.
    d. the human rights perspective.
    e. antiappeasement.

29. Opponents of the Gulf War were supportive of American intervention in Kosovo, suggesting a shift to the _____________ paradigm of foreign policy.
    a. isolationist
    b. containment
    c. disengagement
    d. human rights
    e. antiappeasement
30. Political polarization is quite evident in public opinion regarding
    a. World War II.
    b. the Korean War.
    c. the Vietnam War.
    d. the War in Iraq.
    e. C and D.
31. When Saddam Hussein sent forces into Kuwait in 1990, the United Nations
    a. condemned the behavior.
    b. passed a resolution calling for a truce.
    c. debated the move, but took no action, symbolic or otherwise.
    d. authorized the use of force to repel the force.
    e. supported his decision.
32. After the 1990 invasion of Kuwait, U.N. inspectors were sent to Iraq to look for weapons of mass destruction (WMDs) because
    a. of intelligence reports later proved to be false.
    b. the government of Kuwait insisted upon such inspections.
    c. the U.N. was pressured by Iraq and Syria to conduct such inspections.
    d. international treaties called for such inspections for a period of 5 years.
    e. there was no doubt Hussein had dropped chemical weapons in the past.
33. When U.N. inspectors found evidence of programs to develop weapons of mass destruction in Iraq,
    a. Hussein had them expelled from the country.
    b. Hussein explained that the programs had been abandoned.
    c. they failed to report it for almost 20 years.
    d. they considered their work done and returned to their respective homes.
    e. Iraqi officials blamed Syria for "planting" the materials.
34. The size and the division of the defense budget represent, respectively
    a. entrepreneurial and majoritarian politics.
    b. client and entrepreneurial politics.
    c. majoritarian and interest-group politics.
    d. interest-group and client politics.
    e. reciprocal and club-based politics.
35. The reason for the great increase in the defense budget in 1950 was the
    a. Korean War.
    b. Cuban missile crisis.
    c. escalation of the U.S.-Soviet arms race.
    d. U2 spy plane incident.
    e. oil embargo in the Middle East.

36. In a typical poll, a majority of Americans say that
    a. we are spending far too much on military spending.
    b. we are spending too much on military spending.
    c. we are spending too little or just about the right amount on military spending.
    d. they have no opinions regarding military spending.
    e. they oppose military spending except in a time of war.
37. The text suggests the campaigns in Afghanistan and Iraq made it clear that the United States
    a. was a consensus choice to play the role of "world policeman."
    b. would no longer need to engage in military buildups.
    c. could not operate a military campaign without assistance from other Western democracies.
    d. was vulnerable in the air but superior with respect to ground forces.
    e. had reduced its armed forces sharply and was hard pressed to carry out a sustained military campaign.
38. Bill Clinton promised to lift the official ban on gays and lesbians serving in the military if he were elected, but
    a. the Joint Chiefs of Staff lifted the ban before he had the chance to.
    b. he instead settled with a compromise "don't ask, don't tell" policy.
    c. the Pentagon decided the traditional policy could not be modified in any significant way.
    d. the Democratic National Committee insisted that he detach himself from the issue.
    e. he instead referred the question to a bipartisan committee of members of Congress.
39. Among the causes of defense overruns noted in the text are all of the following *except*
    a. the key players' incentive to underestimate costs going in.
    b. the difficulty of estimating the costs of new programs in advance.
    c. the cumbersome process of competitive bidding even for minor items.
    d. the desire to have the very "best" of everything.
    e. "stretch-outs" used to keep annual budgets low.
40. The Department of Defense was created by the
    a. Marshall Plan.
    b. Twenty-second Amendment.
    c. Twenty-third Amendment.
    d. Truman Doctrine.
    e. National Security Act.
41. The creation of separate uniformed services within a single department reflects the concern that
    a. the military budget would not be kept accountable.
    b. the military budget would not be kept below acceptable levels.
    c. interservice rivalry would escalate.
    d. intelligence sources should not communicate.
    e. a unified military might become too powerful politically.
42. President Bush was *not* the first president to act on the doctrine of preemption but
    a. he was the first to launch cruise missile attacks with preemption in mind.
    b. he did elevate the policy of preemption into a clearly stated national doctrine.
    c. Congress first expressed concerns about the doctrine during his administration.
    d. he was the first to invite Congress to a dialogue on preemption.
    e. he was the first to consider international opinion on the doctrine.

43. We did not seek the support of the United Nations in
    a. fighting against North Vietnam (1960s).
    b. occupying Haiti (1994).
    c. assisting friendly forces in Bosnia (1994).
    d. assisting friendly forces in Kosovo (1999).
    e. all of the above.
44. Which of the following does the text suggest is a "lesson" that we have learned when it comes to rebuilding nations.
    a. Unilateral actions are not successful.
    b. The support of the United Nations is critical.
    c. Do not leave a country too quickly.
    d. Widespread support of the European community is essential to success.
    e. Civilian and military agencies should not be coordinated.
45. In Afghanistan and Iraq, there has been conflict between
    a. the Army and the Marines.
    b. the Army and the State Department.
    c. the State Department and Defense Departments.
    d. military leaders and members of the news media.
    e. full and part-time members of the military.

ESSAY QUESTIONS

Practice writing extended answers to the following questions. These test your ability to integrate and express the ideas that you have been studying in this chapter.

1. Explain the specific reasons why Tocqueville thought democracies are at a disadvantage in a time of war.
2. Provide some examples of how foreign policy reflect majoritarian, interest group and client politics.
3. Describe how the kind of foreign policy that is present will determine in large part whether or not the president or Congress will play a dominant róle.
4. Outline the constitutional powers of the president and Congress.
5. Discuss some famous of examples of Supreme Court decisions regarding presidential action in foreign policy related cases.
6. Write an essay on the War Powers Act in which you outline the major provisions of the act and generalize about its impact.
7. Cite 3-4 examples of what the authors call the "rally 'round the flag" effect. In addition, note some historical examples of exceptions to the general rule.
8. Summarize the manner in which elite opinion and mass opinion differ in terms of information levels, volatility and content (or viewpoint).
9. Describe the four worldviews which are discussed in the text with special attention to events which gave rise to those views, or caused a shift in opinion.
10. Explain what the text means by "political polarization" in foreign policy and describe how the concept related to the wars in Vietnam, Korea and Iraq.
11. Summarize the events which led up to the American invasion of Iraq in 2003.

12. Identify the five major sources of cost-overruns in military contracts.
13. Describe how the politics of base closings before and after 1988.
14. Describe how the United States has acted, in the past, both with and without the support of the United Nations.

ANSWERS TO KEY TERMS MATCH QUESTIONS

Set 1

1. v
2. bb
3. q
4. e
5. b
6. t
7. k
8. w
9. dd
10. d
11. z
12. ff
13. n
14. i
15. p
16. u
17. gg
18. ee
19. c
20. g
21. j
22. o
23. ii
24. h
25. hh
26. y
27. aa
28. r
29. cc
30. x
31. a

32. l
33. f
34. m
35. s

Set 2

1. h
2. i
3. e
4. d
5. a
6. j
7. g
8. f
9. l
10. m
11. c
12. k
13. b

ANSWERS TO DATA CHECK QUESTIONS

1. Foreign policy crises are associated with an increase in positive approval ratings for the president.
2. The U2 spy plane incident (1960) and the failed attempt to rescue hostages from Iran (1980).
3. Troops sent to Bosnia (1995) and Kosovo (1998).
4. Public.
5. Leaders.
6. Public.
7. Nixon and Reagan.
8. Carter and Clinton.
9. "Too little/about right."

ANSWERS TO TRUE/FALSE QUESTIONS

1. F Tocqueville thought democracies are at a disadvantage in a time of war because, among other things, they are impatient and cannot act in secrecy.
2. T
3. T
4. F This would be an example of client politics.

5. F When majoritarian politics are involved, the president plays the leading role in policy making.
6. F Congress is the central political arena for entrepreneurial politics.
7. T
8. T
9. F They have signed over a thousand treaties and around seven thousand executive agreements.
10. T
11. T
12. F Kennedy waited for no such declaration.
13. T
14. T
15. T
16. T
17. F It did so between 1974 and 1978, disallowing the sale of arms to Turkey. It also prevented President Ford from giving aid to a faction in Angola.
18. F The Court actually struck down the legislative veto portion of the act.
19. F It has a stake in long standing diplomacy and established relationships. Bold and innovative plans are thus resisted.
20. T
21. F Such activity is usually associated with a bump up in the president's popularity or approval ratings.
22. T
23. T
24. F The public supported the police in the conflict.
25. T
26. F The text suggests such views prevail, in part, because they are consistent with public opinion.
27. F This view was the result of our experience leading up to World War II.
28. T
29. T
30. F Client politics would be the more appropriate category.
31. T
32. T
33. F There has been a steady increase. Women now make up 20 percent of the force.
34. F It used to be an example of such politics.

35. T
36. F It has no command authority over troops. It only plays a key role in national defense planning.
37. F It was not new. Clinton used the approach. But Bush elevated the policy to a clearly stated national doctrine.
38. T
39. F This happened with respect to Iraq.
40. F The text suggests that the United States has a lot of experience doing this, some good and some bad. The rebuilding of Germany and Japan seem to have worked out quite well.
41. F They usually have different opinions.

ANSWERS TO MULTIPLE CHOICE QUESTIONS

1. c
2. d
3. e
4. b
5. d
6. b
7. a
8. d
9. e
10. a
11. b
12. e
13. d
14. d
15. d
16. a
17. e
18. a
19. a
20. b
21. b
22. b
23. d
24. e

25. e
26. c
27. b
28. c
29. d
30. d
31. d
32. e
33. a
34. c
35. a
36. c
37. e
38. b
39. c
40. e
41. e
42. b
43. e
44. c
45. c

CHAPTER 21

Environmental Policy

REVIEWING THE CHAPTER

CHAPTER FOCUS

Environmental policy, like economic or welfare policy, reflects the unique nature of the American political system. Unlike economic or welfare issues, however, environmental issues lend themselves to entrepreneurial politics, which requires mobilizing the media, dramatizing the issue, and convincing members of Congress that their political reputations will suffer if they do not cast the right vote. It is politics in which an unorganized public benefits at the expense of a well-organized group, such as a manufacturer. After reading and reviewing the material in this chapter, you should be able to do each of the following:

1. List three reasons environmental policy tends to be so controversial, providing examples of each reason.
2. Describe the role of the American political system and local politics in shaping environmental policy. Contrast these with environmental policy-making in England.
3. Distinguish among the following styles of politics in terms of who benefits and who pays: entrepreneurial, majoritarian, interest group, and client.
4. Describe the role of entrepreneurial politics in government's efforts to deal with the issues of global warming and endangered species.
5. Outline the major provisions of the Clean Air Act (1970), the Water Quality Improvement Act (1970), the revised Clean Air Act (1990), and the National Environmental Policy Act (1969).
6. Describe the role of majoritarian politics in government's efforts to reduce automobile emissions. Explain why majoritarian politics worked in some cases and not in others.
7. Describe the role of interest-group politics in government's efforts to resolve the acid rain controversy. List proposed alternative solutions, and outline the terms of the compromise that was reached by Congress and the Bush administration.
8. Describe the role of client politics in government's efforts to regulate the use of agricultural pesticides and timber cutting in U.S. forests.
9. Give three reasons why it is so difficult to develop a sane environmental policy in this country. Provide examples of how the EPA is dealing with these problems.
10. Discuss the results of environmental protection measures that have been taken since 1970.

STUDY OUTLINE

I. Introduction
  A. Why is environmental policy so controversial?
    1. Creates both winners and losers
      a) Losers may be interest groups or average citizens
      b) Losers may not want to pay costs
      Example: auto exhaust control
    2. Shrouded in scientific uncertainty
      Example: greenhouse effect
    3. Takes the form of entrepreneurial politics
      a) Encourages emotional appeals: "good guys" versus "bad guys"
      b) May lead to distorted priorities
      Example: cancer versus water pollution
    4. Decisions affect federal and international relations
      a) State laws on greenhouse gases and toxic waste cleanup
      b) Kyoto Treaty and opposition in the Senate
II. The American context
  A. Environmental policy is shaped by unique features of American politics
    1. More adversarial than in Europe
      a) Rules are often uniform nationally (auto emissions)
      b) But require many regulators and rules, strict deadlines, and expensive technologies
      c) Often government (pro-) versus business (anti-)
      d) Example: Clean Air Act, which took thirteen years to revise in Congress
      e) In England, rules are flexible and regional
        (1) Compliance is voluntary
        (2) Government and business cooperate
        (3) Policies are effective
    2. Depends heavily on states
      a) Standards are left to states, subject to federal control
      b) Local politics decides allocations
      c) Federalism reinforces adversarial politics; separation of powers provides multiple points of access
  B. Types of politics
    1. Entrepreneurial politics
      a) Most people benefit, few companies pay costs
      b) Example: factories and other stationary sources
    2. Majoritarian
      a) Most people benefit, most people pay
      b) Example: air pollution from automobiles
    3. Interest group
      a) Some groups benefit, other groups pay
      b) Example: acid rain controversy
    4. Client
      a) Most people pay, some groups benefit
      b) Example: pesticide control

III. Entrepreneurial politics: global warming
   A. Entrepreneurial politics gave rise to environmental movement
      1. Santa Barbara oil spill, Earth Day
      2. Led to the formation of EPA and passage of the Water Quality Improvement Act and tougher Clean Air Act in 1970
      3. Two years later Congress passed laws designed to clean up water
      4. Three years later Congress adopted the Endangered Species Act
      5. New laws passed into the 1990s
      6. Existing environmental organizations grew in size and new ones formed
      7. Public opinion rallied behind environmental slogans
   B. Global warming
      1. Earth's temperature rises from trapped gases in the atmosphere
      2. Predicted result: floods on coastal areas as the polar ice caps melt; wilder weather as more storms are created; and tropical diseases spread to North America
      3. Difficult questions
         a) Has warming trend been mostly the result of natural climate changes or is it heavily influence by human activity?
         b) What would it cost in lost productivity and income to reduce greenhouse gases?
         c) How large would the gains be to mankind?
      4. Elites, ideology and "the facts"
         a) Environmental activists raise money scaring people about the harms global warming will cause
         b) Conservatives raise money scaring people about economic pain
         c) Activists tend to dominate the discussion
   C. Endangered species
      1. Endangered Species Act of 1973 prohibits buying or selling plants or animals on "endangered" species list
      2. Over six hundred species on list with about half plants
      3. Firms and government agencies seeking to build in areas with endangered species must comply with federal regulations
      4. Complaints outweigh public support for law

IV. Majoritarian politics: pollution from automobiles
   A. Clean Air Act imposed tough restrictions
      1. Public demanded improvements
      2. 1975: 90 percent reduction of hydrocarbons and carbon monoxide
      3. 1976: 90 percent reduction in nitrous oxides
      4. Required catalytic converters
   B. Emergence of majoritarian politics in auto pollution
      1. States were required to restrict public use of cars
         a) If auto emissions controls were insufficient—Los Angeles, Denver, New York—parking bans required, implementation of car pools, gas rationing
         b) Efforts failed: opposition too great
         c) Congress and the EPA backed down, postponed deadlines
      2. Consumers, auto industry, and unions objected
         a) Loss of horsepower
         b) Loss of competitiveness
         c) Loss of jobs
      3. The Clean Air Act was weakened in 1977 but revived in 1990 with tougher standards
   C. Public will support tough laws
      1. If costs are hidden (catalytic converters)

2. But not if they have to change habits (car pools)

D. Majoritarian politics when people believe the costs are low: National Environmental Policy Act of 1969 (NEPA)
 1. Requires environmental impact statement (EIS)
 2. Does not require specific action
 3. Passed Congress with overwhelming support
 4. But encouraged numerous lawsuits that block or delay projects
 5. Popular support remains strong: costs appear low, benefits high

E. Majoritarian politics when people believe the costs are high
 1. Increased gasoline taxes
  a) Would discourage driving, save fuel, and reduce smog
  b) Most would pay, most would benefit
  c) But costs come long before benefits
  d) And benefits may not be obvious
 2. Easier to raise gas tax if benefits are concrete, for example, highways, bridges, and so forth
 3. Other approaches
  a) Tax breaks and incentives for companies seeking to develop alternative energy sources
  b) Incentive to car manufacturers to build vehicles that consume less fuel

V. Interest group politics: acid rain

A. Source of acid rain
 1. Burning of high-sulfur coal in Midwestern factories
 2. Winds carry sulfuric acid eastward
 3. Rains bring acid to earth

B. Effects of acid rain
 1. Acidification of lakes
 2. Destruction of forests
 3. Long-term and some short-term effects are unclear

C. Regional battle
 1. East versus Midwest, Canada versus United States
 2. Midwestern businesses deny blame and costs

D. Solutions and compromise
 1. Burn low-sulfur coal one alternative
  a) Effective but expensive
  b) Low-sulfur coal comes from West, high-sulfur coal is local.
 2. Install smokestack scrubbers a second alternative
  a) Costly, not always effective, and leave sludge
  b) But allow use of inexpensive high-sulfur coal
 3. Congress voted for scrubbers for all new plants
  a) Including those that burned low-sulfur coal
  b) Even if plant was next to low-sulfur coal mine
 4. Political advantages
  a) Protected jobs of high-sulfur coal miners; powerful allies in Congress
  b) Environmentalists preferred scrubbers; "definitive" solution to problem
  c) Scrubber manufacturers preferred scrubbers
  d) Eastern governors preferred scrubbers; made their plants more competitive
 5. Practical disadvantages
  a) Imposed scrubbers on plants right next to mines where they could get low-sulfur coal
  b) Scrubbers didn't work well

c) Failed to address problem of existing plants
6. Stalemate for thirteen years
7. Two-step regulation proposed by Bush
   a) Before 1995: some plants could choose their approach; fixed reduction but plants decide how to do
   b) After 1995: sharper reductions for many more plants, requiring some use of scrubbers
   c) Sulfur dioxide allowances could be bought and sold
   d) Financial compensation for coal miners who lose jobs
8. Became part of Clean Air Act of 1990
9. A host of news laws (and potential battles) in 2004–2005

E. Another example of interest-group politics: zoning regulations, residents versus developers
F. New interest groups
1. More fervent and committed than before
2. Able to block change in policies
3. Examples
   a) Environmental protection industry
   b) Environmental Defense Fund
   c) Labor unions
4. Shifts in public opinion
   a) In 1980s and 1990s, public overwhelmingly rated environmental protection more important than economic growth
   b) By the mid 2000s, importance of economic growth had increased

VI. Client politics: agricultural pesticides
A. Issue: control of use and runoff of pesticides; farmers have mostly resisted policy entrepreneurs, with DDT an exception
B. EPA efforts to evaluate safety of all pesticides
1. Given mandate by Congress in 1972
2. Program has not succeeded
   a) Too many pesticides to evaluate
      (1) Many have only long-term effects needing extended study
      (2) Expensive and time-consuming to evaluate
   b) Benefits of pesticide may outweigh harm
3. Political complications
   a) Farmers are well-represented in Congress
   b) Subsidies encourage overproduction, which encourages overuse of pesticides
   c) Damage is hard to see and dramatize
4. The EPA budget is small
5. Few pesticides have been removed from the market; only those receiving heavy media coverage such as DDT in 1972
6. Client politics has won out

C. Environmentalists versus loggers
1. Issue: clear-cutting of forests
2. Congress has supported loggers
   a) Forest Service forced to sell lumber at below-market prices
   b) Subsidizes industry
3. Spotted owl: getting the media involved—entrepreneurial politics

VII. The environmental uncertainties
A. Why is it so difficult to have a sane environmental policy?
1. Many environmental problems are not clear cut
2. Goals are often unclear; public opinion can shift

3. Means of achieving goals (command-and-control strategy) are complicated by
   a) Local circumstances
   b) Technological problems
   c) Economic costs

B. Examples of EPA and politics
1. What is the problem?
   a) The EPA not left alone to define problem
   b) Scandals and congressional demands can shift priorities
2. What are our goals?
   a) Many are completely unrealistic
   b) The EPA forced to ask for extensions and revisions
3. How do we achieve our goals?
   a) Rules have been replaced by incentives
      (1) Offsets
      (2) Bubble standards
      (3) Pollution allowances
   b) Complaints about command-and-control strategy are now coming from environmental groups and government
      (1) Clinton administration is reexamining old approaches
      (2) People are learning from experience

VIII. The results: the environment has improved since 1970 in some aspects
A. Less air pollution
B. Maybe less water pollution but harder to judge
C. Hazardous wastes remain a problem

KEY TERMS MATCH

Match the following terms and descriptions:

1. The type of politics best illustrated by the acid rain controversy
2. An EPA incentive that allows a company to decide how best to reduce air pollution from a given factory
3. A national event held on April 22, 1970, celebrating the new environmental movement
4. Called for a 5 percent reduction world-wide in greenhouse gases
5. A device designed to remove sulfurous pollutants from smoke as it comes out of coal-burning plants
6. The type of politics best illustrated by auto emission control rules
7. Gave the government power to sue any person or company that dumped waste

a. acid rain
b. bank (or pollution allowance)
c. bubble standard
d. catalytic converter
e. Clean Air Act of 1970
f. Clean Air Act of 1990
g. clear-cutting
h. client politics
i. command-and-control strategy
j. DDT
k. Earth Day
l. entrepreneurial politics
m. environmental impact statement (EIS)
n. Environmental Protection Agency (EPA)

8. The setting of pollution standards and rules in order to improve air and water quality
9. The EPA incentive that allows a company higher pollution at one plant in exchange for lower pollution at another
10. A law that includes the compromise reached by Congress on acid rain
11. A pesticide banned by the EPA in 1972
12. Precipitation that may be caused by the burning of high-sulfur coal
13. The type of politics best illustrated by the continued use of agricultural pesticides
14. A law enacted in 1970 that made oil companies responsible for cleanup costs of oil spills
15. A document required before any federal agency undertakes an activity that "significantly" affects the environment
16. A major cause of acid rain
17. An EPA incentive that allows a company to apply credits for low-polluting emissions to future plant expansions, or to sell the credits
18. A law passed in 1969 that included a provision requiring environmental impact statements
19. The type of politics best illustrated by controversies over factory pollution
20. A logging method in which all trees in an area are removed
21. The device used in automobile engines to remove emission pollutants
22. The government agency established in 1970 to implement environmental legislation
23. Landmark environmental legislation that established national air-quality standards with specified deadlines

o. interest-group politics
p. Kyoto Protocol
q. majoritarian politics
r. National Environmental Policy Act (NEPA)
s. offset
t. scrubber
u. sulfur dioxide
v. Superfund
w. Water Quality Immprovement Act of 1970

DATA CHECK

Figure 21.1 (Page 564): Which Should Take Precedence: Environmental Protection or Economic Growth?: 1984–2006

1. In what years did the highest percentage of respondents choose "environmental protection?"

2. In what years did the percentage of respondents choosing "environmental protection" fall below 50 percent?

3. In what year did the highest percentage of respondent choose "economic growth?"

PRACTICING FOR EXAMS

TRUE/FALSE QUESTIONS

Read each statement carefully. Mark true statements *T.* If any part of the statement is false, mark it *F,* and write in the space provided a concise explanation of why the statement is false.

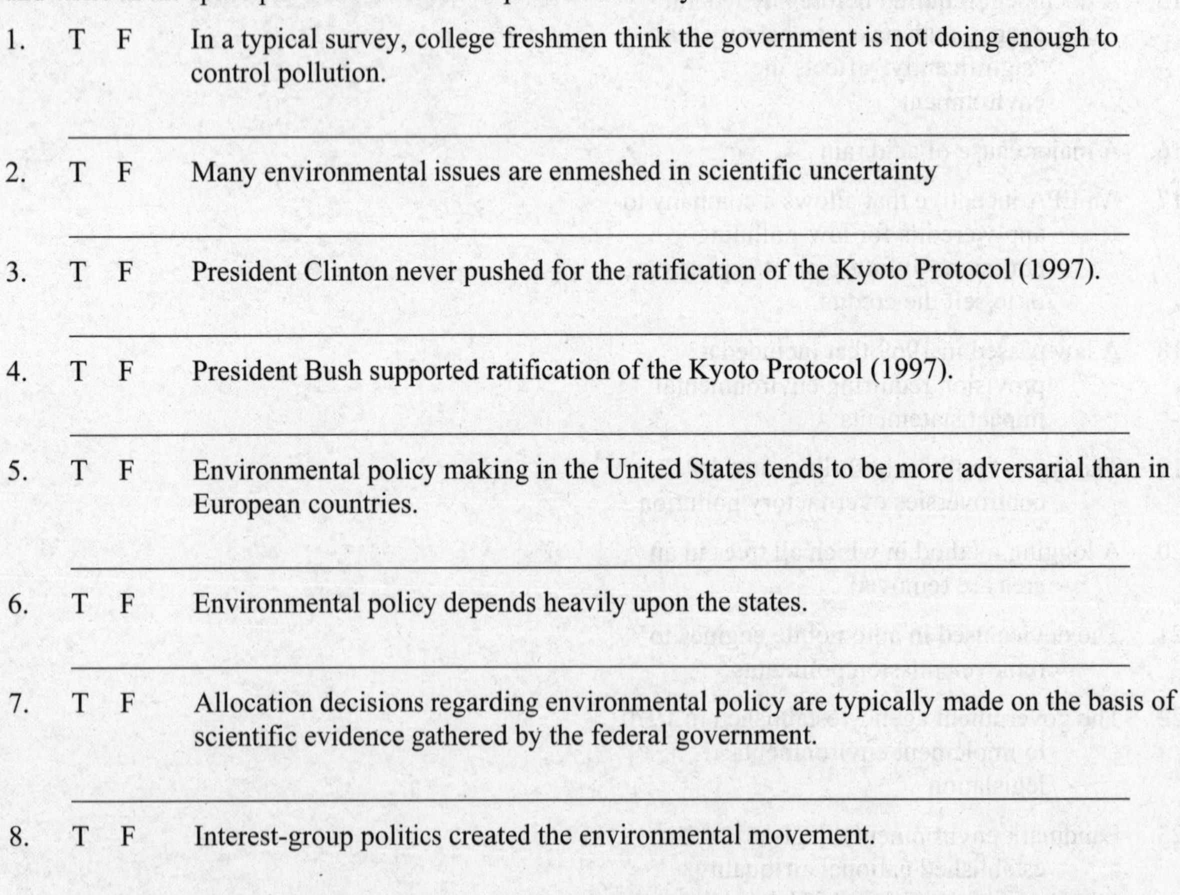

1. T F In a typical survey, college freshmen think the government is not doing enough to control pollution.

2. T F Many environmental issues are enmeshed in scientific uncertainty

3. T F President Clinton never pushed for the ratification of the Kyoto Protocol (1997).

4. T F President Bush supported ratification of the Kyoto Protocol (1997).

5. T F Environmental policy making in the United States tends to be more adversarial than in European countries.

6. T F Environmental policy depends heavily upon the states.

7. T F Allocation decisions regarding environmental policy are typically made on the basis of scientific evidence gathered by the federal government.

8. T F Interest-group politics created the environmental movement.

9. T F The Environmental Protection Agency was formed during the Great Depression as a means of lowering unemployment.

____

10. T F Majoritarian politics best explains the nation's policy approach to global warming.

____

11. T F We do not yet have an accurate measure of how much human activity has contributed to the warming of the earth.

____

12. T F Acting alone, American can eliminate greenhouse gases.

____

13. T F Of the several thousand things categorized by the government as "endangered," about half are plants.

____

14. T F The Clean Air Act of 1970 required states to restrict the public's use of cars.

____

15. T F Most clean air laws passed since 1990 have targeted particular industries.

____

16. T F Popular support for the National Environmental Policy Act of 1969, including its call for environmental impact statements, remains strong.

____

17. T F The average citizen will support increased gasoline taxes if the benefits include cleaner air and a reduction of oil consumption.

____

18. T F The controversy over the problem of acid rain illustrates the importance of client politics in environmental policy making.

____

19. T F The major source of sulfur dioxide in the atmosphere is the burning of low-sulfur coal.

____

20. T F The two major opposing groups in the acid rain controversy are Midwestern power and coal companies and Southeastern environmentalists.

____

21. T F Environmentalists generally prefer reliance on incentives to buy low-sulfur coal to the use of scrubbers.

____

22. T F Under the compromise acid rain plan adopted by Congress, a power plant situated next to a low-sulfur coal mine must nevertheless install smokestack scrubbers.

____

23. T F The text reports the scrubbers which were legally imposed on all new coal-burning plants were generally effective devices.

24. T F A battle between residents and developers over the use of farmland is most likely to involve client politics.

25. T F Entrepreneurial politics often lacks the moral fervor of interest group politics.

26. T F The innovative environmental legislation of the 1970s is less difficult to duplicate today because groups that were once unorganized are now well organized.

27. T F Farmers have effectively resisted the efforts of policy entrepreneurs to restrict the use of agricultural pesticides.

28. T F Thousands of pesticides have been taken out of the market after EPA review.

29. T F Less than one-quarter of the U.S. Forest Reserve is off limits to logging.

30. T F Most forms of cancer have been steadily declining for many years.

31. T F Superfund was created during the administration of Richard Nixon.

32. T F Today, there are about 180 sites that still need to be addressed by Superfund.

33. T F A lot of Superfund money has gone to lawyers not waste removers.

34. T F Offsets, bubble standards, and banks (pollution allowances) are incentives used by the EPA to achieve its environmental protection goals.

35. T F The Clinton administration had the strong support of environmentalists and pushed ahead with a series of impressive command-and-control policies.

36. T F There is now much less carbon monoxide, sulfur dioxide and lead in the atmosphere than once was the case.

MULTIPLE CHOICE QUESTIONS

Circle the letter of the response that best answers the question or completes the statement.

1. One reason environmental policy tends to be so controversial is that
   a. so many environmental policy decisions are based on scientific evidence, which tends to be highly political.
   b. environmental policy often takes the form of majoritarian politics, which requires strong emotional appeals to overcome the political advantage of client groups.
   c. environmental policy creates losers, who must pay the costs without getting enough of the benefits.
   d. most people feel that government is already doing enough to control pollution; new programs are therefore likely to face stiff opposition.
   e. all of the above.
2. The text speaks of the importance of *entrepreneurial politics* in many areas of environmental policy making. This term refers to a style of policy-making in which
   a. an unorganized public benefits at the expense of a well-organized group.
   b. an unorganized public benefits at its own expense.
   c. two organized groups with a material stake in the outcome fight over who will pay and who will benefit.
   d. an organized group benefits at the expense of an unorganized public.
   e. an organized group benefits at the expense of a well-organized public.
3. Which of the following statements regarding the 1997 Kyoto Protocol is *incorrect*?
   a. It called for a 5 percent reduction worldwide in greenhouse gases.
   b. It was strongly opposed by the U.S. Senate.
   c. President Clinton never pushed strongly for its ratification.
   d. President Bush scrapped it completely.
   e. None of the above.
4. An example cited in the text of the adversarial nature of environmental policy making in the United States is the fact that
   a. rules designed to reduce air pollution were written by government and business acting cooperatively.
   b. most environmental issues are settled through majoritarian politics.
   c. the public is prohibited by law from suing the Environmental Protection Agency.
   d. it took Congress thirteen years to revise the *Clean Air Act*.
   e. Congress has not passed a substantive environmental law in over twenty-seven years.
5. Compared with U.S. regulations, rules controlling air pollution in Great Britain involve
   a. strict deadlines.
   b. voluntary compliance.
   c. expensive technology.
   d. a uniform national policy.
   e. rigorous assessments.
6. According to the text, federalism and the separation of powers
   a. have reduced the scope of conflicts in environmental policy making.
   b. ensure efficiency in environmental policy making.
   c. are responsible for the broad-based public support for anti-pollution laws.
   d. reinforce adversarial politics in environmental policy making.
   e. none of the above.

7. What type(s) of politics created the environmental movement?
   a. entrepreneurial
   b. client
   c. majoritarian
   d. interest group
   e. c and d.
8. The Environmental Protection Agency (EPA) was created by
   a. Franklin D. Roosevelt.
   b. Theodore Roosevelt.
   c. Richard Nixon.
   d. Gerald Ford.
   e. Jimmy Carter.
9. Between 1970 and 1990, pollution from cars was cut by between ________ percent
   a. 10 and 20
   b. 25 and 30
   c. 30 and 40
   d. 45 and 55
   e. 60 and 80
10. Currently, there are over ____ species on the "protected" species list.
   a. six hundred
   b. one hundred
   c. fifty
   d. thirty
   e. fifteen
11. About half of the species on the protected species list are
   a. snails.
   b. plants.
   c. fish.
   d. birds.
   e. insects.
12. Most of the debate over the Clean Air Act of 1970 centered on the issue of pollutants
   a. associated with the production of automobile tires.
   b. associated with air conditioning apparatus in new automobiles.
   c. that could come out of automobile tail pipes.
   d. in and around the manufacturers of mini-vans.
   e. affecting air circulation in automobiles.
13. One provision of the Clean Air Act of 1970 required cities in which smog was still a problem, despite emissions controls placed on new cars, to impose rules restricting the public's use of cars. Why did this provision fail?
   a. The EPA adopted an overly zealous command-and-control strategy.
   b. The provision was ruled unconstitutional.
   c. Powerful client groups worked to defeat the provision.
   d. Public opposition was too great.
   e. Legislators vowed to strengthen the measure if there were not immediate results.

14. Congress has limited the impact of the Clean Air Act in various revisions by
    a. extending deadlines for compliance.
    b. decreasing the levels of required reductions.
    c. increasing the level of acceptable emissions.
    d. exempting major metropolitan areas.
    e. forsaking a general interest in reducing smog in big cities.
15. The text suggests that the legislation requiring environmental impact statements (EISs) passed by overwhelming majorities because it was a "pro-environment law" and because
    a. there was no requirement for specific action, only the need to create a "statement."
    b. there was a general sense that EISs would speed up governmental projects.
    c. courts would not consider legal challenges to EISs.
    d. opponents of projects would be silenced by EISs.
    e. federal agencies lobbied Congress intensely for EISs.
16. Which of the following statements about environmental impact statements (EISs) is *correct*?
    a. They were first mandated by a provision of the Clean Air Act of 1970.
    b. They have most frequently been used by businesses to block or change projects.
    c. They require specific action in response to a proposed project.
    d. They apply only to federal agencies.
    e. They apply only to state agencies.
17. Your state proposes an increase in gasoline taxes. The citizens of the state are most likely to support such an increase if the tax revenues will be used to
    a. build a new highway.
    b. reduce air pollution.
    c. pay for measures to reduce traffic congestion.
    d. finance a new crime prevention program.
    e. finance a new weapons-exchange program.
18. Why should many residents of Canada be concerned about the type of coal burned in midwestern U.S. power plants?
    a. Because acid rain caused by these plants affects lakes and forests in eastern Canada
    b. Because the Canadian economy is heavily dependent on the sale of high-sulfur coal
    c. Because the Canadian economy benefits directly from the sale of smokestack scrubbers
    d. Because Canada is a major producer of sulfur dioxide and a source of acid rain
    e. Because the extraction of low-sulfur coal in Canada is quite damaging to farm land
19. If burning low-sulfur coal significantly reduces the emission of sulfurous fumes and therefore reduces acid rain, why don't plants in the Midwest and Great Lakes region burn only low-sulfur coal?
    a. Because it can be burned only if plants are equipped with scrubbers
    b. Because it is expensive
    c. Because it produces far less energy than does high-sulfur coal
    d. Because the major source of low-sulfur coal is Canada
    e. Because the major source of low-sulfur coal is Mexico
20. The compromise worked out by Congress to deal with acid rain calls for
    a. scrubbers in all new plants.
    b. the burning of only low-sulfur coal in all new plants.
    c. both scrubbers and the burning of only low-sulfur coal in all new plants.
    d. both scrubbers and the burning of only low-sulfur coal in all plants, both new and existing.
    e. scrubbers in old plants and the burning of low-sulfur coal in half of all new plants.

21. As environmental policy has become more complex and new interest groups have been formed, it is increasingly more difficult to
    a. interest Congress in environmental policy.
    b. identify who supports or opposes any given policy.
    c. provide cues to members of Congress.
    d. attract public attention to issues.
    e. change existing policy.
22. When Rachel Carson published *Silent Spring* in 1962, she set off a public outcry about the harm of wildlife caused by
    a. a common pesticide.
    b. gas-powered farming equipment.
    c. a variety of synthetic fertilizers.
    d. experimental crops.
    e. Farm Bureau policies.
23. Today, there are well over _____ pesticides in use.
    a. 5,000
    b. 10,000
    c. 15,000
    d. 25,000
    e. 50,000
24. Many policy entrepreneurs favor measures to control the use of agricultural pesticides. One reason they have not been successful in enacting legislation to do this is that
    a. the EPA is opposed to such legislation.
    b. extensive media coverage has lent support to farmers.
    c. the risks associated with the use of pesticide use are undocumented.
    d. farmers are well-represented in Congress.
    e. Congress and the EPA cannot agree on relevant standards.
25. In cases in which pesticides, such as DDT, have been taken off the market, public debate of their effects tends to lend itself to
    a. majoritarian politics.
    b. entrepreneurial politics.
    c. interest-group politics.
    d. client politics.
    e. club-based politics.
26. About ____ of the U.S. forest system is off limits to logging.
    a. 1/8
    b. 1/4
    c. 1/2
    d. 2/3
    e. 3/4
27. Congress orders the U.S. Forest Service to sell timber to the timber industry at below-market prices and thereby subsidizes the timber industry. Such a program best illustrates
    a. entrepreneurial politics.
    b. majoritarian politics.
    c. interest group politics.
    d. client politics.
    e. club-based politics.

28. All of the following are correct pairings of different styles of politics and examples of these styles in environmental policy making *except*
    a. entrepreneurial politics and global warming.
    b. majoritarian politics and pollution from automobiles.
    c. client politics and land-use controls.
    d. interest group politics and acid rain.
    e. a and d.
29. The EPA was given responsibility to administer certain laws governing
    a. air.
    b. water.
    c. pesticides.
    d. all of the above.
    e. a and b.
30. Under this program chemical and petroleum industries would be taxed and the proceeds, along with general tax revenues, were to be used to pay for cleaning up abandoned hazardous waste sites.
    a. Off-set
    b. Superfund
    c. Command-and-Control
    d. Koyoto Protocol
    e. a and d.
31. The inability of Superfund to treat more than 2,000 waste sites by the year 2000 was, in part, attributable to the fact that
    a. Superfund money went straight to the waste removers.
    b. finding and suing responsible parties was difficult.
    c. the government provided little in the way of funding.
    d. President Reagan signed a bill that weakened the EPA.
    e. environmental lobbyists were no longer able to exert pressure on the EPA.
32. The EPA was once instructed by Congress to eliminate *all* pollutants ________ by 1985.
    a. in the air
    b. from automobiles
    c. from factories
    d. entering our water
    e. from pesticides
33. The EPA began to shift from a command-and-control strategy for affected businesses during the ________ administration.
    a. Nixon
    b. Ford
    c. Carter
    d. Reagan
    e. Clinton
34. Offsets, bubble standards, and banks (pollution allowances) are all
    a. pollution control devices that effectively reduce air contamination.
    b. tests conducted by the EPA on agricultural pesticides.
    c. EPA incentives for companies to reduce pollution.
    d. rules devised by the EPA under its command-and-control strategy to improve air and water quality.
    e. standards which are employed in order to control the amount of hazardous nuclear waste that is discarded in waterbeds.

35. Which refers to a total amount of air pollution that can come from a given factory, allowing owners to decide which specific sources within the factory will be reduced?
    a. An air proxy card
    b. An offset
    c. The command-and-control strategy
    d. The bubble standard
    e. A pollution allowance
36. When a company reduces its polluting emissions by more than the law requires and uses the excess amount to cover a future plant expansion, it is taking advantage of
    a. an air proxy card.
    b. an offset.
    c. the command-and-control strategy.
    d. the bubble standard.
    e. a pollution allowance.
37. The Clinton administration has the strong support of environmentalists but
    a. tried to amend Superfund without much success.
    b. pushed ahead with more command and control policies.
    c. sided with lawyers who were being blamed for Superfund failures.
    d. abolished Superfund.
    e. reformed Superfund in a manner that displeased most environmentalists.

ESSAY QUESTIONS

Practice writing extended answers to the following questions. These test your ability to integrate and express the ideas that you have been studying in this chapter.

1. What are four reasons why environmental policy is so controversial in the United States?
2. Compare and contrast environmental policy making in the United States and in Great Britain.
3. What do the authors consider three difficult questions which concerns about global warming must address?
4. What was the most prominent feature of the Clear Air Act of 1970? How did the politics surrounding the act shift from being entrepreneurial to being majoritarian?
5. Why would any politician suggest a gasoline tax and under what circumstances is such a recommendation likely to be more tolerable to the public?
6. Summarize the compromise solution that was reached with respect to acid rain in 1977 and identify its "political" advantages.
7. Explain what *Superfund* refers to and outline the reasons why the results of the program have been somewhat mixed.
8. Identify and explain the types of incentives to improve air and water quality that were created during the Carter administration.

ANSWERS TO KEY TERMS MATCH QUESTIONS

1. o
2. c
3. k
4. p
5. t
6. q
7. v
8. i
9. s
10. f
11. j
12. a
13. h
14. w
15. m
16. u
17. b
18. r
19. l
20. g
21. d
22. n
23. e

ANSWERS TO DATA CHECK QUESTIONS

1. 1990 and 1991 (71 percent).
2. 2003 and 2004.
3. 2004 (44 percent).

ANSWERS TO TRUE/FALSE QUESTIONS

1. T
2. T
3. T
4. F President Clinton supported Kyoto, but did not push hard for Senate ratification. President Bush pushed it aside altogether.

5. T

6. T

7. F They are typically made on the basis of local concerns and practices.

8. F Entrepreneurial politics created the environmental movement.

9. F The EPA was formed during the Nixon administration (1970)

10. F This would, again, be an example of entrepreneurial politics.

11. T

12. F This cannot be done. China and India would need to assist in the effort.

13. T

14. T

15. T

16. T

17. F The benefit needs to be something more concrete, like a new highway.

18. F Acid rain has provoked interest group politics.

19. F We do not know what the "major" source it.

20. F The groups are the residents of Canada and New England and residents of the Midwest.

21. F With respect to acid rain, environmentalists prefer concrete action, like the installation of scrubbers on all new factories, regardless of their location.

22. T

23. F As predicted, they did not work very well.

24. F This would be an example of interest group politics.

25. F Entrepreneurial politics generally has no problem with such. It is interest group politics which tends to lack moral fervor and deep streams of public opinion.

26. T

27. T

28. F Very few are/have been.

29. F It would be more accurate to say 2/3 of the area is off-limits.

30. T

31. F It was created during the Carter administration.

32. F There are more than 2,000.

33. T

34. T

35. F It tried to reexamine this approach and make major changes, without succeeding.

36. T

ANSWERS TO MULTIPLE CHOICE QUESTIONS

1. c
2. c
3. e
4. d
5. b
6. d
7. a
8. c
9. e
10. a
11. b
12. c
13. d
14. a
15. a
16. d
17. a
18. a
19. b
20. a
21. e
22. a
23. e
24. d
25. b
26. d
27. d
28. c
29. d
30. b
31. b
32. d
33. c
34. c
35. d
36. e
37. a

PART 4

Classic Statement: *West Virginia Board of Education v. Barnette* (1943)

INTRODUCTION

Occurring during World War II, the Barnette case presented an explosive issue to the Supreme Court. Under state law, children attending public schools in West Virginia were required to salute the American flag before class. Failure to comply was considered insubordination and resulted in expulsion from school.

Children who were Jehovah's Witnesses refused to participate in the patriotic exercise for religious reasons. They believed that saluting the flag violated the biblical commandment against worshiping graven images. According to their parents, obedience to the law risked the children's eternal salvation. Consequently, the children were expelled from school.

In 1940, the Supreme Court had ruled in a similar case that compulsory flag saluting in public schools was a permissible means of fostering "national unity" and vital to the national security. Much controversy followed this decision. In Barnette, Justice Robert Jackson reversed the earlier ruling and wrote a classic statement about the position of the Bill of Rights in American society.

The very purpose of a Bill of Rights was to withdraw certain subjects from the vicissitudes of political controversy, to place them beyond the reach of majorities and officials and to establish them as legal principles to be applied by the courts. One's right to life, liberty, and property, to free speech, a free press, freedom of worship and assembly and other fundamental rights may not be submitted to vote; they depend on the outcome of no elections.

Struggles to coerce uniformity of sentiment in support of some end thought essential to their time and country have been waged by many good as well as by evil men. Nationalism is a relatively recent phenomenon but at other times and places the ends have been racial or territorial security, support of a dynasty or regime, and particular plans for saving souls. As first and moderate methods to attain unity have failed, those bent on its accomplishment must resort to an ever-increasing severity. As governmental pressure toward unity becomes greater, so strife becomes more bitter as to whose unity it shall be. Probably no deeper division of our people could proceed from any provocation than from finding it necessary to choose what doctrine and whose program public educational officials shall compel youth to unite in embracing. Ultimate futility of such attempts to compel coherence is the lesson of every such effort from the Roman drive to stamp out Christianity as a disturber of its pagan unity, the Inquisition, as a means to religious and dynastic unity, the Siberian exiles as a means to Russian unity, down to the fast failing efforts of our present totalitarian enemies. Those who begin coercive elimination of dissent soon find themselves exterminating dissenters. Compulsory unification of opinion achieves only the unanimity of the graveyard.

It seems trite but necessary to say that the First Amendment to our Constitution was designed to avoid these ends by avoiding these beginnings. There is no mysticism in the American concept of the State or of the nature or origin of its authority. We set up government by consent of the governed, and the Bill of Rights denies those in power any legal opportunity to coerce that consent. Authority here is to be controlled by public opinion, not public opinion by authority.

The case is made difficult not because the principles of its decision are obscure but because the flag involved is our own. Nevertheless, we apply the limitations of thc Constitution with no fear that freedom to be intellectually and spiritually diverse or even contrary will disintegrate the social organization. To believe that patriotism will not flourish if patriotic ceremonies are voluntary and spontaneous instead of a compulsory routine is to make an unflattering estimate of the appeal of our institutions to free minds. We can have intellectual individualism and the rich cultural diversities that we owe to exceptional minds only at the price of occasional eccentricity and abnormal attitudes. When they are so harmless to others or to the State as those we deal with here, the price is not too great. But freedom to differ is not limited to things that do not matter much. That would be a mere shadow of freedom. The test of its substance is the right to differ as to things that touch the heart of the existing order.

If there is any fixed star in our constitutional constellation, it is that no official high or petty, can prescribe what shall be orthodox in politics, nationalism, religion, or other matters of opinion or force citizens to confess by word or act their faith therein. If there are any circumstances which permit an exception, they do not now occur to us.

We think the action of the local authorities in compelling the flag salute and pledge transcends constitutional limitations on their power and invades the sphere of intellect and spirit which it is the purpose of the First Amendment to our Constitution to reserve from all official control.

QUESTIONS FOR UNDERSTANDING AND DISCUSSION

1. According to Justice Jackson, what is the purpose of the Bill of Rights?
2. Does Justice Jackson's position contradict the democratic ideal of majoritarian rule? Explain.
3. According to Jackson, what evils are associated with the government's attempting to compel unanimity at a time of national crisis? Is the justice making patriotism an object of ridicule?
4. Does Justice Jackson imply that the Bill of Rights is superior to the other provisions of the Constitution? Defend your position.

PART V: The Nature of American Democracy

CHAPTER 22

Who Governs?

REVIEWING THE CHAPTER

CHAPTER FOCUS

This chapter provides an overview of American politics and central themes of the text, namely, "Who Governs? To What Ends?" A broad perspective of the history of American politics is utilized in order to provide a basis for understanding the politics of the past and present, and also to allow you to consider what the future may hold. After reading and reviewing the material in this chapter, you should be able to do each of the following:

1. Explain why the size of the federal government and the scope of its power did not increase in many significant ways for almost 150 years.
2. Identify and explain specific historical events and developments that triggered the transformation of the federal government into a common candidate for solving an amazing variety of social and economic problems.
3. Explain the general consequences of the enlarged scope of government activity.
4. Understand how our political culture played a critical role in the foundation of our government and continues to shape political processes and our nation's development.

STUDY OUTLINE

I. Introduction
   A. Assumption the president and Congress are to address social and economic problems
      1. Limited concern of government as recently as the Eisenhower administration
      2. The Founders and the role of the federal government
   B. Constitutional hurdles to effective federal action
      1. Separation of powers and checks and balances
      2. Federalism
      3. Bicameralism
II. Restraints on the growth of government
   A. For first 150 years government grew slowly
      1. Supreme Court defined government authority narrowly
      2. Popular opinion supported a limited governmental role
      3. The political system was designed to limit government
   B. System limiting government makes it difficult to abolish programs
      1. Under Reagan spending increased for many programs
      2. Bush has also proposed programs that would increase spending
III. Relaxing the restraints
   A. Changes in Constitutional interpretation
      1. Bill of Rights incorporated to the states
      2. Special protection of property rights reduced, business regulation increased

3. Congress allowed to give broad discretionary powers to administrative agencies

B. Changes in public opinion
 1. Public demand for government action during Great Depression
 2. Opinions of political elites changed even faster
 3. Some programs have been popular with the masses

C. Changes in the distribution of political resources
 1. Number and variety of interest groups have increased
 2. Funds from organization pursuing causes have grown
 3. Greater access to the federal courts
 4. Technological advances have enhanced the power to communicate ideas

D. The Old System v. the New System

IV. Consequences of activist government

A. Need to assess costs and benefits of programs

B. General political consequences of the enlarged scope of activity
 1. Bureaucratization of all organizations
 2. Rise of competing policies
 3. Less control by the electorate through the decline of parties and turnout and of public confidence
 4. Greater risk of government failure

V. The influence of structure

A. Parliamentary model; if adopted here, would do the following
 1. Fewer legislative restraints on the executive
 2. More bureaucratic centralization
 3. Less citizen participation to challenge or block policies.
 4. Higher taxes and more secrecy

B. U.S. model
 1. More local authority
 2. Greater citizen participation

VI. The influence of ideas

A. Preoccupation with rights
 1. Assumption that affected groups have a right to participate in policy formation
 2. Willingness to resort to courts

B. Effects of rights on government functions
 1. Harder to make government decisions
 2. More red tape

C. Elite opinion influences which rights have priority
 1. Favors freedom of expression over management of property
 2. Mass opinion less committed to freedom of expression

D. Freedom versus equality an enduring tension
 1. Advantages of freedom are remote
 2. Advantages of equality are obvious

E. Fragmentation of political system increases role of ideas
 1. Widespread enthusiasm for an idea can lead to rapid adoption of new programs
 2. Competing ideas make change difficult; change today may require the persuading of thousands of special interests

F. Fundamental challenge: to restore confidence in the legitimacy of government itself

PRACTICING FOR EXAMS

TRUE/FALSE QUESTIONS

Read each statement carefully. Mark true statements *T.* If any part of the statement is false, mark it *F,* and write in the space provided a concise explanation of why the statement is false.

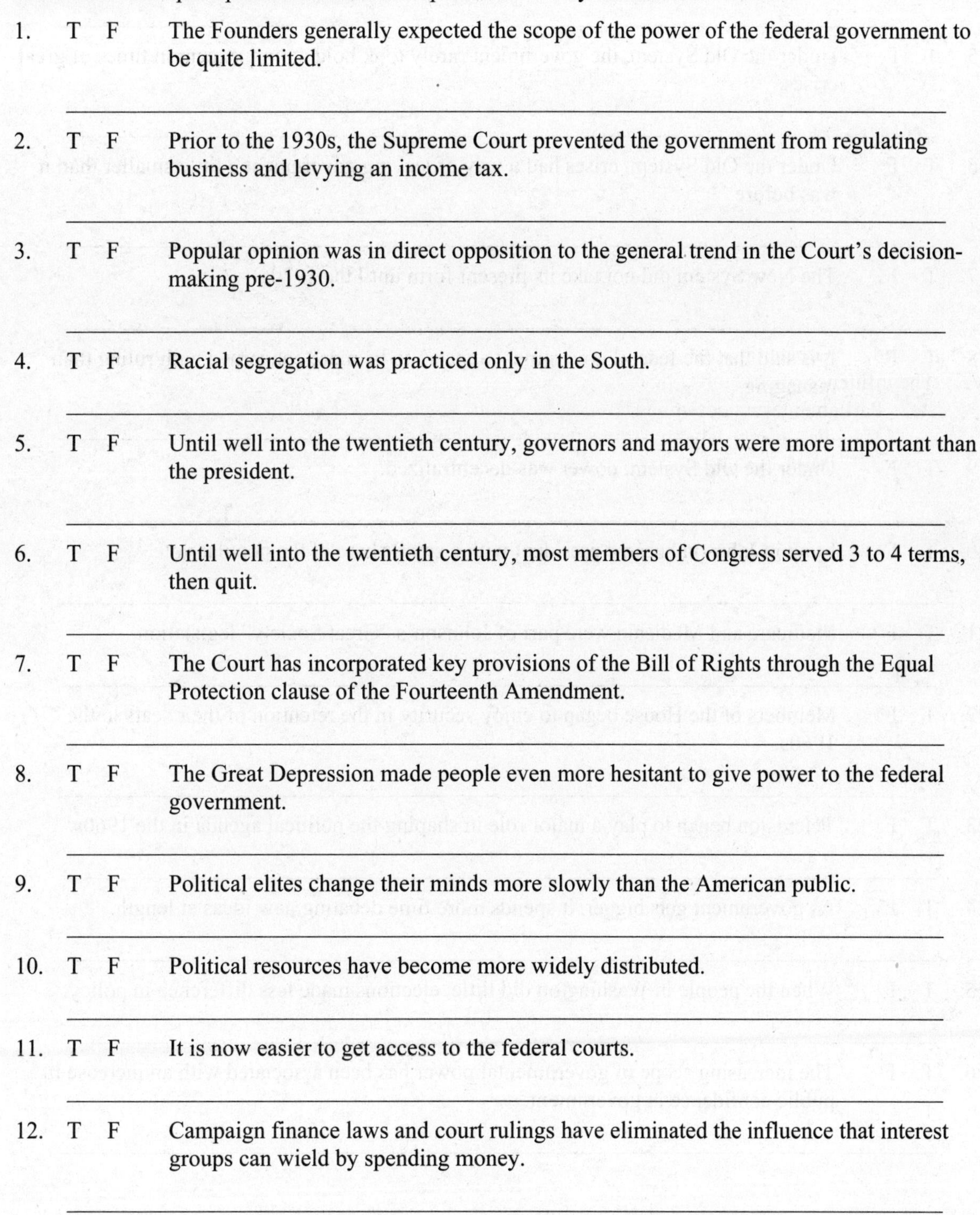

1. T F The Founders generally expected the scope of the power of the federal government to be quite limited.

____

2. T F Prior to the 1930s, the Supreme Court prevented the government from regulating business and levying an income tax.

____

3. T F Popular opinion was in direct opposition to the general trend in the Court's decision-making pre-1930.

____

4. T F Racial segregation was practiced only in the South.

____

5. T F Until well into the twentieth century, governors and mayors were more important than the president.

____

6. T F Until well into the twentieth century, most members of Congress served 3 to 4 terms, then quit.

____

7. T F The Court has incorporated key provisions of the Bill of Rights through the Equal Protection clause of the Fourteenth Amendment.

____

8. T F The Great Depression made people even more hesitant to give power to the federal government.

____

9. T F Political elites change their minds more slowly than the American public.

____

10. T F Political resources have become more widely distributed.

____

11. T F It is now easier to get access to the federal courts.

____

12. T F Campaign finance laws and court rulings have eliminated the influence that interest groups can wield by spending money.

____

13. T F Under the Old System, the presidency was small and somewhat personal.

14. T F Under the Old System, there was a clear understanding that what the president said in a press conference was never to be quoted directly.

15. T F Under the Old System, the government rarely took bold action, except in times of great crises.

16. T F Under the Old System, crises had a way of leaving government a little smaller than it was before.

17. T F The New System did not take its present form until the 1970s.

18. T F It is said that the federal government appears to be more concerned with ruling than managing.

19. T F Under the Old System, power was decentralized.

20. T F Lyndon Johnson became president with a small share of the popular vote.

21. T F Medicare and Medicaid were part of Johnson's "Great Society" legislation.

22. T F Members of the House began to enjoy security in the retention of their seats in the 1960s.

23. T F Television began to play a major role in shaping the political agenda in the 1960s.

24. T F As government gets bigger, it spends more time debating new ideas at length.

25. T F When the people in Washington did little, elections made less difference in policy.

26. T F The increasing scope of governmental power has been associated with an increase in public confidence in government.

27. T F If the United States had adopted the British (parliamentary) model, taxes would probably be lower.

____

28. T F American politics remain far more sensitive to local concerns than does politics abroad.

____

29. T F Party conventions came to supplant primary elections in the 1960s.

____

30. T F The text suggests that, as the political system has become more fragmented and more individualized, it has come more under the sway of ideas.

____

31. T F Individual members of Congress are far more important than congressional leaders.

____

32. T F Forming new issue-based interest groups is much easier than it used to be.

____

33. T F Up until the 1950s, people talked about politics in terms of bargaining among organized interested and "blocs" representing various groups.

____

34. T F We expect more from government but are less and less certain that we are going to get it.

____

MULTIPLE CHOICE QUESTIONS

Circle the letter of the response that best answers the question or completes the statement.

1. As recently as the Eisenhower administration
   a. domestic political issues and foreign affairs were given an equal amount of attention in Washington.
   b. major domestic political issues dominated the attention of Washington.
   c. the national political agenda was short on major domestic political issues.
   d. civil rights were not thought to be a matter of federal policy.
   e. Congress was preoccupied with solving social and economic problems nationwide.
2. For a long time, the Supreme Court prevented the government from
   a. delegating broad discretionary power to administrative agencies.
   b. levying an income tax.
   c. regulating business.
   d. all of the above.
   e. none of the above.

3. The Supreme Court could not have maintained its view of limited government without
   a. general agreement from the public.
   b. allies in Congress.
   c. the support of the American Bar Association.
   d. the cooperation of other federal judges.
   e. life-time appointment.
4. Which of the following was true well into the twentieth century?
   a. Governors and mayors were more important than presidents.
   b. Most members of Congress did not serve more than one or two terms.
   c. Congress wasn't in session long and didn't do much.
   d. The pay for a member of Congress was not very impressive.
   e. All of the above.
5. In recent decades,
   a. the Supreme Court has permitted Congress to give broad discretionary power to administrative agencies.
   b. important provisions of the Bill of Rights have been incorporated to the states.
   c. citizens have been able to alter state policy to a greater degree than before.
   d. court rulings have allowed a greater degree of business regulation.
   e. all of above.
6. Which of the following is *not* an explanation for why there was no rapid growth in the power and scope of the federal government for the better part of a century and a half?
   a. Prevailing interpretations of the Constitution.
   b. Constitutional amendments.
   c. Separation of powers.
   d. Popular opinion.
   e. Checks and balances.
7. Under the Old System of policy-making,
   a. the government's agenda was large.
   b. the legitimacy of federal action was rarely questioned.
   c. states' rights were almost irrelevant.
   d. the president was frequently quoted directly by the press.
   e. the people voted at a high rate.
8. Under the Old System, the dominant theme in debates about the legitimacy of governmental action was the importance of
   a. states' rights.
   b. the Bill of Rights.
   c. federalism.
   d. centralization of power.
   e. nationalism.
9. The texts suggests that the government rarely took "bold action" under the Old System unless
   a. the presidency and Congress were controlled by the same party.
   b. there was a realigning election.
   c. the Supreme Court supported the effort.
   d. it was facing a crisis—such as war.
   e. there was widespread political protest.

10. The "New System" of policy making began in the
    a. 1890s.
    b. 1920s.
    c. 1930s.
    d. 1950s.
    e. 1970s.
11. The "New System" of policy making did not take its present form until the
    a. 1890s.
    b. 1920s.
    c. 1930s.
    d. 1950s.
    e. 1970s.
12. What made it difficult to start a new program under the Old System and makes it difficult to change a new program in the New System?
    a. Checks and balances.
    b. Federalism.
    c. States' rights.
    d. The electoral college.
    e. None of the above.
13. Under the New System, it is much more difficult to resolve conflicts because
    a. individual members of Congress are less influential.
    b. the Supreme Court has limited the impact of interest groups.
    c. the distribution of political resources is shrinking.
    d. power is centralized.
    e. power is decentralized.
14. The shift from the Old System to the New System was, in part, accelerated by
    a. the election of Republican presidents in the 1950s and 1970s.
    b. the election of Democrat majorities in the House and Senate in the 1930s and 1960s.
    c. the selection of Republican Supreme Court justices in the 1930s.
    d. economic instability in the 1960s.
    e. constant turnover in the membership of Congress.
15. Who took office after promising to reduce the size of government, but could only obtain small declines in spending for some programs and actual increases in many others.
    a. John F. Kennedy
    b. Harry Truman
    c. Franklin D. Roosevelt
    d. Dwight Eisenhower
    e. Ronald Reagan
16. The text suggests the consequences of an increasingly activist government include all of the following *except*
    a. members of government spend more time managing.
    b. the government appears to act in inconsistent, uncoordinated and cumbersome ways.
    c. the government is less susceptible to control by electoral activity.
    d. interest groups have lost their influence.
    e. the government is held responsible for more things.

17. If the United States had adopted a parliamentary structure of government, it probably would
    a. be more sensitive to local concerns.
    b. have stronger parties.
    c. be less sensitive to local concerns.
    d. have weaker parties.
    e. experience a decrease in voter turnout.
18. The authors suggest that, had the Founders adopted a centralized parliamentary regime similar to that of Great Britain, the least amount of historical variation would have probably concerned
    a. social welfare.
    b. national planning.
    c. war.
    d. congressional investigations.
    e. taxes.
19. More than the citizens of perhaps any other nation, Americans define their relationships with one another and political authority in terms of
    a. rights.
    b. liberties.
    c. duties.
    d. economics.
    e. social class.
20. According to the text, elite opinion tends to favor freedom of ______ over freedom to manage or dispose of property.
    a. choice
    b. travel
    c. conscience
    d. religion
    e. expression
21. Tocqueville felt that Americans, as a part of a democratic community, were primarily attached to
    a. freedom.
    b. equality.
    c. fraternity.
    d. community.
    e. reciprocity.
22. Perhaps the greatest challenge to statesmanship in the years ahead is to find a way to serve the true interests of the people and, at the same time,
    a. reduce partisan conflicts in Washington.
    b. restore their confidence in government.
    c. increase voter participation.
    d. satisfy the demands of a multiplicity of interest groups.
    e. satisfy the demands of the military-industrial complex.

ESSAY QUESTIONS

Practice writing extended answers to the following questions. These test your ability to integrate and express the ideas that you have been studying in this chapter.

1. Describe the constitutional arrangements that make it hard for the federal government to act.
2. Explain the role that the United States Supreme Court played in the expansion of federal power.

3. Explain what the text means when it says that political resources have become "more widely distributed."
4. Identify the two major differences between the Old and New Systems of politics in the United States.
5. Explain why increases in government activism are likely to be associated with a public that is increasingly dissatisfied.
6. Why does the text suggest that an activist government is less susceptible to control by electoral activity than a passive one?
7. What are some of the ways that the American political system would differ had the Founders adopted a centralized, parliamentary system of government? In your opinion, is it better that the parliamentary form was rejected?
8. Cite 6-7 "rules of politics" as outlined by the authors.
9. Explain how the fragmentation of the political system had an impact on the influence of ideas and the possibility of change.

ANSWERS TO TRUE/FALSE QUESTIONS

1. T
2. T
3. F *Laissez faire* politics was popular with the public.
4. F It was practiced throughout the nation.
5. T
6. F Most served just 1 or 2 terms, then quit.
7. T
8. F The Great Depression raised Americans' expectation with respect to government.
9. F Elite opinion is more volatile than public opinion. It is held more strongly and changes more quickly.
10. T
11. T
12. F If anything, they have had the effect of increasing interest group activity and influence.
13. T
14. T
15. T
16. F Such crises had a way of leaving the government larger than it was beforehand. Government was not typically reduced to its previous size in the aftermath of crises.
17. T
18. F It appears to be more concerned with managing than it does with ruling.
19. F Power was much more centralized under the Old System.
20. F Johnson came to the presidency with a larger share of the popular vote than any president in modern history.
21. T
22. T
23. T
24. F As it gets bigger, it spends less time debating at length new ideas.
25. F When government did less, elections mattered more.
26. F Increase in the scope of governmental power has been associated with a decrease in public confidence in government.
27. F Taxes would probably be higher if we had adopted something like the British system.
28. T
29. F Primary elections supplanted the conventions as the critical decision-making point.
30. T

31. T
32. T
33. T
34. T

ANSWERS TO MULTIPLE CHOICE QUESTIONS

1. c
2. d
3. a
4. e
5. e
6. e
7. e
8. a
9. d
10. c
11. e
12. a
13. e
14. b
15. e
16. d
17. c
18. c
19. a
20. e
21. b
22. b

PART 5

Classic Statement: "Why Democratic Nations Show a More Ardent and Enduring Love of Equality Than of Liberty, and How That Leads Them to Concentrate Political Power," from *Democracy in America,* by Alexis de Tocqueville[1]

INTRODUCTION

Earlier (in the Classic Statement section for Part II), we read of Tocqueville's concern about the power of the majority. Here he examines another problem that democracies face—how to preserve freedom when it is more natural, he argues, for people to love equality more than freedom. He makes a subtle argument about why equality should be more attractive than freedom; read it closely and see whether you agree. Then he turns to one consequence of a love of equality—its tendency to promote the concentration, or centralization, of political power. Tocqueville was writing in 1840; see whether you can think of present-day examples that support or contradict his argument.

WHY DEMOCRATIC NATIONS SHOW A MORE ARDENT AND ENDURING LOVE OF EQUALITY THAN OF LIBERTY

The first and most intense passion that is produced by equality of condition is, I need hardly say, the love of that equality.

It is possible to imagine an extreme point at which freedom and equality would meet and blend. Let us suppose that all the people take a part in the government, and that each one of them has an equal right to take a part in it. As no one is different from his fellows, none can exercise a tyrannical power; men will be perfectly free because they are all entirely equal; and they will all be perfectly equal because they are entirely free. To this ideal state democratic nations tend. This is the only complete form that equality can assume upon earth; but there are a thousand others which, without being equally perfect, are not less cherished by those nations.

Although men cannot become absolutely equal unless they are entirely free, and consequently equality, pushed to its furthest extent, may be confounded with freedom, yet there is good reason for distinguishing the one from the other. The taste which men have for liberty and that which they feel for equality are, in fact, two different things; and I am not afraid to add that among democratic nations they are two unequal things.

---

[1] Alexis de Tocqueville, *Democracy in America* (New York: Knopf, 1944, first published in 1840), Book 2, Chapter 1, and Book 4, Chapter 3.

Freedom has appeared in the world at different times and under various forms; it has not been exclusively bound to any social condition, and it is not confined to democracies. Freedom cannot, therefore, form the distinguishing characteristic of democratic ages. The peculiar and preponderant fact that marks those ages as its own is the equality of condition; the ruling passion of men in those periods is the love of this equality. Do not ask what singular charm the men of democratic ages find in being equal, or what special reasons they may have for clinging so tenaciously to equality rather than to the other advantages that society holds out to them: equality is the distinguishing characteristic of the age they live in; that of itself is enough to explain that they prefer it to all the rest.

That political freedom in its excesses may compromise the tranquility, the property, the lives of individuals is obvious even to narrow and unthinking minds. On the contrary, none but attentive and clear-sighted men perceive the perils with which equality threatens us, and they commonly avoid pointing them out. They know that the calamities they apprehend are remote and flatter themselves that they will only fall upon future generations, for which the present generation takes but little thought. The evils that freedom sometimes bring with it are immediate; they are apparent to all, and all are more or less affected by them. The evils that extreme equality may produce are slowly disclosed; they creep gradually into the social frame; they are seen only at intervals; and at the moment at which they become most violent, habit already causes them to be no longer felt.

The advantages that freedom brings are shown only by the lapse of time, and it is always easy to mistake the cause in which they originate. The advantages of equality are immediate, and they may always be traced from their source.

Political liberty bestows exalted pleasures from time to time upon a certain number of citizens. Equality every day confers a number of small enjoyments on every man. The charms of equality are every instant felt and are within the reach of all; the noblest hearts are not insensible to them, and the most vulgar souls exult in them. The passion that equality creates must therefore be at once strong and general. Men cannot enjoy political liberty unpurchased by some sacrifices, and they never obtain it without great exertions. But the pleasures of equality are self-proffered; each of the petty incidents of life seems to occasion them, and in order to taste them, nothing is required but to live.

Democratic nations are at all times fond of equality, but there are certain epochs at which the passion they entertain for it swells to the height of fury. This occurs at the moment when the old social system, long menaced, is overthrown after a severe internal struggle, and the barriers of rank are at length thrown down. At such times men pounce upon equality as their booty, and they cling to it as to some precious treasure which they fear to lose. The passion for equality penetrates on every side into men's hearts, expands there and fills them entirely. Tell them not that by this blind surrender of themselves to an exclusive passion they risk their dearest interests; they are deaf. Show them not freedom escaping from their grasp while they are looking another way; they are blind, or rather they can discern but one object to be desired in the universe.

I think that democratic communities have a natural taste for freedom; left to themselves, they will seek it, cherish it, and view any privation of it with regret. But for equality their passion is ardent, insatiable, incessant, invincible; they call for equality in freedom; and if they cannot obtain that, they still call for equality in slavery. They will endure poverty, servitude, barbarism, but they will not endure aristocracy.

This is true at all times, and especially in our own day. All men and all powers seeking to cope with this irresistible passion will be overthrown and destroyed by it. In our age freedom cannot be established without it and despotism itself cannot reign without its support.

THAT THE SENTIMENTS OF DEMOCRATIC NATIONS ACCORD WITH THEIR OPINIONS IN LEADING THEM TO CONCENTRATE POLITICAL POWER

If it is true that in ages of equality men readily adopt the notion of a great central power, it cannot be doubted, on the other hand, that their habits and sentiments predispose them to recognize such a power and to give it their support.

As the men who inhabit democratic countries have no superiors, no inferiors, and no habitual or necessary partners in their undertakings, they readily fall back upon themselves and consider themselves as beings apart. Hence such men can never, without an effort, tear themselves from their private affairs to engage in public business; their natural bias leads them to abandon the latter to the sole visible and permanent representative of the interests of the community; that is to say, to the state. Not only are they naturally wanting in a taste for public business, but they have frequently no time to attend it. Private life in democratic times is so busy, so excited, so full of wishes and of work, that hardly any energy or leisure remains to each individual for public life.

As in periods of equality no man is compelled to lend his assistance to his fellow men, and none has any right to expect much support from them, everyone is at once independent and powerless. These two conditions, which must never be either separately considered or confounded together, inspire the citizen of a democratic country with very contrary propensities. His independence fills him with self-reliance and pride among his equals; his debility makes him feel from time to time the want of some outward assistance, which he cannot expect from any of them, because they are all impotent and unsympathizing. In this predicament he naturally turns his eyes to that imposing power which alone rises above the level of universal depression. Of that power his wants and especially his desires continually remind him, until he ultimately views it as the sole and necessary support of his own weakness.[2]

. . . The hatred that men bear to privilege increases in proportion as privileges become fewer and less considerable, so that democratic passions would seem to burn most fiercely just when they have least fuel. I have already given the reason for this phenomenon. When all conditions are unequal, no inequality is so great as to offend the eye, whereas the slightest dissimilarity is odious in the midst of

---

[2] In democratic communities nothing but the central power has any stability in its position or any permanence in its undertakings. All the citizens are in ceaseless stir and transformation. Now, it is in the nature of all governments to seek constantly to enlarge their sphere of action; hence it is almost impossible that such a government should not ultimately succeed, because it acts with a fixed principle and a constant will upon men whose position, ideas, and desires are constantly changing.

It frequently happens that the members of the community promote the influence of the central power without intending to. Democratic eras are periods of experiment, innovation, and adventure. There is always a multitude of men engaged in difficult or novel undertakings, which they follow by themselves without shackling themselves to their fellows. Such persons will admit, as a general principle, that the public authority ought not to interfere in private concerns; but, by an exception to that rule, each of them craves its assistance in the particular concern on which he is engaged and seeks to draw upon the influence of the government for his own benefit, although he would restrict it on all other occasions. If a large number of men applies this particular exception to a great variety of different purposes, the sphere of the central power extends itself imperceptibly in all directions, although everyone wishes it to be circumscribed.

Thus a democratic government increases its power simply by the fact of its permanence. Time is on its side; every incident befriends it; the passions of individuals unconsciously promote it; and it may be asserted that the older a democratic community is, the more centralized will its government become.

general uniformity; the more complete this uniformity is, the more insupportable the sight of such a difference becomes. Hence it is natural that the love of equality should constantly increase together with equality itself, and that it should grow by what it feeds on.

This never dying, ever kindling hatred which sets a democratic people against the smallest privileges is peculiarly favorable to the gradual concentration of all political rights in the hands of the representative of the state alone. The sovereign, being necessarily and incontestably above all the citizens, does not excite their envy, and each of them thinks that he strips his equals of the prerogative that he concedes to the crown. The man of a democratic age is extremely reluctant to obey his neighbor, who is his equal; he refuses to acknowledge superior ability in such a person; he mistrusts his justice and is jealous of his power; he fears and he despises him; and he loves continually to remind him of the common dependence in which both of them stand to the same master.

Every central power, which follows its natural tendencies, courts and encourages the principle of equality; for equality singularly facilitates, extends, and secures the influence of a central power.

In like manner it may be said that every central government worships uniformity; uniformity relieves it from inquiry into an infinity of details, which must be attended to if rules have to be adapted to different men, instead of indiscriminately subjecting all men to the same rule. Thus the government likes what the citizens like and naturally hates what they hate. These common sentiments, which in democratic nations constantly unite the sovereign and every member of the community in one and the same conviction, establish a secret and lasting sympathy between them.

Thus by two separate paths I have reached the same conclusion. I have shown that the principle of equality suggests to men the notion of a sole, uniform, and strong government; I have now shown that the principal of equality imparts to them a taste for it. To governments of this kind of nations of our age are therefore tending. They are drawn thither by the natural inclination of mind and heart; and in order to reach that result, it is enough that they do not check themselves in their course.

I am of the opinion that, in the democratic ages which are opening upon us, individual independence and local liberties will ever be the products of art; that centralization will be the natural government.

QUESTIONS FOR UNDERSTANDING AND DISCUSSION

1. In Tocqueville's opinion, in what ways do the pleasures of freedom differ from the pleasures of equality?
2. Why does democracy tend to make its citizens nonparticipants in the affairs of their state?
3. Why does a centralized government prefer that all citizens have the same rights and duties?
4. Tocqueville states that "the government likes what the citizens like and naturally hates what they hate." Do you think this observation is still valid in light of all the controversial issues, protests, and debates of today?
5. Has the course of government in the past century and a half tended mostly to confirm or to refute Tocqueville's ideas in these segments? Give examples to support your answer.

Practice Examination, Chapters 1 to 14

TRUE/FALSE QUESTIONS

Read each statement carefully. Mark true statements *T.* If any part of the statement is false, mark it *F,* and write in the space provided a concise explanation of why the statement is false.

1. The Framers of the Constitution did not think that the "will of the people" was synonymous with the "public good."

2. The Framers hoped to create a representative democracy that would act swiftly and accommodate sweeping changes in policy.

3. The self-interest of individuals is often an incomplete guide to their actions.

4. Revolutionary colonists largely held that the legislative branch of government should have a greater share of governmental power than the executive.

5. The Constitution of the United States is the world's oldest written national constitution still in operation.

6. Today, an effort is being made to scale back the size and activity of the national government.

7. Federalism was intended by the Founders to operate as a protection for personal liberty.

8. From the time of its founding, to today, America has been among the most religious countries in the world.

9. Since the 1960s, there has been a fairly sharp drop in internal political efficacy in the United States.

10. The process whereby the United States Supreme Court applies provisions in the Bill of Rights to the states is known as "incorporation."

11. In America, it is generally much more difficult for public figures to win a libel suit.

12. The Court applies the strict scrutiny standard to gender discrimination cases.

13. The right to privacy is nowhere mentioned in the Constitution.

14. Since 1952, the major polls have a modest record with respect to predicting the winner in presidential elections.

15. Younger voters have a weaker sense of partisanship than older ones.

16. The Nineteenth Amendment nearly doubled the number of eligible voters in the United States.

17. Most scholars believe voter turnout did decrease somewhere around the 1890s.

18. Split-ticket voting is on the increase in the United States.

19. Most Americans would resent partisanship becoming a conspicuous feature of other organizations to which they belong.

20. In a typical House race, the incumbent receives over 60 percent of the vote.

21. Most of the money for congressional campaigns comes from big business and PACs.

22. Interest groups are an accurate reflection of the high degree of unity that exists among politically active elites.

23. Members of interest groups tend to work primarily with legislators with whom they agree.

24. America has a long tradition of privately owned media.

25. Today, journalists are far less willing to accept at face value the statements of elected officials.

26. Newspapers knew that Franklin Roosevelt had a romantic affair in the 1930s but did not report it.

27. Senators are more likely to lose bids for reelection than members of the House.

____

28. Democrats tend to do exceptionally well in low-turnout districts.

____

29. The Framers expected that the House of Representatives would frequently select the President.

____

30. A president rarely knows more than a few of the people that he appoints.

____

MULTIPLE CHOICE QUESTIONS

Circle the letter of the response that best answers the question or completes the statement.

1. Americans seem to agree that the exercise of political power at any level is legitimate only if, in some sense, it is
   a. systematic.
   b. democratic.
   c. bipartisan.
   d. partisan.
   e. traditional.
2. Which of the following is a basic tenet of representative democracy?
   a. Individuals should acquire power through competition for the people's vote.
   b. It is unreasonable to expect people to choose among competing leadership groups.
   c. Government officials should represent the true interests of their clients.
   d. The middle class gains representation at the expense of the poor and minorities.
   e. Public elections should be held on every issue directly affecting the lives of voters.
3. In the Marxist view government is a reflection of underlying ________ forces.
   a. economic
   b. political
   c. ideological
   d. social
   e. teleological
4. Max Weber felt that the dominant social and political reality of modern times was that
   a. "the Establishment" was dominated by Wall Street lawyers.
   b. all institutions have fallen under the control of large bureaucracies.
   c. capitalism is essential to modern-day forms of government.
   d. conflict increased between the government and the press.
   e. a dialectical process made communism inevitable.
5. The view that money, expertise, prestige, and so forth are widely scattered throughout our society in the hands of a variety of groups is known as the
   a. pluralist view of American society.
   b. economic theory of democracy.
   c. elitist view of American society.
   d. dispersed power theory of American politics.
   e. monetary displacement theory of American politics.

6. The original purpose of the Constitutional Convention was to
   a. draw up a bill of rights.
   b. discuss regulations on intrastate commerce.
   c. levy taxes.
   d. build an army.
   e. revise the Articles of Confederation.
7. The philosophy of John Locke strongly supported the idea that
   a. government ought to be limited.
   b. property rights should be subordinated to human rights.
   c. the state of nature was without flaw.
   d. reason is an inadequate guide in establishing a political order.
   e. equality of goods and income is necessary to political order.
8. The Great Compromise
   a. required Supreme Court justices to be confirmed by the Senate.
   b. based House representation on population and Senate population on equality.
   c. solved the conflict between those who wanted a powerful House and those who did not.
   d. provided that the president be selected by the electoral college.
   e. dealt with, without mentioning by name, "slavery."
9. The American version of representative democracy was based on two major principles:
   a. self-interest and institutionalism.
   b. separation of powers and federalism.
   c. commerce and competition.
   d. liberty and equality.
   e. unification and centralism.
10. Sophisticated statistical analysis of the voting behavior of the Framers of the Constitution suggests
    a. they generally pursued the interests of wealthy land owners and businessmen.
    b. they generally acted in a manner to protect the interests of the poor.
    c. they consciously ignored the interests of the commercial classes.
    d. they generally represented the interests of their respective states.
    e. they consciously ignored the interests of the slave-owners.
11. A system is not federal unless local units of government
    a. are the official distributors of the national government's resources.
    b. exist independently and can make decisions independent of the national government.
    c. answer solely to the national government.
    d. make decisions in conjunction with national goals and needs.
    e. are mere administrative subunits of the national government.
12. According to the text, the most obvious effect of federalism has been to
    a. modify ideological conflicts.
    b. protect the interests of the upper classes.
    c. facilitate the mobilization of political activity.
    d. reverse the democratic tendency in the states.
    e. increase the scope of the president's power.
13. Most federal mandates concern
    a. sexual harassment.
    b. civil liberties and civil rights.
    c. civil rights and environmental protection.
    d. waste management.
    e. law enforcement.

14. The text suggests the growth of mandates has been fueled by the fact that
    a. local citizens can use a federal court to change local practices.
    b. Congress has taken a greater interest in busing, state prisons, and police brutality.
    c. few courts have an interest in hearing cases related to mandates.
    d. the Reagan and Bush administrations supported them so enthusiastically.
    e. none of the above.
15. The text suggests devolution was actually an "old idea" that acquired "new vitality" because
    a. courts no longer stood in the way of state policies.
    b. state constitutions were modified in accordance with federal policies.
    c. governors and mayors supported the effort.
    d. Congress, rather than the president, was leading the effort.
    e. Democratic leaders spearheaded the effort.
16. Which of the following is *not* among the important elements in the American view of the political system?
    a. Civic duty
    b. Individualism
    c. Equality of opportunity
    d. Democracy
    e. Equality of condition
17. Compared with people in other democracies, Americans are particularly preoccupied with
    a. elections.
    b. the assertion of rights.
    c. social harmony.
    d. institutions.
    e. equality.
18. While there has been no established religion in the United States, there has certainly been a dominant religious tradition. That tradition can be best described as
    a. Catholicism.
    b. Protestantism.
    c. Protestantism, especially Lutheranism.
    d. Protestantism, especially Puritanism.
    e. none of the above.
19. The culture war is basically a conflict over
    a. economic issues.
    b. foreign affairs.
    c. international norms.
    d. differing religious ideologies.
    e. private and public morality.
20. The increase in cynicism toward our government has been specifically directed at
    a. government officials.
    b. the system of government itself.
    c. the Constitution.
    d. the Declaration of Independence.
    e. capitalism in America.

21. Blackstone argued that the press should be free
    a. from any restrictions whatsoever.
    b. only when it published the truth.
    c. from censorship prior to publication.
    d. from seditious libel restrictions alone.
    e. from libel laws regarding government officers.
22. The Supreme Court struck down a 1996 law that addressed the issue of child pornography because it attempted to ban images that were
    a. graphic.
    b. violent.
    c. psychologically harmful.
    d. in the public domain.
    e. computer simulated.
23. The phrase "wall of separation" between church and state comes from
    a. the pen of Thomas Jefferson.
    b. the Bill of Rights.
    c. the debates in the First Congress that drafted the Bill of Rights.
    d. the 14th Amendment.
    e. George Washington's farewell address.
24. Instead of using the exclusionary rule, our courts might do as European courts do and
    a. refuse to include illegally obtained evidence at a trial.
    b. ignore the legality or illegality of the method used to obtain the evidence.
    c. levy civil or criminal penalties against law enforcement officers who obtain evidence illegally.
    d. refuse to hear cases tainted with official illegality.
    e. use the rule only when cases do not involve murder.
25. All of the following are true of the USA Patriot Act (passed in the aftermath of the attack of 9/11) *except*
    a. the penalties for terrorist crimes were increased.
    b. the government can seize voice mail without a court order.
    c. information in secret grand jury hearings can be shared by officials.
    d. non-citizens who pose a national security risk can be detained for up to seven days.
    e. the government can tap Internet communications with a court order.
26. According to the text, the authors of the Fourteenth Amendment
    a. intended to outlaw segregated schools in the Washington area.
    b. intended to outlaw segregated schools throughout the United States.
    c. may not have intended to outlaw segregated schools.
    d. were pleased four years later when a civil rights act proposed an end to segregated schools.
    e. thought desegregated schools would cure certain social ills.
27. *Brown* called for the desegregation of public schools
    a. "with all deliberate speed."
    b. as soon as the state legislatures could fund the enterprise.
    c. "in an acceptable amount of time."
    d. "immediately."
    e. immediately following the next school year.

28. *Roe* v. *Wade* held that the state may regulate abortions to protect the health of the mother
    a. in the first trimester.
    b. in the second trimester.
    c. in the third trimester.
    d. at any point in the pregnancy.
    e. in cases involving rape or incest.
29. In the highly publicized cases involving affirmative action programs at the University of Michigan (2003), the Court struck down the use of a ________ but was sympathetic to the use of a so called ______.
    a. quota … goal
    b. goal … quota
    c. quota guideline … bonus points
    d. racial label … ethnic categorization
    e. fixed quota … plus factor
30. Under the "quid pro quo" rule pertaining to sexual harassment
    a. the employer is "strictly liable" even if he/she did not know that sexual harassment was occurring.
    b. the employer cannot be held liable if he/she did not know that sexual harassment was occurring.
    c. an employer is never liable for the sexual harassment of an employee.
    d. a pattern of sexual harassment must be proven before the employer is liable.
    e. the employer is liable but not the employee in sexual harassment cases.
31. The Framers of the Constitution understood that ________ would be the chief source of opinion on most matters.
    a. the general public
    b. elected representatives
    c. factions and interest groups
    d. political theorists and educators
    e. intellectuals
32. When political scientists see how accurately they can predict a person's view on one issue based on views on a different issue, then the focus is on
    a. "constraint."
    b. "salience."
    c. "congruence."
    d. "linearity."
    e. "robustness."
33. In a typical ideological self-identification survey, the largest group of Americans will
    a. classify themselves as liberal.
    b. classify themselves as conservative.
    c. classify themselves as moderate.
    d. refuse to classify themselves in any manner.
    e. None of the above.
34. The rate at which governments adopt policies supported by majorities in polls
    a. has increased dramatically.
    b. has increased somewhat.
    c. has remained the same for some time now.
    d. has decreased.
    e. suggests politicians often pander to constituents.

35. Which of the following is an *incorrect* assessment of elite opinion?
    a. Elites influence which issues will capture the public's attention.
    b. Elites are unified in their interests and opinions.
    c. Elites state the norms by which issues should be settled.
    d. Elites raise and frame political issues.
    e. Elites influence how issues are debated and decided.
36. VEP measures of turnout may have an advantage over VAP measures because
    a. VEP measures attempt to remove ineligible voters from the data.
    b. VEP measures are based on actual census data.
    c. VEP measures include prisoners, but not felons or aliens.
    d. VEP measures include felons, but not prisoners or aliens.
    e. VEP measures are verified by each state legislature.
37. In surveys, about what percentage of respondents claim to have voted in an election when they did not do so?
    a. 2 to 3 percent
    b. 8 to 10 percent
    c. 20 to 25 percent
    d. 30 to 35 percent
    e. 40 to 50 percent
38. In states that have instituted same-day voter registration, the effect on voter turnout has been
    a. a major decline.
    b. a slight decline.
    c. a slight increase.
    d. a major increase.
    e. no effect at all.
39. The best evidence suggests Americans
    a. are voting less, and participating in politics less.
    b. are voting less, and participating in politics more.
    c. are voting and participating in politics at about the same rate.
    d. are voting more, and participating less in politics.
    e. are voting more and participating more in politics.
40. The number of elective offices in the United States, compared with European nations, is
    a. much lower.
    b. slightly lower.
    c. about the same.
    d. slightly higher.
    e. much higher.
41. Why should George Washington, among other Founders of our nation, have been so opposed to political parties?
    a. Because the Constitution made clear the dangers of partisanship in government
    b. Because political parties during the early years of the republic were both strong and centralized
    c. Because disputes over policies and elections were not easily separated from disputes over governmental legitimacy
    d. Because political parties during the early years of the Republic represented clear, homogeneous economic interests
    e. Because Washington was concerned that Hamilton would win the White House as a result of party mobilization

42. The formulas for apportioning delegates to the national party conventions are such that the Democrats give extra delegates to ______ states and the Republicans give extra delegates to states that are ______.
    a. small … large
    b. Midwestern … heavily populated
    c. large … loyal
    d. Southern … heavily contested
    e. conservative … liberal
43. Almost all elections in the United States are based on
    a. the plurality system.
    b. the majority system.
    c. proportional representation.
    d. retention and recall.
    e. a combination of systems.
44. The disadvantage to parties of the current system of presidential nomination is that it
    a. affords little opportunity to minorities to voice their concerns.
    b. decreases the chances that a faction will separate itself from the party.
    c. decreases the chances of a realigning election.
    d. increases the chances of nominating a candidate unappealing to average voter or the party's rank and file.
    e. increases the chances that a faction will separate itself from the party.
45. The text suggests Democrats have had some difficulty in competing for the presidency, in part, because
    a. they have typically had little experience in government.
    b. redistricting which has created an advantage for Republicans.
    c. slanted reporting by media.
    d. of recent changes in electoral laws regarding placement on the ballot.
    e. of the views their candidates have had on social issues and taxation.
46. All of the following statements about presidential and congressional races are true *except:*
    a. Presidential races are more competitive.
    b. More people vote in presidential elections.
    c. Congressional incumbents usually win.
    d. Presidents can rarely take credit for improvements in a district.
    e. Presidents can distance themselves from the "mess" in Washington.
47. In 1911, Congress fixed the size of the House of Representatives at ______ members.
    a. 50
    b. 100
    c. 435
    d. 535
    e. 537
48. Campaign contributions by PACs generally favor
    a. Republicans.
    b. conservatives.
    c. incumbents.
    d. supporters of organized labor.
    e. challengers.

49. In recent presidential elections the independent vote has usually favored
    a. a third party.
    b. the Republicans.
    c. the Democrats.
    d. no one party.
    e. male candidates.
50. With respect to the seemingly "negative" tone of today's campaigns, the authors suggest it
    a. is not a new feature of American politics and it has been much worse.
    b. is not a new feature of American politics, but it is worse now than it has ever been.
    c. is a relatively new feature in American politics.
    d. became a feature of American politics when pro-choice and anti-abortion groups grew in influence.
    e. tends to disappear when the nation is at war.
51. Interest groups with large staffs are likely to take political positions in accordance with
    a. rank-and-file opinion.
    b. editorial commentary in the media.
    c. the view of the general public.
    d. staff beliefs.
    e. government policy.
52. Probably the best measure of an interest group's ability to influence legislators and bureaucrats is
    a. the size of the membership.
    b. the dollar amount of its contributions.
    c. the occupational sketch of its members.
    d. its organizational skill.
    e. its contacts.
53. The revolving door between government and business raises the possibility of
    a. poor communications.
    b. revenue sharing.
    c. conflicts of interest.
    d. duplication.
    e. ticket splitting.
54. The most significant legal constraints on interest groups currently come from
    a. the 1946 Federal Regulation of Lobbying Act.
    b. the tax code and campaign finance laws.
    c. antitrust legislation.
    d. state labor leaders.
    e. the Supreme Court.
55. Joint Operating Agreements are important to consider when assessing the competition and diversity of viewpoints among newspapers because they
    a. encourage the hiring of minorities.
    b. have increased the sales of newspapers in major metropolitan areas.
    c. are usually biased in a conservative direction.
    d. allow businesses to own more than one paper in a large city.
    e. do not allow the expression of political opinion without prior consent.

56. Once something is published, a newspaper may be sued or prosecuted if the material
    a. is libelous.
    b. is obscene.
    c. incites someone to commit an illegal act.
    d. all of the above.
    e. none of the above.
57. In general, the Supreme Court has upheld the right of government to compel reporters to divulge information as part of a properly conducted criminal investigation if
    a. the president has pardoned a defendant for contempt of court.
    b. a jury is unable to reach a decision.
    c. it has not been reported publicly.
    d. it has been reported publicly.
    e. it bears on the commission of a crime.
58. In an age in which the media are very important, who of the following is best positioned to run for president?
    a. A House member
    b. An innovative person with a business background
    c. A senator
    d. A state governor
    e. A big-city mayor
59. Which of the following does the text suggest is one of the consequences of intense competition in media today?
    a. Reporters are more easily manipulated by sources than once was the case.
    b. The requirements for citation of sources are more rigorous than ever.
    c. There are few incentives to rely on sensational news stories.
    d. Reporters are less confrontational with public officials than they once were.
    e. none of the above.
60. Until 1913 senators were
    a. popularly elected.
    b. picked by state legislatures.
    c. appointed by state governors.
    d. selected by the state judiciaries.
    e. elected by the electoral college.
61. In the 1860s, being a congressman was not regarded as a "career" because
    a. the federal government was not very important.
    b. travel to Washington, D.C., was difficult.
    c. the job did not pay well.
    d. Washington was not generally considered a pleasant place to live.
    e. all of the above.
62. According to the text, most categories of pork spending have _____ in the last ten or fifteen years.
    a. decreased
    b. remained at approximately the same levels
    c. increased
    d. slightly increased
    e. dramatically increased

63. The process of "double tracking" allows
    a. committees to consider recently rejected legislation within a limited time frame.
    b. members of the House to filibuster two bills at the same time.
    c. the president to influence congressional votes at the beginning and end of the legislative session.
    d. members of the Senate to focus on other business during a filibuster.
    e. freshmen members of Congress two chances to pass their first piece of legislation.
64. In the House, a stalled bill can be extracted from a committee and brought to the floor by means of
    a. a discharge petition.
    b. an extraction bill.
    c. a committee rule.
    d. cloture.
    e. a unanimous consent vote.
65. In a parliamentary system the prime minister is chosen by the
    a. people.
    b. signatories.
    c. electors.
    d. legislature.
    e. monarch.
66. The text makes which of the following statements about the effect of divided government?
    a. Divided government produces worse gridlock than does a unified government.
    b. The end of gridlock is accomplished by a divided government.
    c. Important legislation is produced about as much with divided governments as with unified governments.
    d. Divided government slows the progress of necessary legislation and, in a time of crisis, almost ensures there will be no consensus.
    e. Divided government is a myth.
67. The greatest source of presidential power is found in
    a. the Constitution.
    b. Congress.
    c. public communication.
    d. the bureaucracy.
    e. politics and public opinion.
68. Once in office a president can expect to see his popularity
    a. increase over time.
    b. remain about the same.
    c. fluctuate in a manner that admits of no generalization.
    d. decline over time.
    e. be dependent on the actions of Congress.

69. A president suffers a stroke that leaves him or her partially paralyzed. The vice president, with the support of a majority of the cabinet, declares that the president is unable to discharge the duties of the office, but the president disagrees. What happens next?
    a. Congress decides who is president.
    b. Because the vice president has the support of a majority of the cabinet, the vice president assumes the presidency.
    c. Because the president is still alive, he or she remains president.
    d. Because the president and vice president disagree, a new election is held, allowing the people to decide who should be president.
    e. The Supreme Court decides who is president.
70. Which of the following statements is *incorrect*?
    a. Sixteen persons have been impeached by the House.
    b. Seven persons have been convicted by the Senate.
    c. No federal judge has ever been removed by impeachment.
    d. The impeachment case against Andrew Johnson was "flimsy."
    e. Clinton's impeachment led to the expiration of the office of independent council.

ANSWERS TO TRUE/FALSE QUESTIONS

1. T
2. F The separation of powers and checks and balances were utilized to ensure, if anything, a slow, deliberative process.
3. T
4. T
5. T
6. T
7. T
8. T
9. T
10. T
11. T
12. F The Court announced the "reasonableness" standard in *Reed.* More recently, in the V.M.I. case, it appears to utilize a standard somewhere between "reasonableness" and "strict scrutiny."
13. T
14. F The major polls have an outstanding record in the same period, predicting all of the winners correctly.
15. T
16. T
17. T
18. T
19. T
20. T
21. F Most of the money in a congressional campaign comes from individual donors.
22. F If anything, they are a reflection of the disagreements among the middle classes and those who are more active in politics.
23. T
24. T
25. T
26. T
27. T
28. T
29. T
30. T

ANSWERS TO MULTIPLE CHOICE QUESTIONS

1. b	2. a	3. a	4. b	5. a	6. e	7. a
8. b	9. b	10. d	11. b	12. c	13. c	14. a
15. d	16. e	17. b	18. d	19. e	20. a	21. c
22. e	23. a	24. c	25. b	26. c	27. a	28. b
29. e	30. a	31. c	32. a	33. c	34. d	35. b
36. a	37. b	38. b	39. b	40. e	41. c	42. c
43. a	44. d	45. e	46. e	47. c	48. c	49. b
50. a	51. d	52. d	53. c	54. b	55. d	56. d
57. e	58. c	59. a	60. b	61. e	62. a	63. d
64. a	65. d	66. c	67. e	68. e	69. d	70. a

Practice Examination, Chapters 15 to 22

TRUE/FALSE QUESTIONS

Read each statement carefully. Mark true statements *T.* If any part of the statement is false, mark it *F*, and write in the space provided a concise explanation of why the statement is false.

1. The federal civil service as a whole looks very much like a cross section of American society in the education, sex, and race of its members.

2. People with conservative viewpoints tend to be overrepresented in defense agencies.

3. Congress rarely gives any job to a single agency.

4. Iron triangles are much less common today than once was the case.

5. The Supreme Court has declared thousands of federal laws to be unconstitutional since 1789.

6. The Constitution sets the number of justices on the Court at nine.

7. The influence of law clerks on the selection of the Supreme Court's cases and the rendering of its decisions is considerable.

8. The text suggests that there has been an increase in politically conservative judges who accept the activist view of the function of courts.

9. The expansion of government has been the result, fundamentally, of a non-partisan process.

10. The Founders deliberately arranged things so that it would be difficult to pass a new law.

11. Our antitrust policy is perhaps the strongest found in any industrial nation.

12. Client politics appear to be on the increase in the United States.

13. Low-income people are more likely to vote Democrat.

14. A "sociotropic" voter votes on the basis of his/her own pocketbook.

15. "Reaganomics" was not dictated by any single economic theory.

16. Voters consistently say they want a balanced budget and lower government spending.

17. The Constitution is silent on whether the Congress has the power to spend money on welfare.

18. President Bush has called for further restrictions and limitations for so called Charitable-Choice provisions.

19. Key votes on the Social Security Act pitted a majority of Democrats against a majority of Republicans.

20. Charles Murray's position was that social welfare programs actually increased the number of people living in poverty.

21. Tocqueville argued that democratic nations were the best adapted to handle foreign affairs.

22. It would be accurate to say the president has the power to "make" war, but Congress has the power to "declare" war.

23. U.S. presidents have less freedom in foreign affairs than do most other Western heads of state.

24. Most executive agreements are authorized by Congress in advance.

25. Before Pearl Harbor, most Americans seemed to oppose U.S. entry into World War II.

26. Environmental policy making in the United States tends to be more adversarial than in European countries.

27. The major source of sulfur dioxide in the atmosphere is the burning of low-sulfur coal.

28. Less than one-quarter of the U.S. Forest Reserve is off limits to logging.

29. American politics remain far more sensitive to local concerns than does politics abroad.

30. The text suggests that, as the political system has become more fragmented and more individualized, it has come more under the sway of ideas.

MULTIPLE CHOICE QUESTIONS

Circle the letter of the response that best answers the question or completes the statement.

1. American bureaucracy is complex because
   a. federalism encourages the abuse of power.
   b. it is heavily dependent on career employees.
   c. the Constitution determines its structure and function.
   d. authority is divided among several managing institutions.
   e. civil servants are immune from firing.
2. The basis of appointments to the bureaucracy during most of the nineteenth century and the early part of the twentieth century was
   a. financial.
   b. patronage.
   c. nepotism.
   d. technical expertise.
   e. support for the president's policies.
3. Wars have generally caused the federal bureaucracy to
   a. become more decentralized.
   b. shrink in size, but increase in efficiency.
   c. respond more quickly, but make inefficient decisions.
   d. increase in size.
   e. neutralize the power of Congress.
4. Which of the following is the *most* important consideration in evaluating the power of a bureaucracy?
   a. The number of employees in it
   b. The importance of its functions
   c. The extent to which its actions are supported by the public
   d. The social status of its leaders
   e. The amount of discretionary authority that its officials have
5. A steady transfer of federal jobs from the patronage to the merit system was initiated by the passage of the
   a. Seventeenth Amendment.
   b. Eighteenth Amendment.
   c. Pendelton Act.
   d. Hatch Act.
   e. Civil Service Reform Act.

6. Which of the following statements concerning the Senior Executive Service is *incorrect*?
   a. It was created by the Civil Service Reform Act of 1978.
   b. It consists of eight thousand top federal managers who, in theory, can be fired more easily than ordinary civil servants.
   c. It consists of eight thousand top federal managers who, in theory, can be transferred more easily than ordinary civil servants.
   d. Its members are eligible for substantial cash bonuses if they perform their duties well.
   e. none of the above.
7. All of the following statements concerning the legislative veto are correct *except*:
   a. Congress made frequent use of it for many decades.
   b. It required an executive decision to lie before Congress for a specified period of time.
   c. Resolutions of disapproval could be passed by either or both houses.
   d. The Supreme Court ruled such vetoes unconstitutional.
   e. Congress has not passed a law containing a legislative veto since the Court considered its constitutionality in 1983.
8. Bureaucratic conflict and duplication occur because
   a. large organizations must ensure one part of the organization does not operate out of step.
   b. Congress often wants to achieve a number of different, partially inconsistent goals.
   c. Congress can be unclear as to exactly what it wants an agency to do.
   d. of the need to satisfy political requirements.
   e. of the need to satisfy legal requirements.
9. The dramatic and sometimes bitter conflict surrounding some Supreme Court nominations can only be explained by the fact that
   a. there are only nine people on the Court at any given point in time.
   b. the Court plays such a large role in making public policy.
   c. the partisan balance of the Court is quite skewed.
   d. Presidents rarely seek the "advice" of the Senate.
   e. nominees are rarely qualified for the job.
10. There are ____ U.S. District Courts.
   a. 11
   b. 12
   c. 13
   d. 50
   e. 94
11. When politicians complain about the use of "litmus tests" in judicial nominations, they are probably
   a. Democrats.
   b. Republicans.
   c. Liberals.
   d. Conservatives.
   e. not part of the group that is currently in power.
12. What percentage of appeals court cases is rejected by the Supreme Court?
   a. 1 or 2 percent
   b. 20 percent
   c. 30 percent
   d. 50 percent
   e. 99 percent

13. *Amicus curiae* is generally translated as meaning
    a. "friend of the court."
    b. "amicable but curious."
    c. "let the decision stand."
    d. "to reveal."
    e. none of the above.
14. *Stare decisis* is generally translated as meaning
    a. "friend of the court."
    b. "amicable but curious."
    c. "let the decision stand."
    d. "to reveal."
    e. none of the above.
15. A political question is a matter
    a. involving voters.
    b. that the Constitution has left to another branch of government.
    c. that an elected state judge has dealt with.
    d. that causes conflict among average voters.
    e. that must first be acted on by Congress.
16. A major reason that the courts play a greater role in American society today than they did earlier in the century is that
    a. government plays a greater role generally.
    b. lawyers are more influential than ever.
    c. public opinion is less focused.
    d. judges are better trained.
    e. the courts are more representative of American society.
17. The Occupational Safety and Health Act of 1970 was passed at a time when
    a. the number of industrial deaths had increased steadily for a decade.
    b. the number of industrial deaths had been dropping steadily for twenty years.
    c. industrial fatalities had remained the same for several years.
    d. data on industrial fatalities were unavailable to Congress.
    e. data on industrial fatalities were unreliable.
18. The text's explanation for the urban riots in the 1960s centers on
    a. white radicals who mobilized blacks.
    b. organized special-interest groups in urban areas.
    c. followers of Marcus Garvey.
    d. blacks' sense of relative deprivation.
    e. the Black Panther movement.
19. Which of the following statements *best* describes government bureaucracy today?
    a. It is a tool of big business.
    b. It is a major source of policy proposals.
    c. It is an impartial institution.
    d. It is an appendage of the political parties.
    e. It is without significant influence in the policy-making process.
20. An example of client politics is
    a. social welfare.
    b. labor legislation.
    c. licensing of barbers.
    d. antitrust legislation.
    e. All of the above.

21. An example of entrepreneurial politics would be
    a. agricultural price supports.
    b. Social Security.
    c. a tariff on imported cars.
    d. requirements for antipollution and safety devices on cars.
    e. None of the above.
22. The Reagan administration broke up ________ forcing it to compete with other companies of its kind.
    a. IBM
    b. Standard Oil
    c. AT&T
    d. Microsoft
    e. Northern Songs Ltd.
23. The Clinton administration was notable for its antitrust suit against
    a. IBM.
    b. Standard Oil.
    c. AT&T.
    d. Microsoft.
    e. Northern Songs Ltd.
24. The text speaks of the "power of ideas" as a key force in the deregulation of several industries that has occurred over the past two decades. Where did these ideas most often originate?
    a. With academic economists
    b. With the courts, especially the Supreme Court
    c. With broadcasters in local news stations
    d. With the national media
    e. With Congress, especially the Senate
25. Choices about economic policy are shaped most significantly by the
    a. party affiliation of politicians.
    b. occupational status of legislators.
    c. seniority of legislators.
    d. predictions of economists.
    e. ideology of cabinet members.
26. Democrats tend to be more worried than Republicans about
    a. inflation.
    b. international politics.
    c. unemployment.
    d. business investment.
    e. recessions.
27. Politicians have a strong tendency to get reelected by
    a. decreasing taxes.
    b. lowering the deficit.
    c. cutting expenditures.
    d. spending money on specific programs that are popular.
    e. raising taxes.

28. Milton Friedman takes the position that inflation is caused when
    a. there is too little money chasing too few goods.
    b. there is too much money chasing too many goods.
    c. there is too little money chasing too many goods.
    d. there is too much money chasing too few goods.
    e. the government has a predictable increase in the money supply.
29. Keynesians believe that if people save too much
    a. they will pay too little in taxes.
    b. they will invest too little.
    c. production and money supply will increase.
    d. demand will decrease and production will decline.
    e. demand and production will increase.
30. Which statement about the Federal Reserve Board is *incorrect*?
    a. It has fifteen members.
    b. Each member is appointed by the president and confirmed by the Senate.
    c. A member's term is fourteen years.
    d. Since its founding in 1913 no member has ever been removed.
    e. The Chairman serves a four-year term.
31. The most important part of the economic policymaking machinery is the
    a. Federal Reserve Board.
    b. Congress.
    c. Council of Economic Advisers.
    d. General Services Administration.
    e. Secretary of Labor.
32. In the first half of the twentieth century, Republicans expressed bitter opposition to
    a. high marginal rates.
    b. tax loopholes.
    c. incentives.
    d. income adjustments.
    e. tax exemptions.
33. The biggest problem facing majoritarian welfare programs is
    a. their cost.
    b. their legitimacy.
    c. their goals.
    d. who will benefit.
    e. how should clients be served.
34. The biggest problem facing client-oriented welfare programs is
    a. their cost.
    b. their legitimacy.
    c. their goals.
    d. who will pay.
    e. how will costs be determined.
35. The __________ government program provides medical assistance for poor people.
    a. Medicare
    b. Poverty Fund
    c. Medifund
    d. Medicaid
    e. Temporary Assistance to Needy Families (TANF)

36. A national advisory commission examined the Social Security crisis and proposed to President Clinton that
    a. the retirement age be raised to eighty-five.
    b. retirement benefits be increased.
    c. Social Security taxes be lowered.
    d. the program be privatized.
    e. citizens be allowed to invest some portion of Social Security taxes in mutual funds.
37. Although AFDC involved giving federal aid to existing state programs, Washington insisted that states
    a. use a federal calculation for applicants' incomes.
    b. establish mandatory job-training programs for many recipients.
    c. provide child-care programs for working AFDC parents.
    d. identify the fathers of the children of recipients.
    e. all of the above.
38. Which statement accurately describes the ultimate fate of AFDC?
    a. It was reformed in 1996 but is scheduled to expire in 2008.
    b. It was abolished in 1996 and replaced by a block grant program, TANF.
    c. It was restructured in a manner that eliminated fraud and increased federal control.
    d. It was supported by so many special interests there was no hope of significant change.
    e. Congress incorporated the program under three categorical grants.
39. The big debate in 1935 and 1965 over Social Security and Medicare was over
    a. whether the public wanted them.
    b. whether they were too costly.
    c. whether they constituted unnecessary duplication.
    d. whether they were needed.
    e. whether it was legitimate for government to provide them.
40. The division of constitutional authority between the president and Congress is *best* characterized as
    a. congressional dominance.
    b. presidential dominance.
    c. an "invitation to struggle."
    d. "provocative silence."
    e. a true case of controversy.
41. The most important congressional check on the president in the area of foreign affairs is the power to
    a. impeach.
    b. control the purse strings.
    c. approve ambassadors.
    d. reorganize those federal agencies that make foreign policy—the State Department, the CIA, and so forth.
    e. restrict access to the White House.
42. According to the text,
    a. the Director of the CIA authored the War Powers Act.
    b. the Pentagon whole-heartedly supported the War Powers Act.
    c. every president has obeyed the War Powers Act.
    d. every president but Clinton has obeyed the War Powers Act.
    e. no president has acknowledged that the War Powers Act is constitutional.

43. The only war in which public support remained high was
    a. the Korean War.
    b. the Vietnam War.
    c. a and b.
    d. World War II.
    e. World War I.
44. The "rally 'round the flag" effect and boost in presidential approval ratings which typically accompany foreign policy crises were *not* evident when
    a. John F. Kennedy accepted responsibility for the failed invasion of Cuba.
    b. George W. Bush responded to the attack of September 11.
    c. Ronald Reagan invaded Grenada.
    d. George Bush sent troops to fight Iraq.
    e. Bill Clinton sent forces to Bosnia or launched bombing attacks on Iraq.
45. A careful study of public opinion has concluded that, as American lives are lost during a time of war, the public tends to
    a. desire escalation and swift victory.
    b. seriously rethink the general premises behind our involvement.
    c. withdraw support from its political leaders.
    d. lose faith in our ability to "win."
    e. none of the above.
46. The disengagement worldview was adopted by younger elites as a result of experience with
    a. the War Between the States.
    b. World War I.
    c. World War II.
    d. the Korean War.
    e. Vietnam.
47. The text suggests the infamous $435 hammer was
    a. a major source of reform in the process for procuring military contracts.
    b. responsible for several high-ranking military officials losing their jobs.
    c. a myth created by critics of the military who opposed intervention in Kosovo.
    d. a myth resulting from a complex accounting procedure and exploited by a member of Congress.
    e. actually $754 once the handle was attached.
48. We did not seek the support of the United Nations in
    a. fighting against North Vietnam (1960s).
    b. occupying Haiti (1994).
    c. assisting friendly forces in Bosnia (1994).
    d. assisting friendly forces in Kosovo (1994).
    e. all of the above.
49. One reason environmental policy tends to be so controversial is that
    a. so many environmental policy decisions are based on scientific evidence, which tends to be highly political.
    b. environmental policy often takes the form of majoritarian politics, which requires strong emotional appeals to overcome the political advantage of client groups.
    c. environmental policy creates losers, who must pay the costs without getting enough of the benefits.
    d. most people feel that government is already doing enough to control pollution; new programs are therefore likely to face stiff opposition.
    e. all of the above.

50. Compared with U.S. regulations, rules controlling air pollution in Great Britain involve
    a. strict deadlines.
    b. voluntary compliance.
    c. expensive technology.
    d. a uniform national policy.
    e. rigorous assessments.
51. According to the text, federalism and the separation of powers
    a. have reduced the scope of conflicts in environmental policy making.
    b. ensure efficiency in environmental policy making.
    c. are responsible for the broad-based public support for anti-pollution laws.
    d. reinforce adversarial politics in environmental policy making.
    e. none of the above.
52. Which of the following statements is *incorrect*?
    a. Most scientists agree the earth has gotten warmer over the last century.
    b. Global warming is caused when gases are trapped in the earth's atmosphere.
    c. Global warming "activists" have had significant impact on policy-making.
    d. Almost all scientists agree that global warming will occur in ways that hurt humankind.
    e. The United States signed the Kyoto Protocol pledging to reduce greenhouse gas emission.
53. Currently, there are over ____ species on the "protected" species list.
    a. six hundred
    b. one hundred
    c. fifty
    d. thirty
    e. fifteen
54. When is the average citizen most likely to support tough environmental protection measures?
    a. When people believe the benefits are great enough
    b. When almost everyone benefits from the measures
    c. When costs of the measures are hidden or deferred
    d. When benefits are deferred to some later date
    e. When benefits are perceived as legitimate
55. The inability of Superfund to treat more than 2,000 waste sites by the year 2000 was, in part, attributable to the fact that
    a. Superfund money went straight to the waste removers.
    b. finding and suing responsible parties were difficult.
    c. the government provided little in the way of funding.
    d. President Reagan signed a bill that weakened the EPA.
    e. environmental lobbyists were no longer able to exert pressure on the EPA.
56. Offsets, bubble standards, and banks (pollution allowances) are all
    a. pollution-control devices that effectively reduce air contamination.
    b. tests conducted by the EPA on agricultural pesticides.
    c. EPA incentives for companies to reduce pollution.
    d. rules devised by the EPA under its command-and-control strategy to improve air and water quality.
    e. standards which are employed in order to control the amount of hazardous nuclear waste that is discarded in waterbeds.

57. Which refers to a total amount of air pollution that can come from a given factory, allowing owners to decide which specific sources within the factory will be reduced?
    a. An air proxy card
    b. An offset
    c. The command-and-control strategy
    d. The bubble standard
    e. A pollution allowance
58. When a company reduces its polluting emissions by more than the law requires and uses the excess amount to cover a future plant expansion, it is taking advantage of
    a. an air proxy card.
    b. an offset.
    c. the command-and-control strategy.
    d. the bubble standard.
    e. a pollution allowance.
59. As recently as the Eisenhower administration
    a. domestic political issues and foreign affairs were given an equal amount of attention in Washington.
    b. major domestic political issues dominated the attention of Washington.
    c. the national political agenda was short on major domestic political issues.
    d. civil rights were not thought to be a matter of federal policy.
    e. Congress was preoccupied with solving social and economic problems nationwide.
60. Under the Old System of policy-making,
    a. the government's agenda was large.
    b. the legitimacy of federal action was rarely questioned.
    c. states' rights were almost irrelevant.
    d. the president was frequently quoted directly by the press.
    e. the people voted at a high rate.
61. What made it difficult to start a new program under the Old System and makes it difficult to change a new program in the New System?
    a. Checks and balances
    b. Federalism
    c. States' rights
    d. The electoral college
    e. none of the above.
62. Under the New System, it is much more difficult to resolve conflicts because
    a. individual members of Congress are less influential.
    b. the Supreme Court has limited the impact of interest groups.
    c. the distribution of political resources is shrinking.
    d. power is centralized.
    e. power is decentralized.
63. Once enough proposals for new government programs were passed, former debates about legitimacy shifted to arguments about
    a. reciprocity.
    b. costs.
    c. effectiveness.
    d. popularity.
    e. creativity.

64. Under the Old System, the dominant theme in debates about the legitimacy of governmental action was the importance of
    a. states' rights.
    b. the Bill of Rights.
    c. federalism.
    d. centralization of power.
    e. nationalism.
65. The texts suggests that the government rarely took "bold action" under the Old System unless
    a. the presidency and Congress were controlled by the same party.
    b. there was a realigning election.
    c. the Supreme Court supported the effort.
    d. it was facing a crisis—such as war.
    e. there was widespread political protest.
66. The "New System" of policy making began in the
    a. 1890s.
    b. 1920s.
    c. 1930s.
    d. 1950s.
    e. 1970s.
67. The "New System" of policy making did not take its present form until the
    a. 1890s.
    b. 1920s.
    c. 1930s.
    d. 1950s.
    e. 1970s.
68. The text suggests the consequences of an increasingly activist government include all of the following *except:*
    a. Members of government spend more time managing.
    b. The government appears to act in inconsistent, uncoordinated and cumbersome ways.
    c. The government is less susceptible to control by electoral activity.
    d. Interest groups have lost their influence.
    e. The government is held responsible for more things.
69. If the United States had adopted a parliamentary structure of government, it probably would
    a. be more sensitive to local concerns.
    b. have stronger parties.
    c. be less sensitive to local concerns.
    d. have weaker parties.
    e. experience a decrease in voter turnout.
70. Perhaps the greatest challenge to statesmanship in the years ahead is to find a way to serve the true interests of the people and, at the same time,
    a. reduce partisan conflicts in Washington.
    b. restore their confidence in government.
    c. increase voter participation.
    d. satisfy the demands of a multiplicity of interest groups.
    e. satisfy the demands of the military-industrial complex.

ANSWERS TO TRUE/FALSE QUESTIONS

1. T
2. T
3. T
4. T
5. F On average, the Court has exercised judicial review over federal legislation once a year since 1789.
6. F Congress can enlarge or contract the size of the Court at will. It started with 6 members and has had as many as 10.
7. T
8. T
9. T
10. T
11. T
12. F Client politics has become harder to practice in this country unless a group is widely thought to be a "deserving" client.
13. T
14. F Sociotropic voting is consistent with other-regarding theories of voting behavior. The sociotropic voter is concerned about the state of the economy as a whole.
15. T
16. T
17. T
18. F Bush's call for expansion of such provisions created a political firestorm early in his presidency.
19. T
20. T
21. F He argued just the opposite, contending that—among other things—democracies were too fickle, impatient, transparent and unable to endure protracted and difficult wars.
22. T
23. T
24. T
25. T
26. T
27. F The major source is unknown.
28. F Two-thirds of the Reserve is off limits to logging.
29. T
30. T

ANSWERS TO MULTIPLE CHOICE QUESTIONS

1. d	2. b	3. d	4. e	5. c	6. e	7. e
8. b	9. b	10. e	11. e	12. e	13. a	14. c
15. b	16. a	17. b	18. d	19. b	20. a	21. d
22. c	23. d	24. a	25. a	26. c	27. d	28. d
29. d	30. a	31. b	32. a	33. a	34. b	35. d
36. e	37. e	38. b	39. e	40. c	41. b	42. e
43. d	44. e	45. a	46. e	47. d	48. e	49. c
50. b	51. d	52. d	53. a	54. c	55. b	56. c
57. d	58. e	59. c	60. e	61. a	62. e	63. c
64. a	65. d	66. c	67. e	68. d	69. c	70. b